Stan Rudick

JEAN H. BAKER

MARGARET SANGER

Jean H. Baker is the author of *Mary Todd Lincoln: A Biography*; *James Buchanan: The Fifteenth President, 1857–1861*; *Sisters: The Lives of America's Suffragists*; *The Stevensons: A Biography of an American Family*; and other books on American history. She is a professor of history at Goucher College in Baltimore, Maryland.

MARGARET SANGER

MARGARET SANGER

A LIFE OF PASSION

JEAN H. BAKER

📖 HILL AND WANG

A DIVISION OF FARRAR, STRAUS AND GIROUX

NEW YORK

Hill and Wang
A division of Farrar, Straus and Giroux
18 West 18th Street, New York 10011

Copyright © 2011 by Jean H. Baker
All rights reserved
Distributed in Canada by D&M Publishers, Inc.
Printed in the United States of America
Published in 2011 by Hill and Wang
First paperback edition, 2012

The Library of Congress has cataloged the hardcover edition as follows:
Baker, Jean H.
    Margaret Sanger : a life of passion / Jean H. Baker. — 1st ed.
        p.   cm.
    Includes bibliographical references and index.
    ISBN 978-0-8090-9498-1 (cloth : alk. paper)
    1. Sanger, Margaret, 1879–1966.   2. Women social reformers—
United States—Biography.   3. Birth control—United States—History—
20th century.   4. Women's rights—United States—History—20th century.
I. Title.

HQ764.S3B35 2011
363.9'6092—dc22
[B]
                                                             2011008439

Paperback ISBN: 978-0-8090-6757-2

Designed by Jonathan D. Lippincott

www.fsgbooks.com

1 3 5 7 9 10 8 6 4 2

For Bricks, again

CONTENTS

MARGARET SANGER

INTRODUCTION

Passion: the suffering of pain as in the passion of Christ; a painful disorder or affliction of the body; a strong barely controllable emotion; a sexual urge; a strong enthusiasm for a specified thing.

—*Oxford English Dictionary*, 5th edition

Margaret Sanger died in 1966, one of those rare, signal reformers who live long enough to celebrate the acceptance of their cause. Yet, in an ironic demonstration of her primacy in the movement she named in 1915, went to jail for in 1917, organized in 1921, and led in the United States for a half century and internationally for fifteen years, her name currently serves as a target for opponents of women's reproductive rights. Today the antichoice pickets carry their angry homemade signs as they parade in front of the Margaret Sanger Center on lower Manhattan's Bleecker Street. "Don't Kill Babies," "Down with Abortion," they protest, as they try to engage the women hurrying inside for abortions, but more often for contraceptive advice and education about sexually transmitted diseases. Nearby, in one of the Expectant Mother Care Centers where antichoice advice is deceptively rendered, Margaret Sanger, who focused on contraception, not abortion, is described as a supporter of the Nazis.

This is purposeful propaganda: it employs a caricature of Margaret Sanger in order to discredit Planned Parenthood of America, the most important private provider of reproductive health care for women in the United States. It is an effort as well to prevent the liberalization of restrictive federal legislation that hinders funding of both national and international family planning programs. By distorting Sanger's views, by attaching the label "racist" to her name, and by, in the most ridiculous, hateful version of her demonization picturing her as the woman who inspired Adolf Hitler, critics of reproductive rights seek to challenge not just legal abortion but access to contraception.

They also seek to drive a wedge between black and white women. To intimidate African American women from seeking legal abortions, Georgia Right to Life and the so-called Radiance Foundation recently advertised on roadside billboards outside of Atlanta that "black babies are an endangered species." The billboards were eventually taken down, but references to Margaret Sanger remained on the Georgia Right to Life website. There, condemned by inaccurate misrepresentations about her life and work, she is labeled a eugenicist who worked to eliminate the black race. So intense and pervasive is this campaign to repudiate Sanger that even a staff member at Planned Parenthood of New York admitted that he did not talk much about Sanger—though a clinic named in her honor was on the floor below—because, after all, she was a racist and eugenicist, those lazy "ist" labels that obscure and, in this case, defile.

In 2009 such was Sanger's reputation that when Secretary of State Hillary Clinton received Planned Parenthood of America's annual Margaret Sanger Award, there was intense criticism. Few remembered that Martin Luther King Jr. had accepted the same award in 1966. On that occasion his wife, Coretta King, acknowledged striking similarities between the civil rights movement and Margaret Sanger's efforts to obtain contraception for all Americans.

Doubtless, Margaret Sanger would not be surprised at her enduringly controversial reputation among detractors who would limit women's freedom. She lived an acknowledged "tumultuous" existence amid her critics, though she would certainly protest the inaccuracies, misrepresentations, and sound-bite misquotations that now encrust her historical reputation. Nor would she, a woman who spent most of her life trying to liberate women, be shocked by the continuing controversy over women's reproductive rights that makes her memory a contested one in which her name is employed as a despised symbol. What might astound her is the way that, unlike heroes of other reform movements, she has been written out of history, thereby easily caricatured and denied the context required for any fair appraisal of her life and work.

Other women reformers, especially those associated with voting and temperance, have emerged as women worthies of unassailable virtue, their good works respectfully chronicled in the context of their times, their faces memorialized on coins and in history books. Sanger is different. Until recently, with the publication of Ellen Chesler's *Woman of Valor: Margaret Sanger and the Birth Control Movement in America* and Esther Katz's edited volumes of *The Selected Papers of Margaret Sanger,* she has attracted not only critics who find her useful for their antichoice endeavors, but also, from a different, more nuanced perspective, progressive detractors.

Held to a paradoxical double standard by the latter, Sanger is accused of deserting her early feminist principles, at the same time that some historians have discovered in her persisting radicalism and confrontational tactics, especially against the Catholic Church, an obstacle to the progress of the birth control movement. She deserted her working-class friends in the 1920s, goes this indictment, for the rich society women of New York who contributed the financial support for her fledgling American Birth Control League (ABCL). She is accused of being antiblack, though she spent time and money establishing birth control clinics for African Americans both in Harlem and in the South. But these very clinics are considered examples of her desire to eradicate the African American population.

An entire book published in 2005 focused on her supposedly rabid eugenicism without considering the context of a now heretical, but earlier popular, progressive effort to limit the number of dysgenic Americans. During Sanger's time, eugenicism—the belief that it was possible to improve the qualities of the human race through science—enrolled American presidents, from Theodore Roosevelt and Woodrow Wilson to Herbert Hoover; Supreme Court justices, including Oliver Wendell Holmes and Louis Brandeis; along with scientists from the most prestigious institutions in the United States. It promoted enlightened parenthood and raising healthy children, and also, in its darker side, supported involuntary sterilization—all in the name of improving heredity. It is no defense of Sanger to place her within the conventional wisdom of her times on this matter, though it is important to have a more nuanced view of her perspectives and the reasons she accepted aspects of a mainstream movement dedicated to improving human beings.

Sanger's reputation suffered in several biographies and studies of the history of birth control written shortly after her death. Her sins were manifold. Ardent feminists of the 1970s complained that she medicalized birth control, delivering the authority over contraception to physicians when it should have stayed under the authority of women. If it had not been for Margaret Sanger, according to recent critics, the pill would not require a doctor's prescription and health plans could not deny coverage, as some do now, without violating the due-process rights of women to health care. Moreover, in her one-dimensional approach promoting birth control, she failed to create a broad-based, sustainable feminist organization. Nor, goes another complaint, did she comprehend that separating sex from reproduction, one of her enduring contributions to women's (and men's) lives, did not spell liberation for all women.

And as for Sanger's character, some earlier historians portray her as a selfish woman, pathologically interested in power, who promoted her uniqueness but who in fact had a minimal effect on sexual behaviors and fertility rates, which were changing during the first decades of the twentieth century because of material forces, not because of Margaret Sanger. In this criticism, Sanger was a difficult woman who enjoyed her later role as a prima donna, and was responsible for the factions within a marginalized movement at a time when unity was essential. She should have positioned birth control as a free speech issue, as did her rival Mary Ware Dennett. Even her tactics failed: a string of patchwork clinics could never bring birth control to the poor, and in another of the contradictions surrounding Sanger's reputation, if establishing clinics was her intention, such tactics revealed eugenic designs. Moreover, before the pill, she supported her favorite contraceptive device, the pessary, far too long, though contradictorily, she also promoted ineffective spermicides. As a sex educator, she considered only traditional heterosexuality and publicly supported one of the pillars of women's oppression—traditional marriage.

Such judgments—lurching between the should-haves and should-not-haves—abound in the story of Margaret Sanger, and they are not tethered to the realities of her purposes and her often changing attitudes—whether toward human betterment through eugenics, the role of physicians, or the technology of contraception. According to one view, which makes all biographical considerations of pioneers in other fields useless, birth control would have come without her. Indeed, such a point goes without saying, though few observers find it necessary to declare that slave emancipation would have come without Lincoln or the automobile without Henry Ford. Sanger herself often applied to birth control Victor Hugo's dictum that "there is nothing so important as an idea whose time has come." But, as this biography seeks to illuminate, she was well aware that she had shaped the timing, the technology, and the way in which contraceptive access was recognized and acted upon throughout not just the United States but the world.

Margaret Sanger: A Life of Passion places Margaret Sanger at the center of the birth control movement and its derived benefit of separating sex from reproduction. It focuses on her significant work as a sex educator, mostly accomplished through her writing and lectures, and her efforts to repeal her generation's harmful reticence about sex. Of course there were others who contributed, and certainly fertility would have declined without her. But by changing established law, she popularized the attitudes of the future— that Americans could have sex without babies and that couples, especially women, could plan when those babies came. This book also emphasizes her role as an international advocate and the ways in which, through her conferences, she hastened the global debate about population trends.

Margaret Sanger also emphasizes the degree to which she personified aspects of American culture: the poor girl who made good; the middle-class housewife who, ahead of her times, got a divorce; the activist of a generation of women in which, with the exception of the suffragist Alice Paul, everyone stayed home; the sexual enthusiast who lived and helped shape attitudes toward women's sexuality; the internationalist who took her reform overseas; and, in a neglected personal area, the woman who suffered from a variety of illnesses that might have led someone of less fortitude to abandon any energetic commitment to a public cause. In an attempt to see her life from her perspective, I argue that her triumphs over sickness served as a life-affirming inspiration, as did that other unusual aspect of her life— her many sexual affairs.

This biography also seeks to interlard the personal with the political, not as hagiography but as authenticity. I hold no expectation that the angry defilers of Sanger will revise their misinformation, nor do I believe that Sanger deserves sanctification. But I do hope that a new generation of Americans will consider the life of an important American from her perspective and on its own terms. Accordingly, this biography focuses on Sanger's means of ascent, from the invisibility of her birth as one of eleven poor Higgins children in Corning, New York, to, by her early fifties, one of the most influential women in the world. While modern Americans savor those who perpetually reinvent themselves, shedding their earlier beings like crocodile skins, Sanger was different. She kept adding various lives and talents

to what became an effective public temperament. In 1940 the writer Garth
Cate wrote to his friend Margaret Sanger:

> The thing which if recognized and taught would make over the life
> of thousands is that you won your battle in spite of the fact that when
> you started you were not a strong woman, that you did not have
> the advantages of a complete or formal education, nor training as a
> speaker and that you did not have an organization to back you up,
> but you won because you had consecration, devotion, compassion and
> a ceaseless desire to be of the greatest service to mankind. That is
> the inspiring lesson of your life.

1

MAGGIE HIGGINS: DAUGHTER OF CORNING

I hate all these biographies that go back and forth over your childhood, dragging out this and that, that has nothing to do with your recent life.
—Margaret Sanger to Mildred Gilman, February 11, 1953

In the fall of 1879, when Anne Purcell Higgins's time came, she called for neither midwife nor nurse. There was no hospital in Corning, New York, where the Higgins family lived in a tiny ramshackle cottage on the western edge of town. Instead, it was her husband, Michael Hennessy Higgins, who eased her labor pains with his inimitable charm and a little whiskey from his flask. To save money and because he believed himself to be as knowledgeable about medicine as any expert, Michael often doctored his family. By this time both parents were experienced in matters of childbirth and took great pride in the size and health of their blemish-free, ten-pound babies. "They had a eugenic pride of race," wrote their famous daughter Margaret Sanger, who later held her own views on that subject.[1]

These Catholic-born parents never considered the number of their offspring, for they believed it was the purpose of marriage and the nature of sex for women to bear children. According to the injunction from the family Bible where the names and birth dates of all the Higgins offspring were conscientiously recorded, "Lo, children are the heritage of the Lord." This new blessing—promptly named (but not baptized) Margaret Louise after a Purcell relative and a Catholic saint—was the couple's sixth child in eleven years of marriage, and she remained their youngest for an unusual four years of special attention before another daughter replaced her.

Usually, the Higgins babies arrived every two years and sometimes more frequently, in lockstep fashion after their mother stopped nursing, and thereby lost a natural means of preventing ovulation. After one of the longest hiatuses from childbirth in her married life (though the period included one nearly deathly miscarriage), Anne Higgins delivered another five children in eleven years. Eventually, the ravages of disease and the deliverance of menopause ended her childbearing years, but not before she had given birth to eleven children in twenty-two years and suffered seven miscarriages. She had been pregnant eighteen times in thirty years of marriage. Six years after her last child was born in 1892, Anne Higgins succumbed to the tuberculosis that had made her last years an agony of fitful coughing, bloody expectoration, and persistent enervation. "My mother died at 48," wrote Margaret Sanger in sentences that needed no further explanation to make her point. "My father lived to be 80."[2]

Born in 1845 in Cork County with an archetypal Irish name, personality, and, eventually, drinking habits, Sanger's father had come to Canada as a six-year-old with his mother and his younger brother, part of a massive exodus that began in the 1840s. Throughout Ireland, a strange fungus had shriveled dependable potatoes into inedible roots, and the pressures of English landlords with their demands for rent had become intolerable. With uncertain prospects for a better existence across the seas, but nothing to gain from staying, over a million and a half Irish immigrated to the United States from 1846 to 1852. Many left from Cork, the seaport on the Irish coast in the county where Michael and Anne Higgins were both born.

The Irish mostly settled in the coastal cities of the United States, but some, as much because of the shipping routes as for any other reason, came to Canada, where Toronto, with its access to the Atlantic through the St. Lawrence River, emerged as the favored port of entry. But the Higgins family had another reason to choose Canada: they were following relatives, including Michael's older brother, who tended sheep, cattle, and horses on a stock ranch, probably in the southern part of Quebec province. Here Michael Higgins grew up.

By 1861 the American Civil War offered exciting prospects for a bored and restless teenager. In 1863 Michael Higgins crossed the border and came to New York City. There, offering his experience with animals to eager recruiting officers who needed to fill President Abraham Lincoln's call for 300,000 additional Union troops, he volunteered for service in the elite Twelfth Regiment of the New York Cavalry, lying about his age and his name (he is listed as Michael Hennessy in the rosters) in order to join as an underage drummer. As many as 150,000 Irish fought in the American Civil War, some drafted, others bought for three hundred dollars as substitutes for draftees, and still more, especially in the famous Irish Brigade, served as volunteers.

Unlike the soldiers in that brigade, Michael Higgins saw little of either the glory or the gore of battle that his daughter later claimed he had. In fact, he was sick with tonsillitis for his unit's first muster, and eventually ended up in Union-controlled North Carolina, where he undertook an exciting reconnaissance mission behind enemy lines at Bachelor Creek. An inspiring storyteller, Higgins spun this incident and others into heroic and often mythical tales of military adventures that delighted his children: the time he captured a Confederate soldier on a mule, his unlikely journey across Georgia with Sherman's Union army, and the episode when someone tried to steal the gold coins that were his paternal inheritance.[3]

The Civil War made Michael Hennessy Higgins into an American, though a persistently critical one. He never returned to Canada, a colonial possession despised by many Irish for its devotion to the detested English monarchy. He lost all contact with his mother and brothers. Instead, with great expectations, Higgins settled first in New York City, and then on Long Island, where he was apprenticed to a stone cutter. Perhaps he hoped for a career as a sculptor, for he could craft the most exquisite roses out of obdurate stone with his tools.

What Michael Higgins found in America was a lifetime as a graveyard stone and marble cutter, usually of monuments for children's graves, fashioning lifelike angels and saints and meticulously wrought flowers. For adults, he adorned handsome slabs of marble and granite, with the resurrectionist hopes of the survivors (which he considered absurd) chiseled below family names into epigraphs such as "May you rest in Heaven" and "Dwell with Christ in paradise." When it came time to decorate the graves of his own wife and child in Corning's St. Mary's Cemetery, he used no churchly sentiments, only their names and dates under the surname Higgins, on polished granite topped with a rough, unfinished rock. Perhaps the latter was a testament to the challenges of his own life as Corning's best-known iconoclast.

In Flemington, New Jersey, where he had gone to stay with friends from his regiment, Michael Higgins met and in 1869 married Anne Purcell, the Irish-born daughter of an ambitious day laborer. The Purcells, like Michael Higgins, had emigrated from Cork County during the Great Famine.

After working for a time as potters in New Jersey, Anne's brothers had been apprenticed to a lawyer in Flemington and been admitted to the bar; they then headed west for successful careers in North Dakota. In time both were wealthy ranchers who remembered their more impecunious Higgins nieces and nephews in their wills. After amassing a fortune, William Purcell ran for the state legislature and subsequently filled a vacancy in the United States Senate, where he lobbied successfully for an increase in his brother-in-law Michael Higgins's veteran's disability pension, claimed on the basis of failing eyesight. The pension, awarded first in 1896 as an annuity of six dollars a month, was raised in 1911 to thirty dollars a month.[4]

The first four children of the notably fecund Anne and Michael were born in four different towns in New Jersey, Ohio, and New York, before the fifth child, Thomas, arrived in 1877 in Corning, New York. There, in a town that had prospects of becoming the largest inland city in the United States, Anne and Michael Higgins settled in a community of nearly six thousand, over a thousand of whom were foreign-born, mostly from Ireland and, in fewer numbers, Italy.

The specific reasons for their final destination are unclear. But surely an itinerant life with four children and a perpetually pregnant wife had become impossible, and there may have been Purcell cousins in the community. So many emigrants from Michael Higgins's native county in Ireland had gathered in Corning that one small section of shanties was nicknamed "Corktown." Besides, in a practical test often undertaken by artisans like Michael Higgins, the smoke, soot, and noise of this small industrial city meant jobs and prosperity. Soon, because there were twelve other families with the surname Higgins, Michael became known as "Marble" Higgins.

Corning took its name from its founder, the merchant capitalist and land speculator Erastus Corning. Impressed with the village's location as a port on the Chemung River and anxious to incorporate southeastern New York, with its resources of coal and lumber, into a commercial nexus that he controlled, Corning had bought more than a thousand acres in Steuben County along the river in the 1830s and 1840s. By the time of America's market revolution and capitalist expansion, the land was profitable investment property, eventually returning Erastus Corning's speculative capital many times over. The business blocks on Market Street and the clock tower in Corning's center were located on his land, as were the new railroad tracks that crisscrossed each other along the river flats.

At first, feeder canals to Lake Seneca and then to the Erie Canal transformed the village of Corning into a significant transportation center, as tobacco from the farms in Steuben County, marble and granite from nearby quarries, and coal from the mines near Blossburg in Pennsylvania's Tioga County were transshipped east and south. But even before the Civil War, faster, more dependable railroads had begun replacing river commerce. Again, Erastus Corning, intent on creating a central New York railroad system connecting the west (he had already bought land in Michigan) to New York City, emerged as a financial leader, consolidating the lines in the Gilded Age, a time when, as in Marxist prediction, one capitalist's mergers often killed off many others' businesses. But in time this centralization—and particularly Erastus Corning's giant industrial creation, the New York Central Railroad—condemned the town that bore his name to second-rate status.[5] No longer even a large inland city or hub station on any main railroad line, as town fathers had hoped, instead Corning would forever be associated with another industry—glassmaking. By the 1890s Corning had earned its permanent nickname, Crystal City.

In 1868 the Houghton family had accepted a subsidy of fifty thousand dollars from the ambitious town fathers to move their glassworks from Brooklyn to Corning, where there were promises of excellent transportation, abundant coal and water, appropriate sand, and cheap Irish workers, the latter the human detritus left over from canal and railroad building. After the firm created a means of mass producing the tubes for Thomas Edison's new electric lightbulbs, its factories employed half the workers in town. Smoke belched from the local marvel of hundred-foot brick smokestacks.

Children as young as twelve labored in the glassworks, where the eldest Higgins sons—Joseph, John, and Thomas—at various times supplemented the family income with their wages. In a system widely accepted in the community, the Higgins boys went to school for a few hours and then spent the rest of the day and part of the evening in the glassworks. There they worked as laborers sweeping up and, more dangerously, carrying on long poles the molten globs, the result of silicates fused with sand, soda, lime, and wood ash, from furnaces heated to fifteen hundred degrees, to be fashioned into glassware by the more skilled and higher-paid gaffers.

As in other communities in the United States, the distribution of wealth in Corning's version of the Gilded Age became more skewed: education, wealth, family size, even clothing and leisure activities separated the residents. The local newspaper the *Corning Daily Democrat* under the heading "Town Talk" featured news and gossip of the smart set—trips to Florida and New Orleans during the cold months by the Houghtons of the glassworks and the Drakes of the banking family, social events organized by "the Club," weddings, railroad outings to nearby Elmira, and presentations by the girls studying in the privately funded Corning Academy.

Among the latter was Katharine Houghton, daughter of Amory Houghton, who had founded the Corning Glass Works. A year older than Maggie Higgins, these two never knew each other as girls growing up in stratified Corning. But later, as a fervent supporter of suffrage, the now married Katharine Houghton Hepburn served as a lieutenant in Sanger's birth control movement, though she was best known as the mother of the movie star Katharine Hepburn.

Corning's striking geographical feature, its steep southside hill rising from the river valley, symbolized these differences. The wealthy few who had lived in substantial houses on First Street now moved up the hill on the south side of town, building grand stone and brick homes with turrets, music rooms, and libraries. Young Maggie Higgins did not need any instruction from her father to recognize the contrasts between an existence she later characterized as "strange, hard, and barren, materially speaking" and the softer, gentler life of the wealthy.[6] As she later described the town that along with her father had taught her lessons in America's class structure:

> The people who lived on the hilltops owned their homes, had few children, dressed them well, and kept their homes and yard clean and tidy. Mothers of the hills played croquet and tennis with their husbands in the evening. They walked hand in hand with their children through the streets to shop for suitable clothing. They were young looking mothers, with pretty, clean dresses and they smelled of perfume. I often watched them at play as I looked through the gates in passing.[7]

Meanwhile, the workers lived at the bottom of the hill, in shacks on the fringe of the town or squeezed into the congested area between the river and the railroads. Corning had its share of the late-nineteenth-century version of today's homeless in the itinerant tramps who had no permanent homes and who occasionally slept in the Higgins home. There seemed to be no middle class, though as a skilled worker Michael Higgins might have joined the cobblers, clerks, and grocers who resided along First Street.

Despite this stratification, Corning's opinion makers held to democratic ideals. The *Corning Daily Democrat*'s masthead proclaimed, "We go where Democratic principles point their way; when they cease may we cease to follow." Its proprietors also asserted that "part of the village may be built on the hill, but her citizens do not look down upon those living on flats at their feet. Corning is a homely looking village and in some parts decidedly sloppy but she is attractive to those who know her best and [is] full of business."[8]

In the early 1880s Michael Higgins endured some devastating bad luck: within months a partner ran off with profits from his business and his shop burned down. Still, there was opportunity. Rural country graveyards in garden settings with substantial plots had created a growth industry for sculptors in the late nineteenth century, and every year nearly one hundred residents of Corning died. But Higgins's commissions became increasingly sporadic, and his large family was consigned to the category of poor—never even lace curtain—Irish. Consequently, Maggie spent her childhood as an outsider, classified as a redheaded southside Irish girl. Of course, looking back, she knew why: "Very early in my childhood I associated poverty, toil, unemployment, drunkenness, cruelty, quarreling, fighting, debts, and jails with large families."[9]

After the Civil War, St. Mary's Roman Catholic Church—located on Corning Hill, midway between the rich and the poor—replaced its former wooden structure with a stone building, complete with an organ and stained glass windows, to accommodate the city's Catholic population of two thousand, most of whom were Irish. By 1880, the church, with the financial help of poor but generous parishioners, had added a brick schoolhouse. In an unusual, surely unconstitutional, and soon challenged arrangement, St. Mary's School received public funds from the state of New York and Steuben County, serving for a time as both a parochial and a public "free" school. Here Maggie Higgins and her seven brothers and three sisters attended school for varying lengths of time with differing amounts of attention, sitting obediently in long, crowded rows along a wooden planked bench, careful to avoid the wrath of the Sisters of Mercy and Father Colgan, who was known to use the strap on unruly pupils.[10]

In the shadow of St. Mary's, in a city where the phrase "the bottom of the hill" replaced "the wrong side of the tracks" as a designation of social and economic standing, the Higgins family lived at the foot of Corning Hill, first in a home that Michael had rented after selling one of his finest sculptures, then above his business on Main Street. Later, Margaret Sanger romanticized the shack into a house in the pines, with fresh air that might improve her mother's tuberculosis. In fact, the first of many Higgins residences was dangerously close to the Fall Brook Railway line. In part because of the growing number of Higgins children, and in part because of their father's uncertain support, the family moved as often as every two years, never owning a home but always boarding in various locations on the flats or along First Street. The Corning directories track the family's movements, and by 1890 they lived in a rented home on Second Street.[11]

By the mid-1880s, with her elder sisters gone from home, eight-year-old Maggie had taken up the routinized, inside-the-house female chores. She tended to her younger sister, Ethel, and then to four younger brothers born in quick succession. She stirred the big pot of soup that simmered on the wood stove and sustained the Higgins children; she helped her mother with the extra laundry taken in to supplement the family income; and she even cleaned up the afterbirth when her youngest brother was born. Meanwhile, her older sister Mary took a permanent position as a live-in, lifetime domestic servant in the wealthy Abbott family's home up the hill, and Nan fled to New York City and then Buffalo to become a secretary and later a translator. With lives familiar to many firstborn daughters of immigrant Irish families, neither married.

Plying his trade as a stone cutter, "Marble" Higgins alienated his conservative neighbors with his views on labor unions during a time of violent antagonism between labor and management. The Higgins family had arrived in 1877, a year in which railroad workers staged a nationwide walkout following a reduction in wages. In the United States that year, more than a hundred workers died in pitched battles with security forces hired by companies before federal troops moved in to quiet the fears among the propertied classes of a forthcoming revolution. During the years between 1881 and 1905, 6 million American workers left their jobs for better wages, and 36,757 strikes erupted in the United States. The prosperous classes in Corning believed glassworkers, given their higher wages, would remain well behaved and impervious to what many Americans considered the illegal action of leaving work in order to protect wages. But in 1891 strikers closed down the glassworks, and two years later the nineteenth century's worst depression devastated Corning.

Michael Higgins applauded the strikers and joined the Knights of Labor, a popular labor organization that supported an end to private ownership of the means of production. Yet he never became an officer or even a member of the mainstream organizations that glued the community together, such as the Grand Army of the Republic and the Independent Order of Odd Fellows. Still, Michael Higgins was never invisible like his wife. (Years later, when Margaret Sanger was famous, a dentist who had lived in Corning during her childhood wrote that he remembered her father well, but he did not believe that he had ever seen her mother.)[12]

With his wiry, electric red hair worn longer than customary and his lack of the facial hair favored by this generation of bewhiskered and bearded gentry, Michael Higgins fashioned himself into an outsider—an Irishman who hated the Catholic Church in a religious community of believers, a supporter of the nation's most prominent social dissidents, a union man in a company town, and an unreliable breadwinner with a large family to support. Michael saw himself as an intellectual but, in one resident's memory, "many thought him a lazy, drunken, loud-mouth who would sit around and drink rather than work."[13]

He talked socialism and agnosticism in the town pubs and even invited his hero, the popular orator and freethinker Robert Ingersoll, to speak in Corning, probably in 1885, when Ingersoll was delivering his blasphemous views across the Northeast. Ingersoll was well-known as a critic of both capitalists and priests. And sometimes he even delved into matters of sex and the importance of physical love. Ingersoll talked about sexual desire— "the tender flame"—at a time when few Americans welcomed any discussion of an off-limits topic. Most found it more threatening than even Ingersoll's frequent jokes about the obscenity he found in the Bible.

As retold in Margaret Sanger's *My Fight for Birth Control*, the following episode illustrated the importance of free speech and commitment to principles—even those despised by others—that anticipated events in her own life: The pastor of St. Mary's had interceded to prevent any lecture by the infidel Ingersoll. Reluctant to permit such apostasies, Father Colgan had persuaded officials to padlock the doors of Corning's only public hall in order to prevent such a meeting. As her father so often did in Maggie's memories, Michael Higgins triumphed in the end. Taking Maggie by the hand, he led the audience full of cheering supporters and jeering objectors to a clearing in the woods. There, standing on a tree stump, he introduced his friend "Colonel Bob." In a lecture titled "Why I Am an Agnostic," Ingersoll inveighed against the superstitious practices of all churches. He left his audience with the heretical question "Does God create us or we God?"[14]

Similarly intolerable to most of Corning was Michael Higgins's support of Henry George's radical solution to the inequitable distribution of wealth in America. George proposed a single tax for landowners on the unimproved value of land. In a home with few books, George's exposition of this idea in *Progress and Poverty*—published in 1879, the year of Maggie Higgins's birth—held an important place in a small family library that included the Bible, *Aesop's Fables*, *Gulliver's Travels*, Thomas Moore's *Lalla Rookh*, and Michael's medical books on physiology. But in a city where the Catholic Church held extensive and untaxed property as well as community respect, George's positions were anathema. Articulated loudly by Michael Higgins, such convictions and his invitation to George to speak in Corning ended any commissions from the church, though in his early days in the town Michael had sculpted the church's altar and many of its gravestones. No longer would he decorate the graves of St. Mary's faithful; instead, he would have to look to faraway places for his business.

At home his agnosticism created troubled waters with his devout Catholic wife. All the Higgins children acknowledged the loving relationship between their parents; still, disagreements erupted when Michael Higgins prevented his children from becoming members, through the rituals necessary for a proper Christian life. Maggie, born in 1879, was not baptized until 1893, and according to the priest who officiated, her entrance into the church was accomplished without her father's knowledge. The next year she was confirmed, after parental negotiation.[15] Years later, she remembered her father's challenges to the givens of the church and his ridicule of her nightly repetitions of the Lord's Prayer. When she intoned the traditional "Give us our daily bread," her father interrupted, asking to whom she was speaking. When she replied the obvious, her father then asked whether God was a baker who could feed the Higginses. Retrospectively, Margaret admired her father's lifelong efforts to teach her to think for herself and to challenge conventional wisdom. Such a legacy—her father's way of sanctifying and underwriting the defiance that characterized her life's work—

became her inheritance, for there would be no monetary one. Still, as a child she could never "pray in the same way," and soon would not pray at all.[16]

Certainly the Higgins family presented a challenge for the fathers of St. Mary's Church. Vividly, Maggie recalled standing in line in the Parish Hall for a gift at Christmastime. When she approached, the priest called her "a child of the Devil" with a disgraced father and promptly sent her home empty-handed. When the priests came to encourage Anne Higgins to come to church, sometimes bringing baskets of food to the family, Michael turned them away. After Anne became too enervated from tuberculosis to walk up the hill for services, Michael objected to any priest delivering the sacrament of communion in his home. Only on his wife's deathbed did he relent. According to Sister Mechtilde, a nun who was an eyewitness, a priest gave the last rites on Good Friday to Anne Higgins, who murmured, "My Heaven begins this morning." In Corning lore that forever stigmatized the infamous Margaret Sanger, young Maggie had refused to kneel in prayer as her mother died, though in her own remembrance, she was not in the house.[17] Michael did bury his wife in St. Mary's Cemetery, where as a contumacious, insubordinate nonbeliever, he could never join her in consecrated ground.

While Maggie's younger sister, Ethel, prettier than she, claimed her mother's special attention as the youngest of four daughters, Maggie was her father's favorite. When her younger, unbaptized brother Henry George Mc-Glynn Higgins died—this son bore the name not just of Henry George but of an excommunicated Catholic priest who supported Henry George—her father picked Maggie to help on a secret project. Intent on consoling his wife with a death mask (for the family had no picture of the boy), Michael Higgins walked with Maggie, carrying a wheelbarrow, shovel, and pick, two miles to the graveyard at midnight. Maggie was to swing the lantern as a warning if anyone approached: exhuming a body was a crime.

Meanwhile her father dug up the coffin, opened it, and made a mask of the boy's head and shoulders. "For two nights I worked with Father while he modeled that head. I remember the queer feeling I had when I discovered some of the hair which had stuck in the plaster."[18] The conspirators—father and daughter—then proudly presented a realistic plaster bust of a dead son to a grieving mother consoled by the remembrance.

So close was Maggie to her father that it was he who awoke her earliest erotic feelings. "Sex knowledge" might be "a natural part of life," as she once wrote, but specific aspects of sexual physiology and behavior remained mysterious. Neither Michael nor Anne Higgins discussed sex with their children, though their crowded living quarters assured some understanding. In the more spontaneous first version of her life published in 1931 as *My Fight for Birth Control*, Margaret Sanger recounted the story of her sexual awakening. The incident did not reappear in the sanitized, polished version of her youth published seven years later as *Margaret Sanger: An Autobiography*.

Feverish with a case of typhoid fever, Maggie Higgins lay in her mother's bed. At some point during the night she became aware of her father's heavy breathing beside her. He intended to nurse her through the night, but instead he lay down on the bed with his clothes on and soon was asleep beside her:

It was Father. I was terrified. I wanted to scream out to Mother to beg her to come and take him away. I could not move, I dared not move, fearing he might move toward me. I lived through agonies of fear in a few minutes. Then Father's breathing changed—he was about to awaken. I was petrified. But he only turned over on his other side with his back toward me, taking all the bed clothing with him. I was cold; I began to shiver; blackness and lights flickered in my brain; then I was falling, falling and knew no more.[19]

Hardly an example of familial incest, the episode nonetheless remained an enigmatic tale of an acknowledged sexual coming-of-age that has been interpreted, in Freudian terms, as a classic female dream of defilement and in another view as her initial association through her father of the masculine "aggressive, threatening . . . sexual instinct." In fact it was probably no more than an uninformed recognition of her father's erection and nightly dreams.[20]

Other early memories involved battles to wage and win, whether against illness or the poverty that separated the Higgins children from their contemporaries whom Maggie envied—"the children of the well-to-do . . . free to romp and play wherever they chose . . . secure in their right to live and be just what they were."[21] Still, she respected her own familial legacy of a "rich, colorful [childhood] abundant in things of the spirit." In fact, all the Higginses hated Corning and, save for Joe, left as soon as they could. But the family held great affection for one another and a belief in their mutual exceptionalism. Throughout her life, Maggie remained a loyal Higgins, help-ing her sisters financially when she could as they had helped her, buying a cottage on Cape Cod in Truro, Massachusetts, for her aging father, visiting and entertaining her younger brothers. She did numerous favors for her nieces and nephews, taking one to Europe and paying for another's college tuition. But during her childhood in Corning she lived, as did her father, as an outsider. "We . . . knew not where we belonged. Everything we desired most was forbidden. Our childhood was one of longing for things that were always denied."[22]

Post–Civil War Corning offered an expanding range of consumer goods. But the Higgins children always dressed in hand-me-downs; a younger brother once wore a dress to school. At Christmastime the *Corning Daily Democrat* advertised the elegant new goods that had arrived just in time for the holidays, but unlike her classmates, Maggie could expect no gifts. In-stead, she used her younger siblings as doll babies. Nor did the Higgins children have time or quiet or even a place to study their lessons. Yet ever optimistic, young Maggie Higgins held no crippling sense of bitterness nor guilt about these circumstances, only a comprehension of reality and a de-sire to triumph over obstacles and press forward. Conflict inspired; it rarely intimidated.

Once lacking the necessary ten cents to pay for a ticket to the popular traveling performance of a musical version of *Uncle Tom's Cabin*, Maggie nearly stole ten cents from an open purse and, in the end, snuck into the Corning theater without paying. That night she contemplated the "remem-brance of the power which had seized me, the escape and the victory. I began to think of the stories of the devil and his temptations."[23] Such childhood recollections became inspirational triumphs.

Fifty years later she recounted at length the story of her crossing the narrow Erie Railroad Bridge that spanned the Chemung River. Forbidden to cross the bridge alone, previously she had been lifted by her brothers over the gaps in the tracks. Now she created a risky challenge for herself: "I had to cross the bridge unaccompanied. I had to take that walk alone. I trembled as I drew near. The more I feared it; the more I determined I had to do it."[24] But when she was midway across, a train approached. She stum-bled, fell through the tracks, and dangled dangerously over the river as the train passed over her until she was rescued by a fisherman. As her future life became a journey of challenges and adversity overcome, such memories of girlhood, the stories she chose to include in her autobiography, offered a

melodramatic prelude to adulthood and a reinforcement of triumphs discovered in her early life.

In September 1895, sixteen-year-old Maggie Higgins went away to boarding school. In one of those extraordinary contingent happenings that ac-
company every human existence, what she later termed her "mutiny" began
when her teacher had ridiculed a new pair of gloves, a gift from her sister
Mary. The gloves were too pretentious for the daughter of a poor stone cutter, the teacher implied, as the class tittered. Although her classmates remembered Maggie as polite and quiet, giving, as one said, "no indication of
the bizarre career she would follow," this day she angrily left her seat, ran
home, and promised herself that she would never return.[25] Only two weeks
remained until she would complete eight grades of school—as only about a
third of all the daughters of Corning accomplished. And there was no
schooling for girls available in town after the eighth grade. Nearby Elmira
College for women required completing ten grades in order to qualify for its
newly established secretarial program.

The bleak alternatives for an undereducated girl were domestic service
or early marriage to a factory worker. In fact, her younger sister, Ethel, was
already courting and at seventeen would marry a glassworker. Prudence demanded that Maggie abandon such headstrong behavior and at least complete eight grades, especially since her dreams included going to nearby
Cornell in Ithaca, which had started admitting women in 1870. Her purpose
was to become a doctor. In the private mantra that sustained her life: "When
once I believed in doing a thing, nothing could prevent it."[26]

And little did. She never returned to St. Mary's School after the family
debated her future during the summer. In the fall, sisters Nan and Mary
somehow came up with $50 to pay part of the annual $225 tuition (ap-
proximately $2,250 in today's dollars), and Maggie Higgins, who had never
been farther away than Lake Tioga outside of Corning, enrolled at the Claverack College and Hudson River Institute, a coeducational boarding school
near Hudson, New York. As a middle child, she had benefited from her
family placement. Her elder sisters, whose own ambitions had shriveled,
saved her. Now they projected their dreams of the future, stifled by what
she called their "cruel immolation at the shrine of family duties," onto their
capable younger sister.[27]

By the time Maggie Higgins arrived, Claverack College and Hudson
River Institute had a long history as a respected institution—first as a girls'
school, then as that rarity in the nineteenth century, a coeducational col-

lege preparatory boarding school, with males making up more than two-thirds of its pupils.[28] Predating the elite northeastern single-sex boarding school, it attracted, along with mostly New Yorkers, students from Panama and Venezuela. It offered, as its Methodist mission, to give "a thorough and systematic education to young men and women and at the same time furnish them a comfortable, cultured Christian home." Unlike many schools in this age of harsh corporal punishment, Claverack promised a gentler discipline whereby "government is actually secured more by fixing a high standard of morality, honor, and politeness than by resort to painful discipline."[29]

In Maggie's time Claverack enrolled more than three hundred students in a huge, four-story Greek Revival structure with two wings of rooms for girls and boys, separated by faculty apartments. The campus, which included an armory, drill house, and gymnasium, sprawled across twenty acres a few miles from the Hudson River. Ambitiously, Claverack divided its curriculum into eleven departments, offering traditional subjects along with a strong conservatory and art program, as well as chemistry and biology, military training, and commercial and agricultural training. One could study everything at Claverack, and Maggie Higgins first enrolled in the mostly female commercial department, where she studied penmanship and bookkeeping, and attended lectures on accounting. Later, forgoing any practical considerations, she moved into the literary program.

The expense of such an elaborate facility, as well as declining enrollments because of improving high schools and the impracticality for boys of its transfer college program—its students had to transfer as junior-year students to institutions such as Yale—soon caused its demise: only four years after Maggie left, Claverack closed down permanently. But as schools aspire to do, it had transformed Maggie Higgins of Corning into a more sophisticated, better-educated young woman whose vision of her future life had broadened. Later, in a graphic depiction of this process, she informed a biographer that in her second year she had scratched the name "Maggie" from the register and written over it "Margaret." But like many of the stories created in her selective memory—like her father, she would become an adroit fabulist—this was fiction. What was not false was the college's effect on her rising expectations.

At Claverack College, Maggie entered the world that she had only glimpsed through the fences enclosing the homes of Corning's wealthy. As a work-study scholarship student who paid part of her tuition, she waited on tables and washed dishes, but there was far less such domestic work than there had been in the Higgins home. Unlike life in Corning, in Claverack there was running water, electricity, elegant furniture, and books in the library. Maggie felt less discrimination as a scholarship student than she had in her hometown as a poor Irish child-of-the-devil, and she had more time.

She read, studied arithmetic, painted, and watched the military drill of the handsome cadets, a group of male students who a few years before had included the novelist Stephen Crane. She debated, appeared in plays as the female lead, and gave speeches about Helen of Troy, Cleopatra, and women's rights, while the boys guffawed and drew pictures of her in men's clothing, smoking a cigar. But she did not mind such foolish ridicule. She wrote papers approving of Robert Ingersoll's agnosticism and women's suffrage, though the latter cause remained in the doldrums. On June 11, 1897, in Claverack's chapel, she gave a dramatic reading of the curse scene from *Leah, the Forsaken*, in which Leah believes incorrectly that her lover, Rudolf, has forsaken her and utters a curse on him. Proudly, Maggie sent her essays and speeches home to her father, whom she still acknowledged as "the spring from which I drank."[30] And of course she took up the regnant political issue of the day—the silver question, throwing her support to William Jennings Bryan's inflationary notions of monetizing silver, though few of her classmates agreed.

In the classic manner of learning, Maggie also absorbed a full curriculum in gentrification from her classmates—how to dress, how to fix her lovely auburn hair in something other than pigtails, how to dance (which she enjoyed for the rest of her life), how to take tea, and how to fall in love with boys and girls, employing the appropriate rituals of courtship. Her first crush entangled her with the most popular girl in school, who came from a blue-blooded New York family. A platonic relationship, as Maggie described it in her *Autobiography* after she had become a recognized expert on sexual matters, such an affair of the heart was necessary for all adolescent girls and—sadly, in her view—was profoundly misunderstood by the advice experts. "The depths of its chastity, the simplicity of its fulfillment are part of the girl's growth. Seldom does sex expression enter into the relation . . . I have lived with girls for years and only after I was well along in maturity did I come into contact with homosexual problems," concluded this self-taught informant who rarely used the word "homosexual."[31]

With her delicate oval face, even features, gray eyes, and abundant red hair, Maggie attracted fellow students of both sexes. Many years later friends from Claverack were still writing their news to her and complimenting her on her great work for humanity. Intrigued by another female soul mate who went into the theater and encouraged impressionable Maggie to do the same, she had a boyfriend as well—handsome Corey Albertson from Long Island. With a stilted air and in their best clothes, the two posed one spring day for a photograph, his hat on her lap. All Claverack College knew a secret she both subscribed to and denied: Maggie Higgins and Corey Albertson were engaged to be married. Years later, to her English lover the novelist Hugh de Selincourt, Margaret Sanger acknowledged that she had gone on several vacations alone with Corey and in fact had enjoyed "a real marriage" with him.[32]

In the closed community of a boarding school, Maggie Higgins emerged as a fun-loving leader, organizing activities and, on more than one occasion, illegal escapades off campus. In an episode recounted in her *Autobiography*, she encouraged her friends to sneak off campus and attend a dance in nearby Hudson. Near midnight amid the hilarity, Claverack's principal, Arthur Flack, walked in and marched the sheepish students back to the school. The next day he summoned Miss Higgins to his office. There he accused her of being the ringleader who had led classmates into trouble. Presciently, to her mind, he had noted her influence over others. "You must make your choice—whether to get yourself into difficulty or else guide yourself and others into constructive activities which will do you and them credit."[33]

Maggie Higgins did not graduate from Claverack. Her sister Nan, now living in Buffalo, had paid part of her tuition for three years, which Maggie acknowledged by listing her hardworking sister, not her father, as her guardian in the student register. But by 1898 neither Nan nor Mary could afford the money, and their parents, still feeding four younger Higginses, had no funds to spend on one child's education. Family duty now required that Maggie help support the family, as all Higgins children must. And so after three years, she left Claverack, abandoning her far-fetched plans for medical school at Cornell. Soon she was teaching at a New Jersey school in a classroom of eighty-four pupils, many of whom were non-English-speaking Hungarians, Poles, and Italians. They tested her patience. She was not "suited" for teaching, and so one of the natural, acceptable occupations for women disappeared.[34] Then, in the winter of 1899, she returned to Corning to nurse her dying mother and run a household with four children under fourteen.

Conflict with her father over her boyfriends immediately erupted. After his wife's death, the progressive views of Michael Higgins disappeared into the paternalistic monitoring of "an aggravating, irritating tyrant." Now nineteen, Maggie chafed at her father's discipline, despising his constant monitoring of her social activities and critical evaluations of her suitors. One night, Maggie missed her curfew, and Michael Higgins locked his favorite daughter out of the house. In her dramatic telling of the episode:

> I was left on the verandah in the dark. It was a chilly night in October. I was stunned by such a surprise. I did not know this monster father. I was less than sixteen years old [she was nineteen] and was left out in the streets at night for being three minutes late! Hurt beyond words, I sat down on the steps, concerned over the children at home with this new kind of father . . . I walked away from the house, trying to decide where I should go and what I should do. At first there seemed no one to turn to.[35]

Taken in by a friend and later reconciled with her father, Maggie Higgins nevertheless knew that she must leave Corning and never go back. Returning home became the symbolic expression of defeat. Yet as birthplaces inevitably do, Corning had taught her about class divisions and the arrogance of the Catholic Church. Her conflicts with the church, begun when she was the loyal daughter of a nonbeliever, would forever spur her endeavors. Corning had also instructed her in the ways that convention limited the ambitions of women. After her marriage she would return only three more times during her long life—once to bury her father, a notable occasion when no one came to his wake except family, once for her brother Joe's funeral, and in 1932, when she was mocked by some as that "wicked Sanger woman," to deliver a speech on birth control. "I can never look back on my childhood with joy . . . Even when I am passing through Corning at night by train, my body knows I am there and I become sick at my stomach. I could endure all hardships—anything but remain at home. I wanted a world of action."[36]

2

MRS. WILLIAM SANGER OF HASTINGS-ON-HUDSON

Some lives drift here and there like reeds in a stream, depending on changing currents for their activity. Others are like swimmers knowing the depth of the water. Each stroke helps them onward to a definite objective.

—Margaret Sanger, *My Fight for Birth Control*

A year after her mother died, Maggie Higgins entered nursing school in the White Plains Hospital outside of New York City. Refusing to run the Higgins household, as was expected of Irish daughters in motherless families, Maggie spurned a life with a widowed father whom she believed had "slid into the small town rut of propriety." Besides, as she complained to her older sister Mary, in recent years her father had "never even said that I was a good daughter (after all the washings & scrubbing I did too)."[1] She carried higher aspirations than housekeeping and serving as a permanent surrogate mother to three younger brothers, especially since her success at Claverack College.

Even in a period when only 5 percent of American doctors were female, Maggie Higgins still hoped to attend the only medical school she knew about—Cornell University in nearby Ithaca, New York. But she was too poor and undereducated for admission—even if her sex had not disqualified her. Cornell still "called" to her, as she searched for something to do. Somehow she must support herself and find a worthy vocation.[2]

But what could she do? Certainly this twenty-one-year-old woman with so many male admirers could marry. Her younger sister, Ethel, aged seventeen, had just eloped with a handsome, heavy-drinking Irish glassworker from the Corning factory named Jack Byrne in what soon became a brief, unhappy marriage. Maggie intended a different life. Yet she rejected the traditional occupations for young single women. For this ambitious daughter of Corning there would be no stigmatized domestic service such as her sister Mary endured as "the hard years tending to Mrs. Abbott." Nor would she become a secretary, doing the salaried but subordinate office work that sister Nan so disliked. And Maggie despised teaching after her brief encounter with a classroom of unruly first-graders in New Jersey. In 1900 such were the designated occupations for respectable single women, especially those who, at least temporarily, disdained marriage in a new century that seemed to promise better possibilities for working women.

Another opportunity for girls like Maggie Higgins had recently opened in the burgeoning, haphazardly monitored occupation of nursing, with its training administered through unregulated programs. A natural extension of the female role of caring for sick family members—all women were considered instinctual nurses in this generation—the field had received exciting publicity during the Spanish-American War when an Army Nursing Corps had served overseas in the Philippines. Clara Weeks-Shaw, the author of a popular textbook on nursing, promoted the field as "a new activity for women—congenial, honorable and remunerative and with permanent value to them in the common experience of domestic life."[3]

In readable language, Weeks-Shaw presented nursing as an artful balance between self-reliance and submission. Overall its practices were an extension of maternity, requiring the classic female behaviors of cheerfulness (to the patients) and obedience (to the doctors). "Never leave a doctor alone with a gynecology patient except at his request," went one injunction. "Never present your views unless asked," was another in a book that included chapters on surgery, internal medicine, orthopedics, and gynecology. "Happily," assured Weeks-Shaw about the latter, "ignorance of her own anatomy is no longer regarded as essential to a woman's refinement," though no drawings of the female body were more mysterious to nineteenth- and twentieth-century Americans than those of the reproductive organs. There was nothing on urology—a discipline in its infancy compared to the more established practices of obstetrics and gynecology, on which Maggie concentrated.[4]

In their homes and in the increasingly popular hospitals no longer associated with almshouses for the poor, Americans were hiring nurses to tend them during their illnesses. Ever since the field's great transatlantic priestess Florence Nightingale had laid out the necessary criteria for nurses—they must be disciplined and devoted, and deliver self-sacrificing service in starched uniforms and caps—training programs had proliferated. In the last decade of the nineteenth century, four hundred new nursing schools opened in the United States. Just fifteen had existed previously. Most were in small hospitals, similar to the privately owned White Plains Hospital, where girls in training like Maggie Higgins provided cheap labor.

In this new field, these young women cooked, cleaned, and treated a generation that benefited from few cures, only palliatives. By World War I an astounding four thousand schools—some no more than hiring halls, others boasting a demanding scientific curriculum—were training over ten thousand nurses a year.[5] Most served as private-duty nurses who never worked in a hospital but who registered on a list, as in a longshoremen's hiring hall, to be called out for employment in private homes. Isabel Hampton, who presided over the rigorous program developed at the Johns Hopkins Hospital Training School for Nurses, acknowledged that "a trained nurse could mean anything, everything or next to nothing."[6]

Some physicians protested this innovation of placing patients' lives in the hands of barely trained young girls. Issues of contested territoriality emerged: everyone agreed that female nurses could take temperatures and give enemas, a popular feature of this generation's therapeutic healing. But should female nurses insert catheters in males and give hypodermics and take blood pressure, or were these the domain of male doctors? Indeed, should girls take care of male patients at all? American folklore held that hired nurses were promiscuous, and such a view, however erroneous, influenced the intention of schools to hire only genteel, well-behaved young women. But there was little controversy over the assignment of young women to care for male patients with contagious diseases such as gonorrhea and tuberculosis.

In time, nurse administrators, especially those connected with hospitals and medical schools, standardized training programs and provided the professional rigor that doctors were adopting as well. In the future, associations and state legislatures licensed nurses in what became a dignified vocation, and only programs with a formal curriculum of three years' duration with clinical apprenticeships qualified for accreditation. Only then did nursing leave behind its unsavory reputation, as nurses gained control over their work, although autonomy was always limited because nurses were overwhelmingly female and doctors male.

In 1900 Maggie Higgins discovered this calling of rising prominence, and she benefited from its lack of standards. But no matter how simple her program, from her perspective, nursing irrevocably shaped her future. "I have often said," she wrote an official in the National Youth Administration in 1940,

> that if I had a family of twenty daughters I would encourage every one of them to take a course of nurses' training in a nearby hospital . . . it develops her own personal sense of responsibility. It develops accuracy, cleanliness, order, punctuality. It removes from her consciousness the prejudices of race, creeds and sex, enabling her to administer and to give service to old and young, black and white, Jew and Gentile . . . She is taught to observe not only the dust in corners, but the pupils of the patients' eyes.[7]

The White Plains Hospital and its practical system of nurse training remained typical of many programs. What had been an old stone manor house of three stories had been transformed into a general hospital by a board of managers. The downstairs parlor and sitting rooms became the male ward with six beds; on the second floor nurses tended six female ward patients as well as those in three private rooms. And on the third floor the student nurses lived in the tiny former servants' quarters. One bathroom on each floor served as many as twenty patients and nurses. Without electricity, there was no efficient call system; instead, patients needing attention rang bells or simply yelled. In a dramatic change, because the Hungarian-born, German-trained obstetrician Dr. Ignaz Semmelweis's discoveries on the importance of cleanliness had penetrated medical care in the United States, the hospital's huge laundry boilers sterilized the medical tools—the forceps, clamps, and retractors—of this generation.

"I am only on probation until July 1," wrote an apprehensive Maggie Higgins to her sister Mary in June 1900. "Then if I am accepted I shall continue to take the three year course of four lectures by different Doctors a week and training by our head nurse who is an unusually capable woman."[8] (On reflection, forty years later in her *Autobiography* this same head nurse reappeared as "truly diabolical.")[9] There were no resident physicians. The two attending doctors commuted during the day, allowing precious opportunities, at least at night, for the nurses' independent judgments about the care of patients. Several nights, Maggie presided alone over the delivery of babies, as obstetrics and gynecology had become her specialties.

Drawn to dramatic tales, Maggie described to her sister Mary horrifying incidents of deranged patients wielding knives, her attendance at an autopsy, and the angry young doctor who once chased a nurse out of the operating room, leaving the patient with a needle and catgut sticking out of his nose and Maggie on the floor. The latter episode was the only time she ever fainted.[10] Every day there were dreaded challenges: "An operation soon on a man," she informed Mary, "& how can I stand the smell of ether?"[11]

The White Plains Hospital also provided its trainees with occasional lectures by the attending physicians, covering readings on physiology, anatomy, and medical treatments. Sometimes it was difficult to stay awake, but this knowledge was important for Maggie's future. Among the assignments were those in the emerging field of gynecology, as she absorbed material on pregnancy, childbirth, and how to repair injuries sustained during childbirth. Maggie kept the essential text, Weeks-Shaw's *Text-Book of Nursing*, throughout her life. Well thumbed and with the sections on gynecology underlined, it was in her library in Tucson when she died in 1966. But she also learned by watching and doing. Neither Weeks-Shaw nor the attending physicians mentioned abortion or contraception, both of which were illegal. Had the latter information been covered, local vice committees and the U.S. Post Office would have classified Shaw's textbook as obscene matter.

For Maggie, general nursing was hard but satisfying and esteem-building, yet familiar to a young woman accustomed from her own family life to the physical intimacy and often profane debasing of human bodies that nursing and doctoring require. Nurses' training tested her character. She gave it credit for lessons learned in "integrity, nerve, patience, and endurance," which she believed had "equipped me to organize myself for the battle of life."[12] Like Claverack College, the White Plains Hospital represented another confidence-building challenge met and surmounted— another swimming stroke taken toward an as-yet-undefined goal.

It was certainly not remunerative, for she could hardly afford to buy a new pair of shoes. Nor was it leisurely: "I slept just four hours out of 74 and about ten hours all last week." But by July 1900, manifesting the superior organizational talents that marked her later career, she had become the head nurse of the women's six-bed ward. "I feel complimented to think they feel I am capable."[13] Years later when everyone in America knew her name and letters addressed simply to "Margaret Sanger, New York" were deliverable, several former patients gratefully acknowledged her midwifery skills at the

White Plains Hospital. Some of these, she remembered, had asked for advice on how they could prevent another pregnancy.

By the end of the year she was as sick as the patients. "The girls say I am very thin and have lost my red cheeks," Maggie Higgins wrote in December, not mentioning to her sister the afternoon fevers and night sweats, familiar to all the Higgins children as symptoms of their mother's illness. "But at least there's only a short time to go until we get a New Year's vacation."[14] In fact, she was suffering from more than exhaustion: she had tuberculosis, the airborne bacterial contagion, not in her lungs like her mother, but in her tonsils and lymph glands. This rare, less lethal form of tuberculosis frustrated her plans for the next twenty years.

In the spring of 1901, one of the attending physicians at White Plains Hospital removed some of Maggie's swollen lymph nodes. But small pockets of the bacterial infection remained in the fissures—the crypts, as doctors called them—of her tonsils, where they continued to drain into her sinuses and intermittently bring on the anorexia, fever, and exhaustion symptomatic of this plague that killed more Americans every year than any other disease. Doubtless, surgery had improved, though not cured, her condition and changed it from a death threat into a capricious presence that waxed and waned. In fact, not until 1921, when after several operations an English surgeon removed her tonsils, was Margaret Sanger completely cured, another obstacle overcome.

In the summer of 1901, Maggie worked in an apprenticeship program at the New York Eye and Ear Infirmary. One of the New York doctors, himself a tuberculosis sufferer, warned that she would always have the disease and must expect the life of an invalid. "You see," she wrote Mary, "I am having a fight if I can only get through the three years I can go out & nurse in the west where the animals [a reference to the bacteria] cannot exist."[15] This doctor had mentioned Colorado, the great out-of-doors hospital for thousands of tubercular patients where one-third of the state's population had migrated for the clean air, low humidity, and high altitude.

To deliver such advice to a woman with a family history of tuberculosis remained standard practice until the discovery of streptomycin in the 1940s. In this generation's medical bags there were neither cures nor even palliation, only advice to rest and live quietly in dry, thin air, which was considered hostile to her bacterial "animals." Perhaps Maggie had contracted her own capricious version of tuberculosis from her mother. If this was the case, however, she would most likely have suffered from the more lethal pulmonary version in which microorganisms concentrated in the air sacs of the lungs destroyed the tissue until the lungs resembled sticky glue. Living for years with a woman mortally ill with the disease, apparently the other Higgins children—although the medical history of three brothers is unknown—had built up immunity to infection during their exposure to their mother's airborne bacteria, disseminated by her coughing and spitting. Theirs was not the typical diseased family, whose maternal germs, in the understanding of this generation, made tuberculosis into an inheritable disease with implications for the public health of the community.

More likely, Maggie's tuberculosis of the tonsils and adenoids came from drinking the milk of infected cows—a condition identified as bovine tuberculosis, typically seen among children who drank unpasteurized milk. Perhaps she had been exposed as a child when she and Ethel went to the free milk stations in Corning, before pasteurization was required, and her infection had remained dormant. Possibly she was infected at the White Plains Hospital, where none of the doctors were aware that tuberculosis could be located in the tonsil.[16] Whatever the cause, for a young woman who had nursed her mother to a miserable death, the diagnosis of tuberculosis anywhere was devastating.

Six months after her first operation, Maggie Higgins met a handsome, "intense, fiery-eyed" freelance draftsman, an aspiring architect and artist, at a dance at the New York Eye and Ear Infirmary. William Sanger had come to discuss his architectural plans for a doctor's home in the suburbs; Maggie was dancing with that doctor. Immediately and irrevocably, William fell in love with the charming, slim, auburn-haired nurse; so smitten was he, in fact, that he began waiting on the bottom step of the hospital every morning and afternoon to take walks with her during her few hours of leisure. "When I first saw your lovely self—I came under the rays of your sunshine, basked in the beauty of your mind," William Sanger wrote. "I revelled in your vivacity your intellect your womanlyness, your very feminine qualities."[17] Inclined toward pessimism and depression, he adored her gaiety and resolve. Maggie Higgins recalled a first embrace, when he "tilted my face for a kiss," and left four telltale finger marks on her face from the poison ivy on his hands.[18]

Such intimacy was rare: nurses of this generation lived like cloistered nuns with little time or energy for romance. In an occupation aspiring to respectability, they were often chaperoned. No matter what the restrictions, William Sanger never hesitated to pledge his troth to Maggie Higgins. In the end he was successful at a time when the object of his desires, given her health, was especially vulnerable to his pleas.

During a courtship marked by lavish attention and gifts of jewelry and flowers, Maggie Higgins wavered. It was the classic dilemma of ambitious young women who wanted a career and knew from their experience the constraints that marriage and the subsequent housekeeping and child-bearing brought. On the one hand, after a few months of "my Sanger Lad's" devotion, she was thinking about bridesmaids and all the sentimental accoutrements of fancy weddings that she could not afford—the dress, the honeymoon trip, even the place and time of the nuptials. On the other hand, she was not ready to marry anyone and certainly not until she finished her training. To do so was to abandon her future. "I am not prepared to marry anyone—I hate long engagements myself but I would rather finish training—and when I think of all the hard work . . . the lonesome nights I passed waiting for some tramp to die—then when it is finished—without a laurel to get married—"[19]

Still, the romance enthralled, as William Sanger nudged, gingerly and with appropriate respect, against the nursing career that, given her tuberculosis, threatened her life: "You have given the best time of your life in your present professional vocation—and I thank God that I came, that our souls met [and] that you will give up this strenuous life." As her savior, he promised, in a vow only fitfully fulfilled, to be a reliable breadwinner: "You will be able to have all the leisure and enjoy life—we will soon be on easy street . . . A home with [you] as presiding Queen . . . dearest. A real home—with love the necessary utensil . . . The little home nestled among the trees—we shall build it, of course we shall!"[20]

William Sanger attracted Maggie Higgins because he was different from any of the boys she had previously known—the ones she labeled "dull" from Corning and even Corey Albertson, "that same old boy" from Claverack who casually placed his hat in her lap when they had their picture taken together. Five years older (not the ten that she later fabricated when she began taking her younger sister Ethel's birthdate), he was sophisticated, urbane, and sexually adroit. He earned a middle-class wage from his drafting job at the well-known New York firm of McKim, Mead and White, while pursuing an architectural degree at Cooper Union, the inexpensive People's Institute college where New Yorkers earned professional degrees at little cost. At night he studied painting, one of her favorite subjects at Claverack and part of her intellectual inheritance from her father.

Despite her special relationship with her father, as a middle Higgins she had received from neither of her parents the extraordinary affection that William Sanger so spontaneously bestowed, stopping to buy a scarf she admired or sending flowers on a whim. Of course, Bill Sanger also reminded her of her father with his socialist ideas, anticapitalist talk, and casual irreligion, but despite his principles, he seemed to promise affluence or at least financial security. With his wild hair he even resembled Michael Higgins.

When Michael Higgins finally met his new son-in-law, he gave his enthusiastic endorsement. More of an activist than her father, Bill had recently joined a Socialist Party local in the Bronx, where he lived with his father, Edward Ely Sanger; his mother, Henrietta Wolfberg; and his younger sister, Cecilia. Most heretically appealing for the rebellious daughter of a Catholic from a town without a synagogue, William Sanger was a Jew—by heritage, not conviction.

The Sangers had emigrated from Berlin in 1878 when William was four years old. His father represented a growing stream of Jewish immigrants from Germany as well as, in greater numbers, Eastern Europe, pushed across the Atlantic by increasing pressure from the Prussian state. When the census taker came to their apartment in the Nineteenth Ward two years after their arrival, in 1880, Bill Sanger's father gave his name as Edward, a proper Anglo-Saxon name, and his occupation as a wool manufacturer. Twenty years later, living in a diverse neighborhood of mostly German Jews who sold real estate and insurance, he was listed as Elzia, an unusual contraction of the Hebrew name Eleazar.[21]

At first Maggie Higgins and Bill Sanger shared their alien status: she the migratory, rebellious daughter of a poor Catholic family, he a Jewish immigrant still living at home at twenty-six years of age. Then, for the rest of their lives, they both obscured the facts of his family heritage, which became easier to do when his father died in 1903. Finding Bill's background exotic at first, she later erased it, lest it compromise the fragile birth control movement and her credibility to lead it. To be married to a Jew in the first decades of the twentieth century was to be associated with the radical political views of socialists and to invite the pervasive smear of anti-Semitism.

In her *Autobiography*, Margaret Sanger transformed her father-in-law, Elzia, a wool manufacturer in the garment industry in New York, into

Edward, a wealthy English sheep rancher who had moved to Australia. During one of his trips to Europe, though he was sixteen years her senior, Edward had fallen in love with the mayor of Königsberg's fourteen-year-old daughter, Henrietta. Smitten, he had waited for her to grow up and then returned to marry her. It was "from this talented mother that Bill had derived his fondness for music and his desire to paint," wrote Margaret Sanger.[22]

Meanwhile, Bill Sanger concealed his ancestry because the rampant anti-Semitism of the times, particularly pronounced among New York's architects, threatened his employment in a field that, like so many others, was infected not just with casual rhetorical ridicule against Jews, but with discriminatory hiring practices. Years later Bill's daughter Joan (from his second marriage) confessed that she never knew about her Jewish grandparents. When she sought admission to Barnard College in the 1940s (which like so many colleges at the time had informal quotas for Jewish students) and requested a letter of recommendation from her famous stepmother, Margaret Sanger wrote that Joan Sanger was "a Protestant of a long line of American citizens."[23] Nor were Margaret's two sons, Stuart and Grant, aware that their father was Jewish, although their cousin Olive Byrne Richard recalled visiting the Sangers in New York when relatives in traditional religious garb came to visit.[24]

Certainly Maggie Higgins had discovered Bill's heritage when the two were courting, but his background never inhibited the anti-Semitism she casually expressed throughout her life. Nor did it affect her feelings about him. In a letter written after the two were informally engaged, she wrote of an "at home" to be hosted by "his people . . . oh ye gods I dread to meet them. I wonder if they will have long noses—and own flashy diamonds."[25]

Six months after Maggie Higgins and William Sanger had met, on a hot August day in 1902, during a two-hour break from her nursing duties, Maggie Higgins and William Sanger abruptly married. He had arrived at the hospital with wedding plans but no agreement from the future bride. He had hired a carriage to go to a waiting magistrate and insisted there was time to get married before she went on duty. Still she hesitated. As they drove through the streets of New York, he told his beloved "Peg" that she must decide. Finally she agreed. There was little of the romance that had fueled their courtship in this hasty ceremony, the bride wearing an old blue dress and returning to the hospital twenty minutes later for the rest of her shift.

"I am no longer a Higgins," she informed Nan. "That man of mine simply carried me off—he made me marry him 'now or never' he said . . . I vow I will not live with such a beast of a man. I cannot give up my training." And then later in the same letter, "I am sure I could not have a better husband—he is my ideal in many ways."[26] Nurses were still forbidden from marrying and expelled from training programs if they did so. The marriage temporarily became a secret, a comforting thought for a woman who was not sure she wanted to be married just then anyway.

Leaving before finishing her degree became an early subject of marital disagreement. "As for the hospital arrangement," wrote William to his new sister-in-law Mary Higgins, "I can say that when we were married I did not think the diploma question would loom up in such prodigious proportions. But since then I have persuaded Margaret to change her mind and she will send in her resignation in the next few days."[27] Without graduating, she left the program to live with her husband in his family's apartment in a Bronx tenement.

Five months after her marriage, she was pregnant, and as had been the case with her mother, pregnancy exacerbated her tuberculosis. No longer was the disease in remission. Desperate, the young couple decided that if Bill used some of his savings, she could afford the famous rest cure, not in Colorado—for she could not bear to leave Bill—but closer to home, in the isolated Adirondacks village of Saranac, New York.

By 1900, Americans understood the contagious possibilities of the airborne tubercle bacilli during what was considered a national epidemic. Reaction to the coughing and spitting of the diseased became Margaret Sanger's introduction to the ways in which a formerly private illness emerged as a threat to the community, a plague, requiring the intervention of professionals and local officials. A new category of experts—municipal employees, medical doctors, and state commissioners of health—argued for the removal of the sick from the healthy for the benefit of both. But first, it was necessary to find those who were diseased, encourage them to volunteer for X-rays, register them, and then segregate the infected from the rest of society.

Nothing could be done for the thousands of sufferers living in the less sanitary, more congested parts of New York who could not flee to magic mountains possessing supposed curative powers. For the working classes of New York there was only information about preventing the spread of tuberculosis and unrealistic advice to rest and eat rich food. Lillian Wald's famous settlement house on Henry Street sent visiting nurses into the tenements with information about hygiene. By 1900 health officials had confirmed impressionistic evidence that tuberculosis had social roots: rates in the poorer districts of New York City's Lower East Side—such as the notorious "Lung Block" near Hamilton and Market Streets—were five times those in the uptown neighborhoods. Some experts were beginning to talk of the necessity of sterilizing those in tubercular families, but no one was certain if the disease ran in families because of some genetic predisposition or because of contagion in close quarters. In any case, marriage and especially pregnancy were to be avoided, as the ubiquitous sputum cup along with posters sternly enjoining spitting became the emblems of this generation's crusade against tuberculosis.[28]

For those with means, the tuberculosis sanatorium emerged for refugees from this frightening plague, and there was no better known hospital than the Adirondack Cottage Sanitarium, soon to be renamed after its founder, Dr. Edward Trudeau, who had been cured in the pine-scented, crisp atmosphere of the Adirondacks of the disease he had contracted after caring for a tubercular brother who died in his arms. By the time Mrs. William Sanger arrived in the spring of 1903, the sanatorium consisted of individual cottages where patients followed a strictly enforced regimen of rest and special nutrition.

Endless regulations, characteristic of all sanatoriums, required that patients drink eight glasses of milk a day, along with eating six raw eggs and the despised creosote, a thick, brown, oily concoction made from wood tar that was believed to have antiseptic properties. Trudeau also recommended developing a tranquil mind—(what else was there to think about in the imposed silence than one's impending death?)—while lying on special reclining chairs on porches, "living," as the brochures promised, "outdoors while indoors," no matter what the temperature. Only then, it was believed, could the body's own defense mechanisms reassert themselves and destroy the bacteria.

Trudeau was an effective proselytizer, convinced that a doctor's optimism could rally a depressed patient. Meanwhile, he struggled in his primitive laboratory to discover some sort of vaccine. Unsuccessful, he nonetheless had no difficulty demonstrating the social and economic implications of this disease of the poor: rabbits infected with a strain of tubercle bacilli placed in dark, humid cages with inadequate nutrition in his cellar suffered far higher rates of death than those living in healthier environments with more food. For the humans who came to his sanatorium—a few from tenements, many from more affluent homes, and still others prominent Europeans such as Robert Louis Stevenson—Trudeau charged only what they could afford.[29]

For six months a miserable, pregnant Margaret Sanger rested, ate, and slept in one of Saranac's cottages. She remembered a gloomy environment, talking to patients one day, only to have them disappear the next, with the dead removed quietly at night.[30] When she could stand the confinement and the strict regimen no longer, she fled to New York to have her baby.

It was a difficult delivery. The inexperienced doctor who presided over the birth of Stuart Sanger later inquired what "bearing my lack of knowledge of obstetrics may have had upon this profound movement that is so essentially yours . . . It was a hard night for both of us."[31] Although Margaret Sanger disdained any connections between her personal life and her public cause, in this exception she agreed that her own painful childbirths influenced her commitment to a movement intended to make childbearing voluntary.

Shortly after Stuart's birth, Margaret Sanger had a relapse. The capriciousness of her disease frightened her more than her earlier encounter with the so-called great captain of death. After consultation with several doctors, including Trudeau, "it gradually dawned upon me that preparations were really being made for a long lingering illness, and eventually death."[32] She agreed to return to Saranac with the baby and a wet nurse—the latter required because breast-feeding was considered a possible means of transmission. There she remained for over a year—a dismal period with the enforced invalidism and the germs draining away her natural energy, enthusiasm, and ambition.

One day, after she demonstrated to the Saranac staff her depression and the indifference she felt even toward her baby, a young doctor intervened: "Don't be like this! Don't let yourself get into a mental condition like this! Do something! Want something! You'll never get well if you keep on this way!"[33] Against doctor's orders she abruptly refused to remain an invalid: "I decided to give old Death a run and if he was to outdistance me I'd call it square, but at least I'd die in an atmosphere of love."[34]

Now began the brief domestic phase of Margaret Sanger's life. After her husband's impassioned promise that he would not let her die, and the remarkable improvement in her health, the couple bought land on the Hudson River in the woody hills above upper Broadway. They lived in a rented cottage in the area until their dream home was built. "We wanted something more than a mere house. We wanted space, we wanted a view, we wanted a garden."[35] They found it in the Columbia Colony, a suburban community of professionals who, like Bill, commuted to the city from Hastings-on-Hudson. The husbands left their wives at home to garden, join literary groups, and raise their children. Some were university professors from Columbia University; others worked as doctors or lawyers. All were participating in America's first great suburban housing boom, when a home surrounded by a yard beyond the congested cities of industrial America emerged as the ideal for middle-class families.

Using money inherited from his father, Bill designed and supervised the building of a three-story stucco house on Edgar Street on an acre of land, with views of the Hudson River, a large playroom, several fireplaces, and a large library. Bill had an artist's studio, and Margaret and Bill spent hours together crafting a stained-glass rose window to embellish the head of the staircase, "our keystone of beauty . . . symbolizing the stability of our future." Eight years earlier as Maggie Higgins, she had been living in her father's overcrowded clapboard cottage in Corning; now as Mrs. William Sanger, she took pride in showing visitors her new home built in the style of a grand Italian villa. But in the first glimpse of her husband's unpredictability, Bill was having trouble paying the bills.

In keeping with her newfound domesticity as a full-time homemaker and child raiser, Margaret was pregnant again, despite doctor's orders. Her second son, Grant, was born in July 1908, and with her tuberculosis still dormant, she was defiantly pregnant again thirteen months later. Margaret—nicknamed Peggy—was born in May 1910. After that, Margaret Sanger was never pregnant again.

No doubt the couple employed some form of birth control. Certainly she knew about the illicit, but ubiquitous and often unsound, artificial devices sold in pharmacies or delivered in brown envelopes through the booming mail-order market, though during her life she refused to endorse any means of contraception based on her own personal use. Still, Margaret Sanger knew more than most Americans about male and female physiology, and her training as a nurse had freed her from any self-conscious timidity about matters of sex and reproduction. Yet no public arena existed in which to discuss such matters. By federal law, contraception was labeled obscene matter. Sexual matters must remain private, and indeed were not spoken of at all in some marriages.

Amid declining birthrates—by 1900 the typical American woman had

3.2 children compared to 7.4 a century before—contraception was still associated with promiscuity. Sex was sanctioned for purposes of reproduction, not pleasure. Those who limited their families by artificial means were warned about the probability of bad health, permanent infertility, and, because contraception always came with moral judgments, their sinful interference with God's will.

Meanwhile, doctors saw birth control not as an opportunity to improve women's health, but rather as a hazard threatening their professional practices. Overwhelmingly they opposed any forms of artificial contraception for women, although exceptions were made for men, who were encouraged to use condoms to prevent venereal infection when they visited prostitutes. Still, in some doctors' offices insistent female patients received covert information, as a growing sexual awareness, especially among the upper classes, spurred an interest in limiting the size of their families. By 1900, according to one study, Harvard men had fewer than two children, too few for the well-being of the nation, according to the university's president, Charles Eliot. To this the great American suffragist Elizabeth Cady Stanton responded that it was just as well, because Harvard men made bad fathers.[36]

From his bully pulpit, another Harvard graduate, the then president of the United States and national preacher of righteousness Theodore Roosevelt, spoke for many of this generation when he predicted an impending "race suicide," the result of selfish upper-class women's unwillingness to undertake the pregnancies necessary for their historic role as mothers. The future of the republic and its heritage as an Anglo-Saxon nation rested in their wombs. "The worst evil," asserted Roosevelt, the father of six children, was "the greater infertility of the old native American stock especially in the North East."[37]

For couples like the Sangers, voluntary parenthood accomplished through some sort of birth control was simply smart economics. Children no longer represented useful farm labor. Rather, in the urban middle and upper classes, they were expensive projects of venture capital to be nurtured and educated and only after years of support sent out to their own destiny. Accordingly, more couples controlled their fertility in a variety of ways: by abstinence or a rhythm method often based on an inaccurate understanding of female ovulation. Others used withdrawal—the coitus interruptus called by French peasants *le retrait*, and commonly practiced in 1900 in the United States. Upper-class women depended on an array of post-coital douches, spermicidal suppositories, womb veils, and cervical caps and, in contrarian fashion, took the herbal remedies advertised as "bringing on the monthlies." For men, the ancient condom, now no longer fashioned from thick sheep's bladders but manufactured in smooth galvanized rubber, was the contraceptive of choice.

Such devices were hardly new; they had existed in primitive form in ancient Egypt, where crocodile dung was considered a spermicide. In the Roman Empire, vinegar, along with mule's and eunuch's urine, was recommended, and in medieval Europe a whole series of magical practices to prevent conception found ready believers. In the United States during the nineteenth century, underground literature covertly discussed the practices of birth control. In 1830 the Boston doctor Charles Knowlton had written about some methods in his book *Fruits of Philosophy; or, The Private Companion of Young Married People*, in which he argued that sex must not be treated as a moral issue but rather as a physiological matter. "Mankind will not . . . abstain." To limit family size, "the fecundating property of the sperm" must be destroyed by chemical agents, and for this purpose Knowlton recommended douching. Arrested on the grounds of his book's obscenity, Knowlton was convicted on obscenity charges and imprisoned for three months.[38]

There were other freethinkers imparting sexual knowledge in the United States during the nineteenth century, though none were well-known. A self-anointed British physician who immigrated to the United States in the 1840s, Frederick Hollick, included drawings of female and male sexual organs in *The Origin of Life: A Popular Treatise on the Philosophy and Physiology of Reproduction* and *Married Guide or New History of Generation*, the latter published in 1845. Hollick, like Knowlton, celebrated sex, separated it from reproduction, and recommended douching. Soon he was arrested, tried in a Philadelphia court, and sent to prison for publishing a scandalous book that encouraged promiscuity.

Despite such censorship, American attitudes and behaviors were quietly changing. A survey undertaken in 1910 by a California physician, Dr. Clelia Mosher, revealed how far reality for upper-class Americans diverged from the conventional wisdom that children were the gifts of God. A sample of forty-three wives of professional men, all with high school diplomas, revealed that they enjoyed sex and experienced orgasms. Over 90 percent of these couples used some form of birth control—for the women various forms of pessaries and douches, for the men condoms, and for both partners withdrawal.[39]

With the birth of Peggy in 1910, the Sanger family, fulfilling the national average of three children, was complete. Life seemed tranquil during this brief interlude in the first decade of the twentieth century, though Margaret Sanger remembered it as a period of bad health "given over to constant consideration of recovery . . . years of combat—unending, discouraging, impossible except for the indomitable optimism of youth."[40] She spent her afternoons in a playground with other mothers discussing problems with servants (the Sangers had a live-in German maid), her garden, her children, sometimes politics, and possibly sexual knowledge. She joined a literary society where the wives read papers on George Eliot and Robert Browning. The group was a forerunner of the Women's Club of Hastings, which not many years later refused to let its most famous former member deliver a talk on birth control. Her days revolved around the children in soft, easy routines enlivened by trips to the New York opera and theater. Yet whether in retrospect or at the time, Margaret Sanger believed that "there was an inclination among both husbands and wives, to sink back into a complacent suburban attitude, to enjoy petty middle class comforts."[41] Understanding herself as a special human being, she intended to resist such an inclination.

Then a fire, started one cold winter's night from an overheated stove, destroyed the house. With the children, Margaret watched the flames crack, shatter, and then melt the iron moldings of the rose window that had symbolized the stability of her home and her love for Bill: "I stood silently regarding the result of months of work and love slowly disintegrate," contemplating "the futility of material things."[42] The house was rebuilt, but her attachment to Hastings, the Columbia Colony, and her home died in the fire. Dramatically, just as she had closed the door on Corning and her childhood, now she did so on Hastings and her brief episode as a traditional wife and mother. "My scale of suburban values had been consumed by the flames, just as my precious rose window of leaded glass had been demolished . . . A new spirit was awakening within me; a strong, insistent urge to be in the current of life's activities. I felt as if we had drifted into a swamp and had to wait for the tide to set us free."[43]

Sometime in 1910, the year of his third child's birth, William Sanger quit his full-time job as a draftsman and began a career as an artist. Now he worked mostly in his studio. Meanwhile his wife had no such focus, only the profound understanding that she must leave the suburbs that had briefly seemed paradise. In 1911, over her husband's objections, the dream home was sold and the Sanger family moved back to the city. Later William regretted selling the house where he had lived during the best years of his life.[44] But for Margaret, the best times lay ahead.

3

COMRADE SANGER

It is not hard to laugh about it all now, but no one could have been more serious
and determined than we were in those days.

—Margaret Sanger, *Autobiography*

Before Christmas, in the winter of 1910, the Sanger family—thirty-six-
year-old William, thirty-two-year-old Margaret, and their three children,
all under nine—moved into New York City. They came mostly on Margaret's urging, for she had grown restless and bored with suburban life. She
had tired of "the tamed domesticity of the pretty hillside suburb" and worried
about becoming "kitchen-minded."[1] Bill acknowledged that his wife disliked
the routines of domesticity, even with the help of a German housekeeper.
Intent on her superiority in all things, Margaret demurred: housekeeping
"with its endless details was [never] drudgery to me. There was always the
interest of conquering the problems, which made it fun."[2]

But the Sangers also came to the city because their income had shrunk
now that Bill no longer worked full-time as an architect and draftsman,
and instead, captured by the possibilities of life as an artist, spent his days
in a studio in Greenwich Village. Bill's widowed mother joined the family,
frequently watching the children in an arrangement that Margaret both
appreciated and resented. They rented a flat in a four-story freestanding
"railroad" tenement with large, open rooms on upper Manhattan's West
135th Street. Although they were less than ten miles from their former
residence along the Hudson River, they might well have been in a foreign
country.

•

Margaret had first discovered New York during her exile from home, when she had found sanctuary in Manhattan with her wealthy Claverack friend Esther Farquharson before entering nursing school. When she married Bill in 1902, the newlyweds briefly shared an apartment in the Bronx with his parents. Even during her suburban years she had entertained the children and herself with trips to what was undeniably America's commercial and cultural center and, as well, the nation's hub for radical ideas. According to one of her new acquaintances, the writer Walter Lippmann, "at some time everyone lived in New York [where] it was easy for a young man to believe in the inevitability of progress, in the perfectability of man and of society."[3] Lippmann's "everyone" referred to the intellectuals, writers, and artists who clustered along the narrow, twisted streets of Greenwich Village, living in converted stables and boardinghouses previously inhabited by Italian immigrants. During the decade before World War I, in both their work and their behavior, the self-conscious residents of Greenwich Village experimented with boisterous ways of liberating themselves from the imperfect ways of the past.

The foreign-born accounted for the spectacular increase in the numbers of New Yorkers during this period. Earlier, the harbor, featuring since 1886 the 151-foot Statue of Liberty, with its female figure holding aloft the golden torch of an anticipated freedom, had welcomed Germans and Irish. Now the nationalities of these future Americans shifted. During the first decade of the twentieth century, 155,000 Catholic Italians, 78,000 Poles, and 181,000 Russians, most of the latter Jews, entered the city through Ellis Island, gathering on the Lower East Side in overcrowded dumbbell-shaped tenements with little light and ventilation. The area bounded by the Bowery on the west, the eponymous East River on the east, and Houston and Monroe Streets on the north and south soon became, as a reform society reported, "the filthiest place on the Western continent with a population density worse than sections of Bombay."[4] By 1910, as this new immigration surged, New York's five boroughs contained a population of nearly 4 million; by 1930 that number had doubled.

Conditions on the Lower East Side occasioned Margaret Sanger's earliest professional writing, published in September 1911 in the socialist daily *The New York Call*. In the first of several articles, she described the miser-

able living conditions of immigrants, and in graphic prose outlined the problems of ghetto children and their mothers during these years before she
discovered the solution to their despair:

> Everything is thrown out of the windows; garbage is rolled up in news-
> papers and thrown . . . into the streets . . . where the toilets are in
> use by the many families on the same floor, the mother allows the
> children to use paper as toilet receptacles and it too is thrown out of
> the windows . . . And the vermin . . . kitchens swarming with, not
> thousands but millions of roaches . . . Bed bugs are everywhere . . .
> thousands of mothers leave their little children in the care of the
> older boy and girl (usually not over nine years old) and go to work
> early in the morning in the factories or work shop to return at night
> to do the work of the family . . . the washing which takes until two
> in the morning, the next night the ironing, which takes the same time
> and so on with the scrubbing, cleaning and mending . . . in this ter-
> rible existence day after day this worn out and half famished mother
> continues her burden of life.[5]

Two decades later, Margaret Sanger disliked the city that she had first
embraced as "a great Pageant of Living," the place where through the simple
process of observation she clarified the purpose of her life. By the 1930s she
detested New York's crowded streets, bone-chilling winter weather, and
grimy, sooty air so damaging to her lungs, and especially its dark days, when
the sun, increasingly obscured by skyscrapers, disappeared for weeks. But
in 1910 New York offered exciting possibilities for personal experimentation and professional activism.

The Sangers had lived in the city only a few months when in April 1911,
a fire at the Triangle Shirtwaist Factory near Washington Square killed
146 garment workers, mostly young Jewish girls, who either died of smoke
inhalation or jumped to their deaths from the sixth floor. The doors to the
fire escape had been locked by the owners; short fire hoses had failed to
deliver any water to the upper floors. The tragedy became an epic example
of unsafe working conditions during a period in American history when in-
dustries operated with few regulations. The headline in *The New York Call*
after the fire read "Let the Guilty Answer" for this "holocaust," though there
was no punishment of the owners of the Asch building.[6] No doubt Margaret

and Bill joined the solemn funeral parade of more than 150,000 New Yorkers marching silently down Fifth Avenue to demonstrate their solidarity with
the families of the dead women.

Mass protests during this decade before World War I were unavoidable.
There were parades organized by the suffragists as the New York legislature, yet again, prepared to take up proposals for a state referendum to consider votes for women. During this period of union activism it was not
unusual to pass pickets outside of factories, especially in the garment district, as the battle between labor and management that Margaret Sanger
had first observed in Corning intensified. For her, New York was politics
observed and engaged.

Immediately after the family was settled, Margaret resumed her
nursing career: the family finances could not depend on the intermittent
mortgage payments from the purchaser of their Hastings home. Life in the
distant suburbs had choked off her nursing career. Now, in a city with
rapid transit where she was minutes away from the Lower East Side and
only a telephone connection removed from a doctor or patient, she took
advantage of methods of communication unknown in Corning during her
childhood. And there were more patients to nurse. Now she must take advantage of her professional opportunities as she discovered in her husband
the improvident ways of her father.

Yet Margaret Sanger had not finished her degree and was not a registered nurse. Initially she worked as one of Lillian Wald's growing band
of visiting nurses who, with their heavy black leather bags, carried to the
residents of the Lower East Side both traditional treatments and new hy-
gienic information about how to avoid the white plague of tuberculosis.
By 1910, fifty mostly unmarried visiting nurses sallied forth every day but
Sunday from the Henry Street Settlement House that Wald funded from
private donations to offer various services to the poor, with married nurses
expected to stay at home and work only at night and on the weekends. Too
independent for Wald's program and too impatient for public health nursing, which preached long-term preventions and not solutions, Sanger soon
left to establish her own practice. For some referrals, she turned to her
younger sister, the now divorced Ethel, who was finishing her nursing degree at Mount Sinai Hospital; for others she depended on the word-of-mouth
recommendations of her patients on the Lower East Side who skimped so
that they might pay a few dollars for her services.

Mostly she accepted obstetrical cases. Such commitments could be roughly scheduled and were of shorter duration than a medical case such as pneumonia, or a patient's lengthy recovery from the increasingly invasive surgery practiced by this generation of doctors. Often she served as a mid-wife, delivering babies by herself as she had learned to do at White Plains. Always, as her mother's daughter, she attempted to respond to the notice-able anxiety of postpartum mothers and their repeated questions about how they could avoid another pregnancy. More often than not, she offered ele-mentary information about the two cheapest means of contraception: con-doms and coitus interruptus, saying nothing about the complex pessaries used by wealthy women who learned how to insert these so-called womb veils in the offices of their private-practice gynecologists.

Her patients on the Lower East Side knew all about this class-based system of birth control: "It's the rich that know the tricks, while we have all the kids," they told her.[7] Sanger learned other lessons from these mothers of the Lower East Side. While she despised "the wretchedness and hope-lessness of the poor," she never experienced the satisfaction of "noble women" who brought parcels of food and bags of clothes along with their kind, patronizing words. "I could see that much was wrong with [these mothers] which did not appear in the physiological or medical diagnosis. A woman in childbirth was not merely a woman in childbirth. My expanded outlook included a view of her background, her potentialities as a human being, the kind of children she was bearing, and what was going to happen to them."[8]

One night in the summer of 1912, Margaret Sanger experienced a life-altering epiphany while nursing one of these women. A doctor had called about a patient on the Lower East Side who had an infection from a botched abortion—a common enough, though illegal, procedure that cost five dol-lars and attracted scores of women to shady practitioners. Some women tried to save a few dollars by inserting wires and hangers into their vaginas or in-gesting the abortifacients advertised in newspapers. When this patient, Sadie Sachs of Grand Street, recovered, her first question to her doctor was one Sanger had heard before: what could she do to prevent another pregnancy?

Already the mother of three and only twenty-eight years old, Sachs wanted no more. The doctor replied indifferently, "Any more such capers, young woman, and there will be no need to call me." Sachs persisted: "What can I do to prevent getting that way again? Another baby will finish me." The doctor laughed, and then delivered his profession's frivolous objection

to the use of artificial means of contraception: "You want your cake while
you eat it too, do you? Well it can't be done. I'll tell you the only sure thing
to do . . . Tell Jake to sleep on the roof."[9]

Months later Margaret was called back to the Sachs apartment. Again
Sadie had become pregnant and again she had resorted to a dangerous,
self-inflicted abortion. This time she died from septicemia, leaving a devastated husband and children. Disgusted with herself and the doctor for their
inability to help, in her retelling of this incident, Sanger left Jake and the
children weeping and with characteristic drama underwent her "Revolution":

> I walked and walked through the hushed streets. When I finally ar-
> rived home . . . I looked out my window and down upon the dimly
> lighted city. Its pains and griefs crowded in upon me, a moving pic-
> ture rolled before my eyes with photographic clearness; women
> writhing in travail to bring forth little babies; the babies themselves
> naked and hungry, wrapped in newspapers to keep them from the
> cold; six year old children with pinched pale wrinkled faces old in
> concentrated wretchedness pushed into gray and fetid cellars crouch-
> ing on stone floors, their small scrawny hands scuttling through rags,
> making lamp shades artificial flowers, white coffins, black coffins,
> coffins, coffins interminably passing in never-ending succession . . .
> The sun came up and threw its reflection over the house tops. It was
> the dawn of a new day in my life also . . . I was resolved to seek out the
> root of the evil, to do something to change the destiny of mothers
> whose miseries were as vast as the sky.[10]

Now she must abandon the palliative care of nursing individuals and
instead treat humanity. "I was now finished with superficial cures, with
doctors and nurses and social workers who were brought face to face with
this overwhelming truth of women's needs and yet turned to pass on the
other side . . . I resolved that women should have the knowledge of contraception . . . I would tell the world what was going on in the lives of these
poor women. I *would* be heard. No matter what it should cost. I *would* be
heard."[11]

At the time she was an improbable leader of such a cause. Others, especially the well-known radical Emma Goldman, were earlier, better-known
advocates of contraception. A decade older than Sanger and a self-taught
nurse and midwife, Goldman had fled her native Lithuania in order to avoid

a forced marriage. She arrived in New York with five dollars, a sewing machine, and an ardent sexuality that matched Sanger's, though her love affairs usually ended in heartbreak. Goldman had already served a year in jail for her role in the attempted assassination of Henry Clay Frick. As a committed anarchist she published the subversive magazine *Mother Earth*, whose first issue she dedicated to Leon Czolgosz, President McKinley's assassin. Most Americans considered her a repugnant threat to society; *The New York World* dismissed her as a wrinkled, ugly Russian peasant. But Goldman was a powerful speaker on the lecture tours that drew hundreds, and for a time she became a model, though never a mentor, for Sanger's future.[12]

Sanger lacked any training in the process of how to change opinion or even how to create a durable reform movement, the latter tentatively achieved in this decade before World War I by unionists and suffragists. Nor did she have money or influence. "I was not trained in the arts of the propagandist. I had no money with which to start a rousing campaign. I was not a trained writer nor speaker . . . I had no influential friends, and I was digging deep into an illegal subject."[13] Yet, through the various means of her ascent, she became a quick study and a shrewd observer, and so spent these years as an apprentice in the radical movements of the day—learning how to write effective propaganda, working as an activist in the streets, growing accustomed to stinging criticism, and listening, on a more positive note, to those who would change the world in a multitude of ways. Her friend, the leader of the Industrial Workers of the World, Bill Haywood, appreciated her ambitions: "Girl," he told her one night. "You are getting ready to kick over the traces."[14]

Sadie Sachs's death, representing in Sanger's mind that of thousands of women, became a constant theme in her writing and speeches. Like many reformers, she often referred to this episode, her burning vision on the way to Damascus, as a way of making obvious to her what must be done for humanity. Possibly a conflation of the medical histories of several different patients, especially given her fabulist predilections, the event became the creation story of her movement, as she retold the sad medical history of Sadie and her family, an uninterested physician, and her own realization of the crucial importance of separating sex from pregnancy. Controlling conception now became the plot of Margaret Sanger's life. At first it clarified her search for a life beyond domesticity. In time, as a hero's tale, it offered enemies to overcome, challenges to navigate, and, as well, international acclaim accorded to a pioneer.

Margaret Sanger soon discovered just how different her struggles were from the battles of those who sought more traditional and acceptable re- forms: the progressives who worked for more playgrounds for city children and public toilets for women, the temperance workers from the Woman's Christian Temperance Union who wanted to end the sale of liquor and in their social purity division raise the marriage age for young girls, and the suffragists from the National American Woman Suffrage Association who lobbied for voting rights for women. Sanger's self-help reform was a revolu- tion because it involved public discussion of secret matters of sex, consid- ered unspeakable and obscene. Her vision of preventive medicine required Americans' exposure to, and acceptance of, intimate matters of sexuality and anatomy, even though ears and tongues had long been sealed to such matters by the mandates of priest and legislator.

But unlike suffrage, temperance, and urban reform, there was not even a solution, for no efficient means of female-controlled birth control existed in 1912. There would not be any safe, inexpensive, and convenient contra- ceptive for another fifty years. Sanger's movement did not even have a name until one evening during a discussion with friends at her apartment the eu- phemism of family planning and voluntary parenthood gave way—simply, irrevocably, and consensually—to "birth control." When she became the doyenne of birth control and would share neither credit nor leadership, Margaret Sanger claimed, with her selective memory at work, sole author- ship of the name.

Nursing obstetrical cases left time for Sanger's superabundant energy, and through her husband she was swept into the world of New York social- ism. Before their marriage Bill had joined Branch 5 of the Socialist Party, encouraged by his father, Eleazar, who considered Eugene Debs, America's homegrown revolutionary and founder of the Socialist Party of America, a friend as well as a hero. The German Jews of Eleazar's earlier generation of New York immigrants had freed themselves from their home country ties to Old World Judaism; some had become ardent advocates of socialism and, to a lesser extent, anarchism. Certainly their observations of capitalism in New York—and especially in the garment industry, where her father-in-law worked—reinforced commitments to the necessity of systemic economic and political change in their new country.

Some of those who would transform America supported anarchism, an imported set of beliefs promoting the overthrow of the state and the substitution of local governing communes. Rules were anathema; deeds of propaganda, sometimes through violence, were necessary to persuade the indifferent. By 1910 anarchism was associated by mainstream Americans with terrorism, and the connection would be reinforced during the coming decade. Most advocates for transformative change focused on the revolutionary proposals of theoretical, Marx-accepting socialists for class warfare. For a time Sanger was attracted to both, preferring "the individualist, anarchist philosophy . . . but it seemed to me necessary to approach the ideal by way of Socialism—as long as the earning of food, clothing and shelter was on a competitive basis, no man could ever achieve independence."[15]

By the spring of 1911 Margaret Sanger had joined Branch 5 of the Socialist Party of New York, located only a few blocks from the Sanger apartment. "Almost without knowing it you become a comrade," she wrote, though of course, given her paternal heritage, her husband's embrace of socialism, and her own rebellious instincts, she needed little persuading.[16] As an official fifteen-dollar-a-week organizer for the New York Woman's Committee for Propaganda for Socialism and Suffrage, she arranged events for an organization that, amid much controversy over the issue, only in 1908 had established a separate women's division. European socialists disapproved of what was thought by purists to be a diversion, diluting attention from male wage earners and the need to create a proletariat who chafed with revolutionary consciousness.

But Branch 5 was well-known for its acceptance of women and the extraordinary amount of socialist literature it disseminated. It boasted a Committee on Propaganda that met weekly at headquarters "to fold, assort, stamp, and count" thousands of pamphlets and newspapers. As a new member, Margaret Sanger stood on the street corners of New York handing out this publicity, overlooking the taunts of objectors and patiently explaining the cause to the curious. She also went door-to-door, hoping to enlist the Scandinavian women in her neighborhood. The result of this effort to communicate socialism's lofty goals was heralded in a letter from a comrade to *The New York Call*: "The present committee on distribution with its assistants have accomplished more in the past seven months than any time in the history of the Harlem Socialist organization. From January to July 114,000 pieces of Socialist literature went into the homes of about 15,000 families, and never before has such a Socialist sentiment existed."[17]

During the municipal elections of 1911, Margaret handed out materials touting her husband. Bill Sanger, a leader in his local, was running for alderman in the Twenty-third Assembly District on the Socialist Party ticket. At the time, official strategy incorporated plans to install local socialists in municipal governments. Socialists had been elected to local positions in several American cities, notably in Milwaukee, where Victor Berger now served in Congress. These were the optimistic years of possibility for American socialists, who believed that their movement, founded in the United States only a decade before, represented the electoral future of America. All that was needed was time and the means to spread the message. "Socialism in New York advances," headlined *The New York Call* before the election. "The socialist vote is becoming gigantic"—a point demonstrated to the faithful a few years later when Meyer London, a hero after his activity in the New York cloakmakers' strike, was elected to Congress and numerous socialist mayors took office throughout the United States.[18]

Despite these expectations, there were never more than a few hundred socialists in Bill's district, where he received 352 votes, the least among three other candidates in a district that polled 10,000 votes and where the Tammany Hall candidate won, as usual. The next year, in 1912, when Eugene Debs ran for president, the Sangers were disappointed when he received only 6 percent of the national vote in an election contested by four presidential candidates and won by Woodrow Wilson. The laws of New York and the nation prevented Margaret from voting for her husband and Debs. But years later, when she finally could cast a ballot and was a wealthy woman living on an estate in Fishkill, New York, she consistently voted for the Socialist Party presidential candidate Norman Thomas, the only voter in her precinct to do so.

Soon Margaret had her own ideas about how the affairs of Branch 5 should proceed. "My Dear Comrade Gerber," went an undated letter to one of the party leaders. "We have been having excellent success at the meetings . . . I also left word for you that we are out of literature. Could you rush that order of the 'New York Woman' and have five thousand sent directly to my home . . . We need speakers so badly and I hope you can get some who understand the Woman question. I trust I am not giving you too much trouble." She signed herself with the socialist watchwords "fraternally yours."[19] At night she listened to the long theoretical arguments that radicals of this generation relished. "They really came to talk to Bill and I made the cocoa," Margaret later wrote in the age-old acknowledgment of female service rendered to male reformers who preached equality, but never noticed who served the cocoa.[20]

Margaret had been attracted to Bill for his knowledge of revolutionary theory, and she remained an eager student. Even as she was listening to those she deemed "a very superior group," and feeling herself inferior to these college graduates and intellectuals, Bill was encouraging everyone "to listen to Margaret. Margaret has something to say on that. Have you heard Margaret? She has some ideas about that."[21] Never a profound thinker, she spent hours at home and in the library of Branch 5 headquarters absorbing the basic socialist texts of Marx, Engels, and Karl Liebknecht. The latter, a German Marxist, founder of the Spartacist League, and a vehement antimilitarist, had impressed her three years earlier during his speaking tour of the United States. In Yonkers, where she had heard him, he had repudiated the American Constitution, arguing that it was not worth the paper on which it was printed: "No other country save America compares to the waste of the citizenship of human life and the trampling on the rights of man."[22] Yet the future plans of these critics still seemed too remote and utopian for a woman who wanted action.

Her new socialist comrades included the most talented writers and activists of this generation—Jack Reed, the Harvard graduate, poet, and journalist who moved to the Soviet Union during the Bolshevik revolution and died there of typhoid fever in 1919; Alexander "Sasha" Berkman, the Russian-born anarchist and attempted assassin of Henry Clay Frick, so beloved of Emma Goldman; and "Big Bill" Haywood, the mesmerizing one-eyed leader of the Wobblies, officially the Industrial Workers of the World, a group that promoted strikes and industrial, not craft, unions. Haywood died an exile in the Soviet Union, after his intentions for overthrowing capitalism foundered.

There were female role models besides Emma Goldman, among them Elizabeth Gurley Flynn, the oft-arrested Irish firebrand who spoke at labor rallies, and Jessie Ashley, the wealthy socialist lawyer who had graduated from New York Law School and was now spending her family inheritance supporting radical magazines and providing bail for jailed anarchists. Crucial as well was Sanger's friendship with Anita Block, who, with her husband, John, published the socialist daily *The New York Call*, circulation twenty thousand, whose masthead carried the slogan "Devoted to the Interests of the Workers."

Impressed with Sanger, Block enrolled this new member as a speaker at

open-air meetings and as a writer for her popular feature "The Woman's
Page." Shortly thereafter, a nervous Margaret Sanger found herself on a
stage in the Labor Temple on Eighty-fourth Street, delivering her first public lecture on the benign subject of "Social Conditions of Today as Seen by
the Trained Nurse."[23] Gradually she expanded her lecture topics to include
more subversive themes of sex education, and soon *The New York Call*
was advertising her apartment on West 135th Street as the place to go "for
all information concerning the Work of Margaret H. Sanger."[24]

The turn-of-the-century Socialist Party offered its members more than
weekly study groups immersed in the finer theoretical points of Marx and
Engels and the deficiencies of modern capitalism. Branch 5 organized outings and dances; it held masquerade balls and picnics in Pelham Bay Park
and, once, a moonlight excursion down the Hudson River. It sponsored
debates, such as the one Bill Sanger arranged between trade unionist Morris Hillquit and the socialist leader Eugene Debs over how best to transform capitalism in America. It supported an adult school and, most important
for the Sangers, was affiliated with the new educational endeavor of the
Modern School movement, organized around the martyrdom of the Spanish anarchist Francisco Ferrer.

In 1909 Ferrer, intent on reforming Spanish education by establishing
so-called Modern Schools, had been convicted with little evidence and
executed for his role in fomenting a riot that had broken out earlier that
year in his home city of Barcelona. Ferrer's real threat to the authorities lay
in his educational reforms that rejected the traditional church- and state-
run schools in a nation where two-thirds of the citizens were illiterate. The
Catholic Church immediately recognized Ferrer's threat. Its clergy had little
difficulty in persuading the authorities to close up Spain's Modern Schools
on the grounds that they trained revolutionaries. Thereafter Ferrer was a
marked man. His death, considered a judicial murder by anarchists and socialists in Europe and the United States, created a spontaneous movement
in New York that led to the creation of a Francisco Ferrer Association.

Self-styled freethinkers and socialists including Emma Goldman, Leonard Abbott—the lawyer and head of New York's Free Speech League—as
well as the Sangers, raised money for a school dedicated to his educational
ideals. By 1912 the Ferrer Center on Twelfth Street in Greenwich Village
offered lectures to adults. Rosa Phelps Stokes, the factory girl who married a millionaire, taught socialist theory. Authors Upton Sinclair, Eugene

O'Neill, and Theodore Dreiser lectured on writing and literature, and Margaret Sanger spoke on sex education and preparing for marriage.

The central focus of the Ferrer Association agenda remained the creation of schools for children, and when such a school opened, all three Sanger children were eventually enrolled. In January 1912, nine-year-old Stuart Sanger, the eldest of the children, joined eight other children in the Modern School located first in Greenwich Village and later in an old brownstone building on East 107th Street. Twenty-seven-year-old Will Durant, later the author of the popular seven-volume *Story of Philosophy,* served as the school's head, teaching most classes himself, with time left over to court the school's only other teacher, his future wife, Ida (Ariel) Kaufman.

Following Ferrer's precepts to make "the boys and girls well-instructed, truthful, just and free from all prejudices," Durant challenged the dogmas of the past: women must not be restricted to the home; evolution was proper scientific theory; the unequal distribution of wealth must be overturned. While it is not clear how deeply such ideas penetrated the minds of its youthful student body, the children enjoyed freedom from the traditional pedagogy practiced in American public schools. According to Ferrer's principles, there must be neither tests nor punishments nor, in the standard practice of the day, recitations of memorized material. Each day the children chose their own activities in a type of learning that, in a less exaggerated form, the philosopher John Dewey made acceptable as progressive education. Later, Stuart Sanger, who graduated from the elite, traditional Peddie School in New Jersey and then Yale University, complained that he had never learned anything in the Modern School.

Margaret Sanger did more than enroll her children in a school that supported radical values. She led a brigade of automobiles flying the anarchist's black flag, filled with women, to the courthouse to protest their socialist friend Frank Tannenbaum's sentence of a year in jail. Tannenbaum, later a respected sociology professor at Columbia, had broken the windows of St. Alphonsus Church when its priests refused to open its doors to the homeless. But most of her activism came from her association with her friend Bill Haywood.

The first opportunity for sustained service arrived during the brutally cold winter of 1912—the coldest since the blizzards of 1888. In Lawrence, Massachusetts, textile workers, many of whom were Italian and Polish women and children, went out on strike after their pay was cut, and management instituted a speed-up requiring faster work on the weaving machines. The strike, led by Bill Haywood's Wobblie organizers, simmered on, with neither side ready to negotiate. A striker was accidentally shot; arrests of pickets followed. Elizabeth Gurley Flynn gave fiery speeches encouraging civil disobedience and was arrested. Then, by late winter, the funds raised to support the workers ran out. Strikers informed union leaders that they must return to work: their children were starving.

According to Sanger: "The primary reason for the failure of all labor rebellions was the hunger cries of the babies; if they were only fed the strikers could usually last out."[25] Duplicating a tactic used in Italy, Haywood and his anarchist comrade Carlo Tresca mapped a solution: they would transport the children to New York, where sponsoring parents from the Ferrer Association and Socialist Party would serve as foster parents, boarding the children for the duration of the strike.

Haywood chose Sanger, along with two other comrades, to lead this expedition, in part because he had observed her previous exploits, and in part because she was a nurse sympathetic to the cause. She was also a native-born American woman who brought propaganda value to the Wobblies. Haywood and his followers suffered from their association with immigrants, believed by mainstream Americans to be infecting the nation with their dangerous ideas. Traveling to Lawrence, Sanger supervised the railroad journey of 119 children, from two-year-old babies to teenagers. When they arrived in New York, the children walked from Grand Central Station to Webster Hall near Union Square, singing, with frosted breath into the bitter cold air, "La Marseillaise" and "The Internationale" in a cacophony of languages—Italian, Polish, Hungarian, Russian, and English. "Who are we, who are we?" Those who spoke English shouted the answer, "Strikers, strikers."

As Sanger and her assistants left the train, members of the crowd pushed forward to take the children into their arms and homes for the duration of the strike. The following week, more children came to New York, though by this time mill owners opposed what they considered an illegal union tactic and a mere publicity stunt. There was police and militia violence against the strikers and their families when this second group tried to leave Lawrence.[26]

Before long the children's exodus became a national issue. Using the clichés of a good socialist, Sanger contributed an article, "The Fangs of Lawrence," to *The New York Call* in which she attacked the police as "on every corner with guns bayoneted ready to plunge this deadly instrument into the flesh of the working man or woman who has rebelled against these degrading conditions of wage slavery which has reduced them and their families to human machines used only to pile up enormous profits for the bosses of the mills."[27] Congressman Berger prodded Congress to begin an investigation into the strike and the removal of the children.

Within weeks a poised Margaret Sanger was sitting before the House Rules Committee in Washington, responding to the sometimes hostile questions of congressmen. Many legislators were intent on demonstrating that the children were mere pawns exploited by the strike organizers and "paraded" before the public. Identified as a nurse and soon to be known in the press as "the little nurse from New York," Sanger informed the committee of the "pitiful circumstances" of emaciated children wearing only shredded coats—though they lived in a community famed for the manufacture of heavy wool—with no underclothes and, sometimes, no shoes. When she was asked to compare the circumstances of the Lawrence children with those of others, she made her case succinctly:

> I have been brought up in a factory town where there are glass blowers and children of glass blowers and I must say I have never seen in any place children so ragged and so deplorable as these children were. I have never seen such children in my work in the Italian [slum] districts in New York . . . these children were pale and thin . . . every child showed the effects of malnutrition . . . I would like to say that when they had supper (the first night) it would bring tears to your eyes to see them grab the meat with their hands and eat it.[28]

Unable to withstand the negative press and public opinion (even President Taft's wife, Helen, had attended the hearings and listened to Sanger's testimony), within weeks the mill owners offered the workers a small raise and the Lawrence strike ended with a victory for the workers in the form of increased wages.

Sanger was involved in another epic, but less successful, strike in 1913 when twelve thousand Paterson, New Jersey, silk workers closed down their factories, over cuts in their wages and hours. Again Wobblie organizers led by Bill Haywood sent personnel and financial help, and in the winter of

1913 Margaret Sanger worked the picket lines. When silk workers from nearby Hazelton, Pennsylvania, walked out, Haywood envisioned a general strike by all American workers. He sent Sanger, his third-best woman rebel (after Flynn and Goldman), to picket in Hazelton, where she was promptly arrested for loitering. Refusing to pay any fine, she spent five days in jail and immediately returned to the picket line. When a policeman called her "a New York Bowery bum," Sanger demanded that he be arrested, and in the ensuing fracas, according to the local newspapers, "as she attempted to land a blow, [the policeman] dodged and sent her to jail." But to avoid publicity, the authorities released her after her arraignment.[29]

When the Paterson and Hazelton strikes failed to bring about negotiations with mill owners, the creative minds of Greenwich Village decided on a new tactic: they would organize a pageant to gain attention and raise money. The pageant had emerged as a popular art form for this generation, intended both to entertain and to express a political agenda. New York's suffragists staged many such symbolic representations of their cause with banners, stationary human figures, and occasionally spoken words. Jack Reed wrote the script; members of New York's Ashcan School of painters, so named for their lowlife subject matter, created the backdrops for a money-making event to be held in Madison Square Garden.

On June 7, 1913, thousands of Paterson workers boarded the ferries from New Jersey to lower Manhattan. From there they marched to Madison Square Garden, where a huge, ten-foot sign of red lights spelled out the initials IWW (the abbreviation for the Industrial Workers of the World). Before an audience of thousands the workers themselves became actors, dramatizing their lives as underpaid laborers toiling fifty-four hours a week. The event culminated in a reenactment of the strike and a speech by Jack Reed. At the end the audience stood, cheered, and along with the players sang the "The Internationale" and "La Marseillaise." Designed as a fund-raiser for the strike fund, the pageant instead lost money, and the Sangers, among others, paid a painful fifty dollars to cover its bills.

Nor did the pageant have any effect on the mill owners. After five months the strikers returned to work with neither shorter hours nor larger paychecks. Some said, though it was not obvious at the time, that this failure signaled the end of Haywood's Wobblies. But for Margaret Sanger, participation in the strikes served as instruction in the uses of subversive publicity, even if a few nights in jail were required. But never again would she serve as either labor organizer or socialist recruiter, and she resigned from the Socialist Party sometime during this period. Not only had Margaret Sanger found birth control by this time, but "it seemed to me that the whole question of strikes for higher wages was based on man's economic need of supporting his family and that this was a shallow principle upon which to found a new civilization . . . woman and her requirements were not being taken into account in reconstructing this new world about which all were talking."[30] Margaret Sanger's early radicalism had led directly to observations on the plight of the female poor, and from there to a birth control agenda grounded in feminism.

Contacts with socialists and unionists, no matter how brief, earned Margaret Sanger a reputation among the writers and intellectuals living in Greenwich Village. In her early years in New York, she did not live in the Village, though membership came easily enough. "Everyone was conscious of every question. No one had any answers, but everyone agreed with you on the importance of your thought," concluded T. S. Eliot. Sanger agreed: "Each believed he had a key to the gates of Heaven; each was trying to convert the others."[31] Some challenged capitalism and religion; others protested censorship of art and books. Almost everyone privately included some sort of sexual emancipation in their recipes for a new society. What was the point of political revolution if personal liberation was not included?

At first Sanger simply listened to these discussions of alternative relationships, especially of homosexuality and open marriages, and ever a diligent student, she read the essential texts of English Malthusians, especially Havelock Ellis's multivolume *Studies in the Psychology of Sex* and Edward Carpenter's *Love's Coming of Age*. But in Greenwich Village sex was more than theory. Couples such as Hutchins Hapgood and Neith Boyce, eccentrics such as Hippolyte Havel, and writers such as Max Eastman of *The Masses* and his sister, Crystal Eastman, enacted their polemics about the need for sexual liberation. Considering monogamy a stifling bourgeois arrangement, they sought sexual freedom, though such promiscuity often created an uneven playing field for women. The titles of their works displayed their keen interest—Floyd Dell's *Love in the Machine Age,* Mabel Dodge's *Intimate Memories*, Eugene O'Neill's *Desire under the Elms,* Hutchins Hapgood's *Story of a Lover,* and Susan Glaspell's *Suppressed Desires.*

Greenwich Village residents often met to discuss sex in Peggy's Restaurant, with its cheap meals downstairs and conversation-enhancing slow service. Upstairs, lecture clubs, including the all-female Heterodoxy Club, debated the vital issues of the day. Sanger spoke to the professional women

of the Heterodoxy on her specialty of sex education. But she had neither
the time nor the taste for the Heterodoxy Club's lengthy personal discourses,
which often focused, given that one-third of the members were divorced,
on their pursuit of true love and satisfying sex. Indifferent to the issue of
birth control, these women soon became a target for Sanger: "Who cared
whether a woman kept her Christian name—Mary Smith instead of Mrs.
John Johns? Who cared whether she wore a wedding ring? Who cared about
her demand for the right to work after marriage . . . When I suggested that
the basis of Feminism might be the right to be a mother regardless of church
or state, their inherited prejudices were instantly aroused. They were still
subject to the age-old masculine atmosphere compounded of protection and
dominance."[32]

Sanger became a regular at another Greenwich Village ritual: Mabel
Dodge's evening salon at Ninth Street and Fifth Avenue, where laboring
men in rough flannel shirts, society women in shimmering satin with fashionable, newly bobbed hair, and village intellectuals in bright ties and sus-
penders gathered to debate everything from Freudian psychology to French
Cubism. At midnight, after the sometimes heated discussions, the doors of
this shockingly all-white apartment in an age that preferred dark mahog-
any were thrown open, and all feasted on elegant buffet meals. Dodge, the
wealthy, twice-married lover of Jack Reed, created a place where new ideas
about everything were welcomed.

Immediately Dodge discovered in Margaret Sanger an intrepid woman
who promoted sex as a positive good. "It was she who introduced to us all
the idea of birth control, and it along with related ideas about sex, became
her passion . . . Margaret Sanger was the first person I ever knew," wrote
Dodge, "who set out to rehabilitate sex and [she] was openly an ardent propagandist for the joys of the flesh . . . Margaret Sanger was an advocate of
the flesh who set out to make it a scientific, wholly dignified and proper
part of life."[33]

One evening before the crowd flooded into Dodge's palatial mansion on
Fifth Avenue, Margaret Sanger talked to Dodge and several other women
about the mechanics of sex. "She told us all about the possibilities in the
body for 'sex expression' and as she sat there, serene and quiet, and unfolded
the mysteries and mightiness of physical love, it seemed to us we had never
known it before as a sacred and at the same time a scientific reality." With
no hesitation Sanger discussed what later generations called the erotic zones

of the female body and "how to heighten pleasure and prolong it," until, according to an enthralled Dodge, "the whole body was sexualized."[34]

In the summers the Villagers moved to Provincetown on Cape Cod, where with great enthusiasm they produced plays and gave dramatic readings. The Sangers followed, renting a small cottage in nearby Truro. Many Americans chose to leave cities during this period when summer resorts were becoming popular sanctuaries. Some left because they disliked the heat; others feared the airborne germs of tuberculosis and, especially for their children, the dreaded infantile paralysis. The Sangers had a special reason to flee the city. In 1910, before her first birthday, Peggy had come down with a fever. Suffering from pain in her leg, she had gradually recovered, though polio left her with a permanent limp. Her mother refused the doctor-recommended leg braces for this daughter, whom she later described as "the most independent child I ever knew . . . vivacious, mischievous, laughing—the embodiment of all my hopes for a daughter . . . She was born to *do*, to act, to lead."[35] In other words Peggy was another Margaret Higgins. Sanger never referred to Peggy's infirmity, believing, as she had during her own battle with tuberculosis, that disease was best addressed by denial and through activity, not the rest and invalidism that doctors recommended.

In both New York and Truro, Margaret Sanger listened to Emma Goldman's theories that women, no longer the passionless objects of male concupiscence, held the same rights and instinctual desires as men to take lovers. She also observed the behavior of men and women who intended to be free from the restraints of bourgeois monogamy. Standing marriage on its head, some married Villagers, such as Neith Boyce and Hutchins Hapgood, practiced free love and made their affairs into a charter for spontaneous sex, though the idea of taking lovers and discussing them with her husband made the more conventional Boyce miserable. A few of the bohemian left pretended they were married; others were married and never said a word. When Max Eastman and his wife, Ida Rauh, placed both their names on their mailbox, others began to follow suit. "Free love in the Village," writes historian Judith Schwarz, "was not illicit self-indulgence, but instead was a serious ethical undertaking . . . the only sin was in living with someone you no longer loved. That was seen as almost a form of prostitution."[36] But such views, however fiercely argued in Dodge's salon, never expunged jealousy in the bedroom.

By the summer of 1912 Margaret Sanger had joined the bohemians and taken a lover. She had first met John Rompapas, a Greek-born anarchist, tobacco importer, and founder of the Rabelais Press, in her upper Manhattan neighborhood before he moved to Greenwich Village. Soon she was dancing at socialist parties with the man Mabel Dodge described as having "a handsome head on a handsome body [with] black hair and the darkest brown eyes far apart in his strong face."[37] In the summer when Margaret and the children (sometimes without Bill) lived in Truro, the relationship turned sexual. Wrote Rompapas in an undated letter, "Although I am sure of your love, the fact that we could [be] apart even for a short period created in me a fear, a strong fear, and while I am glad we did not elope and thus we will have no reason of regret, in reality I am sorry I did not force you to run away. For I wanted you. Yes, dearest, I want you and I am sorry I have knowledge of future feelings through certain acts." But for this lover— and there are no surviving letters from Sanger to Rompapas—as with many of the men in her life, she was "more than sex . . . [I am] a slave before your feet to sing the eternal song of love, of equal love."[38]

So began the first of Sanger's numerous sexual relationships with men who adored her and kept adoring her even after she ended any physical contact. Several relatives, including one of her grandchildren, described her as "a nymphomaniac" who required frequent sex, though for a woman like Sanger the term seems inappropriately clinical and in any case is an obsolete, elusive classification.[39] Certainly her presence in Greenwich Village and her friendships with socialists and unionists allowed for spontaneous, self-affirming alliances with men. And these were not difficult for Margaret Sanger.

She attracted men effortlessly not because of her beauty, though she was attractive, with her long, auburn hair that she twisted up in a tantalizing arrangement in the back. She had neither extraordinary figure nor face, given her square, uneven Higgins nose. At five foot four with eyes that her lovers variously described as hazel, brown, and green, she did not stand out. Her clothes rarely caught anyone's attention. When she first entered a crowded room, no one noticed her—at least not at first. Rather there was a seductive presence—a sex appeal complementing her gaiety, intelligence, and curiosity—that she offered to men. Hers was an ability to charm, a personality exuding laughter and pleasure along with high purpose.

Never a frivolous love object available for men's pleasure, Sanger did not allow her affairs to distract her from her cause. Even as Rompapas became so love-addled that his work was disrupted, she was completing her series on sex education in *The New York Call*. From her Greenwich Village friends, her patients, and her children's innocent questions, Margaret had discovered the need for information about the invisible topic of sex education, not just for children but for adults. Ever a controversial subject, any public discussion of sex had become particularly problematic in a place and at a time when representatives of the privately funded New York Society for the Suppression of Vice censored reading material, along with the behavior of New Yorkers. "I was told that I better keep off that subject or Anthony Comstock would get me."[40]

In articles for *The New York Call*'s Sunday pages devoted to "The Woman's Sphere," Sanger published "What Every Mother Should Know; or, How Six Little Children Were Taught the Truth." She included stories she had told to her own children about frogs, flowers, and, of course, the birds and the bees. The fictional Mr. and Mrs. Buttercup represented the evolution of human marriage. In later articles, Sanger encouraged mothers to talk about sex with, never at, their children, and she discouraged that time-honored, well-traveled avenue of all human sex knowledge, the conversation of children. Her sex-education formulas were age-graded, experiential, and cautious. At this point in her writing the subject was radical, not the substance. "As all the children were still too young to go into the details of either menstruation or venereal diseases, it was considered best to dwell on the early tribes of man up to marriage."

To be sure, she insisted that children learn about "their generative organs. To tamper with this most important part of nature's machinery means not only sickness, dullness of intellect, stupidity and mental weakness but often time disables little children." Earlier generations of Americans had fastened sexual intercourse to reproduction; they had worried about too much spilling of seminal seed from a closed energy system and had therefore rendered masturbation the vice of their times. The latter had emerged as the great temptation for Victorians who believed in a finite amount of semen that, if expelled too often, led to feeble, weak children. Their churches had taught them so, and no church more vigorously than the Roman Catholic Church.[41]

A growing group of dissidents—some scientists, a few doctors, some supporters of the new specialty of social hygiene, and most of Greenwich Village's practitioners of a new sex culture for women—challenged such monastic sexual attitudes. Emma Goldman believed that women must resist the traditional male domination that destroyed their personalities and made them into "sex commodities." Women must refuse to bear children unless they wanted them, and most heretically in Goldman's attack on marriage, they must understand their own "sex cravings." For Goldman and others, sexual pleasure became its own end, essential for human happiness and appropriate for women as well as men.[42]

In Greenwich Village, residents talked about sex and weighed the implications of multiple partners, but the rest of New York provided a living laboratory. Margaret Sanger was surrounded by "a city of eros" with commercial forms of sex visible everywhere, but nowhere more openly than in the Tenderloin district between Gramercy Park and Murray Hill. There were over two thousand brothels in an area where prostitutes sometimes earned fifty dollars a week, compared to six to twelve dollars a week for garment workers.[43] Bill Sanger's friends in the Ashcan School of painters discovered their best subjects among prostitutes. Despite the vice squad's efforts to shut down what it considered "obscene matter"—and in this period that included birth control—rubber pessaries and condoms were displayed on pharmacy shelves, along with syringes for douching and even recipes for neutralizing the reproductive capacities of sperm.

Meanwhile, prostitutes, who interested Sanger because of their ability to avoid pregnancy, solicited customers in every part of the city. In Sanger's view prostitutes were not the fallen women of an earlier age, but rather the victims of economic hardship, who engaged in a form of commercial activity that could be largely curtailed if married couples employed birth control. The sporting press represented by The National Police Gazette published lascivious short stories with titles such as "The Confessions of a Lady's Waiting Maid," along with tales of sexual violence.

Sometime during this period, Sanger, later a prodigious author of nonfiction, wrote a short story about an attempted rape. She played upon her own personal experience in "The Unrecorded Battle," her only piece of fiction. Sanger told, in stilted prose and labored dialogue, the account of a young nurse named Peggy who after helping a doctor in his office, is nearly raped by him. "You knew what you were getting into," the doctor threatens as he locks the door after the last patient has left. But Peggy challenges the doctor: "Your tyranny and boasted power mean nothing to me." Announcing she is a virgin, she escapes through an unlocked door.[44]

The story was never published. Yet the plot testified to Sanger's view that rape, often blamed on women or overlooked entirely, was a woman's issue demanding attention. Two years before, Congress had passed the 1910 Mann Act, making the transport across state lines of "innocent women" for prostitution and immoral purposes a federal crime. But such legislation, to Sanger's disgust, focused primarily on prostitution, not the acquaintance sexual assault described in her short story.

In the sexy New York of the early 1900s, young working women, freed from parental restraint, now made their own, sometimes perilous, choices. Stephen Crane, a short-term resident of the Village, portrayed the temptations of young working women in his 1893 cautionary tale *Maggie: A Girl of the Streets*. A new form of respectable premarital sex called "petting" emerged among young women who gave intimate favors to men in exchange for an evening's treat at a vaudeville show or a trip to Coney Island. Dry-goods stores displayed erotic materials, and an underground press published stories about sex that sold in special bookstores throughout the city. Later, when comparisons were available, statistics revealed what everyone suspected: the rates of premarital intercourse for women doubled in the decade between 1908 and 1918. The writers of the popular magazine *Current Opinion* knew what was going on: it had struck, according to a lead article in its August 1913 issue, "Sex O'Clock in America."

For one New Yorker these promiscuous ways presented a lifetime challenge. Anthony Comstock had moved to the city from Connecticut as a young clerk after the Civil War, and as a fundamentalist member of a Congregationalist church, he was outraged by the sexual mores in the city. In a crusade for social purity that often brought attention to the very taboos he would repress, Comstock, intent on ridding New York of its prurient vices, at first focused on pornography, which he knew when he saw it, even if others did not. Eventually he claimed the single-handed destruction of fifty tons of obscene printed material and over 3 million pictures, and he arrested the most famous abortion provider in the United States—Madame Restell. By the 1870s, Comstock, a believer in a devil "stationed to corrupt, pervert and destroy," amid other traps for the young, was ready for a national campaign against "lust—the boon companion of all other crimes."[45]

In 1873 Comstock traveled to Washington to persuade Congress of the necessity for national legislation. In the waning days of the second session of the Forty-second Congress, he set up his exhibit of dildos, nude female dummies, and pessaries in the lobby of the Capitol. It was easy to persuade weary representatives, recently exposed to the financial and political corruption of the Grant administration, of the need to do something about the deteriorating sexual morals of the nation. Soon the legislation that bore his name had passed and been signed by President Grant into law.

The officially named "Suppression of Trade in and Circulation of Obscene Literature and Articles of Immoral Use" expanded the powers of the U.S. Post Office, giving it broad, vaguely defined powers over specific infractions, which technically included the behavior of married couples. As historian Helen Horowitz has described: "It made it illegal and punishable to send through the mail six kinds of material: erotica; contraceptive medications and devices; sexual implements, such as those used in masturbation; contraceptive information, and advertisements for contraception, abortion or sexual implements."[46] Conviction brought fines of up to five thousand dollars and imprisonment for five years.

Earlier drafts of the Comstock Act had included an exemption for physicians "in good standing" who might exchange information about contraception, but in the hectic, end-of-session congressional chaos, these versions were dropped. As a result, physicians could not provide contraceptive information to their patients. Nor did the "little Comstock laws" that were promptly passed in twenty-four states contain any such exclusion for doctors. Most devastating for Margaret Sanger, as she began her crusade to prevent unwanted pregnancies among married women, birth control had been defined as pornography, and thus could not be sent through the mail. Moreover, Congress had given Comstock the authority, as an agent of the Post Office, to enforce the law by making arrests.

Armed with handcuffs, Comstock enthusiastically embraced his power. Often he employed the tactic of entrapment, first renting a post-office box, then sending a letter to suspicious booksellers or doctors in the name of a woman asking for contraceptive information. When the doctor, midwife, or abortionist responded with suggestions, Comstock pounced. Ensnared in such a trap, Dr. Sara Blakesley Chase sold two syringes that might be used for contraceptive douching and was arrested. Chase offended Comstock for other reasons: women should not work outside the home and certainly not as doctors. But in an indication of changing attitudes, the grand jury refused to indict Chase.

In Greenwich Village they made fun of Anthony Comstock. Max Eastman's *Masses* published a cartoon of a woman dragged before a magistrate by a recognizable Comstock with a mutton-chop mustache and large stomach. The caption read "Your Honor, This woman gave birth to a naked child." After Comstock forced Macy's to remove a nude female wax model from its show windows, Mabel Dodge's salon spent a hilarious evening discussing pornography. Bill Sanger's friends in the Ashcan School and Artist's League hired young boys to put copies of the French artist Paul Chabas's famed nude painting *September Morn* in store windows and then remove them if Comstock appeared. When, on a tip from his agents, Comstock arrived to arrest nude models posing at the Art Students League, they were, miraculously, clothed. Instead, he confiscated sketches and grumbled when the famous Armory Show opened in 1913 that he would remove the show's star exhibit, *Nude Descending a Staircase*. To this single-minded keeper of purity, not even art was immune from the blight of obscenity.

In 1912, with Comstock still prowling the city for violations of the law he had done so much to pass, Margaret Sanger expanded her essays on sex education for adults, writing at night when the children were in bed. In the late fall of 1912 and the early months of 1913, *The New York Call* published her seven-part series titled *What Every Girl Should Know*, dedicated to "The Working Girls of the World." What girls should know, according to Sanger, included their reproductive physiology, about which fears of masturbation had made them ignorant. They needed information about "their sex impulses," venereal diseases, and pregnancy. And, on the kind of practical note that Sanger often included in her advice, they must never wear girdles before they were twenty-one.

Foremost of all, they must understand love, and for a happy sex life, their "sexual impulses and desires . . . which lead a girl to kiss and fondle a man without any conscious desire for the sexual act, whereas in the man to be touched and caressed by the girl for whom he has a sexual attraction stimulates the accumulation of sex cells and the desire for the sexual act becomes paramount in his mind." Girls must "hold in check the sexual impulse" until they feel "a conscious sympathy." As they reach the age of romance—the concept of puberty as a stage of life had been recently defined by G. Stanley Hall's work at Johns Hopkins University—girls must search out the foundations of love in a man they considered an ideal partner. They must never marry before they have a "settled idea of true love," and marriage to any man must never take place until they were twenty-three— Sanger's age when she and Bill had eloped.[47] A paean to the connection of love to sex and sex in the pursuit of love, Sanger's writing was innocently romantic and scientifically inaccurate, though her views certainly reflected those of the few experts in the field.

On several grounds Sanger shocked her readers. She had separated sex and reproduction: "the creative instinct does not need to be expended entirely for the propagation of the race." While at this point she offered no specific birth control advice, she did explore female masturbation and abortion. She referred to sex glands, though at first she did not use the term "penis," a word largely closeted from the American sex vocabulary until the 1980s. She also discussed syphilis and gonorrhea, and the ways in which venereal disease was a public health issue for women.

The response was outrage. *The New York Times* labeled Sanger "an enemy of the young." Even some readers of *The New York Call* were angry at what they termed "obscenities" and canceled their subscriptions. Others applauded, while still another group acknowledged blushing but reading every word. By March, when the last article, "Some Consequences of Ignorance and Silence," appeared, at Comstock's urging, the Post Office suppressed the paper on the grounds that Sanger's extended discussion of syphilis and gonorrhea violated the law. Now the battle was joined between the woman who would liberate sexuality through birth control and the man who, to paraphrase the pundit H. L. Mencken, worried that someone somewhere might be having a good time. In response to the censorship, *The New York Call* printed in bold letters WHAT EVERY GIRL SHOULD KNOW over a blank box under which the word NOTHING appeared.

One of the most radical elements of the series reflected the double standard of the times: as a woman writing about sex, Sanger had entered the domain of males. Only a few women had written or spoken of sexual matters. Emma Goldman was the notable exception, publicizing her views on women's "sexual cravings" and "sex as a creative element in human life" through her lectures, her recently published book *Anarchism and Other Essays*, and her journal, *Mother Earth*. All appeared before Sanger's articles.

But Sanger could never share her reputation as an advocate for enlightened sex and the founder of the birth control movement. Goldman now emerged as a rival; there could not be two rebel queens. Throughout her career Sanger never credited Goldman for her revolutionary view that women must control their own bodies, which was the authorizing premise of the early birth control movement. Although Sanger had adopted Goldman's views and made them the bedrock of the series *What Every Girl Should Know*, Sanger's exposure to the public through *The New York Call* was far greater than Goldman's. It would remain so. And despite Goldman's devastating claim that Sanger was neither sufficiently well-known nor experienced to lead the birth control movement, it was Sanger who first challenged the Comstock laws by delivering the means of contraception in clinics.[48]

Sanger publicly delineated her differences with Goldman. Her rival not only promoted free love, which if connected to contraception would contaminate her efforts; Goldman also lectured on everything from the abstract notions of anarchism to the failure of Christianity. The single-minded Sanger focused on birth control. Writing in 1929, Sanger disputed her rival's importance: "There was no organization . . . connected with Miss Goldman. Miss Goldman's lectures on Birth Control were of her own brand but everyone knew that Miss Goldman was first, last and all the time an anarchist and not a birth control advocate."[49] And Sanger, who harbored slights, never contributed to a fund-raising effort to help the impoverished Goldman in her old age.

Sanger's series *What Every Girl Should Know*, her rising notoriety, and her love affair with Rompapas (whose Rabelais Press published the series in a pamphlet that included the brief "What Every Boy Should Know") all served as epitaphs to Margaret Sanger's marriage. She was moving into her life's work with a philosophy that included the possibility of extramarital sexual affairs, while Bill was becoming more conservative in his social views. In the summer of 1913, Margaret Sanger asked her husband during an argument he termed "a soul-combat" to adopt an open marriage: she would sleep with Rompapas and he would choose another partner. Unable to fathom the idea that his wife had begun an affair of her own free will, Bill held the anarchists responsible. Indeed, he reminded her, they had even thrown another woman at him—"that Becky [referring to a labor organizer] to trot along with me."[50]

Bill Sanger, at first more radical than his wife, had come to despise Greenwich Village and its ways—"that hell hole of free love promiscuity & prostitution appalls me. I hate all their isms," he wrote his "sweetheart" in 1914. "Perhaps you do not realize dear heart how keen has been the mental anguish at times. I cannot change! My family life is not an external symptom. As long as their personalities hover around you, they will constantly endeavor to break—to disintegrate our family life—the contradiction we have lived—in trying to mix in and out with free lovers & expect our relations to remain intact . . . they want you—your body." His anxiety, apparent in long rambling letters, would end only "when you will finish up with the Greek."[51]

There were an increasing number of arguments over the time Margaret spent with the children. At first Bill seemed to understand: "I know you must be released from the family care . . . I want you to have freedom of thought," impossible in an apartment with three young children.[52] Sanger agreed: "The children are so full of life and fun that I am almost besides myself to keep them quiet."[53] Bill, who had been raised in a traditional family by a doting, nonworking mother, was finding grounds for complaint: she had not put a cast on Peggy's withered leg during the summer; she had not been home when Grant was ill with a cold; she had left the children in Truro.

Acquaintances in Greenwich Village recognized Bill as the more engaged parent. Hutchins Hapgood remembered Margaret Sanger as "a pretty woman," and Bill as "a sweet gentle painter who lacked ego and ambition and had a great deal more interest in the children than she . . . she seemed to grant little value to her husband."[54] And in the way of maternally overlooked children, they craved their mother's attention for the rest of their lives, and were often disappointed.

With principles underwritten by convenience, Sanger rejected idealized views of full-time mothering. She had adopted the Greenwich Village mandates of intelligent, targeted mothering rather than mainstream America's views of dedicated, labor-intensive maternalism. She was never embarrassed, as more solicitous mothers might have been, by stories of the children's reactions to her absences. When they found her "at my mending basket, they all leaped about for joy, took hands and danced shouting 'Mother's home, mother's home, mother's sewing.'"[55] One evening, after Grant asked where she was going and she replied that she was headed to a socialist meeting, he responded, with the vehemence and pronunciation of a seven-year-old, "Oh I hate soshism."[56] At first her mother-in-law served as a live-in caregiver for the children. In the summers when her sister Ethel was available, Sanger left the children in Truro while she traveled to the Boston Public Library and the Library of Congress, only to find disappointing materials on birth control, after which she complained she had discovered nothing more in either library than what she had learned from back-fence gossip.

Later, Grant remembered that "mother was seldom around. She just left us with anyone who was handy and ran off we didn't know where."[57] Sanger acknowledged as much with occasional regret, for she was aware of her personal sacrifices: "Gradually, however, there came over me the feeling and dread that the road to my goal was to separate me from their [the children's] lives, from their development, growth and happiness."[58]

To be sure, Margaret Sanger lacked memories of what proper mothering might be. Her own mother offered no pattern of the child-focused, sacrificial maternal routines recommended by a generation of Americans who celebrated the new national holiday of Mother's Day. Instead, Anne Higgins was a distant figure, nearly always pregnant or nursing, chronically ill and ever coughing, overworked and favoring her youngest daughter, Ethel, with whatever energy she possessed. Margaret's older sisters, Nan and Mary, had dressed and fed Margaret when she was an infant. Later they played with her, read to her, and even paid her Claverack tuition. While Sanger's children played an important role in her credentials, they never took precedence over the cause: "I would never give up until I had obtained [contraception,] nor stop until the working women of my generation in the country of my birth were acquainted with its substance."[59]

Bill could not accept such growing differences: "You are a world Lover who can take recourse to most people. I am not—I am a single Lover . . . I love too deep & not broad enough . . . I want to help you in your work loved one—you must help me to help you," Bill wrote in what his wife complained was his overbearing manner.[60] And later, in an acknowledgment of the ambitions she had shared with him and his own appreciation of the goals she had discovered in New York, he wrote, "now you have arrived— you are now able to express yourself yes I pray for you to be the big woman of your generation." Still, there was only one way the family could survive: Margaret Sanger must mend her ways—spend more time with the children and, of course, "finish up with the Greek."[61]

In September 1913, the five Sangers who had come to New York only three years before boarded a steamer from Boston en route to Europe. Even at a moment of increased war tensions on the Continent, there were compelling reasons for the couple to leave the United States. The trip to Europe might heal their marriage. Certainly, distance would remove Margaret from the company of Rompapas. Bill was optimistic, advising, "Peg, my loved one, we begin a new life when we step on board."[62] Margaret intended to investigate the socialist-governed municipality of Glasgow for a series of articles for *The New York Call*. Then the family would move to

France, where Bill, like so many artists and writers, intended to paint in the rarefied artistic atmosphere of Paris. Meanwhile, Margaret would have more time to spend with the children as she studied European methods of birth control publicly advocated by anarchists and Malthusians for years and practiced by peasant women in France for centuries. But three months later, leaving Bill behind in Paris, Margaret Sanger and the children were back in New York City, living in Greenwich Village.

4

CREATING MARGARET SANGER

All revolutions have been brought about by the few militant individuals with forceful characters.   —*The Woman Rebel*, June 1914

After her return from Europe, Margaret Sanger began a new undertaking. Bill Sanger, who had begged his wife to stay with him in Paris, warned that life in frigid New York during the winter with no money and three children "was no joke. But you are a brave woman," he wrote shortly after her departure.[1] The couple had spent the last of their mortgage payments in Europe, and though Bill intended to send some of his paintings for his wife to sell, given that most were four-by-eight-foot canvases, they proved too expensive to ship. Later, when three versions of the Provincetown-inspired *The Dunes* finally arrived, there were no buyers. Her sister Ethel urged Sanger to return to a more dependable source of income—nursing.

Never inhibited by money problems, Margaret Sanger had other ideas. She intended to publish a magazine. Asked by friends how she would raise the necessary funds, she responded with her characteristic insouciance about finances: "I was certain of its coming somehow." Later, she explained her audacious solution to the withering dilemma of many women's associations: "If I had waited for birth control to be financed, it never would have been."[2] In fact, much of Sanger's success came from her own persuasive talents. She made lists of possible subscribers, found sponsors, pleaded for loans from friends, and asked for grants from a special fund of the Free Speech League, set up by the University of Pennsylvania–trained physician Dr. Edward Bliss Foote. Arrested for advertising contraceptives in his

Plain Home Talk, Foote had established a fund to defend others in the battle for free expression over matters of sex. In the process of setting up her magazine, Sanger developed three skills crucial for her future success: writing, organizing, and fund-raising.

Within weeks of her return she was arranging the final details of publishing a magazine dedicated to the interests of working women—"a monthly paper," as she described it, "of militant thought." With the adamant leadership she often displayed but sometimes exaggerated to the exclusion of others, Margaret Sanger became the magazine's editor, publisher, principal author, bookkeeper, manager, and distributor. She was helped by a few volunteers, including more experienced publishers such as John Rompapas and Walter Roberts, who never received much credit. Her lax attention to copyright laws also aided the enterprise, for she borrowed from previously published materials by everyone from Nietzsche, whose antistatist, antichurch positions she applauded (saying nothing of his misogyny), to the English Malthusians, whose attention to exploding birth rates and diminishing resources shaped her own views.

The need for material also placed her in touch with international feminists such as Olive Schreiner, the South African author of the just published *Love and Labour*, and Ellen Key, the Swedish authority on marriage and motherhood. Answering Sanger's invitation to all "rebel women" to participate in this new venture, her rival Emma Goldman contributed a scathing critique of marriage for the first issue. Despite the borrowings and material from others, what Sanger called "her little sass box" remained her creation. It marked her emergence as a writer, for under various pseudonyms she produced most of the material. Only the printing took place beyond the dining room table of the small apartment she rented in the upper Bronx, after spending a few weeks in Greenwich Village.

In March 1914, three months after her return from France, Sanger's eight-page magazine, printed on cheap paper and presented in what she called "the French style" of long parallel columns, appeared in the mailboxes of New York radicals. Disguised in brown wrappers and carried by hand to a few socialists outside the city, it could be purchased as well on the streets of New York, where Sanger hawked it herself for ten cents a copy. Named *The Woman Rebel*, with its masthead slogan borrowed from the anarchists, but pluralized into "No Gods No Masters" so as to cover all religions and men, not just those wielding political power, it joined the fugitive publications that included the more established "little magazines" of Greenwich

Village such as Max Eastman's *Masses*, Emma Goldman's *Mother Earth*, and the Wobblies' *Arm and Hammer*.

In prewar America, reform agendas required transforming turgid public attitudes about everything from the legitimacy of strikes to women's suffrage. From mainstream newspapers and glossy magazines that used sophisticated advertising to stimulate consumer buying, reformers were learning the art of propaganda—the use of glittering generalities and problem-solving exaggerations. Sanger, unlike Goldman and Eastman and the women of the suffrage and temperance movements, targeted a special audience of working women whose "awakening" she would superintend, though such a group had neither the time nor interest, much less the fifty cents, for a half year's subscription. Her friend Caroline Nelson warned Sanger of the difficulty of educating "giggling and blushing" female workers about sex topics.[3] In fact, most of Sanger's subscribers were well-educated members of various radical movements, not the women she had encountered as a nurse on New York's Lower East Side.

In the ambitious timetable for the magazine, she gave herself less than a year to empower women "to decide for themselves" about the timing of their motherhood: "I have six months' time to devote to arousing this slumbered spirit in the working woman," after which she would turn to direct action. In the tradition of the period's little magazines, in the first issue Sanger offered her daring personal manifesto—and challenge to the censors—"to say what we wished." She promised a series of articles on sex education for girls from fourteen to eighteen that went beyond, in a reference to the Mann Act, "all this slushy talk about white slavery." She guaranteed information on anatomy and "sex desires."

Just as suffrage leaders such as Alice Paul encouraged civil disobedience to obtain votes for women, so Margaret Sanger promised defiance of the Comstock laws. She listed fourteen principles that included the right "to look the world in the face with a go-to-hell look in the eyes, to have an idea, to speak and act in defiance of convention, to be an unmarried mother, and to be lazy."[4] When challenged about the last—for self-indulgence and frivolity were standard male complaints about women—Sanger relied on the universal female reality that men worked from sun to sun, but a woman's work was never done. Any revolution, especially for the working class, must include leisure and, for all women, what the suffragist leader Elizabeth Cady Stanton referred to in 1892 as "the solitude of self" was required for female autonomy. In charge of her own household without the oversight of father, husband, or even doctor for the first time in her life, Margaret Sanger was enacting Stanton's feminist conviction that nothing adds to judgment or "quickens the conscience like individual responsibility. Nothing adds such dignity to character as the recognition of one's self-sovereignty."[5]

Intending to provoke a reaction not only among "slumbering" wage-earning women but also among New York's vigilant censors, Sanger included an editorial in the first issue on "The Prevention of Conception." Much to the chagrin of some readers who had hoped for technical information on the means of birth control, not its philosophical ends, *The Woman Rebel* never described any specific methods, only Sanger's commitment to the necessity of women receiving "clean, harmless, scientific knowledge on how to prevent conception."[6] In addition, she challenged the popular myth that the use of artificial means of contraception led to prostitution, promiscuity, sterility, and insanity—the latter applied, in popular opinion, to female, though not male, users. Having arrived at birth control through the principles of anarchism and socialism, Sanger framed her stand-alone reform as a class issue and cast herself as its indispensable leader.

Since 1911, when the family first moved into the city, Sanger had been a member of an informal women's circle made up of unionists, socialists, and anarchists. Her initial presentation of birth control emerged from this context. "The woman of the people is the only one left in ignorance of this information," she wrote.[7] Even as a former socialist, Sanger viewed the endless pregnancies of working women as supplying exploitable cheap labor to the capitalist machine. While traditional Marxists drew the lesson that such increases among the poor led to the contradictions inherent in capitalism and its eventual overthrow, Sanger reached a more humane conclusion. By keeping wages low, a surplus of young workers simply increased human misery, especially for women and children, and she had seen enough of that in Corning and on New York's Lower East Side.

Privileged middle- and upper-class Americans not only had more knowledge than their poorer sisters about birth control, they also enjoyed improvements in sanitation such as indoor toilets and running water that facilitated the privacy necessary for douching and inserting pessaries—the state-of-the-art female techniques of birth control in this period. Nor did poor women have access to the private doctors who, on the sly—for it was against the law—dispensed information about useful devices and douch-

ing recipes. In the next phase of her campaign, Sanger turned her attention
to the establishment of clinics for poor women. But in 1914 such facilities
existed only for women who suffered from tuberculosis.

The response to the first run of two thousand copies of *The Woman
Rebel* was immediate. Sanger had tapped into an amorphous people's movement that had neither leader nor organization, and she was inundated with
agitated calls for advice. In the 1914 September–October edition of *The
Woman Rebel*, Sanger printed an early version of the letters she received
throughout her life: Mrs. J. S. of Chicago, a self-described "feeble" mother
with six children and wife of an unemployed, sick husband, implored: "Will
you please send me the information you speak of in your paper, so I can
prevent having another child? Your [sic] doing a noble work for women."[8]

Other readers—especially the intellectuals from Greenwich Village—
found *The Woman Rebel* too shrilly sarcastic, heavy-handedly ironic, and unnecessarily provocative, the latter at least part of her intention. Sanger attacked
the much-admired YWCA for its "damnable teachings of passivity, charity,
and submission—scab teaching," as she termed it.[9] She lashed out at the
Rockefellers with the primitive rhetoric that marked this stage of her writing: "the leering bloody hyenas of the human race who smear themselves
with the stinking honey of charity to attract those foul flies of religion who
spread pollution through the land." Socialists of this period found their essential enemy in bourgeois normalcy. Sanger found hers not just in capitalism but in what she held as its institutional coconspirator, the American
church, especially its repressive Roman Catholic version, whose dogmas
about the will of God were delivered to submissive women by a "debauched
priesthood."[10]

With marked paternalism, Max Eastman, the editor of *The Masses*,
acknowledged what many thought: "*The Woman Rebel* has fallen into that
most unfeminist of errors, the tendency to cry out when a quiet and contained
utterance is indispensable."[11] Nevertheless, Eastman, convinced that there
must be "no unwanted or unsustainable life," agreed with the importance of
a mission undertaken by "this trained nurse of unusual intelligence and wide
experience."[12] Writers for more traditional magazines such as *The Atlantic
Monthly* were disgusted. Agnes Repplier complained of "an obsession regarding sex which has set us babbling about matters of sex better excluded
from the amenities of conversation."[13]

Emma Goldman, who had been sent copies to circulate on her 1914 lecture tour in the Midwest, grumbled that she had received only thirty-seven copies of the fifty promised. Well aware of her primacy in the revolutionary struggle to which Sanger was a newcomer, as well as her experience as the successful editor of a magazine, Goldman archly advised Sanger on a tactical issue: "It is too bad that you did not get out a very large edition of the first number so that [after its confiscation] we would at least have been able to circularize the first attempt, and thus arouse enough sympathy and interest." Still, Goldman acknowledged the popularity of *The Woman Rebel* and the many Americans

> who are up in arms against your paper; mostly women, of course whose emancipation has been on paper and not in reality . . . [and who spoke] of your brazen method. They would not believe me when I told them that you were a little, delicate woman, refined and shrinking, but that you did believe in the daring and courage of woman in her struggle for freedom.[14]

To friends and family who connected female rebellion to madness, the Margaret Sanger of the 1914 *Woman Rebel* was disorderly and dangerous, too often seeking the public attention that "normal women" avoided. Her sisters believed that she suffered from a nervous disorder and needed rest, and sent her father to persuade her to enter a sanatorium. Convinced that Sanger fit into a Freudian diagnosis of low-grade hysteria, with its histrionic symptoms apparent in her attention seeking, the civil liberties lawyer Theodore Schroeder advised six weeks of analysis of her motives. He hoped that Greenwich Village's popular Freudian psychiatrist, August Brill, might analyze her, after which, Schroeder believed, she would agree to stop publishing *The Woman Rebel*.

From Paris, Bill Sanger sent his congratulations, offered to "help with the writing," and provided pen-and-ink illustrations in the style of the well-known contemporary cartoonist and socialist Robert Minor. When they came, Margaret Sanger declined to print them or in fact any illustrations. Against Bill's advice, *The Woman Rebel* retained its original format—mostly nonfictional material in the form of short paragraphs, some short stories about mothers driven to infanticide and abortion after unwanted pregnancies, and, occasionally, longer articles on public policy such as that on the need for pensions for mothers and widows. In a statement of just how far this couple had grown apart, Bill found the article on the eighteenth-century English writer Mary Wollstonecraft, the most conservative material in the March edition, the one he liked best. And as for her tactics, he cautioned, "Go slow. Be wise and not too brave." Still, he acknowledged her driving ambition, communicated to him from the beginning of their marriage, to be "a pioneer" and "blaze the trail for another generation . . . Few attempt it."[15]

Even with the excitement of the Paris art scene and his personal introduction to the great masters of French Impressionism, Bill longed for his "Peg," sending "soul kisses across the Big Pond." "I live for you," he proclaimed in long, rambling, sometimes incoherent letters addressed to "Peg Sweetheart" and "my own love," though he added a question mark after "my own love." "Has anyone else come into your life?" he worried, though by this time Bill knew the answer. No matter, his love, he insisted, was more "intense" than anyone else's could possibly be, and certainly she had drained him of love for any other woman. Once he had been "the hero of your dreams" and was, after all, the "father of your children." But now, in the habitual politics of their marriage, he was ever more the pursuer, and she the pursued.[16]

As Bill pointed out in his letters, he—and no one else—had liberated young Maggie Higgins from "the respectable bourgeois life of your boarding school . . . I waited until you could outlive the church life . . . You say my personality is overbearing—just the opposite. I have submerged it." Certainly he had needed no trial marriages or experiences as his wife had when "you did not feel sure of yourself." Bill insisted that he was "the best man to support your claim to belong to the world." Perpetually wondering if she had found anyone else, signing himself, as he knew his wife could not, "Your faithful lover," Bill sank into despondency, only worsened when his paintings failed to be accepted into the spring art shows in Paris.[17]

With Bill on the other side of the Atlantic, though distance had proved no deterrent in the past, Margaret Sanger enacted her personal convictions about monogamy's stifling effect on erotic love and the necessity of women's sexual independence. Sex had become something she could study through practice. There were short interludes with the expatriate Edward Mylius, the Belgian-born journalist who had fled England after a year's imprisonment for libeling King George V. There was a longer sexual relationship with Walter Roberts, a Jamaican-born editor and journalist, best known for his work on the popular *American Parade*. Sometime during this period Roberts sent an undated poem to his new lover, probably written in the spring of 1914. Touched by its passion and the validation of her sexuality, Sanger saved it:

> *Marvelous lover, give me leave to sing*
> *Your body's beauty in keen words lay bare*
> *Your breasts for burning kisses and declare*
> *The glory of your eyes unfaltering . . .*
> *Forbid me not that I should call you fair.*
> *Behold I am entangled in your hair,*
> *And at your mouth have found the whole sweet Spring.*[18]

Meanwhile, the U.S. Post Office, in its role as a national censor, wasted neither time nor effort in confiscating copies of *The Woman Rebel*. After March, five of the six subsequent issues were censored in their entirety under section 211 of the Criminal Code of the Postal Laws and Regulations covering obscene materials. Two weeks after the publication of the March issue, with the required agreement of the New York attorney general's office, the postmaster informed Sanger that her publication could not be delivered. A former postal employee remembered being ordered to hold up to the light all second- and third-class mail: "We are looking for copies of an eight page sheet called *The Woman Rebel*," Bertram Wolfe was informed. "The Solicitor has declared it obscene and unmailable . . . but the bitch that edits it, named Margaret Sanger . . . has been trying to fool us by mailing it wrapped up in respectable newspapers and magazines. Don't let any get through."[19]

Copies did get through, some hidden in the suitcases of sympathetic travelers for personal delivery, especially to Wobblie locals in Milwaukee and on the West Coast. Intending "to continue to the end no matter what," Sanger refused to be intimidated by the U.S. Post Office.[20] On the contrary, suppression became the attention-getting catalyst that she anticipated would permit a First Amendment challenge to the Comstock laws. Each month Sanger continued to place copies of *The Woman Rebel* in bundles in different mailboxes throughout the city; each month the New York postmaster confiscated them and each month Sanger disingenuously inquired which articles and what content were considered obscene, though she never received an answer.

In July, just a few weeks after the assassination of Archduke Franz Ferdinand in faraway Sarajevo and amid the gathering storm of an international conflict, Sanger ran a provocative defense of assassination written by Harold Thorpe, a free-speech advocate from New Jersey. Thorpe, invoking respected nineteenth-century Americans such as the abolitionist Wendell Phillips, argued that because "the great mass of people [are] unable to use the same weapons employed by the better educated and privileged class [this] does not preclude the working class from using whatever means of defense at its disposal, such as strikes, boycott, sabotage or assassination." Sanger correctly anticipated that she would get "pinched" for this defiance.[21]

Faithful to her central mission, in the same issue Sanger included the story of a mother of six who had sold her children because she could not afford to feed them. For such women, wrote Sanger, "motherhood is debauched . . . Crumbs of charity are delivered to such mothers but the solution [of birth control] is called indecent, lascivious and a social crime."[22] As her solution she proposed a daring philosophy, still unacceptable to many Americans a century later: "A woman's body belongs to herself alone. It does not belong to the United States of America or any other government on the face of the earth . . . Enforced motherhood is the most complete denial of a woman's right to life and liberty."[23]

She published articles in the August and September/October issues that summed to a complete feminist agenda for women's rights well ahead of its time, with birth control and voluntary motherhood the organizing principles of women's emancipation and the precondition for a reform intended to give women sexual autonomy. Along with such proposals for reform, Sanger attacked the sacred verities of American life—monogamy and its requirement of one sexual partner. By the same logic of singularity, women should have only one child. She disparaged motherhood as women's priority, and, given her targeted audience of working women, the discriminations of unequal work and pay.

In August, after weeks of surveillance by what she called her shadow, federal Post Office inspectors served a warrant for Margaret Sanger's arrest, charging her with four counts of violating the Comstock laws, "by mailing a magazine called *The Woman Rebel*, which contains certain articles alleged to be obscene, lewd, lascivious, filthy and of indecent character" punishable by a maximum of forty years in prison. Typically, Sanger constructed an unlikely personal tale of her confrontation with the authorities as one of triumph over challenge, not defeat from obstacles—a story, like so many others she told, of personal vindication.

Her father had been visiting when the inspectors came. After the knock on the door, she invited the agents in and then, for three hours, "I presented to their imaginations some of the tragic stories of conscript motherhood . . . at the end they agreed that such a law should not be on the statute books." Miraculously, her father, who had earlier thought her cause disgusting, was persuaded along with the postal inspectors. After listening, Michael Higgins embraced his daughter and, in a moment of familial reconciliation enacted over *his* acceptance of *her* principles, announced that her mother would be alive today if "we had known all this then . . . You will win this case. Everything is with you—logic, common sense, and progress."[24]

Sanger pleaded not guilty at her arraignment, but the grand jury promptly returned an indictment, scheduling the trial of *People v. Margaret Sanger* for September. The charges did not contain Sanger's inclusion of specific information about birth control because to the disgruntlement of readers, there was none. Instead, the postal authorities cited her *advocacy* of contraception, her stated intention to defy the law, and her justification of abortion, if prevention, always her first option, failed. The state specifically objected to an article, "The Marriage Bed," whose offense was its criticism of monogamy, an article on whether most Americans could afford large families, and the Thorpe article on assassination. After the arraignment and indictment there were several postponements of the trial, as the state hesitated to make this delicate, attractive mother of three a martyr. Even the presiding judge noted that Mrs. Sanger did not look "like a bomb thrower or an assassin."[25]

In these years before the courts accepted principles of legal realism and the legitimacy of society's interest in a judicial matter (as in the Supreme Court decision on women's protective legislation in 1908 in *Muller v. Oregon* and, more famously, in the 1954 decision in *Brown v. Board of Education*), no one credited Sanger's sociological defense that the adoption of birth control would benefit the nation by producing fewer and healthier wanted babies. Infuriatingly for the defendant, the prosecutors had excerpted only parts of *The Woman Rebel* "that do not dwell on the bigness of the Cause"; they had based their case on matters peripheral to her central vision of birth control. "Man," Sanger wrote in the passionate defense she hoped to deliver in the courtroom,

has seen fit to place the most sacred functions of her body on a foot-
ing with pornography and he calls any education bearing upon it as
"filthy, vile, obscene." Women must undo that crime. She must raise
Man's standards in this . . . and place the function of motherhood
and its physiology where it rightly belongs. She can do this through
education. And this paper *The Woman Rebel* was a pioneer attempt
to give her that education.[26]

Before her arrest, Sanger had begun writing an illustrated pamphlet
with the kind of specific information that she avoided in *The Woman Rebel*
and that women craved. Presented in forthright language, it replaced earlier obscurely titled manuals hidden away on locked shelves in libraries,
such as Charles Knowlton's *Fruits of Philosophy* and John Cowan's *Science
of a New Life*. Overnight, Sanger's *Family Limitation* became the most influential printed material on the subject. Translated into several languages,
with sales of over 160,000 copies in the United States in four years, and
revised in eighteen future editions, it carried her name and message throughout the United States and Europe.

Sanger titled her sixteen-page pamphlet *Family Limitation* because
such a designation, more straightforward than references in the past, was
familiar to the public and for a time might confound the censors, for surely
its contents would not. When Sanger took her material to the printers, even
the most sympathetic refused. One commented, "This is a Sing Sing job."
After she raised the money for publication from her network of socialist and
trade union friends for the first edition of a hundred thousand, Bill Shat-
tuck, a socialist lithographer in New Jersey, agreed to print it in his shop, but
at night, secretly.

Writing to the working women of America, Sanger provided explicit
practical coverage of every known means of contraception as well as side-
view diagrams of female reproductive anatomy. The text was a revelation to
many women, though the science was by no means new. Intent on the dif-
fusion of available methods, Sanger wrote "as a nurse and mother" with self-
help injunctions that women must be active, calendar-keeping participants
in their reproductive lives, keeping track of their menstrual cycles, douching after intercourse, however troublesome, and attending to any late menstruation by taking laxatives and quinine with a hot drink.[27]

Convinced that birth control was the solution to the thousands of illegal abortions performed in the United States every year, Sanger approved of abortion as a last resort, and she made clear the distinction between it and birth control. Such a differentiation was necessary for a generation of Americans whose ignorance about reproductive matters often led to the conflation of abortion and birth control, encouraged by the Catholic Church. And she emphatically denied that there was a reliable sterile period that could be applied to all women. At some length *Family Limitation* introduced women to specific chemical formulas, useful as acidic spermicides in douches, in capsule form, or in cloths inserted in the vagina.

Sanger made clear her personal preference for the Mizpah pessary, available for a dollar and a half at any "reliable drug store," which was the American version of her favorite device, the Mensinga pessary, named after a German gynecologist, but prohibited from importation into the United States by the Comstock Act. Yet such a rubber cap over the cervix required women to insert their fingers into their vaginas, something that custom, fastidiousness, and ignorance made abhorrent. So Sanger, in blunt, uncoded language and drawings of a finger inserted into the vagina, provided profiles of the still mysterious female reproductive system. Knowing that many could or would not follow her instructions, she encouraged women to visit doctors and nurses for instruction on how to insert a cap.

Though *Family Limitation* was intended as a self-help guide for women, necessarily Sanger considered condoms and coitus interruptus, the male practices of contraception, both of which, for many years to come, remained the most popular birth control methods. Moving beyond simply a contraceptive manual into areas of sexuality and female orgasm, Sanger dismissed coitus interruptus as harmful for women. At this point she still accepted the androcentric fiction that male semen deposited in the walls of the female uterus was essential for a woman's health. Wives, it was believed, were refreshed by this elixir and soothed by such baths of semen. Interrupted intercourse had "an evil effect upon the woman's nervous condition, her whole being is on the verge of satisfaction . . . she is left in this dissatisfied state, which is far from humane . . . A mutual and satisfied sexual act on the part of the woman is of great benefit to the average woman, the magnetism of it is health giving and acts as a beautifier and tonic."[28]

In *Family Limitation* Sanger moved into her self-appointed but unavoidable and soon cherished role of sexologist, a new category of specialist in the twentieth century with few American practitioners before Alfred Kinsey. Even in a pamphlet of sixteen pages she had room for some feminist advice about sexual politics. Men, she wrote, often asked for advice from their physicians as "to the cause of sexual coldness and indifference of their wives. Nine times out of ten it is the fault of the man who through ignorance and selfishness and inconsiderateness, has satisfied his own desire and promptly gone off to sleep. The woman in self-defense has learned to protect herself from long hours of sleepless nights and nervous tension by refusing to become interested."[29]

In Sanger's advanced views of female sexuality, those passionless women of the nineteenth century had been replaced by a new American woman intent on fulfillment. And if women weren't interested, men bore the blame. Almost never did Sanger discuss the physical love of women for other women, but when she did, she could fit lesbians into her sexual framework: women loved women because of their disgust at a sexual existence lived in a man's world, without any consideration of their desires.

In *Family Limitation* Sanger's sexual vocabulary was explicit, for she had moved beyond the reticence of her first publications on sex education published in *The New York Call*. To the dismay of some readers she employed medical terms—"penis" (in place of "male organ"), "vagina" and "uterus" (in place of "female canal" and "womb"), and "semen" (in place of "male seed"). Sanger did not restrict her advice to just married women, intending that all working women benefit from this information. And she encouraged readers to copy *Family Limitation* and pass it on to others. It would be, in the manner of the anarchists, a subversive feminist samizdat, circulating underground, beyond the watchful eyes of the censors.

After several postponements, some requested by the state, others by Sanger, on October 18, 1914, the trial of *People v. Sanger* was called again. According to the defendant, she had received no written notification, only a telephone call that morning. Hurrying to court, she expected another delay. This time it was denied. She must present herself for trial the next morning. In the prosecutor's words, "Every day's delay means that her violations are increased," for she had taunted the prosecutors with information that more "good" material (referring to *Family Limitation*) was forthcoming.[30]

Now Sanger faced a turning point in her life. Should she conduct her own defense as so many radicals were doing in order to promote their cause? Many, such as her friends Bill Haywood and Frank Tannenbaum, held the judicial process so tainted that they made their own case without any legal representation. And if they lost, their courage, at least within the radical community, brought glory to the cause through the sacrifice of a charismatic

leader to jail, but one who, with this sacrifice, had clarified the revolutionary purpose in an inspiring courtroom statement. Or should she, a lifelong
admirer of experts, hire a lawyer?

There was also the matter of the legal grounds for her defense. She had
already prepared her impassioned sociological defense. But would the judge
listen? The lawyers she consulted cautioned that such an approach was
naive and utterly useless in the courtroom. And as for a free-speech defense,
the experts from the Free Speech League knew that the courts usually
denied claims based on the First Amendment right of free expression. One
said she should plead guilty and hope for a suspended sentence. Or, advised
another, she might negotiate an acceptable deal with the prosecutor, promising no more publication of *The Woman Rebel* and no more advocacy of
birth control. But most lawyers were simply not interested in associating
with such an embarrassing, hopeless affair.

Sanger denied any fear of jail, admitting only to anxiety over the sacrifice of her time and presence in an emerging cause. But she had heard her
friend the anarchist Alexander Berkman, who had been jailed for fourteen
years after his attempted assassination of Henry Clay Frick, declaim on
the challenges of imprisonment. To be silenced at such a critical moment
and to be imprisoned on the wrong charge—the material in *The Woman
Rebel* rather than that in her new pamphlet *Family Limitation*—would undermine her purpose. "Should I follow the inevitable suggestion of the
'I-told-you so's' & take my medicine? Yes, but what medicine? I would not
swallow a dosage for the wrong disease."[31]

And what about the children? Few women of this or any age voluntarily
abandoned young children to become absentee mothers, and those who did
were vilified in a society that venerated motherhood as a national duty. Yet
Bill, now returned from Paris and war-torn France, was available for parenting at night and on weekends. And two friends—Helen Marot, an
activist and director of the National Women's Trade Union League, and
Caroline Pratt, an educator and founder of the City and Country School—
offered their home in Greenwich Village for Stuart, Grant, and Peggy, if
Bill insisted on living in his art studio. Eleven-year-old Stuart boarded at
a school on Long Island during the weekdays, and the Ferrer Association
had just moved their school from New York to Shelton, New Jersey, where
both Grant and Peggy could stay, though Bill deplored this "slicing up" of
the family. When necessary, Margaret's sisters Nan and Ethel, both living
in New York, could help as well.

There remained the dilemma of how to circulate the hundred thousand copies of *Family Limitation*, "which simply must be published," and as well, how to sustain the enthusiasm of the growing numbers of birth control advocates. A few supporters attended meetings of an informal group, soon to be grandly named the National Birth Control League of America (NBCLA), where they resolved not just to change the Comstock laws. They determined as well to commit themselves to the larger, more indeterminate purpose of fulfilling women's need for complete control of their reproductive function. These women (and a few men) hailed Margaret Sanger as their leader; they bought her magazine, and they gave money to the cause. Who would be their leader while she was in jail?

Sanger laid out the alternatives: "If I must go to jail, I will give them something to send me in on. Everyone has crawled under cover in denying their support of me with an 'I-told-you-so'. . . Fortunately it is good to stand alone, so with sleeves up in true Irish fashion, I'm in the fight to win."[32] Yet she remembered the cautionary tales of those who had gone off to jail even for a year and were never heard from again, either intimidated by their incarceration or forgotten as others took up their battles. Certainly jail would not help her presently quiescent tuberculosis. Still, "going away was much more difficult than remaining," because as a criminal wanted on a felony charge, she must leave not just New York but the United States.[33]

Characteristically, Sanger chose what she designated for herself as the most difficult path. Failing to appear in court for her trial, she became a fugitive from justice. Before she left the United States on October 28, 1914, she sent her followers a hastily written call-to-duty message: "Comrades and Friends: Jail has not been my goal. There is special work to be done and I shall do it first. If jail comes after, I shall call upon all to assist me. In the meantime I shall attempt to nullify the law by direct action and attend to the consequences later. Over 100,000 working men and women will hear from me."[34] She intended to be gone but not forgotten: "I want to let the United States know that I am alive—May my invisible guardians help me to do so & do it well."[35]

The next day Margaret Sanger took a late-night train to Montreal and there, from friends, received fake Canadian papers in the name of Bertha Watson; these were necessary because, as the notorious Margaret Sanger, she might be denied entry into Great Britain. On November 2, 1914, she boarded a passenger ship bound for Liverpool to begin a self-imposed exile that lasted a year. Once at sea, she cabled a coded message to four "trusted lieutenants" to release the stored copies of *Family Limitation*. Immediately, thousands of copies of the most explicit, practical information on birth control in the world began circulating.

As the RMS *Virginian* plied its way across the rough seas of the Atlantic Ocean from Montreal, with munitions stored below its decks, its crew on the lookout for German submarines, Margaret Sanger began a diary. Rarely in her hectic life had she enjoyed the opportunity to be alone or had the time for such an intimate exercise. Now for a year—and sporadically on other occasions, mostly when she traveled—she pondered, among other matters, the religious faith that kept believers "stagnant and stationary" and depended upon "so much false sentiment that has been built up." Given her well-developed autobiographical imagination, she revealed herself in lonely laments for her children, especially Peggy: "Dear Peggy, how my love goes out to you. I could weep from loneliness for you, just to touch your soft chubby hands. But work is to be done, work to help make your path easier." She wrote nothing of Bill, who had opposed her leaving the United States. But she described helpful friends in Montreal and her fellow travelers on the *Virginian*, the physical appearances of new acquaintances in England, and, after she landed in Liverpool, her activities. "Women," she concluded in a December entry, "must be a God unto themselves and stop worshipping at the shrine of other egos."[36]

After ten days of rare introspection, Sanger looked to action when she arrived. No aimless walker during these first dark, rainy days in Liverpool, she instead window-shopped, using the prices listed for goods to become familiar with the exchange rate. Lonely in the cold boardinghouses where she saved money by not using the coal heaters, with typical Sanger sangfroid, as homesickness swept over her, she recalled, "Like my first days in boarding school, I knew it would not do to 'set & think' as the Quakers say, so I set off for the Clarion Café."[37]

There, in a famous radical gathering place, where Bill Haywood, George Bernard Shaw, and H. G. Wells had all signed the guest book, she met the English Fabians—those socialists who rejected Marxist notions of violent struggle and instead sought through democratic elections to effect the nationalization of the means of production and distribution. Many were supporters of birth control, though they did not call it that; others were pacifists who connected war—and especially German aggression—with population pressure, arriving logically at support of birth control. Even as an under-educated provincial from America amid these Oxford-schooled elites, she was welcomed into their circle and even invited to lecture. At the Fabian Society hall in London, on July 4, an apprehensive Sanger gave a windy, autobiographical speech on women's enslavement, the struggle of capital and labor, and the importance of limiting the size of families in an effort to attain the better society that Fabians anticipated.

With the help of the Liverpool Fabians, Sanger soon moved to London. There, aided by the innate grace and charm that made strangers, especially male ones, offer assistance and companionship, she met another group of English thinkers in the Neo-Malthusian League. They, too, provided friend-ship, support, and intellectual stimulation. With these contacts available for her lonely times, Sanger reported in her diary that "it seems almost good to be alone—there is time to get acquainted with ones self [sic], to reflect, to meditate, to dream," to have, as she had earlier demanded in her manifesto of women's rights, "time to be lazy," though she was rarely that.[38]

English Malthusians, especially the famous Drysdale family, who had founded and for two generations run the society on London's Eccleston Square, introduced their American visitor to the founder's essential eighteenth-century insight that populations increased geometrically, rather than as food sources did, arithmetically. Such a view led ineluctably to the conclusion that to prevent starvation, population must be controlled. To address the problem, Thomas Malthus, the Anglican clergyman and author of *An Essay on the Principle of Population,* had recommended continence and late mar-riage. Following his own rules, he had married at thirty-eight and, himself one of seven, fathered only three offspring.

With different solutions, his twentieth-century intellectual descen-dants, the revitalized Neo-Malthusians, led by Dr. Charles Vickery Drys-dale, his wife, Bessie, and his mother, Dr. Alice Vickery, propelled a society of quiescent tea drinkers into more energetic activities such as establishing international branches and publishing a monthly journal, the *Malthusian.* Writing pamphlets on "sex hygiene," the Neo-Malthusians of London sup-ported what they referred to as preventive sexual intercourse.

In their company Margaret Sanger met English intellectuals who became lifetime friends, supporters, and occasional lovers—writers H. G. Wells, Hugh de Selincourt, and the editor of the *Edinburgh Review,* Harold Cox. Among her new friends was Marie Stopes, a paleontologist with a doc-torate from the University of Munich. After an unhappy first marriage caused by both partners' ignorance of sex, the English reformer had replaced her earlier research on ancient rocks with a new fascination—human sexual behavior. Supported by a rich second husband, Stopes was finishing a study, mostly based on her own experience, titled *Married Love*. Sanger promised to find a publisher in the United States for a book that had shocked the English. When Sanger returned home, she carried a copy through customs, stuffed into her girdle.

Among her new friends was the famous sexologist Havelock Ellis, the author of the influential multivolume *Studies in the Psychology of Sex*. Soon Sanger had an invitation to tea at Ellis's Brixton apartment across the Thames, where she met the man who would have the most enduring influence on her life. Well-known in radical circles, in 1914 Ellis, a physician by training, a teacher by early vocation, and a writer by profession, was fifty-five years old, a generation older than his new admirer. His hair and full beard had turned snow-white, and he appeared as an ancient prophet, though his messages were distinctly modern. For Sanger, who had quoted from his writings in *The Woman Rebel*, he became a beloved muse.

At first the usually indomitable Sanger felt like a shy adolescent in his presence, when Ellis engaged in none of the small talk and gossip that usually carries such first meetings beyond initial awkwardness. "You had to utter only the deepest truths within you," she wrote, still in awe two decades later. "No other human being could be so silent and remain so poised and calm in silence . . . Ellis pasted no labels on himself, had no poses, made no effort to impress. He was simply, quite unself-consciously what he was." In time she, more famous than he, found it a privilege to know Havelock Ellis and "to claim him friend, my greatest honor."[39]

Over tea and cakes, they discovered their mutual profundities: the importance of sex as the innate, natural, joyous behavior of human beings; the resulting recognition that all sex was an aspect of humanity that must be examined with dignity (Ellis had published his study of homosexuality, *Sexual Inversion*, in 1897); their interest in controlling the size of national populations; and their problems with censors. These two agreed as well on the stupidity of government repression and the hypocrisy of conventional morality, though they confronted it differently: Sanger would fight to change the laws, use the courts for publicity, and practice civil disobedience, while Ellis, who had temporarily withdrawn *Sexual Inversion* after a court case, had no such pugnacious instincts. Such conflicts only took time from his writing.

The congeniality of Ellis and Sanger as teacher and student heightened their friendship. Proudly she shared with him her writings—*What Every Girl Should Know, The Woman Rebel,* and *Family Limitation.* Ellis appreciated Sanger both as a disciple, having no others, and as a delightful companion. Bluntly he urged her to spend more time on her writing: It was, he wrote, "direct, sincere and much yourself . . . but I do not think you have a special gift for writing."[40] He inspired her, though she needed little encouragement, to read his new material on the sexual impulse in women and *The Sexual Selection in Man,* based, like most of his research, on a few case studies, his own medical observations, and his study of anthropology.

With a far broader education than she, Ellis supported himself through his writing and reviews of plays and books ranging from Thomas Hardy to Sigmund Freud, the latter his contemporary rival for primacy as an interpreter of sex. In fact, Ellis, with his abundant tolerance for various sexual practices—unlike Freud, who tried to change such behaviors—once declared Freud "an extravagant genius—the greatest figure in psychology who was almost always wrong." Freud, in turn, believed Ellis an unscientific amateur observer whose elegant writing was the most praiseworthy aspect of his work.[41]

Faithfully Sanger studied all Ellis's work, and throughout her life she depended on his writings and ideas to fill the columns of her later, more ambitious magazine, *The Birth Control Review.* With Ellis, as with no one else, Sanger was able to discuss the practices and techniques of sex. What she had considered as possibility, he sustained as a scientist. Familiar with the complete literature of sex radicals, he encouraged her to consider the American utopian John Humphrey Noyes's *Male Continence; or, Self-Control in Sexual Intercourse,* which promoted the male practice of sexual stimulation without ejaculation. And he educated her about the American radical Alice Stockham's theory of Karezza, a birth control practice that required husbands to satisfy their wives before they ejaculated outside the vagina. The practice went by several names—Karezza, Magnetation, and coitus reservatus—and Sanger devoted an entire pamphlet to it, as she weighed its feasibility as a birth control technique.

They agreed on the need for female sexual autonomy, and Ellis affirmed Sanger's view that the clitoris was the key organ for female sexual pleasure, and a central aspect of what he called "the erotic rights of women," in a soon-to-be-published book with that title. Like Sanger, he held men mostly responsible for female sexual passivity: "Failing to find in women exactly the

same kind of sexual emotions that they find in themselves, men have concluded there are none at all in women."[42]

They agreed as well that there was no evidence linking masturbation to
any sexual disorder or neurosis, though Sanger remained suspicious that
overindulgence might prevent a successful heterosexual relationship. Ellis
instead argued that masturbation was no more than a practical autoerotic
means of relaxation and the reality of many women's sex lives. Both, as
fervent believers in the virtues of polyeroticism, approved of foreplay, trial
marriages, divorce, and multiple sexual contacts, and they considered abstinence harmful to the human condition, holding Christianity responsible
for the repression of sex and the degradation of women. With sex at the
center of their intellectual universes, Ellis and Sanger also held that married couples should accept each others' affairs amicably. At this stage,
Ellis's reservations about contraception as impeding the reproductive role
of women were not immediately clear to Sanger, though she never shared
his enthusiasm for motherhood and the natural femininity that he believed
stoked the sexual urges of men.

Ellis, with his more expansive worldview and his innocence about what
eugenics might become, had adopted the increasingly widespread view that
bringing an inferior child into the world was an act of cruelty and irrespon-
sibility to society. Parents, he maintained in a gentle precursor to the future's
repressive eugenic engineering, must ask themselves if their offspring would
improve the quality of future generations. Sanger agreed.

Strengthened by a friendship that Ellis acknowledged flamed as swiftly
as any he, a shy recluse, had ever enjoyed, Sanger traveled each day to the
British Museum, studying statistics in the emerging field of demography
and reading the pamphlets that Havelock Ellis piled on her desk in that
august library. Like Virginia Woolf, Beatrice Webb, and even Karl Marx, she
became a graduate of the British Museum's reading rooms, while waiting on
tables in a London tea room to support herself. "Dear Woman Rebel," Ellis
wrote four days after they had met, "if nothing prevents, I expect to be at
the Reading Room on Monday between 11 & 1." Clearly Ellis was capti-
vated by the spontaneity and gaiety of this "attractive Irish American" who,
he wrote in his autobiography, manifested the best characteristics of both
groups.[43]

He appreciated her best features: her boldness, her charm, and her
courage, and used the English poet Matthew Arnold's lines to describe her:
"The wild waves foam and fret / Margaret, Margaret."[44] In just six weeks

a man who had few friends sent fifty notes and letters to "my little rebel," "you wicked woman," and "my dear Twin." He feared he "would be gobbled up." And after she returned to the United States in the fall, he admitted to moments of nostalgic longing when he looked "in the old familiar spots" and saw only an empty desk in the British Museum.[45]

With Ellis's wife, Edith—who led a separate life in Cornwall—currently in the United States on a lecture tour, this unlikely couple went to concerts at Albert Hall, smoked Russian cigarettes, and enjoyed Soho restaurants. Certainly there was an erotic attraction. They complemented each other: she brought sexual experience to an isolated theorist, who, in turn, schooled Sanger in the world beyond heterosexual phallic intercourse and conventional marital arrangements. His own sexual profile encouraged alternative practices, for Ellis considered nothing degenerate, once explaining that spectators, not participants, see more of the game. Indeed, fetishism was the supreme expression of human idealism, he believed, while conventional behavior was no more than a modified version of what society, in other places and previous times, had condemned as distasteful perversions.

For years the British sexologist had supposedly been impotent or at least unable to sustain an erection; his wife was a lesbian and his particular fetish was an erotic interest in urolagnia—observing women urinating—which he had first come to enjoy when as a child he had spied on his mother. This pleasure was, he believed, no more than an expression of "uridinism" rooted in water as a universal sign of life. Later, his longtime partner, Françoise Lafitte Cyon, described Havelock's glee while he watched her urinating behind a bush in Hyde Park. In one of his early letters to Sanger, Ellis described her "leaving her liquid gold behind."[46]

Years later, in his 1939 autobiography, *My Life*, Ellis stunned Sanger by downgrading their relationship into one of insignificance. She was just "a charming and congenial companion," he wrote, but unlike his dead wife, she certainly had "no power to help or comfort me," much less inform his work. "It made no difference at all when she went away," wrote a forgetful Ellis, perhaps intending to make amends to a dead wife's memory and a present partner's sensibilities, rather than affirm reality.[47] He had said, explained an aggrieved Sanger, "such intimate things to me urging closer intimacy and friendship with him, arranging for meetings together, walks, teas, musicals—letters every day . . . and yet I was just M—an American nurse whom he wished at times never to see again."[48] But even this humiliation did not shake Sanger's devotion.

Enthralled with her counselor in sexual matters, emboldened by his philosophical argument for authentic relationships, and exhilarated by her own confidence-building entry into the lecture halls and bedrooms of British intellectuals, just before Christmas 1914, Margaret Sanger decided to divorce Bill. Her complaints to her husband were many and included the sensitive subject of her mothering: "You have given the impression I have deserted my children and have turned people against me. I can wait until the storms in life pass and my love for them will be proven in the future."[49]

In her diary she justified "the parting of our life together" as a choice patiently arrived at: "Only I am very slow in my decisions—I cannot separate myself from my past emotions quickly all breeches must come gradually to me. It took me so long to get a Church out of my system, then Socialism—bougeouise [sic] Society, etc, etc so in everything." As mistaken in her self-appraisal as in her reading of Bill, she decided that her husband would not be surprised, but this judgment proved inaccurate. He felt differently, sending flowers for Christmas, whereas she, he rebuked, had replied with "a stone." Having made the decision, Sanger spent the next seven years fighting both her husband and an intransigent system before she finally obtained a divorce from Bill, who clung to the idea that he and his dear Peg could maintain at the very least "a spiritual marriage—the spiritual bond . . . more important than sexual desire."[50]

Just weeks after his wife had fled to England, Bill Sanger had a visitor to his studio at 10 East Fifteenth Street who introduced himself as a dealer in rubber goods sympathetic to Mrs. Sanger's work. Mr. Heller, who called himself a friend of Margaret's and the movement, asked if she was home and, if not, where he could find her. Then he requested a copy of *Family Limitation*, which he promised to publish in different languages to distribute to poor people. Bill, falling into the trap, found one, and a month later was arrested by Anthony Comstock for violating the law against giving out obscene, indecent literature. "The self-appointed censor of our morality and his agent did not hesitate to use criminal methods to make a criminal out of me," argued Bill in his defense.[51] Briefly jailed, in January Bill was released on bail, although his trial did not take place until the fall.

His wife, hard at work on her new birth control method pamphlets in London, took the news for what it was: an effort to bring her home. Wishing that her husband had never gotten "mixed up in my work," though he had been in Paris when she had written *Family Limitation*, "of course [his arrest] makes it harder for me & for all of us."[52] Still, it was useful "impro-paganda." In a manifesto, "To Comrades and Friends," inserted in her just completed *English Methods of Birth Control*, she proclaimed, "We who have hatred and contempt in our hearts for those authorities whose high-handed officialism is running riot in America are not to be deterred from our cause . . . just as I refused to go meekly like a lamb to the slaughter . . . so do I refuse to be tricked into rushing to the side of my comrade [Bill]." Not-ing her loneliness "for my three little ones" during her exile, still her personal sorrows and those of her children—her version of a sacrificial passion—were "no more deeply burned in my soul than the sufferings and anguish of thousands of other women's loved ones, left alone in sorrow by death from abortion." And then, ever practical after such grandiosity, she asked the comrades to pay for their pamphlets in the continuing fight "for the down-fall of Comstockery."[53]

In February 1915, Sanger left Ellis and the sanctuary of the British Museum and crossed the English Channel on a steamer, at a time when the German navy had tightened its blockade of the British Isles, using floating mines and submarines. Her mission was to do research in the most sexu-ally liberated country in Europe—the neutral Netherlands. With little money and none of the letters of introduction this generation required, Sanger intended to visit the doctors and clinics in a country that had the lowest infant mortality rates in Europe and the most enlightened birth control practices.

First she went to The Hague and interviewed Dr. Johannes Rutgers, a sympathetic socialist and member of the Dutch Neo-Malthusian League. Rutgers taught Sanger the actual physical technique of inserting cervical caps and how to teach patients to do so. He introduced her, as well, to the common-sense notion of child spacing, which finessed the common com-plaint that birth controllers discouraged having any children. Less success-ful were her efforts to consult with Dr. Aletta Jacobs, the physician well-known in medical circles for the clinics she had established through-out the Netherlands. Given the European prejudice that nurses were little more than servants, Jacobs refused to see Sanger, bluntly informing the American that birth control was, and must remain, the province of physi-cians. Instead of seeing Jacobs, Sanger investigated the women's health clinics throughout the Netherlands, where knowledge about birth control was freely disseminated. Here she absorbed practical information about

the variation in female pelvic sizes and the necessity for individualized diaphragm fittings by trained personnel. Dutch clinics thereafter became the
model for the next stage in Sanger's birth control movement.

Returned to London, in the spring of 1915, Sanger found an English
publisher for her new series of pamphlets, one of them *Magnetation Methods of Birth Control*, its name recognizing popular notions of magnetism
and electricity, but referring in this case to prolonged intercourse without
seminal emission. Her other pamphlets discussed more familiar English and
Dutch methods of contraception. Inserting these publications in innocent
English magazines, she mailed them to supporters in the United States.
Some were destroyed on the increasingly dangerous Atlantic Ocean. Hundreds of copies were lost, along with forty-four lives, when the British steamer
SS *Arabic* was torpedoed by German submarines.

Then, struggling with the English weather and a persistent cough,
Sanger left in April on a romantic venture with a friend who suffered, as
she did, from tuberculosis. Lorenzo Portet, a Spanish anarchist in exile and
follower of Francisco Ferrer and the Modern School movement, whom Sanger
described as "full of vigor, confident—quick to understand," had been
teaching in Liverpool when Sanger first arrived in England. Almost immediately these two exiles became lovers.[54] When Portet received permission
to return to Spain, Sanger accompanied him, though they disguised their
sexual liaison to friends and the authorities by displaying a written invitation from his wife and family to visit Barcelona. The reason for the decep-
tion was obvious. As Sanger explained to her sister Nan, "So many tongues
and gossips [are] ready to put a knife in your back."[55] In fact, these two were
mostly alone, as Sanger continued not just to preach a radical lifestyle but
to live one, in sexual arrangements that she insistently kept secret. The personal was, in a very special way for her, the political, but given their nature
and the supposed immorality of her crusade, her liaisons must be kept
private.

Often followed by the police, the couple traveled through Spain, where
her hostility toward the Roman Catholic Church intensified. To her son
Stuart she described the mountain prison Montjuïc outside of Barcelona,
where "the Catholic Church has tortured the people of Spain—tortured
them to death because they would not belong to the Catholic Church." She
visited the grave of Francisco Ferrer and "was proud that my Stuart attended the first Ferrer school in America."[56] Meanwhile, from New York,
Stuart wrote that he wished she would come home.

For these seven weeks in the spring of 1915, Sanger enjoyed a leisurely romantic episode and found her dedication to the cause briefly shaken by her passionate attachment to Portet. Such was the temptation that she considered settling in Paris with Portet, after collecting the children. There, with the Spanish radical as the attraction, she would work as a translator for the Ferrer press. She wavered for a moment in her sacrificial service to the cause, but when Bill's trial revived the significance of her campaign, she made her decision to return to the United States. It was time to go home, though she was warned that she might face a harsh sentence. Two years later, Portet was dead, a victim of tuberculosis.

Bill's tumultuous trial took place in September 1915. The defendant argued his own case on the grounds of free speech, the legitimacy of birth control information, and "the incurable sexophobia" of Anthony Comstock, who was the principal prosecution witness. In this high-profile, widely publicized confrontation, a Comstock agent set the scene, testifying that in his many years as an antivice officer, Margaret Sanger's *Family Limitation* was the worst, most obscene literature he had ever read. Then Anthony Comstock himself testified that Bill had distributed his wife's obscene pamphlet, for which he deserved to go to jail.

In response, Bill, who refused to have a lawyer, shouted that he was not the defendant; rather, the law was on trial. And like other radicals of this era, Bill chose incarceration in New York's vile prison, the Tombs, rather than pay a fine: "I would rather be in jail with my conviction than be free at a loss of my manhood and my self-respect," to which, amid the cheers of Bill's friends, who were soon removed from the courtroom, Judge J. J. McInerney responded, in something of a non sequitur, "then you will go to jail . . . You are a menace to society. If some of the women who are going around and advocating equal suffrage would go around and advocate women having children, they would do a greater service."[57] Though Bill had demanded a jury trial, his ended with the judge's sentence of a fine or a month in jail.

A week later seventy-one-year-old Anthony Comstock was dead from pneumonia—germs, the Sangers and their friends wickedly suggested, contracted in the courtroom where he had testified against Bill. For those who had disputed his cause for nearly a half century, Comstock's death symbolized the decline of his—and society's—puritanical convictions that reflexively linked birth control to obscenity and sexual intercourse to reproduction. Public opinion was shifting. By 1915, after years of silence, some mainstream periodicals, even *Harper's Weekly*, entered the debate about family limitation. As a measure of progress, there were fifteen articles in *The New York Times* during the year on the subject, several using their coverage of Bill's trial as an opportunity to report on the larger issue of what was now universally dubbed birth control. *The New Republic* covered Bill's trial, noting the irony that both Comstock and Judge McInerney, by their efforts at suppression, had only "accelerated the spread of the doctrine to which they were opposed."[58]

On a foggy day in October 1915, on a ship out of Bordeaux in the midst of the war, Margaret Sanger arrived in New York to resume her crusade. To her surprise, the first newsstand she passed featured a popular magazine, the *Pictorial Review*, with the bold caption "What Shall We Do About Birth Control?" Much had changed during her year of exile; now she must move to new tactics and assert her leadership. But first she would have to face a private tragedy and a very public trial.

5

ON TRIAL

If the cause is not great enough to lift you outside yourself, you can be driven
to the point of bitterness by public apathy and, within your own circle, by the
petty prides and jealousies of little egos which clamor for attention and ap-
probation.   —Margaret Sanger, *Autobiography*

Four weeks after Margaret Sanger returned to the United States in October 1915 to face felony charges, her five-year-old daughter, Peggy, died. When
Bill had been sentenced to prison for thirty days, the Sanger children had
nowhere to live. Their mother was still in Europe, and the Winnwood School
on Long Island, where eleven-year-old Stuart was enrolled, did not accept
children under ten. So Peggy and her older brother Grant attended the Ferrer
School in Stelton, New Jersey. It was only a temporary arrangement, with the
tuition paid by a birth control supporter, though both parents, especially
Margaret, approved of the Modern School movement's commitment to
communal living, intended to neutralize the pernicious effects of individual
parenting. And neither parent, given their socialist-anarchist leanings and
their impatience with the time commitments of child raising, had com-
punctions about sending their young children to boarding schools.

The supporters of the Ferrer movement in the United States had grown
weary of the challenges to their radical style of education in expensive New
York, and had found a permanent location outside the city. They had always
held aspirations for a rugged, collective experience for the young, intended
to inspire a lifelong sympathy with the poor. Along with classroom teaching
of the antiauthoritarian philosophy at the core of Ferrer's goals, a Spartan
boarding-school experience would best instill such values.

But the money ran out before an old farm building in New Jersey could be converted into a boarding school with even limited amenities. The students endured harsh conditions—sleeping on straw mattresses in bunk beds, using an outhouse, shivering in a building without a furnace, and eating cheap and insufficient food. One student remembered wearing his overcoat to meals; another recalled waking up during the winter months with his hair frozen to his straw pillow.[1] It was here that Peggy Sanger first developed a cold, a cough, and then a lethal form of pneumonia.

Moved to Mount Sinai Hospital in New York for the special care that her aunt Ethel along with her recently returned mother could provide, Peggy suffered high fevers, followed by chills, coughing fits, and then the massive invasion of bacteria into her lungs that killed her. There was no treatment; in the latest version of his famed textbook—the one that her mother and aunt had read in nursing school—Dr. William Osler still recommended the bleeding of patients with pneumonia.[2] Helpless in this age before penicillin or even the technology to drain pus from the chest, the two sisters sat by Peggy's bed, sponging her forehead, covering her with blankets when she had a chill, and embracing her during the increasingly violent coughing fits caused by fulminating pneumonia. On the morning of November 6, 1915, Peggy Sanger died in her mother's arms. Thereafter, "a great gulf of loneliness set me apart from the rest of the world," Sanger wrote sixteen years later. "It separated me from everybody and everything—from facts— from sunshine, night and day. The joy in the fullness of life went out of it that morning and has never returned."[3]

For a woman hostile to any organized religion, especially her mother's Catholicism, there could be no orthodox consolation of resurrection, and there was none. Certainly her estranged husband provided no support. Instead, he descended into what became intermittent episodes of depression. As Margaret's father had done in similar circumstances, Bill made a plaster of paris body cast of his dead daughter, which he kept in a suitcase for years until he finally buried the crumbled pieces. Meanwhile, seven-year-old Grant was devastated by the loss of his playmate Peggy, who had been the most constant presence in his young life. In later years he held his parents, especially his mother, partly responsible. Even before Bill and Margaret's divorce, the Sanger family had splintered into fragments of guilt and blame that forever destroyed its cohesiveness.

Peggy's death awoke feelings of mysticism in Sanger, a woman who had always credited her Celtic origins for her childhood premonitions and extraterrestrial visitations. As Sanger described the death scene:

> Peggy was sleeping. Her pulse was so soft and slow. I was unable to realize that the end was near and had my fingers on her ankle to get the pulse when before my eyes arose another Peggy horizontally sleeping [who] rose about a foot or more—fluttering and quivering a moment as if taking leave of its bondage and slowly and majestically [she] soared and floated across the bed and out through the iron closed door . . . Peggy had left for the great unknown and beyond.[4]

Her mother spent the rest of her life searching, and often finding, this ethereal, levitating daughter in the spirit world. At the time of Peggy's death, Sanger recalled earlier dreams, now understood as predictions, though she rejected Freud's popular sexualized interpretations of unconscious states. The number six—Peggy died on November 6—figured prominently in these memories, and to discover their significance she consulted astrologists and mediums, attended séances, and educated herself on the mechanics of spiritualism. She discovered the Society of Rosicrucians, an ancient group of mystics whose views had been revised and transported to twentieth-century America. Rosicrucians taught that through private meditation individuals could discover a greater power, their god within, and, significant for Sanger, apply its direction to themselves, thereby becoming a force for good among humanity. In time, ever marching to her own drummers, Sanger created her own personalized belief system, outside of organized religion but with similarly supernatural consolations.

After Peggy's death, Sanger recalled moments between sleep and consciousness during her year's absence in Europe when Peggy had appeared, asking "Mother, mother are you coming home?"—though the question, especially the omission of the word "when," as if her mother might not return at all, might prompt a lifetime of guilt. But later, as a woman who sometimes shaded events to suit her purposes, Sanger denied that she had ever felt guilt over Peggy's death, only regret. She would not accept blame. As she explained to a biographer in 1953, "As to leaving the children I knew it was a necessary sacrifice to leave them to prepare my defense in order to leave them a clear record of their mother's work."[5]

Sanger had always been empowered by a sense of her own destiny, a

conviction now employed as a consolation. After Peggy's death, parapsy-
chological methods of thought transference—popular during the period
as a transformation of primitive nineteenth-century spiritualism into more
rational expression—emerged as a solace for her loss and a support for her
life's work. She read the Harvard psychologist William James, along with
less creditable self-help introductions to the field, and was particularly attracted to the former Anglican J. Hewat McKenzie's just-published *Spirit
Intercourse, Its Theory and Practice.*

In this manual of spiritualist techniques, Sanger encountered a three-
step process of detaching one's own soul from the material body, entering
into a psychic sphere, then materializing the detached soul of the departed,
and, in the final step, joining in communion with the dead—spirit intercourse, as McKenzie called it. It was hard work but available to "sensitive
persons," as Sanger knew herself to be, given that its practitioners must teach
themselves the means of communication "to open one's soul to admit direct
messages of love and good counsel from those who have passed onto spiritual states."[6] Such self-directed spiritualism appealed to Margaret Sanger.
Tawdry mediums and manipulative psychics were not necessary.

Throughout her life she canceled engagements and secluded herself on
May 31, Peggy's birthday, and November 6, the date of her death, in order
to practice spirit recall. Once, Sanger believed that Peggy used the technique of automatic spirit-writing to encourage her mother's work. At other
times her daughter returned as a needy apparition who "wanted me to recognize that she had gone and was no longer here." And occasionally in group
séances such as those organized by the Rosicrucians, when Peggy did not
return, strangers pressed Margaret Sanger's hand and told her to grieve no
more.

In her mother's fantasies, Peggy never succumbed but, over time,
grew into womanhood "in that strange place where imagination and reality
meet . . . [where] she leads an ideal life untouched by harsh realities, immune to these influences which deform mere mortals."[7] As an adult, Peggy
never disappeared from her mother's consciousness, but lived on as an
inspiration, available, as the manuals suggested, for the purpose of spirit intercourse, where she stimulated Sanger, as if that were necessary, "to make
a bolder effort to accomplish some high purpose in life."[8] Sanger, a rational,
purposeful woman, eventually assimilated the supernatural into her life, as
a grown-up Peggy, visiting from the spirit world, came to represent all the
women whom her mother would save.

Initially friends from the movement offered more customary forms of support. Some sent money to the birth control movement as a means of remembering Peggy. From Charles and Bessie Drysdale, her Neo-Malthusian friends in England who had also lost a daughter, came their solution to the paralysis accompanying the loss of a child: "the innocent perfect young" were better off elsewhere, as they were "unfitted for a hard, vulgar world." Emma Goldman, to whom Sanger had expressed rare feelings of guilt, offered stark, even cruel common sense: "I cannot imagine anyone with your intelligence [would] hold herself responsible for something that could not possibly have been in your power. No doubt the child would have been given better care in your home, but whether that would have saved her life is a mere speculation which ought not to take possession of you in the way it evidently has."[9]

Even government prosecutors, ready to serve their court summonses now that Sanger had returned to the United States, offered their sympathies and the practical consideration that her trial on obscenity charges could be delayed. Officially the three federal indictments from 1914 were still pending, but the district attorney, irritated by her yearlong "disappearance," would not wait forever to prosecute a fugitive.[10]

During this acute phase of Sanger's mourning, as she faced the possibility of a jail sentence, the earlier tactical dilemma that had sent her to Europe reemerged: Should she plead guilty to the manufactured charges relating to what she believed innocent material in *The Woman Rebel*, rather than the more definitively obscene *Family Limitation*? Had the latter been the cause of the indictment, the popular pamphlet would have received additional publicity, sold more copies, further spread the birth control message, and been worth a jail term. Or should she plead not guilty and fight the charges on the grounds that her free speech rights had been violated and that hers was a legitimate form of civil disobedience directed at changing a bad law?

During this era of American jurisprudence, judges and juries, confronted by the civil unrest of strikes, socialist and anarchist protests, and even the popular suffrage parades in New York, relied on common-law police powers to protect the status quo. Free speech defenses based on the First Amendment held little creditability when weighed against protecting the community's safety and public order. Perhaps, then, she should follow

her husband's example, appear without counsel, and use the courtroom as
a forum to proclaim the necessity of birth control and the oppressiveness of
a state that prevented the circulation of her ideas. But how long a sentence
might she receive? It could be as long as five years.

Most lawyers, including a sympathetic leader of the New York Bar,
Samuel Untermyer, counseled Sanger on what they considered a reasonable
compromise: a plea bargain requiring her to plead guilty, for she had certainly violated that section of the U.S. Code prohibiting the circulation of
contraceptive information, followed by her promise to never again publish,
send, transmit, or advertise such materials. In return she would receive a
suspended sentence.

An unusually indecisive Sanger appeared to the members of the Free
Speech League, in the words of Theodore Schroeder, "in a very confused
state of mind. She is undoubtedly crushed by her troubles. She wavers between the attitude prompted by her own weaknesses, and her desire to be
consistently radical and revolutionary." Later, and perhaps only for purposes
of her protection in court proceedings, her physician, Dr. Morris Kahn, advised that she had suffered "a nervous breakdown from excessive mental
and physical strain and would be unable to attend to business for about two
months."[11]

The doctors and attorneys misunderstood Sanger's priorities and mental health. While the lawyers considered her forthcoming trial an opportunity to establish a general ruling that all speech was constitutionally protected
unless it resulted in an injury designated as a crime, her purposes were
different: she intended to use her courtroom appearance to publicize birth
control, to pressure legislators to overturn the archaic Comstock Act and
its state versions, and to establish her role as the leader of the movement.
Her radical friend Jack Reed, on the eve of his departure to Russia, appreciated her motives and encouraged Sanger to have a photograph of herself
taken with her two sons.

The result, by the famed New York photographers Underwood and Underwood, was printed in newspapers throughout the United States under
the heading "Mrs. Sanger to Be Tried: Back from Abroad to Face Indictments for Misuse of Mails." The photograph displayed a maternal scene:
Stuart resting his head on his mother's shoulder and a vulnerable, wary
Grant leaning his head on her chest. As for the boys' mother, in the persistent contrast of the physical Margaret Sanger to the vilified stereotype of a
wild, crazy, radical lawbreaker, the portrait revealed a small woman cuddling

her sons, wearing a sensible gray dress with a deep linen collar, her thick, soft hair swept over her forehead and her sad, apprehensive eyes highlighting a wistful expression.

Throughout December and the early weeks of 1916, negotiations with the U.S. attorney's office stalled, until the trial was finally scheduled. Sanger took advantage of the time, thrusting herself into the cause so that she might become its brand name. Always available to reporters, she informed them, "It is not so much Margaret Sanger who goes on trial, but rather [for women] it is your inherent right to own and control your bodies."[12]

The night before Margaret Sanger was to appear for her trial, her followers organized a dinner to display solidarity with the cause and with its principal advocate, who might go to jail the next day. Always nervous before her talks and especially so before this crucial one, Sanger practiced her remarks on the rooftop of the hotel where she now lived since her return from England. On January 17, 1916, delivering her first major speech in the United States, Margaret Sanger confronted not a handful of anarchists or socialists in a gritty Bronx storefront. Instead, speaking in the ballroom of the well-known Brevoort Hotel on Eighth Street, she looked down from the podium on the cream of New York society, as well as the city's intellectual leaders and a few philanthropists.

Walter Lippmann of *The New Republic* and the progressive author and columnist Herbert Croly were there. So, too, were the writer Mary Heaton Vorse, the suffragist Katharine Houghton Hepburn, whom she had observed from afar in her Corning days, the feminist writer Charlotte Perkins Gilman, and Mary Ware Dennett, the latter her principal rival for leadership of the birth control movement in the coming years. The prominence of the audience—"its diverse outlooks and temperaments"—did not escape Sanger's attention, as she deferentially praised the knowledge and intelligence of the gathering in a calm, clear voice that contrasted with her fiery words.

She spoke briefly about the hidden but universal practice of birth control and then touched on society's evils of abortion, infanticide, and foundling asylums for orphans, all the result of an ignorant society's censorship of birth control information. She defined her role as filling a gap between physicians and scientists, who discussed birth control only among themselves, and the working class, who knew nothing about how to prevent babies because the state prevented her from telling them. In a minimalist declaration of her ambitions, she referred to herself as a bridge across this chasm: "I might have taken up a policy of safety, sanity and conservatism—but would I have got a hearing? . . . Some of us may only be fit to dramatize a situation—to focus attention upon obsolete laws, like this one I must face tomorrow morning." And if she went to jail, others must move to the next stage and "organize this interest . . . Only in this way can I be vindicated."[13]

The next day as her followers filled the courtroom, the trial was postponed and then a second and a third time until the *New York Sun* joked about "the anomaly of a prosecutor who was loath to prosecute and a defendant who was anxious to be tried."[14] Sanger believed the delays were efforts to destroy the movement, exhaust her, and deplete the donated funds that provided her living expenses. Meanwhile, the exasperated federal prosecutor, Assistant U.S. Attorney Harold Content, accused the defendant of inaccurate statements about the scheduling of the trial: "[Last week] you left without any understanding on your part or mine that the case would go to trial on Monday . . . You seem to forget that the case could have been tried over a year ago . . . but you left the jurisdiction in violation of the trust that Judge Hazel imposed in you . . . You also forget that within the last three or four months, adjournments have been granted at your request."[15]

Three days later, the government suddenly dropped the case because, as the U.S. attorney for New York explained to both the press and his superiors in the Justice Department, he refused to make a martyr out of Margaret Sanger. Officially the nolle prosequi (not to prosecute) action was entered on the grounds that the indictment was nearly two years old, that Sanger was not a disorderly person, and "that the evidence is not of such a character as to establish the defendant's guilt beyond all reasonable doubt."[16] To U.S. Attorney General Thomas Gregory in Washington, the New York office acknowledged the dangers of prosecuting a woman who had decided to try the case herself, who had just lost a child, and whose articles in *The Woman Rebel* were not particularly offensive.

Unmentioned went Sanger's potent new defense weapon: shifting public attitudes and the support of respectable opinion makers. Many of her followers represented New York's rich and powerful who used birth control themselves and who were beginning to approve its dissemination among the poor. Even President Wilson was aware of Margaret Sanger and her campaign. At her urging a group of English supporters, led by Marie Stopes and including authors H. G. Wells and Edward Carpenter, signed a petition to the American president to use his influence to prevent the criminal prosecution of Sanger for circulating a pamphlet on birth control allowed in most "civilized countries . . . Hence not only for the benefit of Mrs. Sanger, but of humanity we respectfully beg you to exert your powerful influence in the interests of free speech and the betterment of the race."[17]

"I do not mean to say that this lady is quite irresponsible in a legal sense of the word," wrote U.S. Attorney H. Snowden Marshall to his superiors, using the universal diagnosis of mental illness for disorderly, activist women and especially for those who dealt with matters of sex, "but from what I understand, I do not think she is quite normal." In fact, though a "woman of breeding and refinement, she seems to be obsessed with the idea that it is her duty to promulgate her views about what she describes as birth control." Both Marshall and Content considered her mentally unstable after Peggy's death. As for some of her followers, they were numerous, but "they are the queerest lot of cranks that we have had around here for a long time."[18]

While Sanger's followers celebrated her victory over the judicial system in a series of dinners and meetings, she deflated the optimism of those fellow travelers who simply enjoyed a good party. Birth control required sacrifice. Her more realistic critics from the left knew as much. Nothing had changed: state and federal laws still classified birth control information and materials as obscene matter. In their minds, a trial and jail sentence would have furthered the cause, a rebuke to which Sanger promptly responded: "Going to jail or staying out of it was of slight importance to me. My work—my Cause, is the cry of anguish which comes to me from the women of the Cotton Belt—the cry of working women tortured by the dread of child bearing." Of course trials did not change laws. Yet the dismissal "of my case by the Government is of far greater value as a precedent than an acquittal by a jury."[19]

Meanwhile, the Justice Department in Washington rebuked its New York office for exceeding its authority by dropping a case without discussing the matter with Attorney General Gregory. In an internal controversy, the attorney general reminded Marshall of a recent circular requiring all "nolled indictments" to be approved in Washington. The action in New York had embarrassed the department, which, to throttle the growing prominence of Sanger and her cause, wanted the case to proceed. Given the nationwide publicity and the number of letters sent to the attorney general, the case was far too public to abandon. "Mrs. Sanger must stand trial and accept the verdict of a jury," wrote an angry Attorney General Gregory. But in New York, Marshall refused to follow instructions, replying that he could find no such directive about dropped indictments.[20] Thus, Sanger was never tried on the charges that had sent her to England in 1914. But within the year she would give the authorities, this time at the state level, another opportunity to send her to jail.

With an adroit understanding of what must be done to further birth control at a moment when her prestige was growing, Margaret Sanger now began a lecture tour across the United States. Earlier she had written friends, subscribers to *The Woman Rebel*, and members of the IWW to hire the largest halls in their community, organize supporters, and await her arrival: "The deeper I got into the current of thought about me, the more I realized the necessity of a mass movement, to be organized for action," she explained. A national campaign was the next step.[21]

During the next four months, Margaret Sanger delivered 119 speeches in every major city in the United States—from Pittsburgh to San Francisco, from Los Angeles to St. Louis, though she omitted, and would for some time, southern cities where there was intense hostility to birth control and even suffrage. Her message—front-page news everywhere and delivered in private homes, large theaters, municipal halls, and men's and women's clubs—contained no new material, nor technical information about the practices of birth control, though she encouraged the sale of *Family Limitation* outside her lectures.

Throughout her journey, with occasional local variations, Sanger delivered a standard speech forthrightly entitled "Birth Control." When asked how long it had taken to prepare her speech, she responded fourteen years, tracing her crusade to her nurse's training. Her remarks usually began with her personal experience as a nurse, went on to include versions of the Sadie Sachs story, and ended with eugenically suggestive warnings that there was cause for alarm over the number of criminal and feeble-minded children in the United States, born disproportionately to families with too many children. She frequently employed casual, imprecise statistics on the number of abortions and deaths from abortions, though more precise figures were not available until the 1930s. For years Sanger insisted that 75 percent of all diseases in the United States were the result of ignorance about sex functions, and her figures on the annual number of abortions ranged from 250,000 to a million.

Even after two hours of lecturing, she usually ended with a vigorous call to her listeners to sign membership pledges and form local associations. At the time she had no organization, only her resonant name and abilities as a traveling salesperson intent on nationalizing her crusade. Ever positive, she believed her trip a success: "I consider we have a big movement started from coast to coast."[22]

Along the way Sanger charmed local supporters, some of whom had already started birth control leagues and, in the case of Detroit and Cleveland, had raised money to establish a clinic. Like a pied piper, she often led women back to her hotel room after her talks, where she dispensed information not just on the social rationale for birth control, but on techniques not mentioned in her formal speeches. Sometimes she even demonstrated the use of the pessary, as hotel rooms became her private clinics.

During her trip, like any barnstorming politician, Margaret Sanger established durable contacts—useful in the future and heartening in the present. Among them was Dr. Marie Equi, a gynecologist living in Portland, best known for her radicalism and lesbianism. With Equi's help Sanger revised *Family Limitation*, bringing it up-to-date with new information. One of many women whom Sanger inspired during her trip, Equi wrote weeks after their first meeting, "You have brought back into being the very essence of life itself for me in a measure and I know that I can find in the future a larger and fuller conception of the sweetness that is for me—through the strength and sureness of your beautiful love and friendship for me." It was a platonic relationship, with loving words and sentimental actions exchanged between a heterosexual and a homosexual woman. As the mesmerized Equi explained: "The remembrance of you will live as a delicate visualized you— high courage, strength—ideals that you have bravery to put into being . . . My arms are around you. I kiss your sweet mouth in absolute surrender."[23]

What Margaret Sanger said during these spring and summer months of 1916 was not new to those in New York or to those who had heard Emma Goldman's speeches, though Goldman, who had recently been arrested and jailed in New York for lecturing on birth control, usually mixed her birth control themes with anarchist calls for antigovernment action. Nor was the size of Sanger's crowds unusual, though she believed otherwise. Nor were the questions unique, for they came from twentieth-century American women anxious for a satisfying sexual, nonimpregnating relationship with their husbands. And certainly the reaction of the authorities was not surprising.

In St. Louis, Sanger confronted a conspiracy organized by her primal enemy—the Catholic Church—whose priests threatened the theater manager with a boycott if she spoke. After the browbeaten manager locked the door, Sanger knew her part. With journalists present, she walked slowly to the locked doors and shook them, loudly denouncing this violation of her free expression and suppression of an important public health message. Meanwhile her followers—there were hundreds wherever she went—moved her meeting to a City Club and Womens' Dinner Club. Both were filled to capacity; in fact, Sanger exaggerated, "neither Taft nor Roosevelt had had such a big attendance. Forty Catholic members of the men's club resigned that day. I am going back this winter to fight it out with St. Louis."[24]

Besides the usual pickets, Sanger encountered constant opposition from public officials intimidated by the Catholic Church's threats, the latter delivered by bishops, priests, and influential members of the Knights of Columbus. A speech by Margaret Sanger in many communities meant the threatened loss of Catholic votes for any official who did not either close the hall or arrest her. In Portland, Oregon, she, along with six others, including Dr. Marie Equi, who held aloft placards emblazoned with the slogan "Poverty and large families go hand in hand," were arrested and jailed overnight. Found guilty the next day, Sanger was released without paying any fine, after a sympathetic judge declined to exact the penalty of a jail term and local officials calculated the dangers of her martyrdom.

In a time of shifting opinions about sex and birth control, jailing Sanger now held risks: such action might bring more positive publicity to the previously underground topic of birth control. The supporters of family limitation were beginning to offset its opponents in numbers and influence. And Sanger, through her actions, was forcing Americans to take overt positions on a previously invisible, avoidable matter that they practiced in secret.

A triumphant Sanger returned to New York in July, ready for the next stage of the sequential four-part tactical agenda she had borrowed from the anarchists and would now use as the basis for her movement: "agitate, educate, organize and legislate." As she informed the Drysdales, "I hope to open a free clinic here in New York City in September, and also get out a regular monthly paper dealing with Birth Control from all points of view."[25] Modeled on centers she had observed in Holland as well as those serving tubercular patients in New York, her clinics would be the first devoted to women's reproductive health in the United States. At a time when many Americans were still ignorant about matters of reproduction and confused birth control with abortion, she must somehow separate her clinics, intended to prevent pregnancy, from the dangerous abortion mills where pregnancies were illegally terminated. Certainly she expected her dramatic step of opening a clinic to heighten her reputation and establish her leadership of a movement whose future direction was uncertain.

Some of her New York supporters had drifted away while she was in Europe and on her lecture tour. A few now followed Mary Ware Dennett, a former leader of the National American Woman Suffrage Association who, disgruntled at the slow pace of women's suffrage, had left that movement to establish the National Birth Control League in 1915. The square-jawed Dennett, of distinguished New England heritage, who looked like a schoolmarm with her ever-present monocle but acted like a radical, was the mother of two boys. She had survived a much publicized divorce from a philandering husband. Unlike Sanger, who devoted herself to one cause, Dennett supported multiple twentieth-century reforms from world peace to twilight sleep, from sex education to the enfranchisement of women. Presently Dennett was intent on overturning the Comstock laws by lobbying Congress.

Dennett had first come to Anthony Comstock's attention when, in 1915, she published *The Sex Side of Life: An Explanation for Young People*, designed like Sanger's early writings to answer her children's questions about reproduction. Comstock suppressed the pamphlet, under the legal supremacy of "the unlimited and undefinable police power organized to prevent the moral destruction of the youth of both sexes," now threatened by the obscenity of birth control.[26]

Committed to family limitation as "a purely scientific topic," as distinct, by implication, from Sanger's emotional presentation of the subject, Dennett had successfully recruited middle-class wives searching for an avenue for their volunteer aspirations beyond the National American Woman Suffrage Association, the Woman's Christian Temperance Union, and the General Federation of Women's Clubs. She considered Sanger too extreme in her defiance of the law, while Sanger thought Dennett's efforts to change legislation by omitting contraception from the legal definition of pornography an impractical, time-consuming diversion, similar to the now seventy-year-long effort to change the laws on women's voting. Influenced by her nursing career, Sanger viewed the recruitment of doctors—however hostile they might be in 1916—as an essential step in delivering birth control information to women. Dennett rejected physicians' control of the subject.

Initially not rivals—in fact, Dennett had raised money for Sanger's court expenses—in time these two women split the birth control movement in a brief battle that had its beginnings in their differing strategies and its continuation in their personal ambitions. At first, Sanger refused to join Dennett's league in protest of her competitor's claim that her association had preceded Sanger's new creation, the New York Birth Control League (NYBCL). The reckoning of "firstness" was always significant for Sanger, who understood the authority that primacy delivered. Dennett made the case that she wanted only to change the law, whereas Sanger wanted to break it, an appealing distinction for women worried about joining a radical cause on what was, for many, an unspeakable topic. By 1916 Dennett's organization, the National Birth Control League, had a formal structure, a newsletter, and dues-paying members. Envious of the first, Sanger dismissed the last as an organization of volunteers that, like too many others, focused on female sociability rather than the activism that she would now undertake.

Sanger meant her clinics to demonstrate a bold new phase of educating poor women about birth control beyond speeches, meetings, and lobbying. Their establishment would mark the first free health clinics for women in the United States, an event, though largely forgotten today, that Sanger properly recognized as "of social significance in the lives of American womanhood."[27] Additionally, a Margaret Sanger birth control clinic, where self-help techniques were actually demonstrated, would raise her to the national standard bearer the movement required.

Margaret Sanger needed to recruit a physician, which proved impossible even among the handful of female practitioners in the city. None were willing to compromise their reputations, and most male doctors opposed contraception. Yet under Section 1145 of the New York statutes, medical doctors had the authority to give advice "to cure or prevent disease," a loophole in the draconian obscenity provisions that would make Sanger's clinics legitimate—if she could find a doctor.

For years the application of section 1145, exemplifying the sexual double standard practiced in the United States, was confined to the protection of men from prostitutes' venereal disease, rather than women from pregnancy or wives from husbands suffering from syphilis and gonorrhea. Sanger lamented "the indifference and ignorance of the medical profession on the entire subject—the man who was an expert in performing gynecological operations seemed quite unaware of the importance of preventing conception . . . It all seemed such a chaotic state to me—that it was perfectly legal to go through the sufferings of abortion, but illegal to prevent conception."[28]

For the location of her first clinic, Margaret Sanger chose the downtrodden immigrant neighborhood of Brownsville, near the central shopping area of Pitkin Street in Brooklyn. It took time before she raised the money, hired Fania Mindell, a young Jewish woman who served as a Yiddish interpreter and receptionist, and recruited her younger sister, Ethel Byrne, who would serve as a nurse teaching poor women about birth control techniques. For days beforehand, Sanger walked from door to door informing the neighborhood about the opening of her clinic. In stores, shops, and the stations that gave out free milk to Brooklyn's needy, she posted placards, in Yiddish and Italian as well as English: "Mothers: Can you afford to have a large family? Do you want any more children? If not, why do you have them?" These circulars, offering "safe harmless information obtained of trained nurses for a ten cent registration fee," did not use the term "birth control," and in veiled language separated abortion from birth control: "Do not kill, do not take life, but prevent."[29]

After notifying the Brooklyn district attorney of her intentions and without a physician, Margaret Sanger's clinic opened on October 16, 1916, in two rooms in a storefront on Amboy Street, its front windows shielded by thin curtains purchased after a timely contribution from a western supporter. By any measure the clinic was a success: on the first day over a hundred women and twenty men waited in line. Before it was shut down, over five hundred clients were enrolled. "Nothing, not even the ghost of Anthony Comstock could have stopped them from coming," Sanger exulted. "Women of every race and creed flocked to the clinic with the determination not to have any more children than their health could stand or their husbands could support. Jews and Christians, Protestants and Roman Catholics alike made their confessions to us, whatever they may have professed at home or in church."[30]

To make birth control the measurable, scientific subject she intended, the clients paid a voluntary ten-cent registration fee, signed a slip certifying that they were married, gave information about their family, childbearing history, and their husbands' wages, and agreed that the information about birth control they received was for their personal use. This last, as well as Sanger's continuing efforts to collect case studies, blunted any charge of commercialism and dampened any suspicion that she was no better than the money-seeking abortionists who preyed on women. What her clients got in return was a specific education in various birth control techniques, especially pessaries and recipes for spermicide douches. The former had to be fitted by someone with an understanding of female anatomy, because vaginas and cervixes came in different sizes. "Consequently without a physical examination by a qualified person who had some knowledge of anatomy, advice about a pessary is useless," said Sanger, comparing such a gynecological fitting to the individual eye examinations required before the prescription of reading glasses. To distinguish her efforts from those of hack practitioners, she added, "No woman is safe nor reliably protected from conception who obtains information from a general source."[31]

Most often Ethel and Margaret Sanger recommended the Mizpah pessary, providing demonstrations of its use in the back room. They also informed their clients that this form of female contraception was available around the corner at the local pharmacy on Pitkin Street. There, for two dollars, at a time when the average weekly wage was fifteen dollars, these mostly Jewish and Italian women could buy Mizpahs, legally sold to women who suffered from the pregnancy-induced condition of a prolapsed uterus. As with the off-label applications of reproductive products, which included using patent medicines advertised for starting menstruation in order to end pregnancies, Sanger now taught her clients how to use pessaries as contraceptives.

To the reporters who flocked to Brooklyn for interviews and shouted out questions about breaking the law, Sanger insisted, disingenuously, that hers was "an oral clinic . . . The law says nothing about not spreading birth control information orally."[32] Later she insisted that the district attorney had assured her that such was the case. In fact while the New York Penal Code made it a misdemeanor "to sell, lend, exhibit, or advertise contraceptive materials," the law specifically held criminally responsible anyone "who gives information orally, stating when, where, how, of whom, or by what means" contraceptives could be obtained.[33] Sanger's challenge demanded an official response.

Ten days after the clinic opened, among the crowd of immigrant women, a large, well-dressed woman identifying herself as Mrs. White-hurst and her baby (borrowed, as it turned out, for the occasion) appeared. Whitehurst stood out among the other women in both clothes and demeanor, especially after she paid two dollars for a ten-cent pamphlet on sex education. The receptionist, Fania Mindell, was apprehensive and warned Sanger, who did not hesitate to deliver birth control information to this large woman in the back room. The next day Mrs. Whitehurst, an under-cover police detective engaged in a sting operation, returned and arrested both Sanger and her sister Ethel, along with Fania Mindell. During the chaotic scene, three plainclothes men prevented the terrified women wait-ing in the clinic from leaving, took their names, and threatened subpoenas. The police also confiscated records, pamphlets, supplies of tablets, supposi-tories, Mizpah pessaries, condoms for male clients, and copies of *What Every Girl Should Know*, along with the sparse furniture in the clinic.

The raid was front-page news in many papers, including the *Brooklyn Daily Eagle*:

> Mrs. Whitehurst placed Mrs. Sanger under arrest. The little woman [Sanger] was at first taken aback, but in an instant she was in a tow-ering rage. "You dirty thing," she shrieked. "You are not a woman. You are a dog." "Tell that to the judge in the morning," calmly re-sponded Mrs. Whitehurst. "No I'll tell it to you now. You dog, and you have two ears to hear me too."[34]

Always infuriated when women opposed the crusade she was organiz-ing for their liberation, during the last year Sanger had become disap-pointed by female indifference. She scorned the "lack of action on the part of the women in New York who, unlike the suffragists of England, sat with folded hands and stood aloof from the struggle for woman's freedom . . . American women were not going to use direct action, nor were they going to put themselves on record in approving ideas at this controversial stage."[35] They were hypocrites who refused to confront the discrepancy between their own use of birth control and their tacit acceptance of its illegality for other women. Before one of Sanger's several court appearances, the an-thropologist and author Elsie Clews Parsons had proved the point when she asked all the women who used birth control to stand up. Only one had done so in a room full of married women, most of whom had fewer than three children. Still, to have a woman arrest her was infuriating, when it was male legislators, doctors, and priests who were the enemy. "A woman—the irony of it," Sanger complained of Whitehurst's deceptive role in what became her next confrontation with the judicial system.[36]

When the black police wagon arrived that October day in 1916, sound-ing its klaxon as it threaded its way through the crowd around the clinic, Sanger refused to ride. Instead, with that innate sense of drama that was making her a celebrity, she walked the mile to jail, surrounded by the police, a throng of quickly assembled reporters, as well as a few disciples. Later she recalled a woman rushing through the crowd, screaming, "Come back! Come back and save me!"[37]

At the Raymond Street Jail, Fania Mindell was charged with selling the obscene *What Every Girl Should Know*, and Ethel Byrne with circulating birth control information. Sanger herself faced two counts of violating the New York Penal Code—conducting a clinic and disseminating information outlawed by the state's obscenity laws. Sanger learned the next day, shortly before she was released on the exorbitant bail of five hundred dollars posted by her supporters, that she would be tried in the Court of Special Sessions, not a regular city court. Even worse, in a further example of judicial prejudice, her verdict would be determined by a panel of three judges, not a local jury. The latter might well have included a sympathetic husband whose wife had come to the clinic.

Persistently and intrepidly provocative, Sanger promptly released a statement to the press after her indictment: Judge J. J. McInerney, who had been chosen as one of the panel, was "judicially unfit" and should recuse himself from the proceedings. The judge, according to Sanger, held "an unfailing prejudice and exposed a mind steeped in bigotry and the intolerance of the Inquisition."[38] There was justification for the animus: McInerney had presided over Bill Sanger's trial in 1915 and after sentencing Bill, the judge had delivered a revealing obiter dictum on selfish, activist women who should stay at home. And though this point went unmentioned in her statement, McInerney was, like so many others in positions of authority in New York, a Catholic. Declaring she would not attend her trial if he presided, Sanger won a small victory when the judge, denying any bias, nevertheless removed himself.

Meanwhile, her supporters, joined on this occasion by suffragists, petitioned for the inclusion of women on any jury trying Margaret Sanger, and her attorney challenged any trial by a judicial panel. But in the end three judges heard the case of *People of New York v. Margaret Sanger*, with each of the trial's three days bringing more sympathetic publicity to the defendant.

In fact, in the months before her trial, Sanger found it difficult to stay out of the limelight. She began work on a book, *The Case for Birth Control*, and instituted plans for a new magazine. She always had time for interviews with journalists, who thought she made for good copy. "The Police

Cannot Stop Me—Mrs. Sanger to Reopen Clinic," reported the press. Un-daunted, though she was out of jail on bail, she informed reporters that it was her duty to reopen the clinic. "I do not understand why the police and the district attorney keep on hounding me. The most conservative believe that a clinic is the best method for the spreading of information about fam-ily limitation to poor women to whom every child means a tremendous burden."[39]

A woman of her word, within weeks after her first arrest, she reopened the Sanger birth control clinic at a different location in Brownsville. She was promptly arrested again, this time on the additional charge of main-taining a public nuisance where acts that offended public decency had been committed. Thereafter the Brooklyn police patrolled the neighborhood to make certain that there were no more Sanger clinics. "In the Nether-lands," Sanger complained, "a clinic has been cited as a public benefaction; in the United States it was classed as a public nuisance."[40]

By the time the Brownsville trials opened in 1917, Sanger had found a sympathetic lawyer, Jonah J. Goldstein, a Jewish, Canadian-born graduate of New York University Law School and later a judge himself, who promptly fell in love with the client he had accepted in a pro bono arrangement. With such sympathetic, enlightened counsel, Sanger could not refuse legal representation. Soon Goldstein, who at thirty-one was eight years younger than Sanger, was paying the rent on her West Forty-sixth Street apartment, sending gifts and imploring her to marry him. Later, in the diary she kept sporadically, Sanger evaluated Goldstein as "a queer lad . . . with Old Jew-ish reactions" and though of the same background, evidently with more "good sense" than Bill Sanger—"fascinating at times, but does not try to be . . . a good friend and though quite undeveloped emotionally . . . his hu-man intellect is very keen."[41] Such a searching appraisal exhibited a talent for character assessment.

In her late thirties and facing a jail sentence, Sanger had time for an interlude of romance. During a life of many, even concurrent lovers, she discovered her answer to a personal question, rarely asked by most women of her generation. It involved the reasons for the unrequited affection, which did not preclude sex, when "big, generous, devoted men [like Gold-stein] place their strength, labor, energy and talents at our feet," but "do not seem to bring out of us that love they should . . . I am inclined to feel 'chemical love' has a big part to do in our affairs of life." Goldstein, like several other lovers, was one of those "chemically fascinating men [who] must be dismissed from our consciousness. I often wonder if love is not based on chemistry & if that is why married people grow so indifferent as age advances."[42]

Sex, for Sanger, was an essential part of love, but not all of love. Still, it was one of the reasons, unstated at this point in her public campaign but newly developed in her personal convictions, that birth control brought happiness in marriage. Her English tutors, especially Havelock Ellis, had schooled her to believe what she had already experienced in her short marriage: monogamous marriage, without the romance of diverse sexual partners, became a dull pedestrian arrangement eventually destroying "chemical love." To the contrary, she meant to live her life in a blaze of passion, unconventionally and completely. Her lifelong enjoyment of sex with many partners made the practice of birth control a personal necessity, as Sanger, ahead of her times, represented the sexual expectations of her generation's males, not females.

Finally, amid the musings about love chronicled in her diary, the case of *People of New York v. Margaret Sanger* was placed on the docket. Earlier, Fania Mindell had been fined, with the verdict subsequently overturned, while Margaret's sister Ethel had been sentenced to a month on Blackwell's Island, where she began a potentially fatal hunger strike. Such tactics had already been employed by the English suffrage activists, the Pankhurst family, and their radical followers in British prisons in order to protest their treatment as criminal rather than political prisoners. Alice Paul of the National Woman's Party (NWP) was soon to employ similar tactics in her suffrage campaign in Washington. Sanger knew all about hunger strikes and had written about them in the 1914 *Woman Rebel*. But in Ethel Byrne's case the authorities waited too long to implement even the tortures of forced feeding. A doctor called to insert the nasal tubes and force them down her esophagus had been slow to respond, as Byrne continued her hunger strike. Only a dramatic intervention by Sanger with Governor Charles Whitman, resulting in Ethel's immediate pardon, saved her sister. Ethel had gone 103 hours without food or water and was carried out of the Blackwell Island prison on a stretcher, wrapped in the philanthropist Gertrude Pinchot's fur coat.

On January 29, in the midst of her concern for Ethel, Margaret Sanger's trial began in the smoky upstairs of the Kings County Courthouse, in a room crowded with immigrant women from the clinic and society ladies who had arrived in chauffeured limousines. Many of the latter represented the Committee of 100, which pledged to support Margaret Sanger and her efforts "to change archaic and inhumane laws and her campaign to establish the principle of voluntary motherhood."[43] Also among the throng were reporters anxious for a personal interview with the famous defendant, along with several of her male admirers.

Her attorney, Jonah Goldstein, lost all of his motions, including the one he thought most significant: Sanger should be released on a writ of habeas corpus on the grounds that the penal code preventing the dissemination of birth control information violated the defendant's First Amendment right of free expression. The federal Comstock laws and their New York version were unconstitutional. Goldstein's sociological defense about health benefits for women, and therefore the community, failed as well, cut short by the panel of judges. Nor were his expert witnesses allowed to testify, two of whom were willing to attest to the necessity of birth control as a health measure and to suggest the benefit to society of fewer, better children. Instead, the issue before the court involved not so much Sanger's advocacy of birth control, but whether she had actually fitted devices for her clients.

When the prosecution called twenty of Sanger's clients to the stand, each one more miserably deprived than the one before, but all eager to help, they described the technical information they had received from their hero Margaret Sanger, thereby inadvertently helping to convict the woman they would save. Attempting to turn their testimony to the defendant's advantage, Goldstein questioned these women about their dismal living conditions, their large number of children, their crowded apartments, their enervating health problems, and their husbands' pitiful wages. Judge Freschi, the most sympathetic of the justices, interrupted, wanting to hear no more of these depressing irrelevancies.[44]

When the prosecutor introduced into evidence a cervical cap taken in the raid, Judge Freschi inquired if it could not legitimately be used for medical reasons, and therefore was not necessarily a birth control apparatus. The prosecution promptly responded that Sanger was not a doctor and hence could not, under any circumstances, legally prescribe such devices. Then the police gave damaging, false testimony that the clinic was intended to destroy the Jewish race and besides was a moneymaking operation: Sanger, they said, had admitted as much.

After a conference with Goldstein, the panel of judges announced a deal: the defendant was guilty; she had admitted as much on the stand. But she was not well, according to her attorney. In such circumstances the court might be lenient. It went unstated that a harsh sentence was further advertisement of her cause and so there were reasons on both sides for a negotiated settlement. If Margaret Sanger would swear to permanently end her activities relating to birth control, the court would suspend her sentence. Otherwise she must pay a fine of five thousand dollars or go to jail for thirty days.

It was a classic dilemma of the kind she had often wrestled with since childhood, between the difficult path and the easy escape, between abandoning principle and suffering for the cause, between commitment and compromise. In these tests that made her passionate sacrifices worthwhile, she always emerged victorious, having chosen hardship over compliance. Intending that the case reach the U.S. Supreme Court if necessary, Sanger addressed the judges:

> With me it is not a question of personal imprisonment or personal disadvantage. I am today and always have been more concerned with changing the law and the sweeping away of the law, regardless of what I have to undergo to have it done . . . I am not indifferent. I am indifferent to the personal consequences to myself, but I am not indifferent to the cause and the influence which can be attained for the cause.[45]

When, in response to this intransigence, the court sentenced Sanger to thirty days in prison, a single cry to the judges rang out in the courtroom: "Shame!"[46]

Sanger declined to go on a hunger strike. Ethel had already exploited the available notoriety for such a hardship. And why ruin her already compromised health? It took Ethel a year before she finally regained her strength. Moreover, on the eve of a declaration of war against Germany, foreign news— of American ships sunk by German submarines and a possible German alliance with Mexico—was crowding out coverage of the birth control movement.

Initially Sanger acknowledged the respect Ethel had earned among prisoners whose interest in birth control had been awakened "through your hunger strike—naturally so for it was their life & interest & world that you had entered . . . [you] made the finest fight ever made by any woman in the U.S.A."[47] Despite such praise, Ethel subsequently abandoned not the principles of the movement but its hard endeavors, partly because she resented its increasing domination by her sister's rich friends. At first Sanger encouraged Ethel to lecture on the riveting circumstances of her imprisonment. Years later, chagrined after so many strangers mistakenly complimented her for her sister's bravery as a hunger striker, Margaret brazenly asked Ethel to surrender her ownership of the hunger strike and allow her to claim it.

Instead of starving herself in jail, Margaret Sanger created her own rebellions: she refused to be fingerprinted and physically examined, battling the prison warden and winning on both counts in a judicial system that intended no controversies with its famous prisoner. She was even moved from the grim workhouse on Blackwell's Island, where Ethel served her sentence, to the Queens County Penitentiary. Located in Long Island City, the prison, a gray, grim structure with three hundred women and an equal number of men, was far more benign than Blackwell's Island, where the vermin-filled mattresses on cold floors in the workhouse made sleep nearly impossible.

Still, it was a prison. She was assigned cleaning duties. The food, mostly bread and molasses and occasionally a stew for dinner, was terrible. Sanger lost fifteen pounds and later wrote that life in jail had stirred up her dormant tuberculosis germs, though this new episode of infected glands had probably started sometime in 1916. But certainly a month in jail exacerbated her disease. Yet, she insisted with the optimism common to many reformers, jail would not "hurt a bit & the regular life & early to bed makes a restful life at least."[48] Instead of a sufferer, she became an observer.

Many of her fellow prisoners, jailed as alcoholics or drug addicts, some serving indefinite sentences, were pitiful as they scrounged the grounds for the men's discarded cigarette butts. Women did not have the same privileges as men to write letters or read newspapers. Overall, the experience reinforced Sanger's lifelong hostility toward authority: "Horrible liberties a State takes with human lives—for a crime of drink or dope which should be considered diseases."[49]

As with all of the hardships in her life, Margaret Sanger made the best of it. She counseled her fellow inmates on sexual matters, and spurned the feckless offers of assistance by visiting society matrons and Catholic social workers, one of whom pleaded with Sanger to give up the work of the devil and join the Catholic Church. She taught reading and writing to the surprising number of illiterates in her jail section. Convinced of the eugenic principle that criminals came disproportionately from poor, oversized families, she investigated prison records, which at first contradicted her assumptions. But when Sanger interviewed her fellow prisoners, she learned that inmates routinely lied about their siblings, because they were anxious to keep their families from disgrace and "out of the clutch of authority."[50] Actually, her impressionistic conclusion that such families spawned criminals proved largely correct when she discovered, on closer personal observation, that the families of origin of the thirty women on her corridor averaged eight children.

Often during the boring routines of prison life, she thought of Peggy: "I feel there are no pains left on earth again for me again—jails bread & water nothing can give me pain again compared to the torture of the realization of my loss."[51] She had time to consider the status of the birth control movement and what she would do to further its influence when she was released.

Sanger's imprisonment profoundly influenced her, particularly when she learned about the indefinite sentences for minor crimes, mostly given to women. After her release she singled out for harsh criticism the abysmal conditions in prisons, attacking a hero of the progressive movement, the University of Chicago–trained social worker and New York City's first female commissioner of corrections, Katharine Bement Davis. She sued the prison system over the abysmal conditions in a case that Goldstein filed against "the warden and keeper of Queens County Penitentiary"—though nothing came of it. Sanger resolved that after birth control was won, her next great cause would be the improvement of the treatment of prisoners. "If I can't do it now, I'll book it for the next trip."[52]

On March 7, 1917, Margaret Sanger was released from the Queens Penitentiary, her departure delayed by a prolonged physical battle with prison authorities over the fingerprinting she refused on the basis that such an invasion of privacy was required only for criminals. When she finally stepped through the great iron doors of the penitentiary, she was greeted by over two hundred friends singing "La Marseillaise," the anthem of all American radicals who had none of their own. "All the beauty and tragedy and hope of life's struggle seemed crammed in that moment of my life."[53]

As birth control's martyr, Margaret Sanger was now feted at lunches and dinners by supporters, especially by those members of the Committee of 100 whom she had expected to take turns working in her clinic, but who in fact had done little except come to her trial, pass resolutions of support, and organize celebrations. Jail had done nothing to change her mind, she announced. The government could not imprison ideas. In fact, while in prison, she had determined that the first stage of the birth control strategy had concluded; the time of "the tempestuous season of agitation—courts and jails and shrieking and thumbing the nose—should now end." Now she set herself to the task of educating Americans, recognizing that the "public must be educated before the laws could be changed as a result of that organization."[54]

But first Margaret Sanger had to settle her affairs with Bill Sanger, who, after three years, still refused to sign a separation agreement. "I have always hoped that one with your pretended ideas of women's freedom and independence of State interference . . . would respect my personal and private liberty without the aid of a policeman's club," she complained. Well aware of his failure as a provider, she wanted a financial statement about his share of the children's support and a formal division of their common property. "Today I returned your pictures and will be glad to send you any more of yours I find. I wish to wipe from my memory all thought of connection with you and shall appreciate any effort on your part to further that end," she wrote two weeks after her release from prison, signing herself "very truly yours." And so the unsold *Dunes*, a token of better days, appeared at the door of his studio.[55]

A separation agreement, signed by both husband and wife, remained the only practical legal avenue for ending their marriage in New York State, where the divorce codes remained unchanged since 1787. Only adultery was considered sufficient grounds for the courts. Elsewhere in the United States, during a period of shifting moral behaviors and marital expectations, legislatures had liberalized divorce laws, accepting desertion, bigamy, conviction of some crimes, habitual drunkenness, and even the vague category of intolerable cruelty as grounds to end a marriage. Divorce rates had begun to rise. It was, from a modern perspective, not the numbers but the rate of change that bothered Americans, who discovered in these first decades of the twentieth century "a divorce crisis": in 1880 one divorce for every twenty-one marriages, and by 1916 a divorce for every nine marriages, enough to make the best known monitor of national probity, President Theodore Roosevelt, warn against the nation's dangerously lax divorce laws.

Ever since Sanger's return from Europe, the couple had argued, sometimes violently and publicly. She accused him of spreading rumors, no doubt about her affairs, "with your filthy, vile mouth and slanderous onslaught." Meanwhile he entertained the notion that he and his "Peg" would somehow be reconciled, sending flowers and written apologies after their arguments. But Bill Sanger remained angry about her affairs, her year in Europe, which left him as a single parent, and even her share of the mortgage money from their former home in Hastings, which did not take into account his contributions to the house. In the heat of these confrontations, he shouted that he wanted his name back: she had sullied it. But at this stage Margaret Sanger could return furniture and paintings, but not his last name. She had long ago left the Higginses and Corning in name and spirit and would never go back. Besides, by 1917 her name designated the movement to which she had devoted the last four years. It could not be changed.

"I should like to return your name to you, or drop it & unless you will come to a sane & agreeable or mutual understanding with me I shall be forced to proceed in a way much against my inclinations."[56] It is uncertain what Sanger meant. Of course, she could set up residence in a state with shorter residency and easier divorce requirements, such as North Dakota, Wyoming, or Nevada. But to do so for the required six months would mean the loss of the momentum of her crusade. Given her familiarity with the courts and her friendship with Jonah Goldstein, she could have introduced a divorce petition to be voted on as a private bill by the New York legislature. But this was a lengthy process that would certainly get the attention of the press. Or she could admit to adultery and thereby embarrass Bill, herself, and the movement. She could also accuse him of adultery. Such explanations for what was still cause for criticism would taint birth control and destroy her creditability as the leader of a movement that needed, more than most, respectability. In 1910, despite the rising divorce rates and altered perceptions about the durability of marriage, only 83,000 American marriages in a married population of 46 million ended in divorce.

Eventually Bill acceded to her demand for a separation after another ferocious rejection: "If the affection you feel for me is deeper in your being than your love for yourself and the pity that you have for your own loneliness, you will either grant me a separation or go away where we will not be tormented by the presence of each other. There is nothing I have to give you in love, there is nothing to be repaired, there is no way that we can go on together."[57] In the summer of 1917 Bill left for Spain, where he stayed for two years, miserable in his loneliness and poverty. After returning to the United States, he signed the separation agreement necessary for a divorce in Massachusetts. With Margaret using Truro as her residence, the Massachusetts courts certified her divorce in 1921.

Michael Higgins engraving a tombstone in his Corning shop while an apprentice watches. (Sophia Smith Collection, Smith College)

Maggie Higgins and her first boyfriend, Corey Albertson—photographed in 1897 while both were students at the Claverack College and Hudson River Institute. (Sophia Smith Collection, Smith College)

A proud Margaret Higgins poses in her nurse's cap and uniform in 1901 during her training in the White Plains Hospital nursing program. (Sophia Smith Collection, Smith College)

An undated photograph of William Sanger in the early days of his marriage to Margaret Sanger. (Sophia Smith Collection, Smith College)

Peggy Sanger, the youngest of Margaret's three children, with her beloved cat during the summer of 1913 in Truro, Massachusetts, two years before her death. (Sophia Smith Collection, Smith College)

Cartoon from the August 1914 issue of Sanger's first magazine, *The Woman Rebel*. (Library of Congress)

"Remember, Mrs. Judd, another child will kill you—"
"But, doctor, tell me——"
"I cannot."

Margaret Sanger with her sons Grant and Stuart in a publicity photograph reproduced in papers throughout the United States, taken before her first trial in 1916. (Sophia Smith Collection, Smith College)

The bewhiskered Anthony Comstock, author and enforcer of the Comstock Act of 1873, which defined writings on birth control as obscene matter. (Sophia Smith Collection, Smith College)

Havelock Ellis, the famous sexologist and Sanger's instructor in sex and lifelong friend, in a portrait taken around 1910. (Library of Congress)

Mothers and children line up outside Sanger's birth control clinic in Brooklyn, the first in the United States, in 1916. (Sophia Smith Collection, Smith College)

Margaret Sanger and Hugh de Selincourt, one of her lovers, at Stonehenge, Wiltshire, England, in 1925. (Sophia Smith Collection, Smith College)

Margaret Sanger with Senator H. D. Hatfield of West Virginia during her unsuccessful efforts to lobby Congress to repeal the Comstock Act of 1873. (Sophia Smith Collection, Smith College)

Sanger's second husband,
J. Noah Slee, and her father,
Michael Higgins, in Truro,
Massachusetts, circa 1925.
(Sophia Smith Collection, Smith
College)

Willowlake, Sanger and Slee's estate near Fishkill, New York. (Sophia Smith Collection, Smith
College)

Margaret Sanger, Jawaharlal Nehru, and Lady Rama Rau at the Sixth International Conference in New Delhi, India, in 1959, Sanger's last attendance at the international conferences she began organizing in the 1920s. (Library of Congress)

Margaret Sanger with her younger son, Grant, and his six children at their home in Mount Kisco, New York, in 1954. (Sophia Smith Collection, Smith College)

6

THE BIRTH CONTROL REVIEW

> I never consulted. I never asked advice. I just kept going, night and day, visualizing every act, every step, believing, knowing that I was working in accord with a universal law of evolution—a moral evolution.
>
> —Margaret Sanger, *My Fight for Birth Control*

Four weeks after a triumphant Margaret Sanger was released from prison, President Woodrow Wilson stood at the lectern of the House of Representatives to deliver a critical message to a joint session of Congress. Wilson had been elected in November 1916 on the Democratic platform of keeping the United States out of any European conflict, but now, five months later, he called for a declaration of war to punish the German imperial government (though not the German people) and to reaffirm neutral rights, especially the freedom of the seas violated by the U-boat campaign. War was "terrible and disastrous," said the president. But "the right is more precious than peace and we shall fight . . . for democracy." And to the tumultuous applause of congressmen and senators who a few days later voted overwhelmingly for a declaration of war, the president announced that "the world must be made safe for democracy." Along with his eloquence came a stern warning to the millions of men and women of German heritage in the United States and implicitly to others: "If there be disloyalty, it will be dealt with with a firm hand of stern repression."

From its beginning until the final armistice in November 1918, Margaret Sanger opposed World War I, though she refused to join any of the numerous peace groups that sprang up throughout the United States. For the next three years until she left for England in 1920, congressional limitations on free speech, expanded definitions of espionage and sedition, and patriotic calls for national unity rendered birth control for women counterproductive to the national purpose. The need for more soldiers made pleas for fewer children treasonous. Sanger acknowledged that the war halted the progress of the birth control movement, only temporarily, she hoped, though she soon discovered that former advocates had disappeared. As for the radicals, they focused on opposition to the draft. Meanwhile the great flu epidemic of 1918 had "taken off many of our old companions."[1] For the duration and beyond, Americans had lost their reform instincts.

In her public statements Sanger did not often declare her opposition to this war in particular, or the draft, but to all wars, which, in her judgment, should be despised by women, who lived for the creation of human life, not its destruction, and who in a society without birth control served as "mere breeders" of soldiers. "Sex-bondage has made her the dumb instrument of the monster she detests." For humanity, it was "the old story of the slaves kissing the chains that bind them."[2]

Adept at finding contraception's relevance everywhere, she located the cause of the war in Germany's and Russia's failure to control the growth of their populations, and their consequent demand for more land and resources. While experts in the new field of demography pointed to France's falling birth rates as an explanation for that nation's military weakness, initially Sanger applauded France's healthy, competent soldiers, the products of small families, even as the French army was retreating ingloriously toward Paris. More specific in her private letters, she denounced a conflict in which Germany, a leader in science and medicine, "was being torn to shreds" for no purpose, even if it had been the aggressor. Hers was a preview of later historical interpretations that challenged claims of American neutrality and found few national security interests at stake for the United States in World War I.

Sanger also opposed war because as a former socialist, she viewed the conflict as an example of the brutal military encounters fought by workers, of every nationality, to protect capitalist interests. In his famous essay "War Is the Health of the State," the writer and social critic Randolph Bourne, a onetime neighbor of Sanger's in Greenwich Village, argued that war rendered the capitalist state powerful and intrusive. Certainly it diverted attention from domestic change and progressive initiatives. For who could compete with Liberty Loan drives, mobilization calls, and patriotic messages to Americans to serve their country? In both the United States and Great

Britain, suffrage organizations (Alice Paul's National Woman's Party was the exception) briefly suspended their fight for votes for women, replacing it with the womanly tasks of wartime—rolling bandages, joining the Woman's Land Army of America as "farmerettes" to raise vegetables, plant hay, and harvest wheat, and, in a few cases, serving overseas as nurses.[3]

So personally distasteful was the war that Sanger never permitted anyone in uniform in her apartment, although three of her younger brothers were among the nearly 3 million Americans on active duty by 1918: Robert and Richard Higgins in the Allied Expeditionary Force in France and Lawrence in the navy. When Harold Hersey, the poet and writer, and Sanger's probable lover, appeared at her apartment in his army lieutenant's uniform, she refused to let him in until he changed his clothes.

During the war, no reform leader faced as many challenges as did Sanger and her nascent, but still unsavory, birth control movement. For anxious Americans birth control came to summarize an accumulating cascade of alarming social, political, and sexual transformations, exaggerated in wartime and particularly focused on women's roles. In the twentieth century for some Americans, not just those in Greenwich Village, sex had changed in behavior as well as perception, from dutiful procreation to a pleasurable activity now enjoyed by even unwed daughters of conventional parents. Former guardians of the hearth now worked outside the home in growing numbers—some 17 percent earning wages in 1915—a figure that did not include those in domestic service. More young women attended college and volunteered for community activities. But such alterations were still contested.

After she resigned from the Socialist Party, Sanger acknowledged few public issues not directly linked to birth control, believing it the universal reform of transformative power. Her cause surpassed superficial efforts to end drinking, improve labor standards for children, and clean up politics. She calculated as too dangerous the loss of credibility through guilt by association with any controversial cause, especially during wartime. Besides, birth control demanded all her energy.

Yet the war did empower a few reform efforts, such as public hygiene organizations, one of them decorously titled the American Society of Sanitary and Moral Prophylaxis, Victorian-speak for an association trying to prevent the spread of venereal disease. The women's suffrage movement, whose leaders finally persuaded Wilson to support the Susan B. Anthony amendment, successfully publicized the hypocrisy of a war undertaken to make the world safe for democracy, while national policies disenfranchised half the country's population. But with her long memory for slights, Sanger remained silent, recalling the refusal of organized suffrage associations and social workers such as Jane Addams to join an alliance with birth controllers or even deliver a public endorsement. Carrie Catt, the influential president of the National American Woman Suffrage Association, explained why: "Your reform," she wrote to Sanger, "is too narrow to appeal to me and too sordid."[4]

The need for soldiers immediately brought men's contraception into the public arena, especially after 15 percent of all draftees were found to suffer from venereal disease, so many, in fact, that Secretary of War Newton Baker ended the disqualification. "If you were to attempt to get an army without having men who had gonorrhea, you would not have an army," concluded one doctor.[5] Sanger discovered that the army and navy manuals for young soldiers and sailors paraphrased her pamphlets on sex education, the same ones she had been prosecuted for. Five years earlier, copies of *What Every Girl Should Know* and *What Every Boy Should Know* (which had become a pamphlet) had been confiscated because references to gonorrhea and syphilis were considered obscene under the Comstock law. Now, to Sanger's satisfaction, the U.S. Army's instructions on sex education were even "plainer" than hers, though official policy encouraged an unrealistic abstinence for all soldiers.

Pulled from the shadows, the battle against venereal disease became a national priority. "Men must live straight lives if they would shoot straight," according to Secretary of the Navy Josephus Daniels. "The army which is the least syphilized will, other things being equal, win," explained an official of the American Social Hygiene Association.[6] To protect his soldiers from this plague, the popular commander of the Allied Expeditionary Force, General John Pershing, proclaimed continence a patriotic obligation for all his forces. During wartime and especially overseas in France, sexual intercourse, the birthright of young American males, was suddenly not necessary for good health, according to their commander, though, just in case, the army promptly established treatment centers for soldiers suffering from syphilis and gonorrhea. "Be Fit to Win," exhorted posters in training camps, and everyone knew what that meant.

Officials in the army and navy agreed that the danger lay with prostitutes. One of the government's concerns now became protecting soldiers from bad women. To enforce continence in the United States, thirty thousand women, some prostitutes, others so-called "charity girls" who traded sex for an evening out, others simply camp followers, their habeas corpus privileges suspended for the duration, were placed in detention camps. In 1917 Wilson had successfully pressed Congress for an allocation of $250,000 to build centers to detain women suspected of sex offenses. Some were held for weeks without trial or any due process; most were forced to undergo compulsory gynecological exams.

Despite the official demand for chastity and the repression of female suspects, only after discussions at the highest levels, with Secretary of War Newton Baker at first opposed, did the War Department agree to provide free condoms (called prophylactics by doctors and social hygienicists) to soldiers and sailors as a preventive health measure. By the end of the war thirty-five public health clinics in the greater New York area were treating male venereal disease, mostly among soldiers and sailors. Sanger fumed that a government that protected men from sexually transmitted diseases so they could go into battle still did nothing to shield women from involuntary motherhood imposed on them by unhealthy soldiers. "Misguided, masculine-minded Puritans may try to keep women in ignorance, the authorities may fill the jails with women, but the fight will go on."[7]

The war did not end the vigilant application of the Comstock laws against female contraceptives. In January 1918 Sanger was arrested again for violating the obscenity laws by selling pamphlets with birth control information on the streets of New York. Offering a new line of defense at her trial, Jonah Goldstein compared the offending material to the sex-education publications of not just the War Department but the United States Public Health Service. "In the greater light of today, standards are changing," argued Goldstein to the court. And besides, the overturning of the earlier conviction of Fania Mindell for circulating *What Every Girl Should Know* (on the grounds that Sanger's early pamphlet did not rise to the level of obscenity) had set a precedent. This time the charges against Sanger were dismissed.

At this stage, Sanger refused to concentrate on overturning the Comstock laws. To educate the public—to transform public opinion about sex—now became a mission more crucial than to resist the law or to lobby, the latter the strategy her rival Mary Ware Dennett now employed. "The real fight is not in Albany nor in Washington . . . but in the heart of every community, right in the dreadful little tenement rooms, right in the mining districts, the ranches, the schools and colleges where healthy young people go laughing into horrors, because their education fails to educate," wrote Sanger.[8]

Just before the United States entered the war, Sanger had begun organizing for the publication of a magazine intended, in this post-agitation phase of her tactics, to begin this education. *The Birth Control Review*, a monthly magazine that after a year had a twelve-thousand-dollar budget and twenty-five hundred subscribers, and after a decade claimed a circulation of eight thousand, became the principal focus of her wartime efforts, for she still had no organizational base. Compared to Dennett's Voluntary Parenthood League, her own New York Birth Control League had few members and no money. Besides her tactical wisdom, what Margaret Sanger possessed were her name and her contacts, her zeal and her activism, and, by 1920, a successful periodical.

Against the advice of friends, Sanger used the bold words "birth control" in the title of her new monthly, but she carefully monitored its content, especially after it received the cheaper second-class mailing privileges from the U.S Post Office. Granted additional authority to police expression after the passage of the Espionage and Sedition Acts, the Justice Department was now rounding up unionists, Wobblies, socialists, and immigrants. Sanger knew how cautiously she must proceed when Max Eastman's *Masses* was closed down for challenging the conscription laws and Eastman was charged, but acquitted by a jury, of seditious activities against the United States.

Later her friends Emma Goldman, Bill Haywood, and Eugene Debs were arrested and imprisoned, and as a principal target of the government during the Red Scare of the 1920s, because Goldman had refused to become a citizen during her thirty-two years in the United States, she was deported in 1919. Given her own reputation, Sanger was shadowed by agents of J. Edgar Hoover's rapidly growing antiradical division. Some attended her talks; others collected her documents and speeches and read her magazine. But unlike some labor leaders and peace activists, Sanger was never arrested for espionage and sedition, only for the violation of obscenity laws.[9]

In the three years from 1917 to 1920, only one issue of *The Birth Control Review* was confiscated and that for an innocuous review of Marie Stopes's sensational *Married Love*, which was banned in the United States and England. Sanger deplored the discrimination against her when the postmaster general allowed a review of *Married Love* to be printed in the more mainstream *Survey*. Describing the first issues of the magazine as a kind of people's effort—an early Wikipedia—she later admitted that it was not "a very good magazine then. It had few contributors and no editorial policy. Anyone—sculptor, spiritualist, cartoonist, poet, free lance—could express himself . . . in pages open to all."[10] But like all things Sanger, *The Birth Control Review* improved.

Her magazine was properly titled at a time when the concept of a "review" as a collection of information, book reviews, and suggested readings as well as featured articles had emerged as a popular format. Sanger printed everything, from the location and activities of birth control leagues in the United States and Europe to articles on the relation of contraception to the growing eugenics movement, the latter the organized efforts supporting the belief that the human species could be improved through selective breeding. She published samples from the letters to Margaret Sanger (one addressed to "Mrs. Birth Control" and another to "Lady Sanger") with their appeals for help and sad, repetitive tales of too frequent pregnancies, too many children, and too little money. After the promise of financial support from wealthy acquaintances, she even included the activities and essays of her principal rival, praising in June 1918, "the splendid work of Mary Dennett."

In the first issue Sanger grandly announced her purpose to all "the men and women of the United States": birth control was the most vital issue before the country; it was far more important than the war, and no one should mold her life to the "arbitrary commands of the church and state." With the sanguine confidence and sense of persecution that spur reformers to action, she insisted that "the people are waking to the fact that there is no need to bring children into the world haphazard but that clean and harmless means are known whereby children may come when they are desired." But there were enemies everywhere: "the struggle will be bitter. It may be long. All the methods known to tyranny will be used to force the people back into the darkness from which they are striving to emerge."[11]

The seventeen-page first issue—with Margaret Sanger as editor—featured a front-page article, "Shall We Break This Law?" and the law at issue was, of course, the Comstock Act. Published in February 1917, her answer was a classic justification of American civil disobedience, written in Sanger's revolutionary, apocalyptic language, a style leavened over time. "No law is too sacred to break," she wrote, summoning forth a long list of admired law breakers whose dissent had benefited "civilization." As

evidence, she included Moses and Christ, Joan of Arc and George Washington, John Brown of Osawatomie, and the abolitionist Wendell Phillips—
all had lit "beacon lights of human progress." Now with justice based on
precedent and controlled by men and, for those reasons, inattentive to the
suffering of women, and with women's protests unheard, "against the State,
against the Church, against the silence of the medical profession, against
the whole machinery of dead institutions of the past, the woman of today
arises . . . If she must break the law to establish her right to voluntary motherhood, *then the law shall be broken.*"

At this point in its history—there would be other reasons later—the
purpose of birth control was twofold: "to gain woman's freedom and to relieve economically oppressed workers through the limitation of offspring."[12]
From a woman who has been accused of forgetting her earlier radical commitments to working women and replacing them with a reproductive
agenda that depended on experts for its implementation and on the patron-
age of rich adherents for its publicity, such statements suggest otherwise.

In the same issue, Sanger laid out the purposes of her *Review.* She
intended a "herald of new freedom" for women, dedicated to "the principle of
intelligent and voluntary motherhood." She promised a more scientific and
quieter monthly than *The Woman Rebel*, with subscriptions a dollar a year,
but available in some cities, particularly New York, through the necessary
but dangerous street sales. Because the city's corner newsstands refused to
carry the *Review*, Sanger sold it herself in her spare time and was arrested
across from Macy's in December 1918.

Arrested along with Sanger was the indomitable Kitty Marion, the
German-born émigré to Great Britain who had served in the English
Pankhurst suffrage crusade and who had been force-fed in British prisons.
Marion could be found nearly every day on street corners from Macy's to
Grand Central Station, selling the *Review*, where she dodged the umbrel-
las of old ladies and listened to invective (along with some praise) from the
public. Perhaps it was her accent that led many passersby to mistake her
cries of "*Birth Control Review* Here—Buy *The Birth Control Review* for ten
cents" for a call for British control. And when corrected, some pedestrians
replied, "Oh, that's worse."[13]

Occasionally Sanger could be found on a soapbox, usually on the busy
corner of 125th Street and St. Nicholas Avenue, in the kind of open-air
meetings so popular in London's Hyde Park. There, she and her supporters
unfurled an American flag as the backdrop for talks that began with invita-

tions to the ladies and gentlemen to gather around. When they did, advocates of birth control lifted their banners and placards, and Sanger began her standard speech on birth control, which ended by recommending the purchase of the *Review*.

For the next eleven years, this magazine became Sanger's principal means of communication with the public and, as well, the most important source of general information about birth control in the world. It was, she later thought, the only forward step taken during the war. Publicizing birth control's ultimate purpose, to improve society, not its techniques—about which she could legally say nothing but which her audience craved—the *Review* became the headquarters of the American birth control movement—with Sanger as its leader.

Calling this period "the most strenuous work of my already strenuous life," Sanger wrote letters, editorials, and articles, inveigled her friends for free articles, and struggled with layout before taking the material to Max Maisel, the printer of radical material on Brooklyn's Grand Street. "I was solely responsible for whatever it contained. Besides being editor and managing editor, I also handled the proof reading and make-up."[14]

Less strident and more focused than *The Woman Rebel*, the *Review* was also more time-consuming and more expensive, given its fourteen-inch width, and the inclusion of photographs and cartoons. There was never enough money until friends chartered the New York Publishing Company, a joint stock company that became the financial arm of the magazine. Sanger's new friend, Juliet Rublee, who had inherited a fortune from her family's Chicago roofing business, in turn solicited her wealthy friends. Sanger described these rich socialites as "wrapped in orthodoxy," but she took their money and praised them after they paid a hundred dollars to buy a share of stock. Almost overnight ten thousand dollars was raised, the interest and principal available in hard times. But even with this financial cushion, the *Review* was never a moneymaking proposition, and Sanger was forever foraging for funds, with her friend Rublee often the source.

At first Sanger included Mary Ware Dennett on her editorial board. The latter was organizing an association in order to lobby Congress to repeal the Comstock law as it affected birth control. Earlier, Sanger had scorned both the name and intent of Dennett's newly created Voluntary Parenthood League, though she briefly printed its organizational news in the *Review*. Voluntary parenthood conveyed only a woman's right to refuse sex, and that power had been claimed by advocates of women's rights for years, notably by Victoria Woodhull in the decade after the Civil War. Birth control, on the other hand, meant sexual freedom for women to enjoy sex and plan their families. As for Dennett's tactics, Sanger believed that the public must first be educated before Congress was approached. Like oil and water, these two could never work together. Ever suspicious of Sanger's predilection for "an atmosphere of violence," in 1920 Dennett resigned from the board after Sanger called for a five-year "birth strike" by American women.

Sanger's life during these years was dictated by the traditional frenzy of monthly deadlines. She relied on a growing circle of birth control supporters for articles of varying length. Crystal Eastman wrote "Birth Control in the Feminist Program," arguing its necessity for women's freedom: "Whether we are the special followers of Alice Paul or Ellen Key or Olive Schreiner, we must all be the followers of Margaret Sanger."[15] Schreiner's article in the April issue—"Breeding Men for Battle"—excoriated militarism, and that same month the Drysdales, friends from her early days in London, contributed a dry but space-filling article on the history of the Neo-Malthusian movement in England.

Each February, during his birthday month, Sanger paid homage to the man she still called "the King" by devoting an entire issue to Havelock Ellis. In turn, the English sexologist sent essays, usually secondhand recycled ones, agreeing, though he usually declined any editing of his material, to her title change of his article from "The Erotic Rights of Women" to the more provocative, Americanized "Sex Rights of Women." Once, to his irritation, she published something without attribution, and one of his articles was held up by the censors.

Throughout the war, Sanger and Ellis kept in touch, with their personal letters frequently opened by censors on both sides of the Atlantic. She wrote more often than he, perhaps because Françoise Cyon, the French writer and translator, now lived with him. But Ellis did commiserate about the recurring lumps in Sanger's neck. He urged her to be less strident and insisted that the Frenchwoman, whom he never married but who eventually took his name as the anagram DeLisle, would not drive the Irishwoman from his heart. In his lyric prose he wrote about nature and the weather, always applauding her work: "I know you are not happy unless you are doing something daring."[16]

Others contributed to the magazine as well. The disgraced Bill Sanger, who still refused to sign a separation agreement, wrote an awkward paragraph on the importance of "a new race more dynamic in its prosocial impulses, more keen and alert to digest ideas," created by "finer" parenting and wanted babies. Earlier Sanger had refused, but now she printed some of her husband's charcoal sketches of mournful, pregnant women and emaciated children. Later she persuaded the well-known artist of New York's Ashcan school, Robert Minor, to provide illustrations, and eventually the talented Lou Rogers became the principal cartoonist.

Sanger was a woman who inspired her lovers to poetry, and two of them contributed poems of admiration that she, liking the attention, published. Wrote Walter Roberts: "But one clear-eyed amid the selfish throng / Above their praise or blame / To her the vision came / And led her forth / To battle with the strong." Her newest lover, a journalist from Kansas City, Billy Williams, offered admiring literary allusions: birth control revolved around Margaret Sanger and radiated from her like the spokes of a wheel.[17]

Despite contributions from others, *The Birth Control Review* remained the voice of Margaret Sanger, even when she was not in New York and left the magazine temporarily in the hands of trusted lieutenants. Sanger repeatedly drew on her personal story to provide the movement's legends, bringing alive for her readers what might have been the abstraction of contraception. Her photograph was included in several issues as she became the centerfold of the magazine, and with a sure sense of the uses of biography not just as favorable publicity, but as a means of connecting with her followers, she made certain that *The Birth Control Review* featured chapters of her dramatic life: her training as a nurse, her epiphany when Sadie Sachs of the Lower East Side died, the confiscation of *The Woman Rebel*, her flight to England, the opening of the Brownsville clinic, her persistent harassment by the authorities, and her recent trial and imprisonment.

After another confrontation with the legal system, Sanger also included the story of her suppressed 1917 film. Several times she had gone with Billy Williams to the new theater on West Forty-fourth Street in a city where thirty-six other movie emporiums made New York the biggest cinema market in the world. New Yorkers came to see underdressed, erotic stars such as Theda Bara and Geraldine Farrar. Impressed with the power of this new form of entertainment, Sanger decided to make her own silent film. Part biography, part documentary, it was intended to educate the public, make money for the movement and, with her adroit sense of publicity, stamp Margaret Sanger as its leader.

She starred as Margaret Sanger, playing the beleaguered nurse who attended Sadie Sachs's death, and later, the imprisoned victim of unjust laws.

Friends suggested innocuous titles, such as "The Hand That Rocks the Cradle" or "The New World," but Sanger never compromised on the name of her movement. In the first half of *Birth Control*, she re-created her personal saga. In the second half, images of small families happily walking in shady parks were intercut with views of desperate mothers with too many children from the Lower East Side. The film, advertised in *Variety* and *The New York Times*, ended with a shot of Sanger, just released from prison. The caption read, "No matter what happens the work must go on."

On the day that Sanger's film was to open in 1917, George Bell, the New York commissioner of licenses, at the urging of the New York Board of Censors, suspended the license of the Park Theater. *Birth Control*, according to the censors, advertised a commercial product based on perverted tastes, though it was not erotic. It was, however, indecent subject matter. Its second half offended for its radical arguments against existing laws and its incendiary portrayal of class prejudice. It must not be shown.

After a round of injunctions and with no theater owner willing to risk his license to show *Birth Control*, it was shown only once to a private audience and then all copies of the five reels mysteriously disappeared. But as she always did, Sanger fashioned victory from defeat. Justice Nathan Bijur had noted in his ruling that the film dealt with a "great problem of life in which our citizenry has an active interest." The subject matter might be unpleasant, shocking to some, and the portrayal tasteless, but, according to the judge, that did not "warrant the suppression of a prosaic public presentation. [*Birth Control*] was a measured and decent exercise of the right of free speech guaranteed by our constitutions and essential to natural well-being." An elated Sanger printed Bijur's entire decision, along with pictures from the film in the June issue of *The Birth Control Review*.[18]

Through her work as an editor and author, Sanger developed a brisk, prosaic writing style. In the first two years of *The Birth Control Review* she contributed thirteen articles and over twenty book reviews and editorials. It was hard work, but in the process she honed her arguments for contraception, some reactive, others affirmative, yet all important in the battle for public approval. These positions were usually not original, for Sanger's genius lay in the tactical promotion of contraception. She developed these arguments not just for the *Review*, but for her debates with doctors, social purists, and Catholic priests—with the very holding of debates in which she could present the affirmative a sign of progress.

Frequently, Sanger had to react to the proposition that birth control was immoral. Violating the word of God, according to conservatives, it changed the purpose of marriage and led to female promiscuity. To the criticism that birth control interfered with a natural, God-given, and biblically ordained process and that the only justification for sex was procreation, Sanger offered examples of humanity's improvements on nature such as the wheel. To the command from Genesis that mankind must increase and multiply, she responded with a verse from Ecclesiastes: "Desire not a multitude of unprofitable children." Reducing the point to absurdity, on a matter that had been considered by generations of Catholic theologians, Sanger questioned if those who could not have children—the old and the infertile—must then abandon sexual intimacies and even marriage because they could not reproduce.

In the pages of *The Birth Control Review* she challenged the enormous prestige of St. Augustine, the fifth-century reformed libertine and father of a child, who after his Christian epiphany had defined Western traditions about sex in *Marriage and Concupiscence*, views reinforced by the thirteenth-century philosopher Thomas Aquinas. Both men celebrated marital fecundity as human purpose mandated by God. They also held virginity preferable to marriage, citing the New Testament, and chastity a more holy practice than intercourse. Accordingly, only procreative purpose justified inferior sexual activity. In such a utilitarian view, artificial contraception clearly obstructed God's will. Whoever copulated for pleasure and not for the intended goal of procreation acted sinfully, though in fact, as Sanger noted, there was no clear biblical text on the matter, only the interpretation of man-made scripture and the formulation of sexual ethics by bishops of the church.

Over the centuries such religious views had gained unassailable authority. Besides papal injunctions on sex, Catholics, a minority population amid Protestants in the United States, were concerned about their flocks' numbers, an additional reason to oppose contraception. On practical and theological grounds the Roman Catholic hierarchy condemned birth control as sinful—a venial, remittable, and not mortal sin, but one that, amid the changing sexual mores of the early twentieth century, increasingly preoccupied conscientious Catholics and priests in the confessional booth.

For Sanger, lifetime celibacy, rather than any text, explained the Catholic clergy's crabbed notions of sexuality, and she used the pages of *The Birth Control Review* for ridicule. How could priests, needing to elevate their personal sacrifice and knowing nothing about sex, make rules about behavior that they understood only vicariously and often lasciviously? After a priest termed her birth control movement "a cult," she called on that faith's women to defy such ignorance and abandon their clubs, societies, and even membership in the Catholic-sponsored White Cross nurses. Sanger never failed to report the number of Catholic women, usually around a third of her clients, who defied the church's dictates.

In the *Review* Sanger also criticized the Catholic Church for its intrusions into civil rights and its violations of the free speech of American citizens. She provided personal examples—the church's efforts to force theater owners to close down when Sanger came to town, the unofficial sub rosa instructions to Catholic police officers to arrest birth control advocates selling the *Review*, the threatening phone calls by prominent members of the Knights of Columbus to mayors and councilmen to pass special ordinances targeting her literature, the picketing and disruption of her speeches, and the intimidating threats by prominent Catholics to boycott vendors who sold her magazine. Sanger also used the overheated letters she received from Catholics to expose the irrationality of the church's position: "When you stand before the judgment seat of God and before you are hurled into Hell," went one letter signed by "A Catholic" who, like many Americans in this period, conflated abortion and birth control, "those children you have murdered will stand before you and pointing their fingers of denunciation at you demand of God to punish you."[19]

Sanger's opponents also included prominent Protestant Americans such as the former president Theodore Roosevelt, the evangelist Billy Sunday, and the gynecologist Dr. Howard Kelly, all of whom worried about the deterioration of what this generation called "the race" (and meant by that native-born Anglo-Saxons) and who believed birth control would engender promiscuity among the overly prolific inferior classes, especially immigrants. A supporter of positive eugenics—that is, more babies from parents of good stock—Roosevelt became the spokesman for national anxieties about race suicide, a form of self-inflicted class destruction perpetrated by wealthy and middle-class women who refused to have children for selfish reasons. "Race suicide," he wrote, "is more important than any other question in this country," with the decline in the birthrate "the chief cause as well as the chief symptom of what is evil in nations." Roosevelt, a father of six whose first wife had died in childbirth, recommended four children per family "from old native stock or self-respecting daughters and sons of immigrants."[20]

Positive eugenicists such as Roosevelt intended to increase the number of Americans with approved bloodlines by promoting larger families among the "good stock" of the nation. Roosevelt fumed that his eldest daughter Alice's friends, and especially the college graduates among them, were less likely to marry and, if they did, were more likely to produce fewer children than immigrants. It seemed that what the popular writer Madison Grant called "the great race" was passing.

During the war the frustrated fifty-eight-year-old Roosevelt was unsuccessfully trying to persuade President Wilson to grant him a commission so that he could raise a regiment and go off to war himself. For a man who considered it a national duty for "citizens of the right type to leave their blood behind them as a patriotic legacy," a woman who avoided pregnancy was no different from a cowardly soldier who threw down his rifle. A healthy nation required more babies from the fit, and at no time was that more true than during wartime. Yet, by attacking women who elected not to have children, Roosevelt implicitly acknowledged the possibilities, among twentieth-century women, of choosing not to have children. In his monthly column in the 1917 *Metropolitan Magazine* he discussed the threats of "race suicide," blaming birth control for the dangerously low birthrates of Harvard and Yale men, who were not producing enough *sons*. There was no mention of daughters.[21]

Sanger responded to her most prominent adversary in both *The Birth Control Review* and the *Metropolitan*, the latter affording her welcomed exposure to mainstream readers. Addressing Roosevelt, she argued that children of quality, the desired result for positive eugenicists, could be achieved only by the universal use of birth control, and those who opposed its use were simply expanding the slums. Besides, she wrote, so many poor children died and so few from wealthy households that the differential birthrate among the classes, feared by Roosevelt and others, hardly existed. Intrepidly Sanger also challenged the Harvard-educated Roosevelt's historical facts: decline in the populations of Greece and Rome through fertility control had destroyed neither society.

In this exchange, Sanger asserted that women who lived in poverty had inferior babies because they lacked information about how to space their babies. She described the grim circumstances of families with too many children and too few resources who existed in the so-called submerged tenth, a group, she believed, closer in numbers to a quarter of the population. "It is an error to suppose that woman avoids motherhood because she is afraid to die. Rather does she fear to live. She fears a life of poverty and drudgery, weighed down by the horror of unwanted pregnancy and tor-tured by the inability to rear decently the children she has already brought into the world."

Reframing the ethical paradigm of sex conservatives such as Roosevelt, Sanger disputed the decency and justice of unwanted pregnancies and their effects on the health of mothers and the lives of children. The latter were often driven into lifetime factory or domestic work with neither edu-cation nor prospects, in a nation with no protective child labor laws, where 20 percent of all boys ten to fifteen held full-time jobs, as did 10 percent of all girls of the same age. When Roosevelt toured the Lower East Side in 1918 and congratulated, for their patriotism, "half-starved mothers who could not afford 15 cents for a B grade quart of milk," Sanger erupted: where was the rightness of that?[22]

To those—and there were many—who believed that birth control harmed women physically and was therefore a health hazard, Sanger de-nied that birth control induced sterility, citing the work of a rare ally in the medical profession, Dr. Walter Robinson, along with international experts in Holland and Germany. On the contrary, Sanger argued, birth control led to improved sex hygiene, with douching the best example. As for those women with prolapsed uteruses from multiple pregnancies, the means of prevention for a serious medical condition was obvious.

In a rebuttal to another familiar charge, Sanger used the *Review* to ar-gue that birth control obtained by the use of pessaries and other mechani-cal means inserted into the vagina caused neither cancer nor spinal injuries, as her opponents imagined, and as some physicians such as Howard Kelly predicted. On the other hand, sexual abstinence created nervous, unhappy men and women. Surely, wrote Sanger, it was an unjust world that afforded women in their married state only celibacy, abortion, and too many children as their reproductive choices. Every attempt women make "to strike off the shackles of slavery"—whether suffrage, higher education, and now birth control—"has been met with the argument that such an act would result in the downfall of her morality and the breakup of the home."[23] And as for the positive ethics of birth control, they rested with the ability of a free woman to become "the mistress of her body. Just as long as man dictates and con-trols the standards of sex morality," there could be no freedom.[24] In the pos-tulate that Sanger herself lived, autonomous women celebrated love and enjoyed the pleasures of sexual passion.

•

From 1917 to 1920, Sanger also used the pages of *The Birth Control Review* to present her emerging position on the popular topic of eugenics. The view that humanity could be improved by better breeding—one had only to consult animal husbandry and agriculture for confirmation of the success of biological engineering—now extended beyond the laboratories of zoologists and animal biologists into the domain of the general public. Only three decades had passed since the English geneticist Sir Francis Galton (Charles Darwin's cousin) had created, from the Greek, the neologism "eugenic," by which he meant good genes. Darwin's views on natural selection and the survival of the fittest—now applied to humans in the field of evolutionary biology—gave energy to a social philosophy of intervention intended to produce more fit Americans and, in the language of the day, fewer unfit, dysgenic ones.

Darwin's mechanism of species adaptation depended on the environment, not just heredity. But linking nature and nurture, the influential nineteenth-century French naturalist Jean-Baptiste Lamarck argued that animals and humans acquire certain behavioral characteristics in the process of adapting to their circumstances. These traits were then inherited by succeeding generations. According to Leonard Darwin, Charles Darwin's son, predispositions to everything from loving the sea to adultery were passed on from parents to children.

By the turn of the century several American biologists, with impressive credentials and unshakable assumptions about inherited characteristics, had begun research on "racial temperaments." By 1907 a coalition of scientists published the *American Journal of Eugenics*. Forty colleges and universities offered courses in eugenics, and freestanding laboratories such as that in Cold Spring Harbor on Long Island, funded in 1910 by rich philanthropists, studied data on familial inheritance. The deplorable generational plight of the "Kallikak" family of lunatics and criminals became the symbol for negative eugenicism in the press. On the eve of World War I, negative eugenics represented the future, with the United States an international leader in the possibilities of involuntary sterilization.

Two experts in social engineering through better mating—Dr. Charles Davenport, who had discovered a community of "defectives" in the West Virginia hill country, and his disciple Dr. Harry Laughlin—both with doctorates in biology and directors of experimental evolution at Cold Spring Harbor, promoted the next step: the sterilization of the socially inadequate. The latter were expansively defined as the insane, the epileptic and inebriated, the deaf and blind, and even, in some calculations, the tubercular. The largest category of those who must not reproduce because of their heritable disability was that of the feeble-minded—the vague but popular contemporary classification for those Americans with limited intelligence. New intelligence tests developed earlier in the century, with their numerical measures of mental ability, provided benchmarks for classifying human intelligence.

There were political reasons for Americans to accept sterilization that grew out of progressive attempts to provide protection for the poor. Along with criminals whose antisocial instincts were now believed inherited by their children, the unfit were becoming expensive in an era that was installing programs and institutions to support those who could not take care of themselves. In their reports, eugenicists noted how expensive the deficient were, as states spent growing proportions of their budgets on improved social welfare programs. Such costs—certain to increase given the biological argument for inherited degeneracy and the differential birthrate—justified the next step, as state legislatures began to pass laws permitting involuntary sterilization in institutions: California in 1910, followed by Indiana and Illinois, until by 1920 fifteen states had such laws. By 1937 two-thirds of all American states permitted similar coercive practices. In some states involuntary sterilization took place without statutory approval, and nearly all states regulated the marriage of the feeble-minded and diseased.

Two other circumstances fueled the popularity of negative eugenics: first, the rising tide of non-English-speaking Jewish immigrants arriving in the United States before World War I. Like Roosevelt, Davenport used statistics drawn from his "superior" Harvard classmates, who served this generation as a recurring yardstick of the fit. "A Harvard class does not reproduce itself," he grimly predicted in 1915, "and in 200 years 1000 graduates of today will have only fifty descendants and on the other hand, 1000 Romanians in two hundred years will come to 100,000—hence to govern the fifty descendants of Harvard sons."[25] The war also advanced the popularity of applied eugenics, especially after the intelligence tests taken by four hundred thousand army recruits revealed that, as well as having high rates of venereal disease, one-third of the young men scored as thirteen-year-olds in the "moron" category, while two of every five immigrants were considered feeble-minded, and the average black recruit by these measures demonstrated the intellect of a ten-year-old. In the uproar that followed, only controlled heredity could save an imperiled nation.[26]

In the second issue of *The Birth Control Review*, Sanger printed an article written by an exponent of eugenics, Paul Popenoe, at the time the head of the California branch of the American Eugenics Society, the principal force behind that state's active involuntary sterilization program, and soon to become the director of a famous eugenically oriented marriage counseling service, the American Institute of Family Relations. Titled "Birth Control and Eugenics," Popenoe's article attacked birth control. Hard at work on his influential volume *Applied Eugenics*, he defined eugenics as "favoring the reproduction of happier and more efficient parts of the population and discouraging the increase of less capable persons," with the latter collected in "racially" inferior groups. The differential rates of birth between these two groups—Popenoe's more efficient, superior part of the population producing too few children and the less capable too many—must be reversed. It was Popenoe who wrote the sentence that has been falsely attributed to Sanger: "More children from the fit, less from the unfit," which he used in an editorial in the journal *American Medicine* and which Sanger quoted in a review of his work.

Targeting the birth control movement as "making unfounded claims on the merit of small families and delayed parenthood," Popenoe took aim at Sanger's biology: "The quality of a child is determined much more by the character of his ancestry than by the number of his brothers and sisters or the length of interval between his birth and that of his predecessor." Birth control harmed the race by limiting the number of children "in the superior classes," though Popenoe, the father of two children, did support what he delicately defined as "birth release," or coitus interruptus.[27]

For Sanger the article afforded an opportunity to publish her own views on a subject that so obviously intersected with her life's work. Powerful, emotional reasons from her past life might have led her to oppose any form of human improvement through eugenics. All that she was, and had been, seemed under attack. Her early life as the sixth child in an immigrant Irish Catholic family, whose mother died at fifty of tuberculosis, placed her among those overpopulated impoverished families who spread inheritable diseases such as tuberculosis and added nothing to the "gene pool." Her marriage to a Jew placed her in another marginal group, as did her early commitment to socialism, which preached the importance of the environment in improving society, as eugenicists underrated it. For years Sanger had fought government repression. Even her rationale for birth control focused on liberating individual women, not improving the American genetic pool. And as for wayward girls at risk for sterilization, she could surely sympathize with their sexual behavior.

On the other hand, these same experiences sustained the negative eugenic arguments that Sanger was coming to accept: the deprivation of the too-large Higgins family; her own tuberculosis, which most doctors believed the result of an inherited predisposition from her mother; the miserable conditions on the Lower East Side, where families *did* seem to inherit both social and medical pathologies as well as criminal tendencies; and even her observations from her Brownsville clinic. She was influenced as well by Havelock Ellis, who accepted the key principles of the inheritance of—or predisposition to—various characteristics, and who had introduced her to biological determinism. Wrote Ellis in 1912, two years before Sanger arrived in England, "Feeblemindedness is largely handed down by heredity," though Ellis opposed involuntary sterilization programs.[28] Harsher than he, Sanger believed charity hospitals, pensions, and even sewer systems protected "the propagation of what might be race degenerates."[29] In any case there had been none of these progressive features to safeguard the Higgins family when she grew up in Corning and created her personal means of ascent into another world.

Tentatively in these years and then wholeheartedly in the 1920s, Margaret Sanger became a fellow traveler and then a promoter of the eugenics movement. For the most part her acceptance of the movement was a calculated, pragmatic tactic. She needed allies, and eugenics—the expert qualifications of its proponents, the scientific trappings of its evidence, its expanding networks of journals and associations, its general acceptance among Americans, and even its international connections—represented an opportunity to find friends and join a popular movement.

If she could make her case and gain the support of scientists, it would enhance not just the legitimacy but the application of her still marginal reform. "Birth control opens the way for the eugenicist and preserves his work," she argued in her response to Popenoe, titled "Birth Control and Racial Betterment." "By freeing reproduction from its present chains it will make a better race." Without birth control, negative eugenics, with the same ends as her movement but different means, amounted to little more than "a house built on sand in a rising stream of unfit." Ultimately, "neither the mating of healthy couples nor the sterilization of certain recognizable types touches the great problem of the unlimited reproduction of those whose housing, clothing and food is inadequate."[30]

In an effort to gain support, she signed on to negative eugenics, expecting that its proponents would reciprocate and urge birth control as a solution: "I personally believe the sterilization of the feeble-minded, insane and syphilitic, are superficial deterrents when applied to the growing numbers of unfit." Whatever the variable influence of nature or nurture, blood or environment, she held that the underfed, uneducated, and dispossessed, in some measure, passed on their imperfections to their children. She had observed as much, and though Sanger's views were bad genetics, she learned this mix of science and social values from the most distinguished scientists in the nation.

Sanger's support of eugenics, the latter largely unchallenged in the United States during these years, ultimately cost her some of her reputation, while at the same time it revealed her passion for the cause of birth control, along with her pragmatism. Of course she objected to the facile rhetoric of positive eugenicists that women with "better blood" must abandon birth control and have more children in order to prevent the consequences of race suicide. "A woman's first duty was to herself and that was her first duty to the state," whether for more or fewer offspring. Meanwhile, she had the solution in a world that was "filling up."[31]

During Sanger's lifetime, especially in Nazi Germany but also in the United States and Canada, negative eugenics, through its draconian applications of involuntary sterilizations, spiraled beyond its early formulations to horrific outcomes. With the best of intentions scientists and reformers saw themselves as reducing human suffering. But however well-meaning, they went beyond scientific findings to adopt a form of genetic determinism based on social, class-driven prejudice.

Today its atrocities have no justification, though Sanger's acceptance must be put into the context of her times. Her offhand support of sterilization at this point (though she did not specify that it would be state-sponsored and involuntary) is indefensible. But what does remain of race regeneration in the twenty-first century are individual efforts to improve mankind through advances in molecular biology: whether to abort a fetus with a miserable painful physical condition, whether to avoid pregnancy because of some familial inheritable condition such as Huntington's chorea, and whether to chose voluntary sterilization as a means of birth control in order to prevent pregnancy.[32]

During this period of introspection, no desk could entirely capture Sanger. As she ran the *Review* and wrestled with philosophical issues involving religion and eugenicism, she continued—informally, illicitly, and watchfully in order to avoid any sting operation—to give specific information about contraceptive techniques to the five or ten clients who every day found their way to the second-floor rooms in the brownstone off Fifth Avenue near Union Square. There, the words "Birth Control" on the door proclaimed that they had come to the right place. She also devised a way to send her illegal but still bestselling *Family Limitation* to those who sent stamps and self-addressed brown envelopes.

Sanger lived in two rooms on West Fourteenth Street without heat or hot water and with a gas stove in the kitchen. In the bedroom/living room, she enclosed the tin bathtub with a stylish Japanese screen. She walked to her office most days. Sometimes, at night, wearing the hand-me-down dresses of her growing circle of wealthy female friends (she had decided that red was her best color), she went out on the town: sometimes to the opera, sometimes on a dinner date with Walter Roberts or Billy Williams. In the just-opened Orpheum Dance Palace on West Forty-sixth Street, in the days when couples enjoyed music and dancing for ten cents, she and her lovers danced the steps of a new age—the turkey trot and chicken flip and the improvised routines that Sanger created: "Why dance like everyone else?" she once asked a partner. "Do something different."[33]

Introduced by mutual friends to Sanger, Billy Williams not only wrote material for *The Birth Control Review* but also helped her with a new book. In the process he fell head over heels in love with his "Golden Girl." Like his name, the man her sons called Uncle Billy relied on repetition to express his adoration: "I love you, I love you, I love you." "Oh, M., I love you, I love you, I love you. My love cannot hurt your work . . . You are beauty of beauty, golden heart and flame of my soul." "I want to be lying at your feet, with your fingers in my hair . . . Don't wonder that I am persistently and unreasonably presumptuous in the matter of love, Golden Girl—about all we have in this movement is an inability to quit."[34]

Meanwhile, Stuart and Grant attended nearby boarding schools whose tuitions were paid by Sanger's friends—fourteen-year-old Stuart was a work-study student "to reduce the fees" at the Peddie School in Hightstown, New Jersey, from which her brother Robert had graduated, after his unmarried sisters—Nan and Mary—had paid the tuition in the long-standing Higgins tradition. Grant was still at the Winnwood School, soon to follow his brother to Peddie, transfer to the posh Westminster School, and then enter Princeton. Sanger had lived the elevating effects of education and provided the best for her sons. Peddie, she proudly informed her friend Juliet Rublee, "was a preparatory for Princeton," though Stuart, never much of a student, eventually graduated from the Roxbury School in Connecticut and entered Yale as a freshman in 1921.

Even with the boys at boarding school, she remained conflicted about her mothering: "For several years I hung on to this dream of being with [her sons] constantly, but it was a dream." As she defined this dilemma, she either left them to possibly incompetent servants or "sacrificed my maternal feeling" and put them in boarding schools where "they could lead a healthy regular life."[35]

Years before, she had made her decision, just as she had chosen a calling and never wavered. Acknowledging her father and sisters—Ethel, Nan, and Mary—as good "foster parents," she now excluded Bill from any parental role. But she paid a price: "At times the homesickness for [the children] seemed too much to bear . . . When I came in late at night the fire was dead in the grate, the book open on the table, the glove dropped on the floor, the pillow rumpled on the sofa—all the same—just as I had left them a day, a week, a month before. The first chill of loneliness was always appalling. I wanted the warmth and glow of a loving family welcome."[36]

She fashioned herself into a progressive parent, and after her brief sojourn as a suburban mother, she disdained the overprotective maternalism of this generation, believing that children raised in collective settings were better equipped for community life and their future. Her own cursory style of quality-time mothering—Sanger was not aloof, just unmindful and distracted—combined with her life's work for fewer, better babies hardly indicates, as some have suggested, psychological antagonism toward children.

Letters from her sons were often painful reminders of their maternal needs. "Mother," reminded ten-year-old Grant. "Will you come down on Thanksgiving Day? Now you put in your engagement book Nov. 28th. Go down to see Grant . . . I know you are busy or you would come see me," he continued, wondering whether he was coming home for Easter, as all the other boys did.[37] Once, Stuart walked to the train in Truro, on Cape Cod, where the boys spent their summers, expecting to meet a mother who

never arrived. When he contracted mumps at school and wanted to recuper-
ate in her apartment, she resisted. In response Stuart urged daily letters:
"Don't forget to write every day, as I look forward to your letter—that is the
only thing I do." When he did come to New York, he wrote to his mother,
"you won't have to meet me. Just send me a thought wave."[38]

For comfort from her loneliness and chronic worries about her health,
Sanger turned to Juliet Rublee, whom she had met at Mabel Dodge's salon
as early as 1914. Certainly she knew Rublee by the time of the Brownsville
trial, when the woman who became her lifelong best friend and confidante
organized the Committee of 100, raising money for Sanger's defense. A
wealthy socialite married to a prominent lawyer, the childless Rublee had
taken up birth control as her cause, and Sanger as her hero. Rublee brought
money, contacts, and adoration of Sanger to this lifelong friendship. Until
the Depression, when her personal fortune was nearly wiped out, Rublee paid
bills for *The Birth Control Review* and the printing of Sanger's pamphlets,
along with the expenses from Sanger's occasional sojourns at rest homes and
her office on Fifth Avenue. Rublee even sent checks to the impoverished
Havelock Ellis. With her contacts in New York and in her summer place
amid the intellectual colony of Cornish, New Hampshire, Rublee, by a process of respectability through association, brought other wealthy women
into the movement.

Sanger and Rublee shared more than an abiding interest in birth control.
They were kindred emotional spirits, with mutual interests in spiritualism,
the opera, peculiar diets, and dresses worn without girdles. (Once, when
Rublee gave Sanger the gift of a girdle, Sanger, whose weight fluctuated,
immediately began one of her diets.) As Sanger's principal ally, the exotic
Rublee, with long, black hair and wildly colored clothes, provided a disciple's
faithful solicitude. "Don't rush yourself too much," Rublee wrote to Sanger.
"There is immense work ahead of you—you must get well & strong—you
are too frail just now—I feel it—not robust enough—Please eat a great
deal & drink oceans of milk."[39]

In 1918 the United States was reeling from a pandemic influenza, the
lethal worldwide virus affecting millions around the globe. Unscathed by a
disease that killed 675,000 Americans, including 43,000 servicemen, Sanger
was instead suffering from a recurrence of tuberculosis in her tonsils and
the lymph nodes in her neck, with the resulting enervating symptoms of
night sweats, coughing, and fever. In the summer of 1918, on doctor's orders she left for a three-month rest cure in Truro with her sons, but she

stayed only a few weeks. "Of course," she complained to Rublee, "three months will be utterly impossible—I had an old T.B. fight some years ago—Lately about two weeks ago symptoms of it began—temperature, loss of weight—a lump in neck, etc. So I fled to a surgeon who claims it is not T.B. but caused by suppressed, nervous Fatigue. They claim that aviators have the same ailment and a few months rest cures them without an operation."[40]

But this was more than nerves, and for a month in late 1919, after an operation at Bellevue on her lymph nodes and an enervating course of X-ray treatments at New York's Rockefeller Institute for Medical Research, Sanger convalesced at a retreat in Donan Hills in Staten Island, paid for by Rublee. There she practiced her own therapy of diaphragmatic, yogalike breathing, and described her experience to Rublee, with whom she shared intimate personal details of her life often hidden from others:

> First I sleep with all windows open top and bottom . . . I spend time in breathing from the Solar Plexus & filling the lungs with fresh air and concentrating on power, while I do this breathing . . . then [after breakfast] I sink back again into a dreamy state—trying to reach the sub conscious & also trying to commune with my inner self. I talk to it—as to a personality . . . and then I breathe again from the Solar Plexus holding the thought of the Sun as a Power & I as a power radiating love & warmth & joy & Power & wealth, etc etc . . . I want to develop the capacity of my lungs for I could see on Dr. Hirsh's face that day a look that meant my lungs were O.K. but were not in condition to resist in case trouble came."[41]

The key to a healthy life, she recommended to Rublee, who shared her interest in thought transference and sending parapsychic messages through the atmosphere, was "to sink or submerge yourself into the subconscious . . . then commune with your Inner Self," and, as both these women aspired to smooth, rosy complexions, to use Charles Frey's special facial creams.[42]

One night when she was in the quiet Staten Island retreat, with time on her hands and uncertain about how long she would live, Margaret wrote a letter to Bill Sanger to be delivered, she informed her sons, only after her death, which she anticipated, with this new attack of tuberculosis, would come before his. She had been to the exhibition of the paintings he had done in Spain at the Touchstone Gallery. They were an achievement, a judgment with which the art critics concurred in reviews published in *The New*

York Times that complimented his harsh, steely use of color and his authentic depiction of architectural subjects.[43] Sanger knew the suffering her husband had endured to produce them, though, as she learned in one of her life's lessons, "lasting fame comes on the ladder of grief & pain." She acknowledged her part in his unhappiness, but referred to his habitual pessimism and depression as a reason for their separation: "Tragedy is expressed by you in nearly everything you do." In any case in her own life, she was often "in the hands of forces" she could not control. And these forces had become stronger than their marriage.[44]

She believed that his intense nature made any future "friendship & comradeship impossible." Still, the point of this affectionate letter was to share with him her remembrance of their early love, the coming of the children, the saving and planning for their home, and all the things that he had done for her, especially in their sex life. "Your love for me beautified my life and made possible the outlook on love & passion & sex which has given me the courage & strength to go forth to do." As for her love for him, it had never changed, but reflecting the self-perception that had helped destroy their marriage, Sanger wrote, "Sometimes I think it was not to be that I should love too intensely . . . Au revoir, dear one, ever lovingly." Such sentiments could never be delivered to her husband in her lifetime, as his insistence that their affection could be rekindled would make him clamor for a new start—and object to the divorce she longed for. Yet because Bill Sanger died of a heart attack in 1961 at the age of eighty-seven, forty-two years after she wrote this last affectionate letter and five years before her own death, he never read her loving tribute.

Still enervated from the X-ray treatments, which had little effect on her symptoms, in the winter of 1919 Sanger took Grant out of school and traveled to California for a hoped-for cure, or at least remission from her tuberculosis. There she rested in the soft, orange-scented air in Coronado, read Helen Hunt Jackson's popular *Ramona* to Grant in the evenings, visited with Claverack friends of old, worked on the manuscript for the forthcoming *Woman and the New Race*, and tried to get well. Much in demand in radical circles, she gave several lectures, calling her trip a success when three "old Bolsheviks" attended one of her talks. But when she spoke at a noisy socialist meeting in Fresno, all the objections to birth control that had driven her away from the party surfaced: under a socialist regime, insisted her audience, women could have all the children they want. "The fact that they can today never dawns upon them," Sanger responded, "but the fact that women shall not desire to be breeders under a socialist Republic is no more than she wants today." But given their "Marxist blinders," it was harder to change the views of these radicals than those of the average person, which explained why she had turned to wealthy philanthropists for birth control's support. In any case, during the war, everywhere, not just among socialists, "Birth Control had fled the minds of the people."[45]

Depressed—in fact "despondent," as she sometimes was when she traveled or had little to do—Sanger remembered her dead daughter, Peggy, who, she believed, had sent a message by thought transference one night. Sanger mourned as well her former Spanish lover Lorenzo Portet, dead of tuberculosis in Paris the year before. She despaired of the arrests and trials of her friends, especially Eugene Debs, who had been sentenced to ten years in jail for an antiwar speech. And with Wilson's administration enforcing the deportation of aliens who advocated anarchy or belonged to radical organizations or opposed the draft, she believed her friends in the Wobblies "would prefer any country on earth to this one today where every vestige of liberty of speech and press is dead. Thomas Pain [sic] how his spirit must grieve for the beloved land of his dreams—this land that was to be an asylum for liberty seekers!"[46]

The work of editing and composing a monthly magazine also weighed on her. Sanger had hired an experienced fund-raiser and writer, Frederick Blossom, as an editor of the *Review* in 1917. Sharing a commitment to birth control and an understanding of the art of propaganda through written persuasion, Blossom moved to New York to help run the magazine. For a few months Sanger was pleased. He set up the magazine, assisted in her legal battles, took over the faltering NYBCL, gave speeches, and fostered her reputation. In the March issue, while she was in jail, he complimented Sanger's "unsparing efforts for the liberation of the women of America and her first-hand contact with the many sided tragedy of enforced motherhood."[47] He donated his money (and that of his wealthy wife) and built the subscription list of the *Review* to over one thousand readers, described by Sanger as "radicals, the curious, girls about to be married, mothers, fathers, social workers, ministers and physicians."[48]

After Sanger was released from prison in the spring of 1917, the two shared an office. Explaining to her financial supporter Gertrude Pinchot, who may have questioned the need for another editor whose salary Pinchot helped pay, Sanger noted that she felt "a personal obligation to Dr. Blossom for what he has done and sacrificed that I may have this headquarters in

New York. You and many of the women who have come into the movement recently may not realize the tremendous odds and difficulties during the early period of this work."[49]

A few short months later Blossom and Margaret Sanger were at war. He complained that her accounting practices were corrupt, that she profited from the movement, and that she owed him over two hundred dollars. Such a charge—the result of her conviction that she was the personification of birth control and could use funds donated to the movement for personal expenses—was the first instance of a complaint that surfaced several times during Sanger's long, underfunded campaigns for birth control. Meanwhile, Sanger claimed that she and Blossom differed over the war—he enthusiastically supporting the Allies, she opposed to war in general. But there was more to this battle than differences over accounts and international affairs.

By 1917 Margaret Sanger could not share her movement with anyone, especially not someone as ambitious and effective as Blossom. At stake was the possibility of an interloper taking over the magazine and appealing to his followers in the NYBCL to support a birth control movement under his leadership. Even more than the complacent, conservative Mary Ware Dennett, Blossom emerged as a competitor.

Taking the offensive, Sanger demanded a detailed financial report of receipts and contributions. By her accounting he owed her money, and besides he had used up a year's funds on only three issues. By July Blossom "was out as far as representing me," though he had earlier left to become an organizer for the Socialist Party. To her friends Sanger deplored his "fishwife mind and attention to petty details," dismissing Blossom as one of the many

> young crusaders who come galloping to show me the way, joining the processions and blowing horns for "the Cause" . . . willing to teach me how to put the movement on a "social or sound practical and economic" basis. But . . . they became discouraged at the first show of thorny, disagreeable obstacles, retreating or deserting rather than fighting through.

It went without saying that she acted with more resolve than these summer soldiers of the movement.[50]

Blossom responded with personal insults that stung a woman who depended on hard work as the motive of her life: "While you were taking it easy at home and going out to dinner parties and the theater, your admirers were slaving day and night."[51] And when he refused to give her the accounts and subscription lists, pointing out that he was busy campaigning for Morris Hillquit's mayoral campaign, she hired the ever-faithful Jonah Goldstein to file criminal charges against Blossom with the district attorney's office. Later she unceremoniously dropped them, but turning to the courts revealed the critical nature of this high-stakes struggle. In retaliation, given his control of the NYBCL, Blossom orchestrated Sanger's expulsion from the league, telling a reporter that she had been ousted for her outrageous action of turning to the judicial system.

Blossom further escalated the battle by stealing files, furniture, checks, business records, and subscription lists from the office, dismissing Sanger's demands to return them for the good of the movement: "For you to maintain that I owe anything to your movement is amusing. My social philosophy emphasizes much less than yours what we owe to ourselves as compared to what we owe to humanity."[52] Left in the office with a telephone on a soapbox, Sanger demonstrated her survival instincts: "It was a challenge. We hurried over to Third Avenue and for twenty dollars refurnished the office."[53] Hours later she and an associate were working on the layout for the June issue.

In 1918 she hired her first secretary—seventeen-year-old Anna Lifschiz, who like so many of Sanger's employees and associates (but not equals) promptly fell under the spell of Margaret Sanger and happily worked long hours for twelve dollars a week. As Lifschiz described: "It was like a religious crusade. The office was bedlam, volunteers rushing in and out—perfect strangers just dropping in and sitting. Through it all she moved, serenely, confidently, giving us all some added strength that would make us work 13 hours that day when we were sure we could last only 10."[54]

Sanger worked harder than her staff, later assessing this period of routinized labor as one that, even during the war, helped to change American attitudes about contraception. Every day, along with her writing and management of the *Review*, she "dictated hundreds of letters, interviewed dozens of people, debated, lectured—all in twenty-four hours. Day after day I attended parlor meetings, night after night open forums, returning home too tired to eat, too excited to sleep. Frequently at seven in the morning the telephone started ringing."[55] During the war Americans were beginning to awaken to the logic of birth control for women, but Sanger was pushing them to do so.

Such gains were transparent, as Sanger proclaimed a "year of victory." What she celebrated for a movement that gained most of its success in the courts, not the legislatures, was a judicial victory. After her imprisonment Sanger had insisted on appealing her conviction, and she and Goldstein had worked together fashioning the grounds for such a review. Moving beyond the familiar, often rejected appeal to First Amendment rights, in a harbinger of the future, their unique arguments to the New York Court of Appeals and later to the U.S. Supreme Court claimed that the denial of birth control information unconstitutionally forced "conception on every married woman," thereby contravening her personal liberty and violating her private conscience. The state did not coerce women into marriage: hence it was a denial of due process and equal justice under the Fourteenth Amendment to force motherhood on women by denying birth control information. Dismissing the appeal in a short paragraph, the Supreme Court confined its comments to the point that legislatures, not the courts, must provide the remedy.

But Judge Frederick Crane of the New York Court of Appeals had added a surprising obiter dictum: relying on the New York Penal Code that gave physicians the right to cure and prevent disease (and here Crane broadly defined disease and illness using *Webster's Dictionary*), doctors were excepted from the Comstock laws. For years without harassment, physicians had treated male venereal disease, often suggesting contraception in the form of condoms. Now with the doctors' exception affirmed by the court, physicians could diagnose gynecological and even nervous conditions among women and prescribe birth control. Yet as Crane pointed out, Sanger was a nurse, not a physician. Therefore she had no right to do so; her clinic violated New York's obscenity laws; she was guilty as charged, and her conviction was upheld.[56]

Technically Sanger had no legal standing to raise the issue, but Crane overlooked this. Either because of his judicial error or as an indication of the quiet gains of birth control, Crane had given all doctors in New York the right to prescribe birth control to any woman they deemed ill or diseased. It was indeed a gain to be celebrated in the *Review*, though it was a paper victory that came at a time when few doctors were receptive to female birth control. It also made Sanger's categorical assertions that all women were denied legal access to contraception incorrect, for this was no longer true in New York State. The Crane decision came as well with the price of giving doctors control of female contraception, though Sanger later fought for the inclusion of midwives and nurses. Still, with a doctor supplying contraceptive information, she could open another clinic, and that intention became part of the next phase of her crusade.

In 1920, after three years of hard work on *The Birth Control Review*, Sanger left for England. She worried about her resolve during a time when the movement was stagnant: "I am more than ever decided one must rule and direct one's life—drifting can not be the way and yet we wait and drift, waiting for that great force of necessity to force us into the currents of activity before we decide to act."[57] As it had done in the past, a journey might revive her spirits, even in a country still recovering from World War I. Again she must learn at the feet of Havelock Ellis and the intellectuals who had embraced her earlier. Removed from the constant work of the magazine and her other commitments, she also could plan a postwar conference on birth control. Perhaps, as well, she could gain some relief from her chronically infected thyroid gland and tubercular neck nodes.

7

VOYAGES

Never be ashamed of passion. If you are strongly sexed, you are richly endowed.
—Margaret Sanger, *Happiness in Marriage*

In the spring of 1920 Margaret Sanger boarded the luxurious White Star Line passenger ship the *Olympic*, bound for Southampton with its distinguishing four stacks and boasting, in calm seas, a cruising speed of twenty-six knots. After leaving *The Birth Control Review* in the hands of Juliet Rublee and several trusted lieutenants, Sanger was gone from the United States for seven months. In the next five years she returned to England four times, ending her trip around the world there. For these travels she had moved beyond the cheap tramp steamers that had served as troop carriers and hospital ships during World War I. They had taken her to England with Bill and the children in 1913 and then again in 1914 when, alone, she fled from U.S. authorities. In the 1920s, voyages across the Atlantic on newly refitted passenger ships were becoming commonplace and fashionable. With the help of friends and the money she earned as a lecturer and writer, Sanger usually traveled first-class, savoring for seven days the isolation, the fresh air, and, sometimes, the dancing at night.

During this period of her life, England became more than just a convenient travel destination and the location of conferences on neo-Malthusian eugenics. Rather, it was a sanctuary for the soul, away from the incessant demands of running a movement whose goal remained against the law and whose tools to achieve that goal were ancient, though Sanger, concentrating on making birth control legal, did not overlook the search for an effective contraceptive. Still suffering from the intermittent fevers and cough caused by tubercular tonsils draining into the nodes in her neck, she hoped for better health. In these early days of the British recovery from World War I—a time when English poets mourned the nation's youthful dead, food shortages complicated daily living, and Liberals and Tories glimpsed a future Bolshevik revolution in every labor strike, Sanger found what she craved and could not find in the United States—leisure and the intellectual companionship of those who admired her and accepted her cause. She also enthralled three English lovers, as she continued to practice her own libidinous version of "sex expression." Now in her forties, Sanger was still, as Billy Williams knew, "a woman born to be loved."[1] And to retain that status, she had begun subtracting five years from her age.

Never content to be completely idle in a growing tension between obligations to the movement and a desire, as she aged, for personal relaxation and a more normal life—Havelock Ellis once said she used up "at once" the benefits of a vacation—Sanger lectured, mostly in London to working women. In Glasgow she spoke to a mixed audience of women and male boatyard workers, the latter surprised when their stay-at-home wives came to listen to her discussion of birth control. Sanger was never comfortable with the restrained British audiences, who seemed apathetic compared to her more responsive American ones. Forever searching for an accessible, efficient contraceptive method, when she heard of a powerful spermicide developed in Germany, she spent ten days tracking down a commercial operation whose owner refused to divulge his formula and instead referred her to his secret laboratory in New York. Sanger also began work on what she dubbed her "mind" book, *The Pivot of Civilization*, which she described as "a little highbrow and [without] the woman urge of the other books," by which she meant it was more impersonal and less emotional.[2] Earlier she had published her bestselling "heart" book, *Woman and the New Race*, written during her stay in California in 1919.

Though the successes of the Higgins children hardly sustained her position on the dystopic tendencies of large families, she dedicated *Woman and the New Race*, with its tepid introduction by Havelock Ellis, to "the memory of my mother who gave birth to eleven living children." Propelled partly by her celebrity and partly by the popularity of eugenics, it sold two hundred thousand copies in one year. In England Sanger added two chapters, removed a discussion of "foreigners who have come in hordes" to the United States, and provided a different title—*The New Motherhood*. She predicted, inaccurately, that she would never write again. "I am too uncertain of my technique, having never been trained to write."[3] But a lack of training had never stopped her before.

In both books, motherhood, "the most important profession in the world," was a central theme. Childbearing emerged as a natural role, though with the caveat that women must never submerge themselves entirely in maternity. Such attention irritated modern feminists who might have embraced Sanger as a hero. Still, as they did, Sanger despised the fraudulent sentimentalized worship of motherhood that "closed its eyes to the appalling waste of human life and human energy resulting from the consequences of leaving the whole problem of child-bearing to chance and blind instinct."[4] But abstinent women, adopting the only certain method of contraception, drove husbands to prostitutes. In her version of a postabstinence, postabortion, and postinfanticide universe based on birth control, mothers would be free to choose the timing and the number of their children. From women, then, would come a new race, created by enlightened maternity.

Both *The Pivot of Civilization* and *Woman and the New Race*, which together sold 567,000 copies in five years, emphasized woman's complicity— "her error and debt"—in producing the glut of inferior children who now threatened society.[5] "Woman through her reproductive ability founded and perpetuated the tyrannies of the Earth," though such behavior was unconscious, having been imposed by the church and the state, conspiring to keep women powerless and sexually ignorant. Introduced to the work of the iconoclastic English poet William Blake by her intellectual friends, Sanger quoted his verses on Catholic repression: "Priests, in black gowns, will be walking their rounds / And binding with briars our joys and desires."[6]

Just as political revolutionaries fought their struggles with guns, butter, and propaganda, so now in the glow of a postwar age, women must rebel by using their weapon of controlled fertility. With contraception accessible, they would become "the pivot of civilization" and create a "new race." By the latter term she referred to society and humankind, not biologically inclusive groups, as we mean today. In Sanger's feminist eugenics, the creators of this "new race" were women who rejected the traditional position that as mothers they must be "slaves to reproduction."

Large families were "the most serious evil of our times." In mandates repeated from her earlier writings and lectures, women must not have children until they were at least twenty-three, though it was better to wait until twenty-five; they must space their babies; they must have no more children if one child was born mentally or physically defective; and they must have no children at all if either parent suffered from gonorrhea, syphilis, cancer, epilepsy, insanity, drunkenness, or tuberculosis, the latter viewed by this generation as an inheritable disease and by Sanger as "a grave danger to both mother and child."[7] And of course, they must be able to afford their children. In her early years Sanger had broken two of these injunctions, but by this time she knew herself to be exempt from rules. At a time when self-proclaimed experts on how to raise children were offering advice on "mothercraft" in popular magazines and books, Sanger never considered the specifics of effective mothering.

In these two postwar books, her message remained consistent and repetitive: "The basic freedom of the world is woman's freedom," wrote Sanger in stirring feminist sentences that revealed her shifting priorities from an emphasis on class antagonism (rich women had birth control; poor women had babies) to a focus on all women. She had not abandoned the working class by offering a radical program of sexual liberation through contraception. "No woman can call herself free until she can choose consciously whether she will or will not be a mother . . . Birth control will break women's bonds and will enable her to develop her love nature separate from and independent of her maternal nature." The eugenic solution was obvious: "Free women refuse to bring forth weaklings, refuse to bring forth slaves, refuse to bear children who live in poverty."[8]

In *The Pivot of Civilization*, with its introduction by the famous English writer H. G. Wells, she embraced eugenics as a female cause with a female solution, repeating her utopian correctives that women "must prevent the birth of the weak and helpless and unwanted children of the world."[9] For Sanger one purpose of her movement was to oppose institutional obstacles to responsible parenthood. If nothing was done, Americans would be "faced with the ever increasing problem of the feeble-minded."[10] Yet these unfit were never a specific race or religion, only genetic or behavioral unfortunates, though she believed, as did most Americans, that feeble-minded parents produced children who, in future generations such as the storied Kallikaks, produced ever-spiraling numbers of the diseased, the insane, and the criminal.

A veteran of many free speech battles, Sanger acknowledged the dangers of interfering with personal liberty to achieve these goals, and she rejected the right of "the community . . . to send to the lethal chamber the defective progeny resulting from irresponsible and unintelligent breeding."[11] Yet, following contemporary opinion, she approved of the segregation during their reproductive years, presumably in institutions, of feeble-minded "girls [and boys] of the hereditary class especially of the moron class," and she supported, but did not specify, the circumstances requiring, "emergency" sterilizations. But such interventions must never deprive human beings of "their sex expression" through castration, a point of difference with mainstream eugenicists who cared nothing about maintaining erotic feelings.

Earlier, Sanger had accepted the socialist definition of class as an economic category; now she described a multitiered society based on birth control—those, mostly the wealthy, who had private doctors, practiced contraception, and had small families; another group who wanted birth control but had no legal access to it; the uneducated who needed clinics; and, finally, the reckless and unfit who, if they did not stop reproducing, must be disciplined to do so. "Social classes should be synonymous with biological classes, with each individual rising to the level for which he is fitted by the quality of his tissues and his soul," thereby achieving a nation of spiritual and cellular Horatio Algers, some of whom had risen, as she had, above their heritage.[12] In her evaluation of the three contemporary reform movements designed to prevent the catastrophes she anticipated in a postwar society without birth control—philanthropy, socialism, and eugenics—she found the last the most valuable "in its critical and diagnostic aspects and in emphasizing the danger of irresponsible and uncontrolled fertility of the unfit and feebleminded."[13]

In neither *The Pivot of Civilization* nor *The New Race* did Sanger accept the standard eugenic proposition that heredity was absolute. "Environment and heredity are not antagonistic," she concluded. "Our problem is not that of 'Nature vs. Nurture,' but rather of Nature x Nurture, of heredity multiplied by environment."[14] Sanger never made clear what the precise relationship was, just as she never unraveled the contradiction between the freedom of an individual woman who might want a large family and the collective authority of a society controlling fertility. Nor did she address the fact that some women, even with available birth control, would not use it. But she believed that eugenicists who overlooked the importance of the environment as a factor in human development were as shortsighted as socialists who neglected the biological nature of man. And she presented contraception as a complete solution to this philosophical conundrum: "The great principle of Birth Control offers the means whereby the individual may adapt himself to and even control the forces of environment and heredity."[15]

Despite the popularity of her books and the similarity of her ideas with theirs, eugenicists dismissed Sanger, disliking what they termed her notoriety and the means by which she had obtained it. Some, such as the biologist Charles Davenport, believed her a "charming woman" with a serious purpose. "I have no doubt that she may feel very strongly about eugenics. I have very grave doubt that she has any clear idea what eugenics is . . . The whole birth control movement is a quagmire out of which eugenics should keep," wrote the head of the Cold Spring Harbor Laboratory, where researchers were discovering what they were looking for: family patterns of inherited pathology. Paul Popenoe, currently engaged in a campaign to ban the marriage of the blind, was even more disparaging: "If it is desirable for us to make a campaign for contraception we are abundantly able to do so, without enrolling a lot of sob sisters, grandstand players, and anarchists to help us."[16]

Sanger continued to reject the popular position on class suicide that Yankee stock must produce more children to achieve "race regeneration." There was never a woman in any circumstance who, from Sanger's perspective, would not benefit from the use of contraception and the conscious planning of her pregnancies. Sanger avoided the problem of infertility until years later, when, against her wishes, her associates in the Margaret Sanger Research Bureau began counseling couples with problems conceiving. These Americans had learned from Sanger's challenge to sex-as-reproduction the possibilities for human intervention in a process that earlier generations left to nature and God. Such a new understanding brought them to her clinic.

Never an orthodox eugenicist, originally she titled one of the chapters in *The Pivot of Civilization* "The Limitations of Eugenics." In the final version she deleted it, but the American Eugenics Society, aware of her rejection of race suicide and unwilling to accept birth control, refused to publish her submissions to their journals or accept her papers for delivery at their conferences. Still, she was optimistic: "I never had greater confidence in the work than now," she wrote to Juliet Rublee in 1921. "It [birth control] is absolutely the only issue which is alive which is fundamental & which can save civilization from the wreck which charities & other weak & sentimental agencies have made of society."[17]

Sanger heralded science as an ally, even if its experts did not reciprocate. Prominent authorities with doctorates in biology and zoology (in Popenoe's case, an honorary one) commanded her respect because they might provide better methods of contraception. She also had discovered an emerging discipline in her explorations of possible new technologies: "A whole literature has sprung into being around the glands . . . which form a unity which might be termed the generative."[18] Sanger referred to hormones, whose powerful effect on reproduction and sex organs was gaining the attention of researchers in the field of reproductive endocrinology. By 1920 George Papanicolaou of Cornell University was using vaginal smears to study the estrus cycle, while a professor of zoology at the University of Chicago, Frank Lillie, concluded that sex differentiation depended on blood-borne hormones. At the Johns Hopkins University, George Corner had isolated the compound progesterone and was experimenting on its effect on the menstrual cycle of monkeys. But financial support came grudgingly to these researchers in reproductive science, a field that lagged behind the study of other major organ systems.

Never given to flowery or even evocative language in her hastily written, often dictated books, Sanger concluded *The Pivot of Civilization* with one of her favorite metaphors—the need for women to weed and recultivate "the human garden and end the ill-concealed warfare between men and women."[19] Ever practical, she closed the book with an appendix advertising her new organization, the American Birth Control League.

During the 1920s Margaret Sanger not only wrote about a future society; she lived a new life of international travel amid a circle of admiring friends. She discovered an English surgeon who removed the diseased tonsils full of the tubercular bacteria that for years had been draining into her lymph nodes and causing her intermittent fevers, though the surgery did not end her health problems. Throughout her life Sanger continued to suffer from challenging ailments that might have ended her career. But at least by 1922 she had conquered the Higgins legacy of tuberculosis.

In 1920, on her first postwar visit to England, Havelock Ellis introduced her to the handsome, Oxford-educated Hugh de Selincourt, an aspiring novelist drawn to sexual matters in his novels. *One Little Boy* featured society's cruel punishment of a schoolboy's innocent masturbation; another novel focused on a love triangle. Later, de Selincourt sent Sanger his long, floridly written manuscripts with their ever-changing titles but persistently salacious subject matter, hoping that she might find a publisher in the United States. A loyal friend, she tried, but was mostly unsuccessful. De Selincourt and his wife, Janet, a former concert pianist, lived in the Wantley estate in Sussex, where, over a hundred years before, the poet Percy Bysshe Shelley, a champion of radical ideas and unorthodox sexual arrangements, had been born. There, in a classic English manor house with hand-hewn beams in the living room and recessed tessellated windows, on grounds with majestic oaks and elms, the de Selincourts lived a seemingly idyllic life, though there was never enough money. They read poetry, discussed politics and philosophy with weekend guests, and raised their daughter, Bridget. When de Selincourt's novels brought in little income and his wife's inheritance proved insufficient, the family reluctantly moved to a smaller, though similarly attractive, rustic country home in Sussex.

Supporters of open marriage, these English bohemians practiced their conviction that those who loved the same person loved each other. They quoted Shelley that "life and love are one," and after his wife played the piano and his daughter the violin—Chopin and Brahms were favorites—de Selincourt would recite Shelley's epic poem *The Sensitive Plant*, with special emphasis on its sentimental credo: "For love and beauty and delight / There is no death nor change." Influenced by the sensual lifestyles of the Romantic poets as well as their own times and personalities, they had come to understand that the highest form of love was sexual, and so the lover of one's lover was an appropriate sex partner.

Janet de Selincourt's lover Harold Child lived in Wantley and helped pay the rent. Soon Sanger had become de Selincourt's lover, he apparently an especially adroit one with his ability to practice Karezza—the method of rapturous sustained erection and eventual male orgasm achieved without ejaculation that she had written about in her prewar pamphlets. He was, she once wrote, the man of her adolescent dreams whom, previously, she had never found outside of novels. At first surprised by her time-consuming commitments to the birth control movement, de Selincourt came to understand that the reality of a love affair with Margaret Sanger meant "snatched moments and the hustle of departure." Still, that did not make it "less delightful to take off your darling shoes (AND pull the stockings down from the toes!) and make me want any less to hold you in my arms."

He might complain about her devotion to a cause that took her away from him, even as she was encouraging him to write a book about birth control. But like her other lovers, he adored Sanger for her ineffable mix of gaiety and seriousness, her femininity and high purpose, the latter usually associated with men. De Selincourt appreciated her "freedom from the self-importance which women acquired as the result of a little notoriety," and he understood more than most men that "your lovers will serve you more usefully than your useful acquaintances, however practical or named or successful they may be."[20]

The Wantley Circle created not sexual triangles, but rather a revolving interlocking circle of intimacies. De Selincourt slept not just with Margaret but with Françoise Cyon, Havelock Ellis's partner, making the great sexual libertarian jealous. Sanger had sex with both de Selincourt and with Janet's lover Harold Child. Child, a poet and drama critic for the *Times Literary Supplement*, extended himself in letters of adoration that Sanger kept throughout her life: "You have the eyes and brow of a saint—your eyes very far apart and so quietly, unaggressively, immorally brave and candid and simple with the simplicity of a spirit . . . A saint's face, a lover's face, a child's face."[21] To him she was both Aphrodite and Athena. Occasionally, as Sanger wrote to Juliet Rublee, "things became so complicated that I had to fly away from everybody."[22]

Over time sexual civility proved difficult, even for these believers in free love. Some of the circle, such as Ellis, chafed at these casual affairs. Janet de Selincourt later apologized to Sanger for her "jealous rebelliousness . . . it wasn't his [Child's] having found you & and your love that hurt, but that I had lost someone else to whom I have gone out in the same way."[23] When in the summer of 1920, Havelock and Margaret traveled to Ireland together, searching unsuccessfully for the graves of Sanger's dead relatives during the brutal conflict between British troops and Irish patriots, their liaison made Cyon uncomfortable. Sanger, still an intellectual admirer of the sixty-one-year-old Ellis, had begun placing the aging sexologist in that category of men with waning vitality. "They all want to be with women who stimulate them & give them pep & energy."[24]

Although never a member of the Wantley Circle, H. G. Wells, introduced to Sanger through her Neo-Malthusian and Fabian Society contacts, soon had fallen to the charms of this unusual American woman. Earlier, the celebrated Wells, at work on his bestselling *Outline of History*, had been among the first of the English intellectuals to sign the 1915 letter to President Wilson condemning the censorship of birth control and Sanger's threatened imprisonment. Married to the faithful, accommodating Catherine, Wells was, like Sanger, a sexual voyager, and he welcomed her into "the secret places of the heart" (the title of his 1922 novel). In fact, the attractive, adventurous American character of Miss Grammont, described as "having an air of having in some way graduated in life" and who "wanted love as a man does," was based on Sanger.[25] By October 1920, Wells was smitten: "May I come and stay the night . . . I really want to see you. I am rather inclined to bite through chains because you are not coming today. Please, H.G." "Wonderful, Unforgettable," Wells cryptically acknowledged another encounter in a relationship that continued for nearly three decades.[26] Thereafter Sanger invited the English author to speak at her conferences and write articles for *The Birth Control Review*, even as she characterized the world-famous author as a "naughty little boy man."[27]

In these lascivious English circles Sanger discovered affection in what she called "the house of childhood," something that a deprived refugee from hardscrabble Corning had never enjoyed. "I felt young & happy & did such a lot talking about my children . . . I am happy & grateful to know you," she wrote to de Selincourt.[28] And she also discovered a thriving community of English spiritualists who helped her communicate with the never forgotten Peggy, who came and talked to her mother, once lamenting that she could not speak loud enough to be heard. Eclectic in her taste for otherworldly contacts, Sanger employed Kabbalah, an esoteric form of the occult based on Hebrew scripture; Sanger also believed it had Irish roots.

On her visit to Ireland she searched for her grave from a previous life. "You remember," she explained to Juliet Rublee, "that my quabal [a form of medium] said I was Queen Scotia. Well, there was such a person, the daughter of Pharoa supposed to be long before history began."[29]

Sanger believed Englishmen to be better lovers than Americans, but the most important man in her life during the early 1920s, and the one who might provide a different life if she would marry him, was a South African–born, naturalized American millionaire who ran the successful Three-in-One Oil Company. J. Noah Slee had reorganized the marketing system for a company whose formula of oil and rustproof solvents had first been used in the 1890s on bicycles. By the 1920s most households in America had a small oil can, popular in this increasingly mechanical age, for everything from sewing machines to vacuum cleaners, squeaky doors, and even automobiles. By 1920 J. Noah Slee was worth $9 million.

Sanger and Slee met in New York at one of Juliet Rublee's fashionable dinner parties. By 1921, when Sanger was officially divorced, Slee was in the process of divorcing his socialite wife. For purposes of propriety, though she knew better, Sanger claimed he was a widower. Like so many men, Slee had immediately fallen for Sanger, initiating an international courtship during these years of her frequent travels. But she was uncertain, describing to de Selincourt: "For some strange reason two very fine men have been thrust my way. One a millionaire and sixty—terribly American type of respectable business man, church going widower generous—happy—thinks I'm sensible . . . He could with his wealth make life very comfortable & insure the financial success of my cause. Shall I accept him?"[30] Juliet thought it a bad match, and so initially did Sanger: "Mr. [Slee] has not money enough to pay the price—He could not inspire me to love—[and if I marry] it would be for love or money . . . Freedom is too lovely & I want to enjoy it for a time," she advised Rublee during the summer of 1921 when, newly divorced, she had traveled again to England, this time to find a keynote speaker for one of her conferences.[31]

In his sixties, Slee seemed too old for a forty-two-year-old whose subtraction of five years placed her in her late thirties. Even the psychics urged caution. The couple were too different in interests and temperament; neither their stars nor lifelines aligned. Sanger was too independent and headstrong, Slee too brusque and set in his ways. Havelock Ellis, with proper irony, informed Sanger that Slee was a nice man and deserved a more suitable wife. Hugh de Selincourt sent his congratulations but wondered if she would like a husband who was a good churchman, "while if I was the good churchman, I should be rather nervous about marrying the Woman Rebel."[32]

In 1920 Sanger was invited by a postwar Japanese society, the Kaizo Reconstructionists, to lecture in Tokyo on birth control. Anxious for exposure to new ideas, the reform group had already hosted a stunning array of Western thinkers who spoke on contemporary issues—Bertrand Russell, Albert Einstein, and H. G. Wells. If she went, it would be an impressive accomplishment for a woman often treated as a pariah in the United States. Leading an international movement now emerged, in Sanger's mind, as an ambitious possibility. Yet such a long trip would remove her from the conferences and organizations that were becoming the nexus of birth control activities. And she would have to leave *The Birth Control Review* for at least four months. On the other hand she could renew her friendship with the extraordinary Baroness Shidzue Ishimoto, who had come to the United States with her Japanese husband in 1919, studied English at the YMCA, and become friends with Sanger. As an added benefit, the trip would remove her from the repressive political atmosphere at home.

During the 1920s progressive movements of every persuasion in the United States were eroding. Warren Harding had been elected president in

1920 on the platform that America needed "not heroics but healing, not nostrums but normalcy." Former progressives, intent before the war on improving the nation's cities and political structures, had disappeared. Suffragists had accomplished their goal and retired to domesticity, although the indomitable Alice Paul of the National Woman's Party was an exception. Paul had already written an amendment guaranteeing equal rights for women, but as late as 1927, in a rebuke Sanger never forgot, the NWP refused to support a resolution favoring birth control. Like many activists, Paul watched her followers, including those who had shared jail cells with her, dwindle away. Mary Ware Dennett's National Birth Control League had disappeared, and her new Voluntary Parenthood League, directed at lobbying Congress, was losing members. Few Americans had enthusiasm for organized reform, much less what they considered the kind of drastic transformations that Sanger proposed.

The repressive wartime spirit still hung in the air. The leaders of the Wobblies had been arrested for obstructing the draft and sentenced to long terms in Leavenworth. The government deported 249 suspected Communists and anarchists, including Emma Goldman in the so-called Soviet Ark, the *Buford*. Anarchists responded with homemade bombs sent through the mails to, among others, Attorney General A. Mitchell Palmer. The political climate only intensified opposition to the waves of immigrants, many of them Jews from Poland and southeastern Europe. In 1921 the Sixty-seventh Congress, disposed to eugenicism and its corollary of nativism, passed the first of two National Origins Acts, the first allocating immigration quotas according to criteria of superior and inferior nationalities, the so-called lighter-skinned Nordics favored over the darker Mediterraneans. In 1924, a second immigration law, using the same standards for preferred groups, was even more restrictive. According to a Department of Labor official, "Lawmakers were deeply concerned as to the fundamental racial character of the constantly increasing number who came."[33] The concept of race regeneration, begun innocently in the laboratories of biologists, promoted by politicians such as Theodore Roosevelt, and inserted into Sanger's birth control agenda, had found its way into public policy.

In this dispiriting environment of the 1920s, Sanger contemplated the possibility of a global voyage and hesitated, balancing the importance of her presence in the United States against an Asian adventure and the international expansion of birth control. In New York she continued to manage *The Birth Control Review*, and she briefly lobbied for the repeal of New York's obscenity laws. In the third prong of her campaign of activism, education, organization, and legislation, she was beginning the necessary groundwork for institutionalizing birth control with the formation of an association of national scope and authority, a central clearinghouse of research and information to be called the American Birth Control League (ABCL).

Sanger rejected the pleas of her competitor Mary Ware Dennett to join forces. "The time is ripe," Dennett had written to Sanger when she heard rumors about a new league, "for . . . a great joining of forces instead of splitting them by forming still another organization. There will surely be greater strength in every phase of this work if resources are pooled instead of dissipating the energies of the movement by the formation of another national league."[34]

What Margaret Sanger did for the movement, she did alone as birth control's paramount leader and, after 1921, as the director of its most influential organization, the ABCL. There was no room for Dennett. Besides, as Sanger anticipated, Dennett's projects, whether her recent embrace of the idea of birth control clinics or her proposals to overturn the Comstock laws, never materialized. Dennett's appeals to the influential New York Academy of Medicine had only strengthened the opposition of most doctors. Nor did Sanger accept Dennett's argument that the repeal of the national Comstock laws would necessarily mean the end of those in most states. Instead, Sanger initiated her own strategy—a conference, the first ever on birth control in the United States, which, in turn, would spawn the national organization that became her next project.

Sanger also sparred with an earlier friend, Marie Stopes. As a "memorial" to her happier second marriage, Stopes had opened a birth control clinic in London, and now proclaimed it the first such facility in the world. Drawn into the antagonism between Dennett and Sanger, Stopes revealed Sanger's confidence about Dennett as "outside the pale of honesty and decency."[35] When Stopes, firmly in the Dennett camp, came to New York and gave a speech at Town Hall attended by an audience of a thousand, Sanger sent flowers but refused any personal meeting. "You have deeply wounded me," wrote Stopes, recalling their friendship in England in earlier days. Sanger responded that Stopes had violated a confidence and, worse, had taken sides: "Your public declaration in support of the Voluntary Parenthood League's activities places you in my estimation for all time outside the scope of disinterested, international adherents to the cause of birth control . . . you rushed into a partisan support of a group who have constantly denied the use of the very words 'birth control' and have done a great deal in bringing about controversies and disintegration to the cause."[36]

Dennett had already begun a campaign to undermine Sanger, ridiculing her "English, her facts, and her amazing faculty for being the whole 'moomunt,'" even her red dresses. John Haynes Holmes, the Unitarian minister at New York's Community Church, a fervent supporter of birth control and a member of both competing groups, chided Dennett for her petty attacks on Sanger. Explained Holmes, "I have no doubts that [Sanger] has her faults like the rest of us. It still remains true, however, that she is the outstanding champion of the birth control movement not only in our country but in the world, that she has given the cause an intelligence, devotion and a capacity of leadership which put her in the company of the outstanding reformers of all time and that she deservedly challenges the admiration and support of all right-minded people. I am not interested in personal complaints and criticisms of this woman . . . I believe in her and shall be drawn into no conflict against her."[37]

On November 11, 1921, over two hundred physicians, social workers, scientists of the eugenicist persuasion, and the new breed of population experts, along with Sanger's personal following, met in the ballroom of New York's Plaza Hotel. For months Sanger had solicited papers, encouraged her prominent English friends to attend, and raised money for the program. She had timed her meeting to overlap with that of the American Public Health Association, so that the latter's largely female membership of social workers, still suspicious of birth control, might attend her conference. An advocate of dramatic action, Sanger admitted to "a dread" of conferences for "their weaknesses and the stifling effect they could have. They seemed heavy and ponderous, rigid, lifeless, often caught in their own mechanism to become dead wood . . . [run by] rule-and-rote minds and weight-and-measure tactics."[38] Sanger intended hers to be different.

She organized the meeting by herself with the help of a few trusted lieutenants, dividing the sessions into topics such as population, war, maternal problems, health, and the legal aspects of birth control in the United States. It was labor-intensive work at which she excelled. First she recruited well-known experts: Dr. Adolphus Knopf, an authority on tuberculosis and New York clinics; Dr. Lothrop Stoddard, the well-known eugenicist author of *The Rising Tide of Color*; and Dr. Raymond Pearl, a statistician at the Johns Hopkins Medical School, who believed in the sterilization of some convicted criminals. All had been chosen for their national prestige; all had been picked so that she could use their names to enroll others. They delivered papers, after which there was discussion in a format followed by professional groups throughout the twentieth century. As expected, the most crowded session was a discussion of contraceptive techniques chaired by Sanger herself. To an overflow audience she held up for observation the Mensinga pessary. For years it remained Sanger's favorite form of birth control, though it was unavailable in the United States and needed to be fitted by a nurse or doctor. It safely covered the entire vaginal wall, whereas the French Mizpah, also made of black opaque rubber, in Sanger's explicit description to the audience did "not seem to fit so well over the cervix." Less practical, the mizpah also could "be pushed aside."[39]

Before the conference Sanger mailed out questionnaires to an ever-expanding number of contributors and subscribers to *The Birth Control Review*. From this nonrepresentative data she delivered one of the first large-scale statistical reports in the United States on the contraceptive methods employed by 1,250 American families during the previous year. Only about a quarter used either type of pessary, and as was often the case in surveys of contraception, the results were ambiguous because of overlapping practices. Some women douched before intercourse, others after, and some not at all. Others used spermicides on their pessaries but sometimes did not. Many couples employed a multiplicity of techniques, making comparisons difficult. Ten percent relied on coitus interruptus. The most surprising result, especially given the informed, nonrepresentative population surveyed, was the continuing dependence on the condom. Undaunted by the failure of American women to adopt what she saw as a choice that insured their sexual autonomy, the prophet of women's birth control acknowledged that many couples used condoms, now available in softer galvanized latex, an advance over previous centuries' animal intestines and the nineteenth century's stiff rubber.

Sanger's presentation led to spirited debate among the audience, as the persistent misgivings about female contraception surfaced even among these experts: Did it injure women and permanently prevent them from having children? Was it effective? Meanwhile, in the sessions on population, experts reported on the steady decline of fertility in a nation that still outlawed the dissemination of information about birth control and, in two states, even its use by married couples. Rarely disheartened, and then only privately, Sanger never responded to statistics that suggested the possible superfluousness of her crusade. Even without her, Americans were using contraception in order to limit the size of their families. But for Sanger that was never the point: her victory would come with a convenient, cheap, harmless, easily employed, legal means of contraception that women controlled.

Sanger planned a final public session for all delegates on the still contested issue of the morality of using birth control. Opponents, some even at her conference, continued to argue that birth control encouraged promiscuity among the unmarried and adultery among the married. In a strained though timely comparison, Sanger responded that birth control was no more "at fault than any other progressive or advanced idea of the modern day. Henry Ford's automobiles made transportation available for thousands of young people—morality or immorality as a consequence should not be placed at the door of Mr. Ford."[40] At this last session, Sanger intended to announce the formation of the ABCL, the organization that would coordinate birth control activities nationally, with Sanger presiding and its board of directors representing a who's who of American eugenicism.

The night before the final meeting, Sanger experienced one of the nightmares that since Peggy's death heralded a forthcoming crisis. In a possibly fabricated dream, she remembered trying to carry a small weeping baby up a hill, but she could never reach the top, always falling backward. Given this prognostication from her unconscious, she was not entirely surprised the next day when she and her English visitor, Harold Cox, arrived at Town Hall on West Forty-third Street to find the door barred by the police and the streets crowded outside with a restless full house inside. The police refused entrance to Sanger and Cox, who, unobserved in the melee, quickly slipped through the crowd under the barricades and into the auditorium. Sanger, accustomed to such harassment, sent an associate to call New York's Mayor Hylan for information about who had canceled the meeting. But police in the local station house knew nothing. Apparently the orders had come from division headquarters at the request of an official of New York's Catholic hierarchy—Monsignor Joseph Dineen, secretary to Catholic archbishop Patrick Hayes.

Once onstage, Sanger called out to the audience not to leave, and immediately she was carried off the platform and arrested by two of the more than one hundred police in attendance. Then Harold Cox rose to speak: "I come from across the Atlantic," he began, and was immediately dragged from the stage, proclaiming that such treatment would never take place in England. "The stage was in tumult," according to The New York Times. "Mrs. Sanger was in the storm center."[41] "The confusion and tumult continued for fully an hour. First one woman would attempt to speak," described Sanger. "She would be silenced by two or three policemen; then the crowd would boo, roar, hiss, shout, catcall," while the monsignor, in secular habit, watched from the back of the hall, "directing the police by a casual nod of the head or a whisper to a man who acted as a runner between him and the captain on the platform."[42]

Under arrest but accompanied by a crowd singing their ironic version of "My Country 'Tis of Thee," Sanger refused to ride in the police van. Instead, guided by her sense of theatrical drama, flanked by two policemen, she marched up Broadway to the station house on West Forty-seventh Street, where she was put into a patrol wagon, taken to night court, arraigned on the charge of disorderly conduct, and released until the next day, when the charges were suddenly dropped. Meanwhile, the press was reporting what Sanger already knew: the order to shut down the meeting had come from Archbishop Hayes. "Birth Control Raid Made by Police on Archbishops Order," headlined *The New York Times*. The *New York Tribune* described the breaking up of the meeting as "arbitrary and Prussian. If the police deny the right of assemblage to one group of citizens, what is to stop them from denying it to another group against which they or their advisors have a personal prejudice?"[43] The national press, no friend of "that Sanger woman" or of birth control in this controversial phase of its history, began to defend Sanger.

For many observers the Town Hall episode was memorable primarily as a violation of the First Amendment and an astonishing overreach by the Catholic Church. As Sanger later wrote, "Here was a ridiculous thing— the Catholic Church held such power in its hand that it could issue orders to the police, dissolve an important gathering of adult and intelligent men and women and . . . then not feel called upon to give any accounting."[44] Meanwhile, the arrest of Juliet Rublee provoked her prominent husband, George Rublee, who had served as President Wilson's advisor on trade issues, to consider suing the police for false arrest of his wife. Along with his law partners he demanded an investigation of the police, which continued for years with few results.

A week later, at the Park Theater, Sanger held her postponed session on birth control while a group of Paulist fathers protested outside. The headlines in the *New York American* read "Four Thousand Attempt to Batter Their Way into Birth Control Talk," but the meeting itself proceeded without police interference. As usual, repression had increased sympathetic interest. Cox delivered his prepared remarks on the morality of birth control; there was a reading from Henrik Ibsen's play *Ghosts* on the tragedy of venereal disease. Then Sanger presented her arguments for a new standard of morality. The use of birth control was responsible action, she said in a speech interrupted nine times by applause. Immorality rested with behavior based on the impulse of the moment and a careless disregard for the consequences of having children.

Archbishop Hayes never admitted his complicity in the Town Hall episode, but he did release a statement that the Catholic Church had "a public duty to protest against birth control." The church denied any censorship because its divine, infallible, unassailable mandate to guide matters of faith and morals for everyone prevailed. Besides, there were young children at the meeting, though it turned out that these were students from nearby Barnard College. Citing federal obscenity laws, Hayes proclaimed "the law of God and man, science, public policy, human experience are all condemnatory of birth control as preached by a few irresponsible individuals." And then gratuitously, and doubtless unaware that Sanger was the sixth child in a family of eleven, the archbishop described seventh children as exceptional, a familial placement most favored by nature, a point that the lives of Benjamin Franklin, Ignatius Loyola, and even Catherine of Siena demonstrated. "One of the reasons for the lack of genius in our day is that we are not getting to the end of families."[45]

A month later in his Christmas pastoral, the archbishop delivered another pronouncement on the matter: "Children troop down from Heaven because God wills it. He alone has the right to stay their coming. To take life after its inception is a horrible crime; but to prevent human life that the Creator is about to bring into being is satanic. In the first instance the body is killed while the soul lives on; in the latter not only a body but an immortal soul is denied existence in time and in eternity."[46] In Hayes's view the use of birth control was a more serious transgression against God than was abortion.

Sanger invited the archbishop to debate the issue and titled a chapter on the misery of the young in *The Pivot of Civilization*: "Children Troop Down from Heaven." Employing the sarcasm that often served as her best rhetorical weapon, she congratulated the church's advance in reproductive understanding. Finally the church had recognized the difference between abortion and contraception. But it was the assumption of Catholic power that drew most of her attention: Hayes knew no more about immorality than anyone else. He might legitimately speak to his flock, but he must never impose his assumptions on others and interfere with the principles of free expression in the American republic. "What he believes concerning the soul after life," wrote Sanger, "is based upon theory and he has a perfect right to that belief; but we, who are trying to better humanity fundamentally, believe that a healthy happy human race is more in keeping with the laws of God than disease, misery and poverty perpetuating itself generation after generation."[47]

In this controversy the Catholic Church had delivered a great gift to the leader of the American birth control movement. As a source of inspiration, the events at Town Hall took their place alongside other biographical tales in the advancing narrative of American birth control as written, directed, and lived by Margaret Sanger.

Three months later, accompanied by her fourteen-year-old-son, Grant, in his first pair of long pants, and her now ubiquitous suitor, J. Noah Slee, Sanger left San Francisco, bound for Japan by way of Hawaii. Despite her invitation from a group of journalists and reformers and the intervention of her friend the prominent baroness Shidzue Ishimoto, from a wealthy samurai family, the consulate refused to issue the necessary visa. But Sanger was a risk taker. Believing suppression created favorable attention, she embarked with no assurance that she could enter a country whose militarists wanted to increase the population, not restrict it.

On the long voyage across the Pacific Ocean she gave informal talks about birth control to the passengers on the *Taiyo Maru*, who included the Japanese delegation returning home from the Washington Naval Disarmament Conference. The Japanese had protested the humiliating three-fifths limitation on the number of capital ships assigned to their nation, in comparison to the number allotted to the United States and Great Britain. But they listened eagerly to Sanger in the evenings and were too polite to ask about American discrimination against Japanese in the recent Gentlemen's Agreement, which limited the migration of unskilled Japanese workers to the United States.

Once in Yokohama Harbor, Sanger was confined to the ship, as her prominent fellow travelers—the Admiral Tomosaburo Kato and Masanao Manihara, the ambassador to the United States—intervened on her behalf. To this challenge she reacted in customary fashion: "I felt the exhilarating flush that the prospect of a battle always starts in me."[48] After "a series of negotiations that made the [Washington] conference look like child's play," Sanger was granted permission to enter the country, but, by written agreement, she must not discuss birth control.[49] Customs also confiscated forty copies of *Family Limitation* from her trunk. During the next two weeks, she delivered thirteen addresses, mostly on war and population pressure, to an enthralled Japanese public made up of journalists, doctors, nurses, members of the YWCA, and other women.

She spoke of the dangers of uncontrolled fertility and its importance as a cause for reformers inhabiting a cramped island whose population had doubled in the last forty years. A personal sensation because of her sex and topic, she gave countless interviews, sometimes commenting on birth control. "It is very amazing the way interest in birth control has been aroused by my coming. Every paper in the country carried headlines and front page stories and editorials on the subject for a full week," she described to Juliet Rublee.[50] *The New York Times* reported that she had so shocked one Japanese translator that the young woman had fainted. But Sanger's friend Ishimoto later acknowledged that Sanger's speeches were easy to translate because she always gave the same speech.

Briefly Sanger visited Korea and China, lecturing at the University of Peking, in what was the first of four Asian trips during her lifetime. Then she continued by ship through the Indian Ocean, up the Suez Canal, ending in London, just in time for the Fifth International Neo-Malthusian Conference, where she was the first woman to chair a session. Throughout her journey around the world, Sanger was a curious, energetic traveler, despite episodes of dysentery and symptoms of her worsening gallbladder disease. More interested in prostitutes than monuments, health clinics than palaces, and silk factories with female workers than gardens, she was ever willing to look and listen. The benefits to the advancement of the birth control movement in Japan were uncertain, though her friend Ishimoto dated its beginnings from her inspiring visit. Now notorious beyond the United States, Sanger served everywhere as a coach, organizing the team, training its members, and delivering instructions about how to further the cause. Her name and her presence had become a rallying cry throughout the world.

At a rally in Carnegie Hall after she reached home, Sanger, despite her eugenicist leanings, denied any Orientalist convictions: "I did not go as a self-appointed prophet to reform the yellow race . . . I have never tried to shout the message of birth control into unwillingness." But she had learned that birth control was a world problem of international interest, though she urged patience: "No great historical movement can attain maturity in one generation." Complaining of the meddling Christian missionaries who complicated China's problems, she concluded with what she did so well: the vividly told story of the personal challenges and triumphs during her visit.[51]

Before she returned to the United States, on September 18, 1922, Margaret Sanger married J. Noah Slee in the district of St. Giles, Bloomsbury, London. Ever since the beginning of their courtship, she had resisted his romantic solicitations—the daily cables when she was overseas, the red roses in New York, the purchase of a silk kimono in Japan. But Slee had won her affection on their six-month trip with his sentimental generosity, his kindness to Grant, and his businesslike efficiency in what were often hazardous travel arrangements. Her staff in New York insisted that his reorganization of the finances of the *Review* and his purchase of a date stamper and a mechanical letter opener had made the difference. "He could be," Sanger informed the still dubious Juliet Rublee, "a good friend to us all. He needs a woman in his life and is generous and kind and wants to know more about life, it seems," the latter her suggestion that Slee was a sexual naif.[52] Though Sanger insisted that they would be "happy in spite of your money . . . if only we were living on my earnings," Slee offered a luxurious way of life to a woman who had struggled financially all her life. Perhaps even more important, he would support the passion that forever remained closest to her heart—the birth control movement.[53]

The couple kept the news of their wedding secret, only grudgingly revealing it to family, friends, and the national press. An angry Bill Sanger learned of the marriage from Sanger's father in 1923 and remarried two years later. Only in 1924 did reporters track down the rumors, and soon Americans were reading the drama of a poor woman from a factory town in upstate New York, who used to live in Greenwich Village, and her millionaire husband of conservative Republican politics and Episcopalian faith who had chased her around the globe. When questioned by reporters about the reasons for not announcing her marriage, Sanger replied that her private life was none of their business. In truth she was concerned about any scandal that might reflect on the cause of birth control, and she needed more time after her divorce (and his) to make a second marriage respectable. Slee had his own reasons to avoid publicity: he had only recently received a trumped-up, possibly purchased divorce in the French courts on the spurious grounds that his first wife had not accompanied him to Paris.

There were prenuptial conditions that Sanger imposed, though they had nothing to do with Slee's fortune and everything to do with her lifestyle. To assure the autonomy she recommended for all married women, she insisted on separate New York apartments, albeit adjoining, but with different entrances and keys, at their new residence on Gramercy Park. According to one of her early biographers, the couple telephoned and even wrote notes to each other to determine their evening plans. In this second marriage Sanger installed a far different model from the idealized companionate marriages of this generation, in which most wives, especially rich ones, delivered submissive, grateful domesticity to the husbands who supported them in style. Instead, Sanger intended no modifications in her birth control work, which required late hours at the office and long speaking trips as well as voyages overseas without her new husband. She continued to have affairs with other men, and, of course, she kept birth control's brand name of Margaret Sanger.

Throughout their twenty-year marriage, Sanger and Slee were unusual, often fractious partners, but never strange bedfellows, as Sanger became the instructor of a man whose first wife had suffered sex as a wifely duty. She taught him how to dance and flirt and take moonlit walks; he taught her how to keep financial records. Yet Slee had a keen interest and capacity for sex, and his letters to his beloved Margy (she could not be Peg to another husband) often included erotic references: "How I miss you at night," he wrote in 1923. "Good night my darling God-given adorable wife & sweetheart . . . I need you to clasp in my arms always, ever your lover husband."[54] Sanger responded in kind: "How I miss you at night. I awaken a dozen times to see where you are or feel you pull the cover over me—and then lie awake."[55] Of course Sanger also included tales of her travels, while Slee, his relationship with Sanger the great adventure of his life, wished she spent more time at home and exhaustively discussed what he ate, once describing in stupefying detail his meal of onion soup, fried chicken, and cake with whipped cream followed by a bottle of Chianti that cost only $2.50, though during Prohibition his bootlegger usually charged $3.00.

The overt tensions in their relationship arose from her constant travels. "My very adorable wife," he wrote in 1923, "Come home soon please."[56] Though she would never be home as much as Noah demanded, in the early days of their marriage Sanger responded affectionately to the man she called the treasurer of her heart: "Sweetheart mine . . . I love you adorable Noah &

I should not be away from you & then we would never have these horrid dis-
agreeable questions coming between us."[57] Occasionally Sanger made promises she never kept: to retire with Noah to the "garden of paradise" if he just
agreed to one more long trip or supported one more birth control initiative.

Sanger's niece Olive Byrne Richards recalled a lovestruck Slee, years
after their marriage, abruptly remarking after his wife entered the room:
"Did you ever see anyone so beautiful?"[58] There were limits to the adoration, however. In 1924, after Sanger had traveled to London without him
for a three-month visit, Slee warned that he might do "something foolish."
Sanger countered with her version of the double standard, for she had not
ended her affairs with her English lovers, Wells, de Selincourt, and Child:
"Surely you would not go with some other woman without love and respect!
Is it possible that your love for me is only a satisfying physical passion? To
believe that would kill me!" She closed by declaring that her love for her
husband was "so wholly & fully part of me no other man could satisfy me"
and promised to come home soon.[59]

Slee kept his promise about providing financial support for the movement. For years he was the principal benefactor of the ABCL, and after his
wife appointed him treasurer, he offered unsolicited advice about how to
manage the office. He made up the annual deficits of *The Birth Control
Review*, which usually ran to over a thousand dollars, and in five years spent
nearly sixty thousand dollars on birth control activities. When his wife hired
Dr. James Cooper to travel throughout the United States educating doctors
about contraception, Slee paid his ten thousand dollars in salary and
expenses. When his wife needed money for the publication of the proceedings of various conferences, Slee paid the printing expenses. A communicant
of a conservative Episcopalian church in New York, Slee even risked jail by
smuggling Mensinga diaphragms manufactured in Germany into Canada.
There, the devices, in cartons labeled "Three-in-One Oil," were shipped
through customs to his factory in Rahway, New Jersey, and from there to
the clinic office in New York.

Estranged from his own three children after his divorce, Slee became
a loving, though intrusive, stepfather to the fatherless Stuart and Grant.
They called him Pater, and while he paid their college tuitions and even that
of Sanger's niece Olive Byrne, he gave them stingy, contested allowances.
Stepfathering is never easy family business, and Sanger acknowledged their
very different parenting styles. She delivered what she had always intended,

independence and autonomy for the boys under loose, even negligent maternal direction. Mothers equipped their children for the future by turning them loose, though as the boys became young men, she pondered the degree to which mothers "belong to their childhood past [and are] of no importance to their adult life."[60] In any case mothers must never give up their own freedom to become mere attendants to the young. "We radical parents must stand by our children when they give out what we have fed them in the past," she wrote to Ellis at a time when Stuart was spending too much time drinking bootleg whiskey.[61] Stricter and more traditional, Slee expected obedience to parental directives, of which she gave few and he many. Slee was also offended by the boys' noisy friends, took less delight than she in Stuart's making the Yale football team, and brooded about what he considered the boys' extravagance.

Shortly after their marriage and return to the United States, first class on the SS *Aquitania*, Noah Slee planned a grand wedding present for his wife: a new home near the town of Fishkill, along the Hudson, seventy miles from the city. The couple called it Willowlake, and at a cost of nearly $1 million, together Slee and Sanger supervised the building and interior decoration of a three-story country estate made of fieldstone, with a sloping slate roof. Reminiscent of English manor homes, it was set beside a man-made eight-acre lake with willow trees along the bank. Willowlake boasted fifteen rooms, including a master suite of two bedrooms with a fireplace. Like any proper English estate, there were boxwoods in the gardens and maple trees on the grounds that required full-time gardeners to tend over one hundred acres.

Sanger took pleasure in pursuits earlier denied. She oversaw the interior design, and ordered Chinese rugs, brass fittings for the fixtures, and peacock-blue and crimson-red fabrics for the expensive chairs and sofas in the vast living room. She commissioned a full-length portrait of herself wearing a diaphanous rose-colored gown to hang over the fireplace, and a smaller portrait of Noah for the library, where the french doors opened onto the gardens. There were stables, a tennis court, and lake swimming. To de Selincourt, she exulted when the house was finally finished in 1924, "Spring—good health—new house—furnishing it—a new Belgian police dog to be trained . . . besides writing the new book—I go to NY two days each week for BC. If only I could fly by night to London to see you & Havelock & Harold—I'd be ready to say this is paradise."[62]

De Selincourt dubbed Willowlake "Noah's Ark," and the estate became

Sanger's version of the national excesses of the 1920s. She entertained weekend guests, drank the champagne she had come to love, rode horseback with Noah, and welcomed the boys and their friends. She danced on the grass when the moon was full and invested her charm in dinner parties, where she starred. She built a small office in a treehouse, at the edge of a cliff overlooking the Hudson, where she began work on a new book, *Happiness in Marriage*. But Sanger also chafed under a self-imposed dilemma: Would Willowlake's charms and her husband's money tempt her from the expanding work of legalizing birth control, making it available through clinics, and finding better methods of contraception? And after eight long years of struggle did she want to be diverted?

Following the Town Hall episode but before her marriage, she had written to de Selincourt: "But oh Hugh the time it all takes sometimes I think I'll accept the nicest and richest man I know who wants me to marry him & leave all the miserable people to wallow in their misery & learn to fight for themselves." She could have "such a beautiful time," when the cause was won. There were moments when she longed to lie in the sun quietly with someone "nice, very nice, reading Shelley to me."[63] Fighting for birth control was a sacrifice. She had surrendered "home, a loving husband, children, reputation, friends, love, money" and gotten in return "insolent toleration . . . Your name is whispered and the ideal for which you work is mentioned in tones lower still." But there was also praise at the highest levels, from prime ministers and government officials who commended her "ideal & message" and believed that they were "changing the thought of the people of these countries more surely than Darwin changed the thought of the centuries . . . How can one tell the road to go?"[64] She pondered as well the challenges of life as Mrs. J. Noah Slee: "Are all the material things worth one year's bondage of the soul? Perhaps," she wrote to Juliet Rublee. "Just so one can free oneself from material desires & want soul freedom so desperately that it must be had at all costs & sacrifice."[65]

Amid these personal dilemmas, Sanger organized the ABCL, published and edited *The Birth Control Review*, supervised the massive mailings of the league, created birth control clinics that were now legal, if staffed by a doctor willing to define "disease" liberally, and searched for better contraceptive techniques. As the voice of birth control, she spoke throughout the United States, framing birth control not just as a woman's issue but as a population issue. From November 1920 through May 1921 the *Review* listed forty-six talks by Sanger, some out of town, many to younger audiences such as those at Yale, one in a darkened room to the women of the New Jersey Ku Klux Klan, others to prominent doctors in private residences in New York, and several in Harlem.

There were still some places in the United States where Sanger was not welcome. In Boston, Mayor Curley, referring to Sanger's "child murder propaganda," refused her supporters the necessary permits to rent the city's public halls. In Syracuse, where the New York State Birth Control League planned to meet in 1924, the city council passed an ordinance outlawing public discussion of birth control. Once again, Catholics exploited their ties to municipal authorities to censor a meeting on contraception. But under pressure from a growing coalition of supporters—the American Civil Liberties Union, local Protestant clergy, and birth control's large constituency of middle-class female volunteers with prominent husbands—the mayor vetoed legislation he had earlier supported. And so Sanger delivered her scheduled lecture and, in a sign of the times, gave her first radio address, grandly placing birth control on the side of humanitarian progress: "These opposing groups have laughed at Columbus . . . burnt great scientists, said automobiles were impracticable . . . scoffed at aviation." In spite of this opposition, a few, and it went without saying that she was one of these, have been "brave enough, strong enough, courageous enough, to bear aloft and to carry onward the torch of civilization."[66]

As the director of the ABCL, Sanger now ran a paid staff of three, augmented by volunteers. She organized the file system with Slee's help; she created a mailing list of over six thousand names and discovered the utility of her husband's stamp machines for an organization that by 1926 had thirty-five thousand members. She polled physicians throughout the country about the kind of contraceptive information they delivered to their patients, and by the late 1920s she had amassed a list of five thousand physicians sympathetic to birth control. To them she referred the thousands of American women who wrote seeking help. Sanger came to appreciate impersonal form letters, and she curried the favor of experts in the field, often sending unsolicited invitations to her conferences to scientists and physicians and, increasingly, to supportive Protestant ministers and Jewish rabbis. And if these men declined to speak at a conference or write a paper on an assigned topic, she replied with a request for an article in the *Review* or an invitation to the next year's conference or the name of a more sympathetic colleague. Sanger also instructed women's groups about how they might organize the clinics that she believed to be the next wave of birth control activities.

•

Clinics had been Sanger's early, though illegal, inspiration. Years before she had observed their success in the Netherlands and had returned to the United States convinced that "this new idea of clinics" might be adopted by hospitals and dispensaries. She envisioned a chain—"thousands of them in every center of America, staffed with specialists putting the subject on a modern scientific basis through research and education."[67] Sanger had gained notoriety by opening her own Brownsville clinic without a physician, though she had always believed that doctors, nurses, and midwives were the proper professionals to give advice. In 1920 she had considered opening a clinic in England, but reserved her efforts for the United States after Marie Stopes had organized one in a storefront on London's Marlborough Road. By 1923, empowered by the Crane decision, Sanger was ready to take action in the United States: "Theories and solutions are quite all right; printed matter will carry the message to those who have been educated. But women must be told by word of mouth and shown by demonstration standards what to do and how to do it."[68]

The awkwardly but accurately named Birth Control Clinical Research Bureau (BCCRB), separate from the ABCL to protect the latter from any police interference, though located in the same building, soon moved to West Sixteenth Street into a three-story brownstone that Slee purchased. To deliver birth control services, she needed a license to open a dispensary, meaning a freestanding autonomous facility where medical treatment and advice were given, usually to the poor. Sanger applied to the New York State Board of Charities, the regulatory agency that authorized such permits. Denied her license twice on the basis that her clinic offered no treatment and the granting of a license was "inexpedient," Sanger opened anyway.

The clinic did treat the poor; it did offer what she considered treatment and, when appropriate, it delivered advice and contraceptive supplies. But soon an inspector from the state board threatened to close the BCCRB: it was against the law to operate an unlicensed clinic. She must take her large posters down, most of which depicted birth control as an answer to abortion, and then she might continue as a research bureau, the latter the protective label she had included in the title of her clinic. But Sanger's patients were her research subjects; without them there could be no scientific study. Sanger heard from friends that "the real objection was that of certain religious bodies . . . The opposition of the Roman Catholic Church was specifically mentioned, but this statement is elided from the minutes of the hearing furnished," as Dr. Robert Dickinson explained.[69]

There was another hurdle: to provide legal contraceptive counseling required the hiring of a physician who could dispense contraception to "diseased" women, in the definition established in the Crane decision. Earlier, Sanger had excoriated the medical profession for not taking a progressive stand on birth control. The subject might be social and economic, but as she knew from her years as a nurse, it was also medical. For years physicians had avoided birth control, believing it the stuff of quacks and amateurs like Margaret Sanger. Now she must somehow employ a creditable physician to do pelvic exams and measurements in her clinic. The best birth control advice required expert instruction, though it was not lost on physicians that Sanger was changing the meaning of sex: if intercourse was no longer for procreation, then it was an end in itself. Most doctors, conservative by training and social status and seeing themselves as moralists defining women's nature, publicly opposed what they considered vulgar, unnecessary, commercial, subversive, and unsafe. And they objected not only on principle; work in a clinic such as Sanger's meant low pay and even lower prestige.

Obstetricians, representing a well-defined specialty by the 1920s with their own journal and national society, had no financial interest in limiting births; on the contrary, their fledgling practices required more pregnant women, not fewer. Earlier gynecologists, such as Alabamian Dr. J. Marion Sims, who developed his operations by experimenting on his slaves before the Civil War, were dedicated to helping women conceive by surgically repairing vesico-vaginal fistulas and tears of the perineum. The most famous gynecologist in America, Dr. Howard Kelly, pioneered the use of radium to treat cervical cancer and, in a matter of fierce territoriality among physicians, wrested surgical operations on women's reproductive organs from general surgeons, placing them firmly in the domain of his specialty. Doctors studied pelvic size in the context of childbearing and learned how to do cesarean sections. But they remained uninterested in female reproductive physiology. Instead, they were intent on installing themselves as experts in childbearing, preempting what had earlier been accomplished by midwives and nurses. Neither obstetricians nor gynecologists were interested in the social implications of maternal mortality. With a few important exceptions they decried contraception, at least publicly, if not always in the privacy of their offices.

One of these exceptions was Dr. Robert Dickinson, a Brooklyn-based gynecologist and obstetrician in private practice who at first dismissed Sanger as a radical interloper. "If the profession does not do its duty and make scientific studies, then some Sanger group will." Unlike most of his male colleagues, the bearded, bespectacled, intense Dickinson was interested in sex as a matter essential to his profession, and he was also a popular, respected member of his specialty. Elected the head of the American Gynecological Society, in 1920 he shocked colleagues with his presidential address by asking, "Who has or can acquire any considerable body of evidence on these matters but ourselves? What indeed is a normal sex life? What constitutes excess or what is the penalty for repression in the married?"[70] Like Sanger, Dickinson realized the need for research directed toward making contraception, so revolting to his colleagues, a scientific subject. Abruptly in the 1920s, he closed down his practice and set up his own research and birth control clinic, the Committee on Maternal Health.

Sanger applauded such a move, having long pushed for the opening of "the door of the laboratories where our chemists will give the women of the 20th century reliable and scientific means of contraception hitherto unknown."[71] She envisioned her clinics not just as the sites of important research but also functioning "as an integral part of public and racial health, forming an integral part of all prenatal and postnatal agencies for maternal and child welfare . . . centers primarily in contraceptive technique, but schools for all problems of parenthood for men as well as for women." They would be as well-organized, universal, and popular as the American public school system.[72]

Her challenge in the 1920s was to find a doctor for her clinic. On their journey to professional status, male gynecologists discovered their financial futures in private practice and in a growing number of full-time appointments in hospitals, while, according to Dickinson, the rare "women physicians tend to be more socially minded . . . and in this matter have shown more courage than their male confreres and are more impressed with patient needs."[73] Given the nature of the necessary pelvic exam for measuring pessaries, Sanger preferred a woman doctor, since Dickinson had his own clinic. But where to find one? In 1920 women represented a tiny fraction of the licensed graduates of American medical schools during a period when postgraduate training was becoming critical. The few women who graduated from medical school experienced difficulty finding the career-elevating internships and residencies. Most programs, even at the Boston Lying-In Hospital with only female patients, still refused to accept women as house officers; only 40 of 482 general hospitals in the United States did so in 1921.

After several refusals by women doctors, Sanger approached Dr. Dorothy Bocker, a New York–trained physician who was currently the director of the Georgia Board of Health's division of Child Hygiene. Bocker was anxious to return to New York, and Sanger appealed to the physician's "courage":

> I want to be perfectly frank with you . . . there is a possibility of your going to jail or at least of your standing trial, also you state yourself, of losing your New York State License . . . On the other hand, for one doctor to stand up and assert her right under this legal opinion, would give tremendous impetus and encouragement to thousands of other doctors throughout the country to do likewise . . . I cannot assure you a peaceful, harmonious or uneventful year.[74]

The clinic opened on January 1, 1923, with the well-paid Bocker as physician in charge. For protection, Bocker had demanded and, after Sanger raised the funds from her English friends, had gotten the astronomical salary of six thousand dollars. There could be no advertisement of this new venture; even *The Birth Control Review* across the hall made no mention of this epochal event, although many of the sixty-five hundred women who stopped by the ABCL for advice the first year were referred to the clinic. Clients, as Sanger called them, came by word of mouth and because Sanger was famous. There were referrals as well from nurses in the hospitals that were establishing themselves as the safest places for childbirth. At first Sanger had believed that hospitals would naturally assume birth control services, but she soon learned otherwise. After taking two women—one suffering from tuberculosis and one from syphilis—to twenty-eight area hospitals as a test, she discovered that only one would give information on birth control, though there was general agreement that if these two women became pregnant, given their medical conditions, they could undergo a legal abortion performed by the staff.

Some women heard about Sanger's clinic informally from nurses in the new mothers' and babies' clinics established under the auspices of the Sheppard-Towner Act. Passed in 1921 and considered evidence that women's suffrage influenced public policies, this new legislation funded state infant and maternal care programs, until doctors who called it "Bolshevik medicine" persuaded congressmen to repeal it in 1927. The Children's Bureau, the most established national agency in the field, refused to support birth control, believing it too politically dangerous. The Bureau viewed its mission as saving the lives of babies and mothers, not preventing children from coming into the world.

At first, even at Sanger's clinic, attracting a constant flow of patients proved challenging. In Chicago, at the Sanger-influenced Illinois Birth Control League, one disappointed volunteer noted that in three months of activity only sixty women visited the clinic. Reaching "those who need it most" was a daunting task.[75] By the end of the first year Sanger had data on only nine hundred women.

The reasons were obvious: mothers with small children disliked coming downtown, and once in the clinic found the questions intrusive, after which a vaginal exam with a speculum and sometimes ungloved fingers proved embarrassing. Then the doctor measured for the Mensinga pessary by inserting various sizes of pessaries until one fit, with the patient then practicing herself under the observation of the physician, for the fee of five dollars. Such procedures mapped the distance that Sanger, the practice of birth control, and scientific medicine had traveled since the Brownsville clinic days when Sanger sent many women to the local pharmacy for spermicides and, if available, pessaries.

The secret to a successful birth control clinic, Sanger learned, rested in the approach to the patients: there must be toys for the children while the mothers are examined; the staff must be hospitable; the clinic must be attractive and neighborly—a homelike woman's place without the intimidation of a hospital or even a doctor's office. Throughout the United States, where twenty birth control clinics operated by 1925 and fifty-five by 1930, most followed the directions from the ABCL to provide the proper setting for a hesitant population. This was especially important because the growing acceptance of contraception encouraged outlets offering what Sanger-influenced clinics called bootleg birth control. In a measure of the commercial possibilities of birth control, pharmacies, storefront operations, and rented rooms supported by manufacturers of contraceptive products, such as the Lanteen Laboratories in Illinois, now offered competing birth control services.

The gynecologist Dr. Hannah Stone explained that "of all the equipment, the most important is staff with a breath of inspiration, a truly sympathetic attitude and a sincere interest in the work."[76] And she might have added an understanding of statistical research, an area in which Bocker proved inept. The first director of the BCCRB expertly counseled her clients on how they might avoid pregnancy, but her efforts at the data collecting and collating considered crucial by Sanger were primitive. Bocker was also lax about the required follow-up visits essential if any statistical profile was to be completed. The report of her first year's work, *Birth Control Methods*, was criticized, to Sanger's embarrassment, as unscientific. Bocker never discussed contraceptive failures, and worse still, some women did not even receive the necessary pelvic exams.

After two years Sanger fired Bocker. "A sorrowful ending to a great venture," she wrote in her diary, and an acrimonious one during which both women hired lawyers. Determined to start her own private practice and technically owning the clinic records, though Sanger thought otherwise, Bocker had taken data from the office in a reprise of the Blossom affair. Two years of research findings had disappeared. In Sanger's mind it was "a betrayal of trust of faith . . . she sneaked into the office Sunday & took the Cards & names." As always for Sanger, this battle was exciting; obstacles overcome provided opportunities to renew the work more fervidly: "Must begin all over again. Regain faith in human beings. Use greater discretion; trust them less perhaps is the remedy."[77]

Sanger was more successful in her choice of a second director of the clinic. Dr. Hannah Stone had trained in gynecology at the New York Medical College and had a position at its Lying-in Division. Well-grounded in chemistry, this slim, attractive, dark-haired Jewish woman also had a degree from the Brooklyn College of Pharmacy and was married to Dr. Abraham Stone, a gynecologist and the editor of the journal *Fertility and Infertility*. Volunteering after Bocker's departure, Stone asked for and received no salary, only the opportunity to help women, even after she lost her appointment at the Lying-in Hospital. For the next sixteen years until her death in 1941, Stone worked at the Bureau in the morning and in the afternoons at her private office on lower Fifth Avenue, where Sanger referred patients who could afford her ten-dollar fee.

Stone excelled at her work, and the number of clinic patients rose dramatically. Sensitive to those who wanted birth control but had no health reason to receive it, she marked their cards NHR—No Health Reason— but gave it to them anyway. In 1925, 1,655 patients visited the clinic; four years later 9,737 women, most of them mothers from lower-income families and a quarter of them Catholics, along with a few men, did so. The record keeping, which Sanger considered essential, improved. In fictional form Stone appeared in Mary McCarthy's novel *The Group*, a depiction of sexually active but uninformed Vassar women needing birth control during the 1930s: "The doctor's femininity was a reassuring part of her professional aspect, like her white coat. On her hand shone a broad gold wedding ring, which seemed to Dottie serene and ample, like the doctor herself . . . Her skill astonished Dottie who sat with wondering eyes, anesthetized by the doctor's personality while a series of questions, like a delicately maneuvering forceps, extracted information that ought to have hurt but didn't."[78]

Stone also engaged in the kind of research typical of medical laboratories during the 1920s: finding the best ingredients for an effective spermicide that would not burn women's vaginas like Lysol, but that was more effective than the usual homemade vinegar and saline preparations. She also gathered data for the annual clinic report, and she helped Sanger edit *The Practice of Contraception*, a collection of papers from the Seventh Annual International Birth Control Conference. In 1935 Hannah Stone became famous after she and her husband published their popular *Marriage Manual: A Practical Guide to Sex and Marriage*, a comprehensive study of sex, reproduction, and birth control that found its way to many night tables across America. For all these accomplishments she won Sanger's admiration, and at the heart of their friendship rested the mutually held conviction that their work made a difference to women and to society.

At the time, and more vigorously later, Sanger was criticized for her doctor-run clinics. Dennett accused her of accepting the minimal legal revision of the Crane exception to the federal Comstock laws, the latter the target of the Voluntary Parenthood League's lobbying efforts. Later there were complaints that because of Sanger's clinics, male doctors came to control female reproduction, as the possibilities for women-centered self-help initiatives disappeared. To these critics contraception should never have become medicalized, and the prospect of a social movement based on matters of women's health was stanched. Given the temper of the times, however, Sanger had few choices: correctly evaluating the pessary as the safest method of women's birth control, she had to hire doctors or have her clinic closed down. It was a strategic concession, but in these early days of newly visible birth control, she also needed doctors with their growing prestige to make birth control legally acceptable.

In 1925 Sanger organized an ambitious project, a meeting of the International Neo-Malthusian and Birth Control Conference in New York.

An effective organizer and manager, she had worked for months recruiting speakers, raising money, and publicizing the sixth meeting of the group. To use the word "conference" rather than "convention" or "assembly" suggested her educational intention; to number the conference, in the style of nineteenth-century suffragists, gave legitimacy and respectability to the movement. With her husband Noah Slee's financial help along with that of her best friend, Juliet Rublee, Sanger intended the conference to demonstrate how far birth control had progressed. She also wished to advertise the need for more involvement from doctors, not just to assist in clinics but to give respectability to contraception. Here she walked a tightrope, celebrating success but also recognizing the difficult challenges the movement faced in the future.

On a windy March day in 1925, nearly a thousand delegates from eighteen countries from Mexico to Japan assembled in the McAlpin Hotel, the twenty-five-story marvel on Broadway and Thirty-fourth Street, reputed to be the largest hotel in the world. They came to hear over 150 experts, many of whom had given Sanger advice she mostly refused. "I am no more religious than you, but it might be a shrewd move to let some pious old goat open the Congress with a prayer," suggested Raymond Pearl, though Sanger declined to do so.[79] There were professors from universities, specialists in economics, including John Maynard Keynes, statisticians, demographers, and biologists with startling things to say about hormones. There were eugenicists and representatives from increasingly sympathetic Protestant denominations and Jewish Reform synagogues, and, of course, the halls were crowded with Sanger's friends.

Sanger delivered the opening address, emphasizing birth control as a population issue and later cataloging the efforts of her ABCL: 190,982 letters sent from 1922 to 1925, and over a million pamphlets distributed. Sanger also gave a short address on "the children's era," with the playful suggestion that parents take an exam, like a civil service test, answering questions as to their biological and economic suitability for parenthood. Other sessions considered topics such as whether Soviet Russia wanted birth control at all and the organization of women's clinics in Austria. Speakers linked expanding populations with war, and the audience applauded the statement by an English eugenicist that the population problem must be solved "by birth control or mustard gas." In a crowded session Hannah Stone delivered the results of the BCCRB's findings to an audience of doctors, including a new supporter, Dr. William Allen Pusey, a former president of the American Medical Association. Sanger had invited objectors as well. Thomas Dublin, statistician for the Metropolitan Life Insurance Company, complained that birth control was too emotional, unscientific, and individualistic. A revised version of his speech appeared in the following year's *Atlantic Monthly* under the title "The Fallacious Propaganda for Birth Control."

The conference was extensively covered by the press, as the center of a movement that had begun in France, Holland, and Great Britain, where the first international meetings had been held at the turn of the century, now moved to the United States. To demonstrate the point, the indefatigable Sanger immediately began the editing and publication of the papers. Two years later four volumes of the *Proceedings of the Sixth International Neo-Malthusian and Birth Control Conference*, edited by Sanger and funded by Slee, appeared.

The conference represented a high point of Sanger's advocacy, though her courting of the eugenicists backfired. On the last day the conference voted for a resolution favoring "the general eugenic idea," and encouraging larger families among the "persons whose progeny gives promise of being of decided value to the community." For years Sanger had vehemently opposed such a position. Now she must either offend her principal supporters—a member of her advisory board, Dr. Roswell Johnson, had introduced the resolution—or surrender her convictions. Within weeks she had written a press release dismissing the resolution as irrelevant and meaningless—"with a lack of precision and rigorous thinking . . . Birth control cannot be relegated to the background of human thought as a mere secondary aspect of eugenics or described as negative eugenics. Birth control on the contrary is a constructive creative program proffering to suffering humanity an instrument of release, a weapon of liberation."[80] Well aware of the importance of her eugenic friends, Sanger invited their reaction to her statement. All insisted on modifications; all held to the primacy of their programs for better populations, with birth control relegated to a minor status. Warned Dr. Edward East, a biologist at Harvard University and one of the early eugenicists to support birth control, she must edit her editorial "if you wish to retain the sympathies of a lot of people whose names have some value."[81] And so she did, as the woman rebel of an earlier decade learned a painful lesson on how realized ambitions bred caution, and success encouraged diplomacy.

8

SPREADING THE WORD

My name has become a symbol of deliverance.

—Margaret Sanger, *Motherhood in Bondage*

By 1928 Sanger had tired of committee work and resigned from the American Birth Control League, the organization she had created and run for nearly eight years. Adventure had disappeared for a restless pioneer who had already been everything the movement required. As activist, propagandist, organizer, educator, advocate, and occasional martyr, Sanger had no principal focus nor special endeavor from 1925 to 1935. Instead, she concentrated on spreading her message by writing books, opening clinics, arranging conferences, challenging the Catholic Church, and lobbying in Washington. But first she must leave her organizational beginnings. To Havelock Ellis, she acknowledged her boredom with meetings, especially the elaborate lunches at the elite Colony Club on Park Avenue, and what she hated most—the dreary reading of ABCL committee reports and financial accounting. "The old spirit is gone. Now the [League of Women Voters] spirit reigns," she advised Juliet Rublee. "I could have fought them out but what for?"[1] In fact, Sanger was gone too often from headquarters to maintain her authority over a maturing organization. In her absence new leaders reshaped the League into what Sanger criticized as a hopelessly conservative organization. "What some call fanaticism is never dangerous to the life of such an organization as this one. Apathy and languid convictions are."[2]

Margaret Sanger might be the symbol of birth control, but to those in New York engaged in routine matters of mailing documents, responding to queries, arranging speakers, and encouraging birth control clinics, "Mrs. Sanger is too independent in spirit to be what is known as an organization woman."[3] Sanger countered that the new director, Mrs. Robertson Jones, paid too much attention to details and her husband's stifling legal caveats. Worse, Jones accepted the heresy that the cause was won and there was no need for controversy. And most infuriating of all was her insistence that Sanger submit expense vouchers. As the star fund-raiser for birth control, Sanger could never accept such direction: "I don't like working in an atmosphere of rules and regulations."[4]

In 1929 Sanger also resigned as editor in chief of *The Birth Control Review*, citing discord among the board and what Juliet Rublee, who also resigned, called "petty criticism, rebellion, and personal ambition for prestige and power." Angered when the new editors retained the name of *her* periodical, Sanger correctly predicted that "the poor review is doomed unless they find someone who has time to give to it."[5] Without her articles and her ability to attract first-rate writers and raise money, the *Review* gradually deteriorated into a third-rate bulletin, read by a few true believers and members of the League. Glumly, Sanger decided that the whole "organization is disintegrating and the success of the Birth Control movement is being seriously impaired."[6] The new directors were deficient in the kind of aggressive leadership she had delivered for years and that she expected, even in changing times, to continue to provide until birth control was simple, safe, cheap, effective, and legal. "They never go away from New York to know what is going on," she complained.[7] "They usually [lead] in propping up what others create and then killing it."[8]

Sanger stayed on as managing director of the successful Clinical Research Bureau, which she had established in 1923. Her refusal to leave initiated another battle with the new managers of the league. Sanger argued that the clinic was an independent venture, separately incorporated from the American Birth Control League for the legal independence and protection of both; Jones and her executive board considered it a desirable division of the ABCL. Sanger won this contest, and the Clinical Research Bureau (later the Margaret Sanger Research Bureau) emerged as the organizational arm of Sanger's increasingly personalized movement. Still located in the three-story brownstone on West Sixteenth Street, the clinic became the most active and best-known such facility in the world, attracting local medical students, nurses, and visiting doctors. The indispensable Hannah Stone kept the statistics and served as the physician in charge. By

1931 sixteen doctors, five trained nurses, four social workers, and several researchers served a growing annual population of over 18,000 clients who still must be called patients. By 1934 the clinic had records on 49,798 women.

Success brought suitors anxious to affiliate or, in Sanger's fears, absorb the clinic, especially Dr. Robert Dickinson, whose own efforts had failed to attract many patients. For years Dickinson tried to take over Sanger's clinic. She wavered, needing a license for legitimacy and the imprimatur of an established physician. On the other hand, she feared a diminished role for herself and the installation of an unfriendly medical bureaucracy. "Doctors are considering taking over the clinic. Shall we let it go? Will they make a success of it?" Or, in her dreaded distinction, "will they make it an institution?"[9]

When she asked Dickinson to support her efforts to publicize birth control, he demurred. Doctors followed the law, he replied, and left to others its direction. The clinic, not birth control propaganda, attracted his interest, and he remained disgusted with her all-female staff of "low-level doctors" and her unseemly promotion of what he saw as medical treatment and she envisioned as a transformative social and economic reform. Full of plans crafted on his nature walks around Manhattan, he described to a skeptical Sanger his ideas for a reproductive clinic under the name "uterology" that would include infertility services, new techniques of sterilization using both vasectomy for men and the surgically more complicated duct-closing salpingectomy for women, along with therapeutic abortions and contraceptive research. Meanwhile, Sanger's single-minded intention was revealed in the renaming of her facility as the Birth Control Clinical Research Bureau.

In the midst of these negotiations, the police raided the clinic in a sting operation similar to that of the Brownsville raid. One morning in 1929 a policewoman, Mrs. McNamara, registered under an alias and sought contraceptive advice. Three days later she returned with the vice squad, who arrested the unperturbed Stone, two other doctors, and several staff nurses for violating New York's version of the Comstock laws. For six years the clinic had been operating under the Crane exception that doctors could deliver birth control to treat disease. And the undercover policewoman did suffer from reproductive problems that made it dangerous for her to have another child. After hearing her medical issues graphically described at the trial, to Sanger's delight, she returned to the clinic for consultation.

The raid and the ensuing trial indicated how important the involvement of doctors was to the progress of birth control. The authorities not only made arrests but, armed with a search warrant, impounded patient histories and identifying cards with names and addresses. The latter were never returned, raising Sanger's suspicions when Catholics reported that they were receiving mysterious warnings not to return to the clinic. Even the strange contraceptive devices that women crafted for themselves, displayed as oddities on the shelves of the clinic, were swept up in evidence bags, along with books and pamphlets.

The seizure of the doctors' records led to the involvement of the New York medical fraternity. Suddenly physicians who opposed birth control volunteered to testify in the trial. What had been insignificant now emerged as a crucial challenge to a physician's authority to ensure confidentiality. At a hastily called meeting, the New York Academy of Medicine resolved its "grave concern" about "any action of the authorities which contravenes the inviolability of the confidential relations which always have and should obtain between physicians and their patients."[10] Agreeing, the judge threw out the case, pointing to the necessity for good faith when doctors decided that the prevention of conception was necessary for a patient's health and physical welfare. As propaganda in her campaign to spread the word, Sanger used the raid as yet another example of the illicit suppression of contraception. It was, she explained in her *Autobiography*, "one of the worst errors committed by the opposition, because it touched the doctors in a most sensitive spot, the sanctity of records, and they were obliged to stand by us whether they wanted to or not."[11]

After Dickinson defended the clinic during the trial, Sanger placed him on her medical advisory board, where he promptly challenged her as a divisive element. According to Dickinson, she should not have separated the BCCRB from the ABCL. She should have worked with Dennett, and she certainly should never have packed her medical advisory board with eugenicists. Several times, in his absence, she had unfairly rigged a crucial vote against any merger with his Committee of Maternal Health. And he disliked her second-rate associates in the clinic. "Big things doing with the Medical profession," wrote Sanger to her confidante Rublee. "Dr. Dickinson again wanting to take it over—I must be on the spot [she was in Paris] & watch every step."[12]

Eventually Sanger agreed to share her case histories with Dickinson, but the resulting volume, *Birth Control in Practice*, extended no appreciation to Sanger, who had provided the material. If she was mentioned or included as a director, members of his committee would withdraw their names and financial support from the project. Later, in his study *The Practice of Contraception: An Illustrated Medical Manual*, Dickinson thanked the unknown Mrs. Slee (and Mr. Slee) "for the privilege of making records available from their remarkably complete collection."[13] In this full season of familiar but still hurtful humiliations, Sanger complained to Havelock Ellis: "Earlier no one wanted credit . . . but now when they did, they seized it for themselves . . . The reason for the slight is these gentlemen cannot associate with a propagandist."[14] Doctors of this generation, she might have added from lessons learned as a nurse, never tolerated shared responsibilities with outsiders. But sympathizers such as the eugenicist Clarence Little, a zoologist at Cold Spring Harbor, saw the injustice: medical men "had not earned the right to take over the work in a field that others have tilled for them. The medical profession has tried to handle the problem and has made a mess of it."[15]

In time Dickinson and Sanger came to respect and even admire each other, though she retained control of her clinic. He sent her a copy of his book; she acknowledged "your magnificent work." Still, he refused invitations to speak at various Sanger-organized conferences, using the excuse that he was hobbled by the disapproval of the Committee of Maternal Health. And so, in the name of impartial science, Dickinson continued to oppose what she considered essential—the process of public persuasion.

In February 1930, Sanger opened a birth control clinic in Harlem with an all-white staff, soon integrated and financed by philanthropists Carrie Fuld, heir to the Bamberger's department store fortune, and Julius Rosenwald, a Sears, Roebuck investor and generous supporter of projects aiding black Americans. The project was a bold move, encouraged by some black leaders in a community that was divided over the issue and would remain so. She charged three dollars for an exam and two for the purchase of a diaphragm. But as often as not, during these hard times, both white and black clients were unable to pay and received free advice. The numbers were small by downtown standards, and the clinic survived for only three years under Sanger's direction. But during that time, the waiting rooms in both clinics were among the only integrated places in daytime New York. Perversely, part of the impetus to establish the Harlem clinic had been the grumbling of white clients who refused to share the downtown waiting and examining rooms with blacks. Sanger acknowledged that "we are not able to take [those] who apply because of prejudice."[16]

By 1930 Harlem had become a cultural and population center for African Americans. Many of its residents had moved uptown from Hell's Kitchen and Five Points in lower Manhattan; others, after the boll weevil destroyed southern cotton crops and innovative cotton-picking machinery replaced the labor of black sharecroppers, traveled the railroad lines north into New York. By 1930, 224,000 of New York's 330,000 blacks lived in the 150 blocks bounded by the Hudson and Harlem Rivers, 125th Street and St. Nicholas Avenue. Sanger established her clinic on upper Seventh Avenue off 138th Street, without a license, but with the protection of the Crane rule, liberally interpreted in both her clinics, that women with disease could receive contraceptive devices.

Like other whites during the Harlem Renaissance, a time when, in the poet Claude McKay's words, "white folks discovered black magic," Sanger knew its dance emporiums such as the Cotton Club, its speakeasies, lounges, and supper cabarets, where she occasionally smoked the Gauloises cigarettes sent by her English friends. She also knew its poverty, overcrowding, and the need for birth control. In what was becoming a black ghetto, mothers in Harlem were twice as likely to die in childbirth as those elsewhere in New York, and a shocking 111 of every 1,000 Harlem babies died in infancy, compared to 65 per 1,000 elsewhere in the city.

Sanger was well-known among leaders in the community. In 1923 invited by the Harlem Community Forum, she had spoken in the Utopian Neighborhood Club. Soon after, following a Sanger lecture in his church, Reverend Adam Clayton Powell of the Abyssinian Baptist Church endorsed birth control. Support came as well from the National Association of Colored Graduate Nurses, along with a few ministers and many social workers. By 1926 Sanger had received a formal request from the New York Urban League to open a clinic in the Columbus Hill area.

The most influential endorsement came from the powerful W.E.B. Du Bois, founder of the NAACP and proponent of black leadership. In his essay titled "The Damnation of Women," Du Bois wrote as a feminist: "Women are not for themselves, but for men." They were even renamed after the men they married, but their true damnation was uncontrolled reproduction. Du Bois, who was present at the opening of her clinic and served briefly on her advisory board, gained Sanger's attention when he insisted that "the right of motherhood [must] be at the woman's own discretion. Those who would confine women to childbearing are reactionary barbarians."[17] A eugenicist as well as an elitist with his ideas about the "talented tenth," Du Bois described in *The Birth Control Review* the need for a "more liberal attitude" on the part of "negro churches . . . The mass of ignorant Negroes still breed carelessly."[18]

Other black leaders objected to the clinic as a place where experiments on blacks took place. Like those of whites, declining black fertility rates alarmed activists. Marcus Garvey, the black nationalist and founder of the Universal Negro Improvement Association, in exile in Jamaica, cautioned that birth control interfered with the course of nature and was simply a white man's trick to limit the number of blacks. Birth control, according to Garvey in an argument that still surfaces in the twenty-first century, would do little more than weaken the power of African Americans.

More progressive on racial matters than nearly all white Americans in the 1930s—Sanger never applied the term "unfit" to entire races and religions, only to individuals—she nevertheless saw opportunities for research along racial lines, the kind of data collecting suggested by her eugenic friends. Even before the clinic opened, Dr. Edward East requested that Sanger include in her patient histories questions concerning "the amount of racial intermixture . . . [so as to] make a judgment as to whether the person was more or less pure black, mulatto, quadroon, etc.," the information to somehow be obtained without embarrassing questions.[19] With such data, comparisons could be made between the incomes and status of mulattos, "pure blacks," and whites, and conclusions drawn about the effects of black blood, even a drop of it. In this eugenics-saturated climate, northern state legislatures that had repealed miscegenation laws following the Civil War were reconsidering, and even reinstalling, prohibitions on so-called mixed blood matings. Research that Sanger could provide might justify such actions.

East believed the records from the Harlem clinic would substantiate his suspicions of a racial pyramid with Anglo-Saxon Nordics at the top and blacks at the bottom, and members of various ethnic groups and "hybrids" arranged in between. But the Harlem clinic records disappeared, and there is no evidence that Sanger gathered information on anything other than race, religion, nationality, and childbearing history. Yet she did trumpet the possibility of such research to her eugenic friends in order to raise money. And Sanger did compare the mostly black clients of the Harlem clinic to the mostly white ones in the Sixteenth Street clinic in terms of what mattered most to her: their diligence in using birth control. Black women, despite the suspicions of eugenicists such as the Johns Hopkins biologist and statistician Raymond Pearl, were not more negligent in a matter that demanded discipline and planning. Nor did Sanger accept Pearl's proposition that blacks exercised "less prudence and foresight than white people do in all sexual matters."[20]

Carelessness was a function of class, concluded Sanger, and to make the point, she quoted Norman Himes, a sociologist at Colgate, that "whatever differences exist between the races are a consequence not of racial circumstances but of such social factors as differences in intelligence, home conditions, intensity of the desire to apply contraceptive knowledge effectively, etc."[21] But there was one substantial difference between the women of the two races: blacks were less inhibited than whites. "The negro women learn the techniques of procedure with greater ease and facility than does the average white woman."[22] When John Harvey Kellogg, of cereal fame and a staunch supporter of the Race Betterment Foundation, argued in the *Literary Digest* that high fertility rates among blacks proved the futility of birth control, Sanger used her Harlem case studies to refute the point.

In 1934 Sanger turned the Harlem clinic over to the ABCL, which she incorrectly believed had received a grant to run it. By 1936, moved to a single room in the New York Urban League headquarters, it was renamed the Urban League Mother's Health Center. From the beginning there had been too few clients: an impressive 1,760 in eighteen months, which then leveled off to less than 1,000 a year, nearly all subsidized. Typically Sanger soon left to others the executive functions at which she excelled. Perhaps the clinic could have survived these challenges if it weren't for the Depression, which ended her husband's financial support for her birth control projects.

Sanger had been organizing a regional birth control meeting to support her new lobbying organization on Black Tuesday, October 24, 1929, the day the average price of leading stocks plunged forty points and securities lost $14 billion in value. The slide continued during the following weeks with waves of selling, then stabilization, then more selling until by 1931 many stocks had lost 90 percent of their value. The effect was immediately felt in Sanger's household, in part because Noah Slee, with catastrophic timing, had purchased a seat on the New York Stock Exchange as an investment only months before. Earlier he had sold the Three-in-One Oil business and invested in the stock market. Now, as he faced margin calls on stocks purchased with little down payment, Slee sold his sharply discounted stock exchange seat. For a former multimillionaire whose identity was tied to his financial prowess, the slide of the American economy and his portfolio was a terrible blow.

Slee had special problems; he faced legal fees and back taxes after the Internal Revenue Service challenged his charitable deductions to his wife's birth control organizations, which the Internal Revenue Service refused to accept as a legitimate charity. "J.N.'s condition is alarming," wrote Sanger to the de Selincourts, who were having their own financial problems during a worldwide depression. "We have had to cut and cut to keep going and now he is borrowing to keep up his pledges and obligations . . . Everyone is out of work or on cut salaries."[23] As the Depression deepened, the Slee finances worsened. Although he was still a millionaire, "J.N.'s financial affairs are in the way of the wolf . . . tho' he is far away he is in sight. Possibly we can pull thru this year on hopes . . . If the whole financial system does not smash we will all have to work like H."[24]

By 1932 unemployment in the United States reached 25 percent, the year that Herbert Hoover, Franklin Delano Roosevelt, and Norman Thomas were running for president. Slee voted for the past and Hoover; Stuart and Grant, now both in medical school, for the future and Roosevelt; and Margaret Sanger for a supporter of birth control, the Socialist Party candidate, Norman Thomas. By March when Roosevelt took office, over five thousand banks had closed their doors. The new president used his inaugural address to inspire confidence among "stricken" Americans. As Sanger described to the de Selincourts a few days later, "The banks are all closed. The scoundrels have mostly run for cover with their boodle, leaving the honest ones to take the loss. J.N. did not draw out anything before the crash though we were warned to do so . . . J.N.'s patriotism would not allow him to have such fears and so we are without cash."[25]

At first she had hopes for both Roosevelts. Eleanor Roosevelt had briefly supported birth control when the Women's City Club of New York endorsed it. But in the White House birth control was a matter even this progressive First Lady never discussed. To Sanger, Franklin Roosevelt initially seemed "fearless and daring with new solutions." But the president proved unresponsive to her demands that birth control be included in public health programs. To Sanger's further dismay, Roosevelt appointed a Catholic, James Farley, as postmaster general in a department closely watched by birth control advocates, given its control over the mail. By the mid-1930s Sanger emerged as a fierce critic: Roosevelt had "an adolescent mind" and was "experimenting with people's existence, killing pigs, burning wheat and destroying provisions and the necessities of life."[26]

Unlike her husband, Sanger faced the Depression with an equanimity grounded in her habitual optimism and childhood poverty. To Havelock Ellis's partner, Françoise Cyon, she explained that she could no longer afford the thousand dollars she had previously sent the couple every year. Still, "these difficult times are not so hard for me, (I've been brought up with them.)"[27] Renting Willowlake never ruffled Sanger: she could do with less, especially from a husband who complained but still paid for trips to one of her favorite spas, the Hay-Ven Clinic in the Poconos, where she took Grant in 1934 for a week of colonic emetics, sun baths, and lectures on starch and constipation. Nor did the Depression end her overseas or domestic trips, most beyond her personal financial reach, even though she was now charging two hundred dollars for a lecture and five hundred for a debate. When Stuart suffered from sinus trouble, she took him to Tucson, the beginning of her long association with that city. But in hard times Slee was even more the grim accountant, Sanger the insouciant spender.

Arguments over finances, in addition to her absences, were the cause of marital discord. "You are not a happy poor man," wrote Sanger to Slee in the summer of 1934, though her husband was hardly poor, only less rich. "Money is power & you are happier when you have it & you should not be without it."[28] Sometimes when he browbeat and sulked, she reminded him about what he should have known by this time: "My unassuming manner falsely gives people the idea that they can boss or dominate me. I am not aggressive but I will not be bullied or dominated."[29] She could never be home as much as he wished and would no longer be nagged. "It is foolish for you to think that you can ever have me in a routine way."[30]

One reason for her absences was her new lobbying initiative in Washington. For years Sanger had held as her ultimate goal the repeal of the Comstock law. Without such a change most doctors would never participate in an activity that was still illegal. Guided by her adroit tactical sense, Sanger also understood that legislators could easily avoid the issue, at least until she educated the public. Her rival Mary Ware Dennett had preempted any such campaign with what Sanger considered a premature approach. Dennett's

Voluntary Parent League worked during the 1920s to persuade Congress to remove contraception from federal statutes where it was defined as obscenity (and outlawed along with pornography and abortion) and allow all Americans, not just doctors, access to birth control through a so-called open bill.

Freed of earlier commitments, Sanger began working on her version of a "doctors' bill," allowing licensed physicians to exchange information. "We want no wholesale distribution of indecency nor pornography. [We want] to put contraception in the hand of the medical professions where it rightly belongs."[31] But she needed a new platform and during a few hectic months in 1929 formed the National Committee on Federal Legislation for Birth Control (NCFLBC). When it shut down in 1937, its mailings had reached 12 million Americans. "Let every mother in this land help me fight to change vicious laws which condemn us to conditions our Government would not impose on a farmer's cattle," Sanger implored in one of her write-your-congressman solicitations.[32]

Besides a grassroots campaign organized under the auspices of the NCFLBC, Sanger began intensive personal lobbying. From 1930 to 1936, in the corridors of Congress, Sanger sought out senators who promised they would sponsor her doctors' bill but then never did, and representatives who refused to meet in their offices with her lobbyists from the NCFLBC. She faced as well hostile questioners in the hearings that became an annual occasion. Senator William Borah of Idaho, a member of the Judiciary Committee, slammed his office door in her face. The physician and senator Henry Hatfield, who became a reluctant sponsor in 1932, called hers "the most discouraging and disgusting bill he had ever worked on." Hatfield, a eugenicist and former governor of West Virginia, had signed a state bill permitting coerced sterilization, citing "the universal growth in the number of idiotic, imbecilic and epileptic." Now he complained that letters from birth control advocates were "overwhelming" his office.[33] He was further displeased when Sanger sent a letter to his constituents praising his sponsorship of a bill that would find little favor with voters in an election year. Overall, concluded Sanger, "the more I have to do with Congressmen, the more I believe in birth control and sterilization."[34]

In hard-won meetings with congressmen, Sanger presented new arguments about the dangers of an overcrowded nation. She soon discovered that even during the Depression, "they laugh out loud at population theory."[35] Only once, in the closing moments of the Seventy-third Congress and under the same hurried circumstances that had led to the passage of the Comstock law in 1873, did a doctors' bill even reach the floor. Without debate the Senate passed it, until the absent Catholic senator Patrick McCarran recognized the threat, rushed back to the floor, and demanded senatorial courtesy. Immediately the bill was recalled and so Senate Bill 1842, freeing doctors from the restrictions of the Comstock law, was returned to the committee, there to die as the session ended. A dismayed Hazel Moore, Sanger's most effective lobbyist, wrote that there was never any courtesy extended to the women and children affected by the recall, but "men are men and Senators are cowards." But the senator explained that he did not believe in murder by birth control, and besides any federal change would interfere with state laws on obscenity and pornography.[36]

Sanger held the Catholic Church responsible for most of the opposition: "The Senators and Representatives in Washington are not at present disposed to do anything about this question which might offend Pope Pius XI."[37] In 1930 Pius had revisited the church's ancient dogmas about sex in an encyclical titled "Casti Connubii" (Chaste Marriage), the first statement on such matters since the sixteenth century. Reacting to the Anglican Church's cautious acceptance of birth control "for sound reasons and Christian principles and not for selfish ones," the pope repeated the Catholic position. There would be no change from the Augustinian principles of the fourth century; in fact, the pope liberally quoted St. Augustine along with Leo XIII: "Man is the ruler of the woman . . . New doctrines spread unbridled lust." Most dangerously, matrimony was now considered "invented by man," rather than by God. Birth control, a part of this new secular age, remained a sin against God and nature. "Any use whatsoever of matrimony exercised in such a way that the act is deliberately frustrated in its natural power to generate life is an offense . . . and those who indulge are branded with the guilt of a grave sin." God had bestowed generative organs on mankind solely for the purpose of procreation.

But in a subtle change heralded by church liberals, Pius acknowledged several secondary purposes of marriage, including "the quieting of concupiscence" and the mutual companionship of husband and wife. Still, with sex reserved for procreation, only abstinence was permitted for those who wished to simultaneously quiet sexual urges and not have children. And in what had been a hotly debated topic among priests and theologians, given the church's strictures on intercourse, infertile couples, young and old, could now engage in sex without sin. But as for "the advocates of the neo-paganism of today" who spoke in favor of birth control, only the pope, "whom the Father has appointed over His flock," had authority: "We consider it our duty to raise our voice to keep the flock committed to our care from poisoned pastures."[38] The encyclical initiated a period of unanimity among local priests who now spoke with renewed vigor against birth control in their confessional booths.

Sanger responded immediately. "The Pope is afraid and is whistling old tunes to keep up his courage . . . Progressive doctrines are indeed being spread among Catholics," many of whom came to her clinic. As she had earlier emphasized, the pope's insistence that Catholicism—and he its sole arbiter—was the "only authoritative guardian and interpreter of divine law is ridiculous." In a novel twist to her indictment, she shocked readers and listeners: "Evidently the pope believes in birth control," although he countenances only one means, "virtuous continence." But by approving any method, in Sanger's logic, the pope tacitly acknowledged the benefits of contraception. And as for the pope's mandates that contraception violates nature, "nature herself wastes almost all of the millions of sperms."[39]

The Catholics in America might be a minority of the population—Sanger correctly calculated one-seventh—but "it is a minority which our non-Catholic politicians, for various reasons, respect."[40] Even at a time when there was pervasive nativist sentiment among Protestants, Catholic opposition to contraception tapped into traditional attitudes about sex held by non-Catholics. Matters of good behavior and decency transcended denominational boundaries and were timeless, unchangeable, and ordained by everyone's God. Modifying legislation and opinion encountered the kind of moral veto that perpetually handicaps those intent on changing sexual customs and mores. Catholics, with forty-eight members of the House of Representatives in 1929, could never outlaw the practice of birth control, as they would have liked to do and as they had succeeded in doing in heavily Catholic Connecticut and Massachusetts, and nearly in New York. But they could promote the status quo and resist the gathering force of Sanger's movement.

Some non-Catholic congressmen were mortified by the topic and blushed, as Sanger noted mischievously, when she described contraception's techniques and mechanics. The Texas Democrat Hatton Sumners refused to discuss this "subject with a woman. It embarrasses me." His Democratic colleague from South Carolina informed a lobbyist from the NCFLBC, "We should let it alone. It jars me. It is revolting to interfere in people's personal affairs."[41] In fact, these legislators had little organized pressure from the electorate to change the Comstock law, which remained un-repealed (though rarely enforced) until the 1970s. Instead, they heard a great deal from voting blocs organized by Catholics and a group of self-proclaimed patriotic societies. The latter had determined that birth control was un-American and violated standards of decency. Contraception was "a commu-nist trick," testified one member of the Patriots Society.[42] To some members of the general public, it did seem somehow unpatriotic to limit the number of Americans in a nation of supposed boundless opportunity.

Other congressmen, such as the first-term Catholic from Massachu-setts John McCormack, one of twelve children, nine of whom had died in infancy or youth, tangled with Sanger over his church's preference for continence—"the exercise of an affirmative mind," said the childless repre-sentative, to which Sanger demurred, "Not always." But like the rest of Amer-ica, McCormack seemed salaciously fascinated by the techniques whose discussion and dissemination through the mail were outlawed by the Com-stock law but were well-known to the witness. "What kind of drugs do you have in mind?" asked McCormack, and after Sanger answered, he inquired, "What kind of instruments has this bill in mind?"[43] And so for the first time since the Comstock bill had passed sixty years before, talk of condoms, pessaries, and chinosol and quinine suppositories to kill sperm entered the halls of Congress. But there was no action.

Always dismayed when women, the intended beneficiaries of her cru-sade, opposed the means of their liberation, Sanger was particularly angry when one of the seven women in the Seventy-third Congress, Mary Norton of New Jersey, challenged Sanger's assertion that most American women supported the bill. "In fact they know little about it," testified the congress-woman. "The paid lobbyists of the Birth Control League should not be confounded with the free women of America, the vast army of mothers who consider the bearing of children their greatest privilege. The pressure of a baby face against their own is the highest form of earthly happiness." But if the childless Norton had obeyed the laws of nature, Sanger countered, "this competent, educated woman would be home attending to ten or twelve children, not in Congress." In any case Norton's arguments were no more than "a case of personal opinion against the facts, theories against practical knowledge."[44]

So, too, Sanger believed, were the comments of the notorious Catholic priest Father Charles Coughlin, well-known for his Sunday radio show tirades against Jews and blacks. An embarrassment to some opponents of the bill, Coughlin refused to stand before the committee, as was customary; to do so indicated deference to the state. A chair was brought. Coughlin sat and, warming to his subject, described women who used contraceptives as prostitutes and birth control as teaching children to be fornicators. "To the extent that we can still be Christians, [Americans must] increase and multiply . . . according to a regulation that is in the heart of man and not in a bottle in a drug store . . . all this bill means is how to commit adultery and not get caught." Sanger, wearing what her associates dubbed her "Rock of Gibraltar expression," replied that one-third of the women who came for contraceptive advice in her New York clinic were, in fact, Catholics. She followed with the kind of personal attack she used against the Catholic clergy, shocking the audience when she said of Coughlin "that he, as a celibate never knowing the joys of fatherhood, could come here and tell us to increase and multiply. It seems to me that if that is the word of God, certainly he should be on the job."[45]

In the course of fourteen congressional hearings, Sanger chose as additional witnesses eugenicists, doctors, rabbis, ministers, and prominent citizens, most notably Katharine Houghton Hepburn, her contemporary from Corning. Hepburn's daughter Katharine, who won an Academy Award for her 1933 performance in *Morning Glory*, was emerging as a Hollywood star, useful for publicity purposes. "When they ask me what I think," she wrote Sanger, "I say that I stand back of everything that Mother & you say on the subject."[46] Sanger also recruited average Americans such as Vito Silecchia, her one-time coal and ice vendor from Brooklyn and father of four who testified that he was a Catholic. "And Catholics say we must have much children. I say different." He had followed Mrs. Sanger's advice and could support his family. But as for his relatives, they could not afford their families of ten and eleven. Grateful for his prosperity, "I owe everything to Mrs. Sanger."[47]

Of course Sanger played the starring role as the movement's birth mother. She had, after all, named it and nurtured it to its contemporary coming-of-age. In her testimony, she repetitively referred to those action-filled, iconic events of her past: the Sadie Sachs story, her exile and imprisonment, her suppressed writing and lectures, her clinic in New York, and the organizations she had founded. With public opinion shifting in her favor, Sanger introduced the names of seventy-four organizations that now supported her bill. They ranged from women's clubs like that in Nagatuck, Connecticut, to churches such as the Hartford Unitarian Church, national groups such as the Federation of Jewish Organizations, and even the formerly dismissive American Eugenics Society. But she had no answer to questioners who asked why, if hers was a "doctors' bill," was the most powerful medical organization in the United States, the American Medical Association, not included in her list?

As Sanger explained to the president of the Washington, D.C., Medical Association, who had asked the same question:

> It is my deepest concern and ardent desire to have the A.M.A take over, bag and baggage, and lead (not only stand behind) the Birth Control work . . . I have on every occasion in public and in private insisted that the public go to the physician in order to secure the safest contraception. Even when this stand on my part has been the means of breaking up my own organization, I have stood by that principle because I believe it and know it to be true.[48]

But she had to wait until 1937 before the AMA formally endorsed birth control, with the restriction that only in medically supervised clinics could birth control be prescribed.

In her appearances before congressional committees, Sanger sought to educate legislators about the positive work of birth control in clinics that by 1931 numbered 155, most affiliated with her Birth Control Research Bureau. She pointed out the ways in which clinics were hampered by their inability to legally import contraceptive devices, and in her status as America's best-known sex educator, she offered her recipes for a successful marriage, from child spacing to delayed marriage. Adopting the fungible issue of birth control to the Great Depression, she noted how contraception would save welfare costs. Finally she separated birth control from abortion and pornography, making the case that it did not interfere with the development of life, as some confused critics still suggested.

Sanger reserved ten minutes of her time for rebuttals so that she could close with high-minded sentiments and glittering generalities: "I believe we should consider under the Constitution of the United States that every woman should have the right to life, liberty and the pursuit of happiness." "We want children conceived in love, born of parents' conscious desire and born into the world with healthy sound bodies and minds." And to those who persisted with their examples of great men who arrived at the end, not the beginning, of their parents' fertility and therefore with birth control would never have been born—the seventh-child pattern—she responded that Jesus was the firstborn of Joseph and Mary and he had no children. The audience hissed and groaned, as Catholics in the audience crossed themselves at such heresy.[49]

Among the bill's opponents was her persistent antagonist Dr. Howard A. Kelly, the now retired Johns Hopkins gynecologist of international fame. The fact that Kelly's Johns Hopkins colleague Dr. John Whitridge Williams had earlier testified in favor of the bill indicated the growing defection of doctors to the Sanger camp. But Kelly remained intransigent. Noting that he had practiced medicine for thirty years, Kelly spoke not as a physician but as an evangelical Episcopalian, "for the enlightened conscience of the Christian people, Protestant as well as Catholic . . . Birth control breaks down the sanctity of the most intimate human relations. There are functions in life that are private and personal and which instinct teaches us should be barred from common conversation. I speak in defense of the marriage bed and in opposition to those who would subject the most intimate and pure expression of affection between husband and wife to the degradations of manipulations begun in the first intercourse and continued indefinitely." Although this father of nine still believed that even the occasional use of pessaries caused cancer in women, Kelly argued the harder-to-overturn ethical case against birth control: "My plea is wholly on moral grounds—that morality which separates man from beast . . . The proper stand is self-control."[50]

Shifting to scientific arguments in her rebuttal, Sanger described Kelly as a representative of those doctors who opposed birth control because they did not know the facts. "Here is a man like Doctor Kelly who has made his reputation in medicine . . . coming here and talking not on the merits of the bill, but on a defense of 'morals' . . . Dr. Kelly has not been in school in the last twenty or thirty years where he might have learned something of the modern technique of contraception."[51] For Sanger, his view was opinion, like the argument of the Catholic Church that intercourse, the church's only approved sexual practice, must be solely for procreation, while hers was fact, based on scientific, expert evidence of contraception's social and medical benefits to individual women, children, and the community. But no matter how impressive her arguments, no matter how many congressmen she cornered, year after year the bill failed.

Though sometimes mistaken in her statistics, exaggerated in her claims, and vitriolic in her attacks on opponents, Sanger surprised her critics. The contrast between her personal appearance and her views—this demure, slight, conservatively dressed woman looked like any congressman's wife and not the imagined loud-mouthed virago or exotic advocate of free love— shocked both legislators and the press. Still, despite Sanger's appearance, habitual optimism, and determined advocacy, it soon became obvious that Congress would not modify the Comstock Act, even for doctors, much less for everyone, as Mary Ware Dennett had attempted in the 1920s. Change must come from another direction.

In 1930 Dennett, reigniting their old feud, undermined Sanger's lobbying initiative by insisting that her "open bill" would solve the problem of access. In a public letter to the Senate Judiciary Committee, written just as Sanger prepared to testify, Dennett argued that Sanger's legislation was unnecessary. The widespread use of contraceptives already made the Comstock law "a dead letter." Why not then simply remove contraception "in a clean repeal" from the clause on obscenity and allow everyone access, not just doctors, who would now control the process under Sanger's approach? Surely, taunted Dennett in a letter to her adversary, Sanger did not want future "debunking biographers . . . to picture you as a leader whose vision grew dim. People love their popular heroes with wonderful persistence. Don't disappoint them."[52]

For Sanger, there had always been public as well as private reasons to oppose the "open bill." Complete access encouraged the commercialization of inferior products by moneymaking quacks—"the profiteers, the bootleggers and the abortionists" whose frauds damaged the reliability of authentic birth control techniques.[53] Intending that contraceptive research be incorporated into scientific investigations, she identified birth control's future with medical experts. Besides, no Congress would ever approve Dennett's sweeping change. Such a strategy had failed in the 1920s, and Dennett's lack of success had been one reason she had organized the NCFLBC. Her bill, by handing the matter over to doctors, was more acceptable to Congress and the public. Given their previous rivalry, Sanger resented Dennett's interference as a malicious effort to revive the latter's reputation and the Voluntary Parenthood League. Remembering personal insults, Sanger recalled that Dennett had described her as a bomb thrower and, more recently, as a poorly dressed, undereducated woman whose lower-class status and accent hampered her congressional campaign. Writing in her 1926 *Birth Control Laws*, Dennett had even accused Sanger of radicalizing contraception—breaking laws rather than trying to change them—

and when Sanger's domination of birth control became obvious, Dennett trivialized her rival: "Birth Control is your whole career, it is only an incident in mine."[54] Such slights must not go unanswered.

"Many people who received your confusing unsportsmanlike letter," Sanger responded, "agree that if you are out of the running, why not stay out and give others a chance to win out. You had your day, you had the open field, and we are still cleaning up the messy confusion in Washington as a result of the open bill . . . Had I started in the BC movement with all your experience & knowledge it would have been a different story, but I was, as you have repeatedly told strangers, not so clever as you & with not the same background . . . I'm not afraid of biographers . . . It's my own vision I want to keep clear & my own integrity to keep inviolate which makes biography interesting."[55]

Dennett was not the only birth control advocate to challenge Sanger. The influential suffragist sisters Jessie Ames Marshall of New York and Blanche Ames Ames of Massachusetts complained that her bill, by giving doctors authority, would stifle nonmedical approaches. Many middle-class women were able to purchase spermicides and pessaries from pharmacies, diaphragms from Bloomingdale's for $2.50, and contraceptive products mailed under covert labels marked "feminine hygiene." Nor, in Sanger's bill, were there any exemptions "for social and economic reasons, or just plain reasons. How would that help?" Besides, argued Jessie Marshall, no longer did the Post Office interfere with contraceptives sent through the mail "from an authorized sender to a qualified recipient with a worthy intent." Such transformations in the Post Office's policy would be threatened by legislation "tinkering with the present statutes."[56]

Sanger's response made clear the distance between accommodating progressives and single-minded radicals. As Sanger wrote to Marshall, "We should never be satisfied with a Post Office ruling . . . as long as we have a good fighting organization and are daily arousing the public to think of Birth Control and . . . are getting our Congressmen to think on the subject in relation to other social subjects . . . It would be treason and a betrayal of trust to lay down arms with a flimsy ruling based on a case of a diseased man and a tubercular woman," the latter the specific circumstances that the Post Office had approved for the mailing of birth control material. "I know you cannot expect us to stop our work of changing a very old Federal Statute and accepting instead a limited ruling by a Post Office Official." Instead, Sanger urged the Ames sisters to "come down and help us put this

Bill through." Unconvinced, Marshall predicted that Sanger's bill ensured women would remain "apologizing supplicants on the medical door step."[57] But given the currently available methods of birth control for women, her commitment to pessaries, and her expectation that scientists would soon find a better contraceptive, Sanger wondered what she could do differently.

Sanger continued to use censorship to promote her cause. Prohibited from speaking at a forum in Boston, she marched onto the stage with a gag over her mouth, standing silently while the Harvard historian Arthur Schlesinger read her speech: "As a fighting pioneer, I believe in Free Speech. As a propagandist, I see immense advantages in being gagged. It silences me, but it makes millions of others talk about me and the cause for which I live."[58] Later in the program the famous lawyer Clarence Darrow, recent advocate for the defense in the Scopes Monkey Trial, defended Sanger to the audience of over seven hundred: "Error and ignorance [are] often extreme and often entrenched in the law. But no power on earth can stop the work Mrs. Sanger has begun."[59]

Along with her activism and lobbying, Sanger educated the public through her books. During the late 1920s an outpouring of marriage manuals sought to instruct a poorly informed population about sex. Some covered specific reproductive organs in far more anatomical detail than many medical texts. Others focused on modern practices, from recommendations for variety in sexual positions to the importance of mutual orgasm. Male doctors wrote them, although the BCCRB's Dr. Hannah Stone collaborated with her husband, the urologist Dr. Abraham Stone, in their popular *Marriage Manual*, which, for its explicitness, remained unmailable, but very popular, until after World War II.

Sanger had already covered some of these topics in *Family Limitation*, now in its tenth edition. Forever jealous of competitors—even those across the Atlantic—Sanger feared that her English rival Marie Stopes might eclipse her dominant status in the movement. Now allowed into the United States, Stopes's *Married Love*, with its frank description of intercourse, had already sold a million copies in Europe, and Stopes had recently completed another marriage manual, *Wise Parenthood*. Hastily, Sanger published her own romanticized paean to marriage in which birth-controlled marital intercourse became "a dance of soul as well as body, a dance in which two humans are no longer separate and distinct but in which their beings are comingled in a new and higher unity."[60] Published in 1926, *Happiness in*

Marriage, along with its sentimental views of courting and practical tips on keeping hair, "a girl's crowning glory," and teeth clean, promoted a feminist message: women must abandon their prudishness as "docile, passive child bearers," become "comrades and partners," and understand that their sexuality—with the clitoris "the special seat of sensitiveness"—embraced far more than motherhood. "Never be ashamed of passion. If you are strongly sexed," she wrote in a message she lived, "you are richly endowed."[61]

Satisfying erotic relationships, especially relevant in a postwar society with climbing divorce rates, encouraged the ideal of companionate marriage based on mutually gratifying sex for both partners. For years Sanger had detested the antiquated views of suffragists that birth control denied women their power *not* to have sex. Instead, living the benefits of sexual intimacy—in and out of marriage—she enjoyed principled, nonmonogamous, spontaneous liaisons—what some progressives called "varietism," though she never acknowledged any private behavior that might embarrass her cause. In her version of the double standard, men initiated sex and were natural pursuers, while women must direct the process and prevent men from allowing "the marriage relation from drifting into a sort of master and slave relationship."[62]

Like Stopes, Sanger still accepted the controversial view of periodicity, with certain days in the menstrual cycle those of enhanced sexual arousal in women. As for men, disingenuously betraying her own personal behavior, "the man who is notoriously promiscuous is most often he who is unable to awaken the deeper love of any one woman. If the women's side might be heard, we should hear a tale of selfishness and disappointment, of this Don Juan's inability to understand anything but his own gluttonous appetite."[63] Ever practical, for marriage was more than sex, Sanger recommended to these imagined lover-husbands the shared housework that neither of her husbands provided and a mutually agreed upon budget that Noah Slee demanded.

Too conservative for the market, *Happiness in Marriage* never sold well. Ten pages of 230 were too few to spend on what other sex experts such as Theodore Van de Velde, in his popular *Ideal Marriage: Its Physiology and Technique*, emphasized—the explicit practices of intercourse and the significance of vaginal orgasms. Besides, Margaret Sanger was the brand name for contraception, not happy marriage. To a reviewer in *The New York Times*, *Happiness in Marriage* threatened Sanger's reputation as "the terrible

Margaret Sanger whom thousands of the pious have been taught to regard
as the female Antichrist [but who] is engaged in no more iniquitous enterprise than the effort to make people be happy."⁶⁴

Spurred on by this chilly reception, two years later Sanger published
her cautionary tale, *Motherhood in Bondage*. Dedicated to Havelock Ellis,
the book was an edited collection of 470 letters selected from the thousands she received. For over fifteen years, ever since her articles in *The New
York Call*, she had given advice and found the role of counselor gratifying.
These letters, mostly from mothers, but some from sisters, daughters, and
even a few husbands, were separated into sections titled "girl mothers," "the
trap of maternity," "the struggle of the unfit," "the pinch of poverty," "marital relations," and "solitary confinement," the latter a precursor to Betty
Friedan's acknowledgment in the early 1960s of the boredom and isolation
of mothers living with "the problem that has no name."

Sanger's responses covered a range of sage replies to mothers with too
many children who wanted no more, mothers who hated sex because they
feared pregnancy, mothers who complained of bad health after multiple
pregnancies, and mothers who had neither money nor energy to raise another child. *Motherhood in Bondage* celebrated these "uneducated clients"
for their desire to raise better babies: "These mothers reveal themselves
strangely conscious of their duty to the race, of the sacredness of their maternal function, of their realization that the life-stream must be kept clean
and fresh."⁶⁵

Sanger mailed *Motherhood in Bondage* to philanthropists who might
give money to the movement and to public figures, including former president William Howard Taft, currently Chief Justice of the Supreme Court,
and Franklin Roosevelt. She also sent a copy to the most prominent American exponent of the Catholic Church's position on birth control, Reverend
John Ryan. To one recipient, with solemn self-approval, she noted that "never
before in any recorded document has the tragedy of motherhood been so
poignantly or so tragically revealed. That every social problem confronting
American Civilization today is organically bound up with questions of parenthood and home life is illuminated by the cumulative power of the evidence here presented."⁶⁶

Disappointing sales became an incentive for another book. In 1931
Sanger published her controversial autobiography *My Fight for Birth Control*, her third book in five years. At first she had tried to persuade her

English admirers Havelock Ellis and Hugh de Selincourt to write her biography; both had politely declined. Unless she told it herself, for the rest of her life, the story of Margaret Sanger would rest with either harsh critics or admiring idolaters. Preoccupied in 1930 and 1931 with her lobbying efforts, she hired a ghost writer, whom she promptly fired, then hired another who, refusing to remain anonymous after her hard work, insisted, unsuccessfully, that her name appear on the title page along with Sanger's.[67]

Neither gracefully written nor accurate about many events, *My Fight* was aptly titled: it was a nonfictional example of what the Germans call a *Bildungsroman*—an account of how character is formed, with Sanger as the protagonist amid the many tests of her moral fiber, a pilgrim's progress of overcoming obstacles. Fittingly, she had considered the title "Battles and Victories for Birth Control." Sanger spent little time on her early life before she became a disciple of birth control, racing through thirty-four years in 44 pages of a 353-page book. Nor did she credit anyone but herself, even though, as reviewers noted, she had made no scientific contribution to birth control. But who in the early 1930s had?

Sanger, according to Dr. Fred Hankins in a harsh review published in *The Birth Control Review*, boasted that she had created "the wave" of birth control, when in fact she had "merely been caught up by that wave itself . . . This is neither good history nor good autobiography . . . it lacks balance and proportion . . . overall a humorless book, an egotistical book."[68] Sanger replied with ironic pliancy: if Hankins would tell her the names of these other persons to whom full credit must be given, she would include them in the next edition *"which I am already preparing."* Besides, *My Fight* was intended "neither as an autobiography nor a history of the movement, but rather as reminiscences."[69] When the book did not sell as well as expected, Sanger decided that women were too embarrassed to ask for a book with "birth control" in the title. But well aware of how important her story remained to her followers, seven years later Sanger published a smoother version of events. This time she chose the title *Margaret Sanger: An Autobiography.*

She was devastated when her beloved de Selincourt echoed complaints that she had overlooked others in the movement, and that the glossy portrayal of her marriage to Bill Sanger was false. "Now Hugh dear, just be fair, read again those pages about Stopes & see if I was saying 'I've done the whole thing.'" Besides, as far as her marriage to Bill Sanger was concerned, "there is no lie to any caress or kiss I have ever given—Ever." In any case, how could Hugh know her feelings? Only that true diviner of women's emotions, Havelock Ellis, knew her heart, and he liked the book.[70]

Along with popularizing birth control through her writing, Sanger continued her self-appointed task of stimulating research on new contraceptive methods. At her urging, Slee had invested fifteen thousand dollars in the Holland-Rantos Company. By supporting a reputable business, she intended to challenge the black-market trade in worthless goods advertised under the vague label of feminine hygiene. Run by Herbert Simonds, a former Sanger dancing partner, the company manufactured among its other products for gynecological use an expensive, spring-type pessary of handmade latex. Sanger hoped these new devices, made by a respected business that sold to hospitals and physicians, would end the illegal importing of European diaphragms, the latter no longer referring to various medical instruments called pessaries but by 1930 a label increasingly reserved for contraceptive devices. Yet by federal law the Holland-Rantos Company still could not mail diaphragms to doctors and clinics outside of New York.

Sanger also encouraged Julius Schmid, the condom king, to manufacture diaphragms. Schmid, a Jewish immigrant, had been working in a sausage factory stuffing pork meat into casings when he experienced a revelation similar to that of ancient Egyptians and medieval Basque sheepherders: animal intestines, especially those of sheep, made reliable condoms. Soon Schmid was fashioning condoms at night in the cellar of his Brooklyn home, and by 1935 Julius Schmid Incorporated was a multimillion-dollar business. Advances in galvanized rubber and latex molds transformed his Ramses, Sheik, and Forex brands into international bestsellers, with an estimated 150 million condoms sold in 1935. Arrested earlier under the Comstock laws, Schmid had spent too much time on his own research to consider manufacturing female contraceptives that could be neither openly advertised nor marketed.

While encouraging new technology in the United States, Sanger heard rumors that Professor Ivan Tushnov of the Soviet Union's Institute for Experimental Medicine had developed an effective vaccine using spermatoxins, the naturally produced antigens created when sperm was injected subcutaneously into females. In laboratories from Baltimore to Moscow, immunologists were investigating the possibility of a vaccine for women that might deliver a year's infertility. According to reports, Tushnov had already treated thirty women; twenty-two, he insisted, had not conceived for over five months. At a time in medical history when vaccines against diphtheria, pertussis, and tetanus had been successfully developed, an approach based on stimulating the immune system with antibodies seemed scientifically possible.

Sanger hurried to the Soviet Union in July 1934, taking Grant, a first-year medical student at Cornell, with her. They met H. G. Wells and his son in Moscow, and traveled, to Sanger's dismay, in a supervised group to Leningrad and Odessa. Her friend the writer Agnes Smedley had cautioned Sanger not to compare Russia to the United States but only to itself during the time of the czars. Despite the advice, Sanger was disappointed. As with so many magic solutions she investigated throughout her life, her search for an effective spermatoxin immunization turned out to be a fool's errand. Meanwhile, Sanger found Russia cold, inhospitable, and miserable. But in typical fashion she educated herself, visiting Russia's hospitals and clinics, admiring those conveniently placed in railway stations, but decrying the nation's high number of abortions and lack of accessible contraception. Just as depressing as Tushnov's closed laboratory were the claims of Stalinist rulers that Communist regimes could ensure the welfare of all children born in modern Russia.[71]

On her return Sanger confronted a new Catholic approach to birth control. In 1932 Dr. Leo Latz, a Catholic doctor at the Loyola University Medical Center in Chicago, published *The Rhythm of Sterility and Fertility*, a book that drew on familiar knowledge about female reproduction. Along with his heretical belief that having children was not essential to marriage, Latz explained that there were some days in the menstrual cycle in which women were sterile. With a proper understanding of these safe days, women could control their pregnancies. Perhaps the rhythm method, promoted as a natural approach, might satisfy the church's prohibitions against artificial methods. Soon calendars appeared in parish halls, and local priests seized on the technique. Indeed Latz's book included testimonials from prominent American Catholics, including one bishop.

From her work in the clinic Sanger knew all about the erratic nature of individual menstrual cycles. The rhythm method trapped women, she argued, into a dangerous approach whose practitioners had high failure rates. Soon Catholic women recognized the unreliability of the rhythm method, while Latz's claims for any moral differentiation from other contraceptive methods appeared specious to others, and certainly to Sanger. But at last, concluded Sanger, Catholics "have come to say marriage is not solely for the creation of children—nor is sex!"[72]

Dismissing Latz, Sanger continued her search for better contraceptive methods with little success, at least during the 1930s when scientists, mostly in Great Britain and the United States, were using sophisticated cellular chemistry and powerful microscopes to isolate sex hormones. Among an interdisciplinary, international community of biologists, chemists, physicians, and zoologists, the regulatory authority of sex hormones—what in his famous textbook Dr. Edgar Allen called "internal secretions"—was being unraveled. Reproductive endocrinology, no longer a stepchild of other research fields, had emerged as a worthy, if needy, enterprise. An impatient Sanger believed these scientists asked the wrong questions; too many of their experiments focused on the relation of hormones to sex determination, rather than on controlling fertility.

From 1920 to 1940, basic research involving the way in which hormones controlled the female reproductive cycle was deciphering the mysteries of the previously overlooked anterior pituitary gland, with its critical follicle-stimulating and luteinizing hormones, along with the remnant corpus luteum, which, like a timer, gradually secreted more progesterone to end the sequence of egg maturation. All played crucial, interactive roles in fertility. And fertility was still what attracted most endocrinologists. "We don't give a damn about contraception," explained Dr. Earl Engle, a physician who worked on estrogen in Columbia University's anatomy department. "We want a basic study of the basic factors in human reproduction."[73] By this time Sanger, quotes Dr. Adele Clark, a student of the history of endocrinology, "knew what she wanted from the scientists, knew what their research on contraception would likely produce and was still unable to induce any scientist who could make a contribution to engage in such work until the 1950's."[74] The building blocks of investigative understanding existed; the change in social values, which so greatly impact science, had not kept pace.

Initially Sanger recruited the zoologist-physician Dr. F. A. Crew, director of the Department of Animal Research at the University of Edinburgh, who, though partially funded by the Rockefeller-sponsored Bureau of Social Hygiene, turned to Sanger for more money. Crew had attended the Sanger-organized World Population Conference in 1927 and had attracted her interest with his experimental work on animals that suggested some combination of hormone injections might prevent eggs from entering the uterus. Sanger promised Crew five thousand dollars for his research and solicited a new friend and benefactor of the birth control movement, Katharine Dexter McCormick, for more.

One of only two females in her class at MIT, Katharine Dexter had married Stanley McCormick, heir to the International Harvester fortune, shortly after her graduation in 1904. As her husband's moods and erratic behavior intensified, McCormick searched for a cure for his disease, interviewing scientists and the new breed of psychiatrists. Until he descended into hopeless insanity, variously diagnosed as dementia praecox and catatonia, and was permanently confined in the McCormick mansion near Montecito, California, rescuing her husband became the principal motive of her life. At fifty-three, a childless woman with time and money, the virtual widow of "the Mad Millionaire" also embraced feminist causes, including suffrage and birth control. Sanger and McCormick first met in 1917, when Sanger had testified at the Boston trial of a man arrested for distributing *Family Limitation*. Unchallenged by U.S. Customs, McCormick had become one of Sanger's principal smugglers, sewing diaphragms into her clothes and packing others—over a thousand on her frequent European trips—into the eight trunks she ferried back and forth across the Atlantic.

In 1928 Sanger enlisted McCormick's help. "Dr. F. A. Crew believes with me that research on contraceptives is now an important step upon which the future of the movement must wait and he is willing to go ahead and set up a special department for this work. He has already brought from Berlin a clever, brilliant geneticist Dr. Weisner to assist him."[75] But after receiving McCormick's check for five thousand dollars and setting up a lab to study spermicides, Crew shifted his research to experiments on basic questions of reproductive physiology. More interested in broad explorations than targeted applications, he now bristled at Sanger's impositions: "The real scientist is not an employee. He starts out to find something but may discover something on the way that changes the whole course of his investigations. He can't have someone pulling strings and keeping him on course."[76]

Crew disagreed with Sanger on the eugenic benefits of birth control: "You can breed for height and or blue eyes or other presumably controllable traits, but you cannot breed for fitness and all sorts of abstract social qualities. It is only common sense to sterilize feebleminded or grossly defective individuals because they are obviously incapable of raising their own offspring, but it is absurd to think that in doing so we shall breed out mental defectiveness or crime."[77]

Undeterred, Sanger continued to promote eugenics. She courted its leading advocates, such as Henry Fairchild, a professor of sociology at New York University and, in 1930, the head of the American Eugenics Society, along with Clarence Little, the zoologist, now president of the University of Michigan, appointing them to the advisory board of her clinic. She solicited their scholarly papers for her conferences; she asked them to testify in congressional hearings during the early 1930s. In turn former critics came to accept birth control as a weapon in the fight against the high birthrates of the "deficient," though not one as effective as involuntary surgical sterilization. Some eugenicists even urged the merging of their principal journal with The Birth Control Review.

These years were the high tide of the eugenics movement before it fell from popular favor in the late 1930s. Supporters, who believed in the inheritability of everything from promiscuity to tuberculosis, organized traveling exhibits promoting "better babies." "Some people are born to be a burden on the rest," went one slogan. Especially popular was a machine shown at country fairs that lit up every five seconds with the sign "$100 of your money goes for the care of a person with bad heredity." But five minutes elapsed before the light flashed, indicating the birth of a "high grade" American. By 1926 eugenicists had organized a national organization—its symbol a tree with well-defined, healthy roots. Then, in 1927, the U.S. Supreme Court gave its sanction to the harshest of all eugenic proposals: compulsory sterilization.

The case of Buck v. Bell, instituted by its supporters as a test case, involved the legality of Virginia's sterilization laws and, by implication, procedures employed by thirty other states. The plaintiff was Carrie Buck, the mother of a child born out of wedlock and a resident of the Virginia Colony for Epileptics and Feebleminded in Lynchburg, Virginia. Brought by her guardian, the suit involved seventeen-year-old Buck, who had been sterilized, without permission, in an operation in the infirmary that removed an inch of her Fallopian tubes, which were ligated and then sutured back together, with the intended result that she could never have another child. The rationale for such an operation had been obvious to the Virginia doctor Joseph DeJarnette, who, with a large practice based on sterilization, was distressed by the fact that "the Germans are beating us at our own game."[78] Most Americans agreed: a 1937 July poll in Fortune, four years after Hitler had begun adopting American laws to purify Germany's gene pool, found that two-thirds of the nation favored forced sterilization for mental defectives.

Already stigmatized by the authorities' conclusion that her mother was feebleminded and shiftless, Buck, as measured by the Stanford-Binet intelligence test, was not an "idiot," but she did fall into the recently established classification of the unfit—that of "morons"—according to eugenicists. Unless segregated in an institution and sterilized, she would soon be producing more "deficient" Americans. Indeed, her daughter Vivian already gave signs, according to the superintendent, of below-average intelligence in the range of feeblemindedness. As the eugenicist Harry Laughlin, himself a secret sufferer of epilepsy, explained in his deposition to the court, there was no harm in a procedure to which over eighty-five hundred American women and a few men had already been subjected.

The Supreme Court, considering the case in 1927, agreed in an 8–1 vote. The court relied on the police powers; there was no mention of the Fourteenth Amendment's due process and equal protection clauses. Nor was there discussion of the constitutional prohibition of cruel and unusual punishment. The much admired Oliver Wendell Holmes wrote the majority opinion, which was signed as well by both Louis Brandeis, well-known for his advocacy of individual rights, and former president William Howard Taft, now Chief Justice of the Supreme Court: "It is better for all the world, if instead of waiting to execute the degenerate offspring for crime, or to let them starve for their imbecility, society can prevent those who are manifestly unfit from continuing their kind. The principle that sustains compulsory vaccination is broad enough to cover cutting the Fallopian tubes." As Holmes memorably concluded, "Three generations of imbeciles are enough."[79]

After this decision Sanger became an outspoken supporter of involuntary sterilization, though only if it retained sexual instincts and impulses, which it did. Her views, abhorrent by today's standards, should be seen in the context of a time in American history when prominent Americans—from presidents to Supreme Court justices to scientists—believed in genetic improvement through the intervention of the state. In a speech before the New History Society in New York, a group that promoted peace and disarmament, Sanger envisioned her own plan for peace and called for, along with her support for Woodrow Wilson's moribund Fourteen Points, a special federal department for the study of population problems, along with a parliament of population representing the various branches of science.

Their main function would be to improve the American population by "applying a stern and rigid policy of sterilization and segregation to that grade of population whose progeny is already tainted or whose inheritance is such that objectionable traits may be transmitted to offspring . . . The whole dysgenic population would have its choice of segregation on farm lands and homesteads for their entire lives or sterilization." In a rare speech that made no mention of birth control, Sanger promoted the idea of a federal program of lifetime pensions for those who agreed to be sterilized.[80] The need was obvious, she maintained, at a time when philanthropy and welfare were hindering the inexorable Darwinian process of natural selection. In her favorite metaphor, the human garden of weak and incompetent needed weeding.

Five months after the *Buck v. Bell* decision, Sanger attended the First World Population Conference in Geneva. As its main organizer, she had established a planning committee, raised money, solicited papers, arranged housing for participants, hired translators, and designed and printed the program. She had chosen Geneva because the League of Nations, in session at the time, might pay attention to concerns over population. Already she had determined that population experts, like eugenicists, were emerging as an expanding pool of potential supporters, and so she invited biologists, physicians, statisticians, and zoologists, all with prestigious appointments and scholarly reputations. In a measure of her prominence, few declined, especially if she promised travel expenses. From Johns Hopkins the prestigious professor of pathology and member of the American Eugenics Society Dr. William Welch came, and from Scotland her ally Dr. F. A. Crew, the biologist who made, as Sanger noted, hens crow. The Italian government, now under Mussolini's control, sent a Fascist mouthpiece who denounced Sanger and left. And there were Catholic scientists from Spain and Portugal who complained of a display that included books on birth control.

For three days the all-male group of eight hundred delivered and listened to papers mostly on differential national rates of population growth and their economic implications. "The forbidden topic of birth control," Sanger later acknowledged, "was edged about like a time bomb which might explode at any minute."[81] The last day delegates thanked Sanger and sang a rousing chorus of "For she's a jolly good fellow," having first humiliated her.

Presiding officer Sir Bernard Mallet, the registrar general of England and Wales and "a lesser lord," according to Sanger, had made clear that there must be no mention of contraception or even Malthusianism. This was a scientific conference. Far worse, Mallet, announcing that the organizers should never be acknowledged, had crossed off Sanger's name and that of other women who had worked for nearly a year on the conference. The meeting would be the laughingstock of Europe if it was known "that a woman had brought us together." Sanger protested that these "workers" were "in their particular lines . . . just as much experts as the scientists."[82] Outraged at the slight to Sanger and to themselves, the twenty-one female typists, stenographers, translators, and organizers threatened to leave. But Sanger, often accused of selfishness in her desire for publicity, agreed to a conference-saving compromise. Her name would not appear on the program of the conference, but she made sure that after her hard work of editing the conference proceedings, she was listed as a member of the general council.

After ten years of spreading the word through conferences, books, associations with eugenicists and scientists, and her lobbying in Washington, Sanger was ready for a summation of her efforts. She had brought the movement to a higher platform of notoriety and nationalized the debate over birth control through her four-pronged curriculum of agitation, education, organization, and legislation. To do so, on a cold rainy night in the nation's capital in February 1935, she delivered the keynote address to a meeting of birth control advocates, prominent citizens, and ten "pioneers" honored for their dedicated work in legalizing contraception.

The event was intended as a fund-raiser for the NCFLBC, and Sanger had struggled with the arrangements—the invitations, the speakers, the location, and even the size of the audience. Florence Rose, the mercurial daughter of Jewish Hungarian immigrants and since 1930 Sanger's devoted secretary, had helped arrange the event in Washington's Mayflower Hotel ballroom, the only place in town that could hold the crowd of nearly a thousand. They paid ten dollars to hear Sanger, the New York pediatrician Dr. Ira Wile, and the newly famous Pearl Buck, who had just won the Pulitzer Prize for *The Good Earth*, her bestselling novel about China. A recent convert to the birth control movement, Buck, succumbing to both Sanger's public cause and private charm, introduced her friend as "a great name of the present . . . In the future people will be astonished, as we are now astonished, that the things for which Margaret Sanger fights should ever have been opposed or wondered at or taken for anything else than a matter of inevitable human right and reason."[83]

Sanger depended on celebrities such as Buck to attract audiences, though, as often as not, she was the star. For months she had solicited other notables, including her prominent English friends H. G. Wells and George Bernard Shaw, both of whom declined but sent telegrams of support. She contacted Havelock Ellis, who rarely left London and Cornwall and never spoke in public anyway. Sanger planned her Emancipation Dinner for Lincoln's birthday, so as to connect the president's freeing of the slaves with her own movement to liberate American women from their slavery of unwanted pregnancies.

The purpose of the meeting was not just to raise money to finance her lobbying efforts. As always, Sanger campaigned to nudge public opinion toward acceptance of a practice that still lurked in the shadows—publicly censored and unmentionable in polite company. Certainly there had been progress in the twenty-one years since her first indictment for violating the Comstock laws. Yet some observers considered Sanger no more than a symbolic expression of changing American values about sex and family size, her advocacy simply a reflection of a silent transformation occurring in the bedrooms of America.

To the contrary, Sanger and her devoted following insisted that she had created a shift in public opinion that permitted her, in 1935, to promote contraception publicly with prominent citizens at her side, her remarks certain to appear in the next day's *Washington Post* and *New York Times*, and on this special night carried on NBC Radio. Four years earlier she had received an award from the prestigious American Woman's Association, a group of professional and businesswomen, for her "vision, valor, and integrity." (She joked that she was happy to be receiving something other than an arrest warrant.) The well-known sociologist at the University of Wisconsin, Dr. E. A. Ross, had included her, along with Supreme Court Justice Louis Brandeis, the philosopher John Dewey, and New York's governor, Franklin Roosevelt, in his 1930 list of the ten greatest living Americans. Her organization received legacies from ordinary Americans such as Viola Kaufman, whom she had never met but who specified, in a will contested by relatives, that "this bequest is for the greatest reform ever undertaken . . . by the greatest woman of all time, Margaret Sanger."[84]

Now she could lecture to young students at elite colleges such as Mount Holyoke, Bryn Mawr, and Yale without interference from presidents fearful of the corruption of youth and the complaints of parents. More magazines printed articles about contraception; twenty-five years before, according to the *Readers' Guide to Periodical Literature*, there were no articles on birth control, contraception, or Margaret Sanger, though several covered Theodore Roosevelt's views on race suicide and seventeen had featured eugenicism. By 1929 there were fifteen positive articles about birth control and nine mostly favorable portraits of Sanger, two of which cited her bravery. Most surprising of all, she could lecture on birth control in her heavily Catholic hometown of Corning, at the best hotel in town, to four hundred of what her brother Joe Higgins called "the Tony Irish."[85]

On this anniversary occasion in 1935, by attracting a prominent audience of Washingtonians to the Mayflower Hotel, Sanger intended to continue her pressure on hostile and indifferent congressmen, especially those on the Senate Judiciary and House Ways and Means Committees. She titled her talk "Birth Control Comes of Age," its twenty-one years calculated from her first indictment and celebrated by those willing to overlook its earlier history. The forward-looking, ever-optimistic content of her speech was familiar to her followers. By this time many in the audience knew Sanger by heart, and recognized her arguments for the adoption of birth control as a woman's right, a child's future, and a nation's path to an improved population. What had disappeared from this package was Sanger's earlier commitment to contraception as the means of sexual liberation for women who, without birth control, feared intercourse for the very reason that the Catholic Church intended.

For Sanger, there was no such thing as failure: "If any of you think it was the birth controllers who suffered defeat when our bill was tabled by the House Judiciary Committee, you are greatly mistaken . . . Are we too optimistic in hoping for success? No, we can if we just arise and organize in every state in the Union." Calling for fifty workers to go into action within thirty days, she drew on a suffrage tactic—gather a daunting 1 million signatures on petitions in favor of the bill and deliver them to Congress before the end of the session.

Sanger's energy habitually derived from responding to critics, and so her calls to action included accusations against her opponents. On this February night Sanger attacked the members of the Seventy-third Congress "who have defeated themselves. They defeated themselves by going on record as petty politicians, some of them without vision, others without courage or moral stamina, only thinking of elections."[86]

Along with congressmen, she condemned labor unions, especially the American Federation of Labor, which had opposed an earlier version of her "doctors' bill," along with various social and religious organizations, some strongly opposed, others merely indifferent about an easily avoided matter. Sanger protested that they had failed society by not supporting her movement. As federal agencies known by their initials proliferated during the 1930s—most notably in the alphabet soup organizations of the New Deal—she called for the establishment of a Federal Population Bureau to study demographic trends. By 1935, as more middle-class Americans limited their fertility using a variety of methods, the persisting radicalism of Sanger and her movement was to ensure open discussion, end legal prohibitions, use federal public health workers to prescribe birth control, and, in her next frontier, find better methods. There might be more public supporters of birth control than in 1914 (as well as silent practitioners), but Sanger believed this was a dangerous moment when momentum might be lost. Influential opponents remained who believed censorship essential to maintain sexual purity and who still held power. She intended to continue her battles through a program for the future. "I am convinced that on this 21st Anniversary of the Birth Control Movement, it is sound of body and spirit and we may count on it to build beyond itself a true civilization in America."[87]

Her husband had not been in the audience for her triumphant speech. Estranged from his wife and her cause, he had gone to Tucson and had berated her for her absences. Unforgivably in his telephone calls and his letters, he characterized her as nervous and overworked—in fact, a hysterical woman. Sanger replied, "Our last evening's conversation was an outburst of cruelty from you. Cruel, unkind, tactless and insulting to everything I am." Weeks later, after another bitter exchange, she complained, "Noah darling I just cant take it that's all. I've got to have the kind of love I give . . . It has become unbearable to be scolded like a Parent scolds a child, to be treated as tho' I were a half wit & under the management of a cross old father."[88]

Sanger never lost her husband to South Africa, although he threatened to return to the country of his birth. Instead, amid bickering and perils, the marriage survived until Noah Slee's death in 1942. But, in other ways, Sanger's family circle was shrinking. Michael Higgins, the father whom she credited for her revolutionary instincts, died in 1926 after months of incapacity following a stroke. Earlier she had explained her father to de Selincourt: "He loves a good drink of whiskey and prohibition has been hard on him. He is a poet and the spirit of grain makes him eloquent."[89] Then, older sister Mary Higgins, "the stable sympathetic member of a large family," died of a ruptured appendix. "Her passing loosens up the foundation," Sanger grieved in her diary.[90]

Sometime during the early 1930s Sanger had taken a new lover, and like many of the men in her life, he was an unlikely one. Angus Macdonald, an architect and head of a family firm that designed iron modular bookshelves like those in the Library of Congress, was six years younger than Sanger, though he probably did not know it. Neither rich nor handsome, but a good dancer, he was married and the father of two children. He had fallen to Sanger's charms after he heard her lecture on birth control, and for the rest of their lives he remained a passionate, understanding friend, even as distance and age diminished the sexual fire of their early relationship. In the beginning Sanger had explained, as she always did to her lovers, that she was more often absent than available to fit any man's schedule—"Im a wild Irish will of the wisp & can't ever be counted on beyond your sight."[91] To Juliet Rublee she explained, "I think he begins to realize it is not going to be easy to find me available. Most men . . . think a woman is at their beck and call when they like them. They seldom know our kind."[92]

Unlike her husband, Macdonald responded with calm devotion rather than indignation: "I will never willingly give up the largest, richest, most wholesome experience of my whole life . . . I love you with the very best that is in me and that best is being enriched every day that passes whether I see you in actuality or only in vivid, delightful imagination." Absence only made his heart grow fonder as months went by without any contact. "I find myself loving you more and longing for you more all the time . . . You are the greatest woman that ever lived and the most lovable." And then, ever good-humored as her husband was not, in parentheses he wrote "and impossible."[93]

For fifty-four-year-old Sanger, Macdonald represented her persisting fantasy that she might retire from her commitments to birth control—the lobbying, the writing, the lecturing, and the organizing of conferences with their attendant humiliations—for the indulgent pleasures of upper-class women: shopping, reading, relaxing at spas. She shared with Macdonald her impossible dream. Without the movement, she could have time for some dancing at the Harlem supper clubs. "I'll die in this business before I begin to live," she feared. "I want to elope! Cast off all the clutches and break loose—yes?" Still too much of a self-described "cause woman," Sanger never did.[94] Instead she began planning a trip to India, and in January 1936 sailed on the ocean liner SS *Viceroy* for Bombay.[95]

9

ALL THINGS FADE

There will be a gradual pushing of Margaret Sanger out of this and that—her name left out here and there. Watch and Beware—Stand on Guard.

—Margaret Sanger to Florence Rose, 1939

In November 1935, as Margaret Sanger disembarked in Bombay after rough seas and an uncomfortable seventeen-day voyage from England, a courier pushed through the cheering crowds celebrating her arrival to deliver a much anticipated invitation. It came from Mahatma Gandhi, the leader of the nationalist movement in India. After his return to India from South Africa and his emergence as Mahatma, "the Great Soul" who would free India, Gandhi had condemned any separation of sex from reproduction, calling birth control "undignified" and an open door to extramarital promiscuity. At this stage of his political career Gandhi's calls for abstinence mirrored his political initiatives: Indians must achieve personal self-discipline in their sexual lives, a restraint to be matched by their public resolve in a nonviolent struggle for independence against the British. As Sanger routinely did when any world leader stigmatized birth control, she had challenged his position and had begun a brief correspondence that ended in a casual invitation. Now she hoped to meet the man Indians were calling Bapu—Father—and perhaps change his views.[1]

In her ten-week visit to India Sanger covered ten thousand miles, visited eighteen cities, spent twenty nights on bumpy trains, delivered sixty-three addresses, was picketed twice by Roman Catholic priests, and had several meetings closed down. Detailing her experiences in "Hello Everyone" letters to the clinic staff, published in 377 American newspapers in

forty-three states, Sanger described traveling in zigzag fashion across the
country, to the north, then to the east across the thousand-mile waist of
India to Calcutta, then back to Delhi and a visit to the Taj Mahal, where
"the mystic light [seemed] akin to another dimension," and finally to the
southern coast before leaving for China.[2] Everywhere she took her gynae-
plaques, the life-sized rubber models of women's reproductive organs that
could be dismantled and reassembled for the lessons in female anatomy
both sexes needed. She brought along as well a graphic film on the physiology of contraception that elicited great cheers from one audience when an
already fertilized egg rejected a competitive second sperm. And, of course,
she brought her energetic, charismatic advocacy of birth control. Sanger
acknowledged that her audiences craved discussion of methods, not just
theories. Sometimes she provided such specific information in lectures to
Indian doctors and in private consultations in her hotel room, where she
led the social workers and leaders of the women's movement who flocked
to her meetings.

Her standard lecture dealt with population pressures in India and was
innocuously entitled "Making Civilization Healthy." As she wrote to a friend,
"I do not believe that the birth control movement will succeed in any part
of the Orient by use of methods known in this country."[3] In India there
could be no measuring for diaphragms among a population of rural and village women, half of whose children died before they were five. These families subsisted on five cents a day and had neither running water nor access
to physicians. With an exploding population of 370 million in 1930—195
people per square mile who were dependent for food on uncertain weather
conditions and an unmechanized agricultural economy—India required an
inexpensive, easy-to-use method of birth control. Sanger offered the formula for a cheap spermicide foam powder of vinegar, benzoate, and formaldehyde, costing no more than five cents for a six-month supply and taking
advantage of a local product, delivered in a rice paste.

Ever conscious of the uses of publicity, Sanger journeyed with a type-
writer and an American reporter. She had read Katherine Mayo's *Mother
India: Slaves of the Gods*, a popular Orientalist indictment of the treatment
of Indian women. Published in 1927, Mayo's book highlighted the arranged
marriages of children in a divorceless society (Gandhi had married at fourteen, his wife at thirteen), the isolation of women in purdah ("One never
sees women on the street," Sanger noted in her journal), the malnourished
babies, and the widow's notorious suicidal ritual of sati.

Sanger had been invited by the feminist-minded All India Women's Conference, which met in the southern city of Trivandrum in January 1936, and she intended to speak about birth control. But when she arrived, the Catholics objected. The governor's wife insisted that she avoid such a controversial issue as contraception and instead focus on the agreed-upon evils of the nearby brothels in Madras. Aroused by the disagreement, Sanger delivered what she had intended: an explicit talk about contraception to an admiring audience of Indian women. "When they are liberated," Sanger noted of the latter, "they are rather extreme."[4] She listened approvingly as the conference passed resolutions by large majorities supporting contraception in general, the dissemination of devices in particular, and the establishment of women's clinics, after which, she noted, "the Roman Catholics resigned from the conference like spoiled children."[5]

The meeting with Gandhi was the high point of her visit. "Do by all means come whenever you can," he had written in his note delivered by the courier. "And you shall stay with me, if you would not mind what must appear to be our extreme simplicity. We have no master and no servant."[6] Sanger had recognized the significance of Gandhi's support before she arrived in Bombay: "I was sure that his endorsement of birth control would be of tremendous value if I could convince him how necessary it was for Indian women . . . I set myself to the task."[7]

She arrived at Gandhi's ashram in the district of Wardha in the Indian state of Maharashtra on his day of silence. He extended only an enigmatic smile and a message that she might walk with him early the next morning and talk with him throughout the day. So began an extraordinary conversation about sex and marriage between a celibate male and a liberated female, both of whom meant to change the world. They agreed that women should be emancipated, he more interested in their public roles, she their private ones. Gandhi had already successfully appealed to Indian women to join his now famous 240-mile salt march that had ignited the Indian population in opposition to the British. Now, five years after the trek to the Dandi River and his arrest, many of those who flocked to Wardha for an audience with Gandhi were women, any words from him like a god's oracle delivered in ancient Greece. So many came that the government had established both a post office and a train station near his ashram. Some of these women were untouchables from the lowest caste in a system that horrified Sanger and that Gandhi sought to end, having renamed them Harijans— Children of God.

But the means of women's liberation promoted by Gandhi and Sanger differed. She offered her familiar message of contraception as a therapeutic lever for healthier mothers and children, with the added benefit of controlling India's exploding population. He offered abstinence. Opposing contraception for its libidinous possibilities, Gandhi relied on intimate details of his personal life to make the case for chastity as a higher spiritual state. A self-confessed slave of his "animal" passions during the early period of his marriage with Kasturba, when he fathered four sons, after embracing celibacy he had learned the difference between love and lust. "As long as I looked at my wife carnally I had no real understanding . . . The moment I bade goodbye to a life of carnal pleasure our whole relationship changed . . . Lust died, love reigned." To Sanger's suspicions about his ignorance of women, he grandly responded, "In my wife, I studied all women."[8]

Such views were impractical nonsense for Sanger, who offered no personal details of her own sexuality to support her position, but who considered sex a spiritual expression in and of itself. "Seldom are two people drawn together in the sex act by their desire to have children. Do you think it possible for two people who are in love, who are happy together, to regulate their sex act once in two years so that relationship would only take place when they wanted a child?"[9] Such a restriction on intercourse once every two years or more—for surely no woman wanted to have children spaced only months apart—led to "irritations, disputes and thwarted desires," insisted Sanger, as she and Gandhi sat on the ground, lunching on a vegetarian meal of soybeans, rice, tomatoes, fresh radishes, and milk.

And how, asked Sanger, would women in whose hands Gandhi placed the enforcement of his sexual mandate resist their husbands? Surely he understood that most men could not—and would not—match his discipline. Gandhi demurred. Most husbands would concur in any marital decision about childbearing. Women must be educated to challenge those few who did not. In a vague concession, he acknowledged the possibility of using some form of the rhythm method she despised as unworkable and omitted from her later, widely publicized description of this conversation with Gandhi. As the sun set and her interview ended, a hopeful Sanger asked if he had some message of encouragement to help in her work. "I can only say may God guide you . . . Don't go away with the idea that this is a wasted effort. We have certainly come nearer together."[10]

After reading his autobiography, Sanger decided that Gandhi's celibacy emanated from guilt. As a young husband he had been having sex with his

wife at the moment his father died—"a personal experience so shocking
that he can never accept sex as anything good, clean and wholesome," concluded Sanger. In any case she believed Gandhi a noble human being of
simplicity, a true Mahatma—"adored and worshipped by millions but the
same millions disagree with him regarding birth control."[11] A helpful note
from Margaret Cousins, the Irish-born expatriate and in the 1930s the only
female magistrate in India, explained Gandhi's contradictory views about
women: "His built-in asceticism [is] against the common sense and healthy
needs of the general mass of the public to whom your cause makes such
immediate appeal. We women have had to oppose him on several occasions when he wants to make out-of-date distinctions. He does not understand the modern Indian woman."[12]

Sanger left behind a blueprint for her devoted Indian disciples, and they
continued to honor her as their international advocate in the battle for
reproductive rights. They must organize clinics, she told them, raise the level
of sex education, advertise and make available cheap spermicides, and continue to support their respected journal *Marriage Hygiene*. At her urging
Edith How-Martyn, the director of the Sanger-inspired and -funded Birth
Control International Information Centre in London, returned twice to India in the 1930s to organize clinics and deliver contraceptive information
and financial support.

If Sanger gave much of herself during her visit, she received a great deal
in return. Such public affirmation was important as she grew older, and as
the birth control movement in the United States became more respectable,
bureaucratic, and male, and she less central to its organizational identity.
As a woman disposed to eclectic spiritual beliefs, she never forgot the mys-
tical effects of the country on her "romantic Irish soul"—the country's beauty
and diverse geography, its kind people, its erotic Hindu culture, its handsome men with dark eyes, its handful of liberated women always attired in
colorful saris, Gandhi's peculiar commitment to celibacy, along with his ex-
emplary commitment to self-sufficiency and self-denial, and even his commitment to vegetarianism, a nutritional regimen to which both she and Juliet
Rublee intermittently subscribed.

To Noah after her visit, Sanger expressed her admiration for Indian
culture, then warned: "Yes darling, you are right—I have changed. It's some
physical & spiritual change but I feel definitely that the door of Sex Life is
closed for me. It may be a shock for you to hear this but I have a queer feeling about it & prefer to keep it closed."[13] But abstinence was only a temporary

condition for Sanger. When she wrote this letter from a hospital bed in
Hong Kong on her way home to the United States, she was suffering from
a painful attack of gallbladder disease. During her Asia trip, even before
her important speech to the All India Women's Conference, "a pain, a very
old pain began to knaw at me."[14] So severe were these episodes of abdominal pain, so depressingly frequent and alarmingly unscheduled—coming
even during her public appearances—that the fifty-five-year-old Sanger cut
short her trip, acknowledging "the steady tread of Old Father time."[15]

Sanger left India in March 1936 and, on her way home, sailed to the
coastal city of Georgetown, the capital of the state of Penang on the Ma-
laysian Peninsula. There, her gallbladder attack subsided and she enjoyed
a passionate four-day relationship with a new lover, Dr. Hugh Brodie, a handsome Scottish physician in his forties nicknamed "Penang" in her letters to
Rublee. In her journal Sanger described the seductive setting for their first
spontaneous sexual encounter: "We had dinner. The moon came up in a
fascinating color, casting golden reflections on the water. A soft breeze,
languid & romantic enough for my Irish Soul. An amazing place. Ay? This
Penang. Anything can happen here."[16] For her own reputation and that of
her cause, she kept this affair like others "as dark as possible in a spotlight
world."[17] She met Brodie once more in New York, before he disappeared
into her catalog of lovers.

After a short visit to Japan, Sanger sailed for home, promising to return
to China. Fifteen months later she did so, traveling first to Hawaii. By the
time the SS *President Hoover* arrived off the coast of Shanghai, the Sino-
Japanese war had erupted. Japanese planes were bombing the Chinese coast,
and the *Hoover* became an inadvertent casualty. In a swift change of itin-
erary, the steamship turned north, limping into Yokohama, where Shidzue
Ishimoto greeted her American friend with loving enthusiasm. In turn
Sanger dedicated Ishimoto's new birth control clinic in Tokyo, with an expansive speech comparing her Japanese friend to great women in Western
history such as Mary Wollstonecraft, Susan B. Anthony, and Ellen Key.
Ishimoto responded, "You left us a fresh strength to push back all the depressed feelings which are hanging around us. I am writing under dimmed
lights—fear of war planes above us—with a heartful of love, admiration
and gratitude."[18] But war rendered birth control especially subversive at a
time when governments wanted more citizens, not fewer. Four months
after Sanger left Japan, Ishimoto was arrested on the charge of promoting

"dangerous thoughts." Her clinic was closed, and all organized birth control activity in Japan was suppressed until after World War II.

Before she returned to Asia, in the fall of 1937 a reluctant Sanger entered the Harkness Pavilion in the Columbia-Presbyterian Hospital for an operation to remove her gallbladder and several infected diverticula. For over a year she had resisted surgery, employing traditional treatments for a disease that had been variously diagnosed as gastritis, intestinal flu, and, most infuriating, a case of nerves. Throughout her life Sanger gained strength from her successful battles with illness. She remembered curing herself—at least temporarily—after she had fled the tuberculosis cottage in Saranac, against doctor's orders. But after another gallbladder attack in Japan, she must get to the "bottom of this condition," at the same time that she was "furious at myself for getting sick." Surely, despite the crippling episodes, the doctors were "unduly alarmed."[19]

For a time Sanger employed homemade remedies for a disease of at least five years' duration, taking "buttermilk, orange juice, prune juice, lemons, limes, bananas, Swiss Kriss pyssleum concentrate, cascara, citrate of magnesia, enemas, hot & cold . . . massage & colonic irrigations" along with Pluto, America's popular bottled water that advertised "When nature won't, Pluto will."[20] In the past Sanger had also recovered in European spas with their vaunted mineral springs, and in the fall of 1936 she went to a popular American version—Dr. William Hays's clinic in the Poconos—for massages and the colonic irrigations so popular with this generation of Americans.

Nothing worked. On her son Grant's recommendation after another crippling attack—this time with uncontrollable vomiting followed by a fever—she took the advice of Dr. Allen Whipple, the best-known abdominal surgeon in the United States. "Well, it's all decided I guess," Sanger wrote to Noah, whose unresolved tax problems kept him out of New York during the 1930s. "Dr. Whipple is quite certain that both the diverticulum & gallbladder must come out. He says that I can live the life of a semi-invalid, on a diet, going to Marienbad or Karlsbad every year for three months & taking life at half speed . . . But for a woman of my vitality youth & energy & vision I would be only half living—I must be active or sick. I've decided to get it over."[21]

Whipple's alternative therapy of rest exemplified this generation's medical mystique of long hospital stays and lengthy home recuperations, based not on science but ruling cultural views about the body's need for inactivity in order to regenerate. Such a program would never have cured Sanger's gallbladder disease. Nor could she have tolerated an indeterminate sentence of inactivity. Still, her friends were dismayed by her disappearance for nearly a year. Most of them agreed with Dorothy Brush that "the human limitations which apply to most of us just never apply to [Margaret Sanger] at all. She treats her body like a Victorian child—it must be seen but not heard; if it aches it must ache in silence."[22] Chagrined that their hero could not defeat this challenge, assistants in her New York clinic made the best of it. They explained to the public that the operation was necessitated by Sanger's hard work and the subsequent depletion of her strength.

Expecting to stay two weeks in the hospital, Sanger spent five weeks in bed in the Harkness Pavilion, running a fever from an infected seventeen-inch incision after the removal of her gallbladder. She then endured the prescription of six months of rest and a year of relaxation without public meetings. "I've got to put forward my great faith and will power and patience and must take whatever is given me and make the grade as best I can."[23]

There were benefits. Besides the improvement in her health, both her sons—Grant, currently a resident on Allen Whipple's staff, and Stuart, a fourth-year medical student at Cornell Medical School, the institution that years before his mother had wanted to attend—were affectionately and professionally solicitous. Thrilled when Whipple "the big shot surgeon asked Grant what he thought of his mother's condition and his answer coincided with what Whipple thought," Sanger, unaware of the Socratic nature of medical training, "respected a mind so great that he could see the value in a younger mind than his own. Stuart is really more conservative than Grant. He would seek . . . the cause before operating to find the cause. Grant has the Surgeon's attitude 'Let's go in & find out what the trouble is.'"[24]

She recuperated in Tucson in a house that Noah had bought in the Catalina Foothills. Earlier the city had been a wild silver mining town and briefly, though never as popular as Phoenix, a haven for tuberculosis patients with its still, clear air. By the 1930s Tucson had also become a glamorous resort with a population of eighty thousand and a distinguished group of winter visitors who included Rockefellers, McCormicks, and Elizabeth Arden. Sanger had taken Stuart there for his sinus problems in 1934 and had luxuriated in the dry heat and bright sun, so different from New York's dark, sooty atmosphere. As Sanger described to her English friend Edith How-Martyn, "Millions of tall Cactus like trees over the landscape & mountains bare naked & unashamed waiting to be visited." Above all, Sanger appreciated the crisp air, the endless sky, and the changing colors on the distant mountains, with the ten-thousand-foot Mt. Lemmon prominent on the horizon, and at sundown "the sky aflame over the blue mountain tops."[25] The desert was similar to the birth control crusade, its barren sandy soil reminiscent of birth control's unpromising beginnings, only to be followed after the winter rains by an extraordinary blossoming of spring flowers, a symbol of the movement's flourishing. Tucson—"this lovely place"—would be home for the next thirty years.

Among the benefits of her recuperation was the opportunity to evaluate the status of the movement—especially the implications of the recent legal decisions in cases she had initiated. As early as 1932, persisting in her lobbying efforts, Sanger had launched a legal challenge to the Comstock law. Previously the courts had proved allies, inadvertently bringing favorable publicity as well as, in the Crane decision, favorable rulings. Sanger had just arrived in India in 1935 when Florence Rose, wasting no words, cabled JAPANESE CASE VICTORY. CONGRATULATIONS. Rose referred to the landmark decision in *U.S. v. One Package of Japanese Pessaries*, a case in federal district court that both reflected changing mores and shaped the future birth control movement.

To orchestrate her test case, Sanger had asked Dr. Sakae Koyama, a gynecologist in Tokyo, to mail the newly designed, much praised Japanese pessaries to Margaret Sanger in care of the Birth Control Clinical Research Bureau on Sixteenth Street. When they arrived, U.S. Customs officials promptly confiscated the package under Comstock-influenced tariff regulations that prohibited the importation of any article "for the prevention of conception or for causing unlawful abortion."

Morris Ernst, Sanger's longtime legal advisor and veteran of many censorship battles, cautioned that a challenge to the Comstock law using a nurse or layperson as plaintiff would fail. Recognizing her own notoriety and amateur standing, Sanger still hesitated to bring a case in the names of the doctors on her staff, who might be accused of propagandizing what must remain a purely scientific movement. But after she persuaded the heir to the Clyde Steamship fortune, Edith Clyde, to cover the legal costs, Sanger hired Ernst and repeated her request to Dr. Koyama. Under her instructions, this time the Japanese gynecologist mailed a package of 120 pessaries to Dr. Hannah Stone. By 1933 the package had arrived and been confiscated, and Stone, the new plaintiff in the action, had sued for its release.

Sanger waited impatiently for the case to be scheduled; a year passed and then another. She had been warned by a lawyer in Ernst's office that the U.S. attorney's office moved slowly, but as months passed, Sanger suspected purposeful delay, similar to the kind of inconsistent judicial tactics she had experienced before World War I. Unlike those earlier times, she now had public opinion on her side. In a 1938 *Ladies' Home Journal* poll, 79 percent of its readers favored the legalization of birth control, a figure that included 51 percent of the Catholic women surveyed.[26] As Sanger wrote to her friend, the author and commentator Dorothy Gordon, "Such a decision might save us years of effort and much money, and make unnecessary our efforts to accomplish the same results through an amendment to the present Federal laws."[27]

The trial finally began in December 1935. As there were no factual matters in dispute, the jury was dismissed. Then both sides stipulated that it could be heard before a single judge, not a panel, amid rumors that several judges had recused themselves from such an unsavory case. In a stroke of good fortune or judicial discretion, the presiding judge was not John Knox, a man of Sanger's generation who had recently ordered the Hedy Lamarr film *Ecstasy* destroyed after finding its nude swimming scene obscene. Nor did either of the two Catholic judges, Matthew Abruzzo and John Clancy, sit in judgment. Instead, the slightly younger and decidedly more liberal Grover Moscowitz, a graduate of the New York University School of Law, presided. During an earlier censorship case, Moscowitz had stunned his colleagues when he invited three clergymen—a Jew, a Protestant, and a Catholic—"to aid the conscience of the court" during a hearing. Certainly his previous rulings displayed a tolerant position on sexual material in literature that might extend to birth control.

Ernst listed seven doctors as witnesses, including Hannah Stone and the New York City health commissioner. The first, Dr. Frederick Holden, invoked sick mothers, inheritable diseases, and the need for proper spacing of children "to achieve optimum well-being" as the reasons he instructed women in how to insert diaphragms. Dr. Foster Kennedy made clear the general acceptance of contraception among doctors as a treatment for a variety of female complaints. The five other physicians stipulated their agreement with the previous testimony, and the final witness, Dr. Hannah Stone, described the medical significance of testing a highly lauded, new version of an old device in the Birth Control Clinical Research Bureau, where she was the medical director and Margaret Sanger the executive director.

The state's case was simple and required, according to the assistant district attorney, nothing more than a directed verdict: the defendant had violated a law that established "the absolute prohibition on the importation of certain types of articles including contraceptive devices." The state called only one expert witness, Dr. Frederick Bancroft, who, to everyone's surprise, offered exculpatory evidence, admitting under cross-examination that he prescribed contraception to 30 percent of his obstetrical patients. Bancroft, agreeing with Stone, acknowledged that there were many medical conditions warranting the use of birth control.

In his summary Ernst cited recent judicial precedents that required the government to prove that contraceptives were imported for an illegal use. "It is not to be presumed that Congress intended to condemn their use for decent public health purposes." Here the previous assumption of criminality, for years determined by the Comstock Act's application of obscenity to all forms of contraception, had been turned on its head. Now the government must show illegal intent. The language of the tariff act must not be taken "literally," argued Ernst; it was never the purpose of Congress to prohibit articles of medical use for the well-being of Americans. Moreover, a clause for the exemption of physicians had been discussed when Congress passed the Comstock Act but, in the hurried end of the session, had been overlooked.

A showman in the courtroom, at the end of his summation Ernst reached for that one eponymous Japanese pessary to demonstrate the innocent simplicity of this small rubber object that engendered so much judicial activity and political hostility. But the actual pessary—the government's Exhibit A—had somehow disappeared. Had it been lost? Had the state's witness carried it off? inquired Ernst. Had the government delayed the case so long that the rubber in the others had dried up? To laughter, Ernst announced: "What I am afraid of is that someone will use the pessary and it will not work."

Ernst's more serious arguments provided the basis for Judge Moscowitz's prompt ruling. Tariff laws, declared the judge, could not be used to prohibit the importation. Instead, they must be given "reasonable construction," and since the plaintiff had imported the articles in question "for experimental purposes to determine their reliability and usefulness as contraceptives to cure or prevent disease, a lawful purpose, it must be held the libeled articles do not come within the condemnation of the statute."[28] These simple sentences revised the Comstock law that Sanger and her National Committee on Federal Legislation for Birth Control had struggled for years to change. No longer, if the decision held up in a higher court, would Sanger and her friend Katharine McCormick have to smuggle diaphragms through American customs. No longer would doctors have any legal excuse to avoid prescribing birth control to patients. Nor could the government impede the therapeutic purposes of research on contraception by withholding mailed material. The courts had achieved what legislators would not.

Sanger's associates were jubilant; Ernst was optimistic. The birth control movement enjoyed a sudden burst of favorable publicity, mostly focused on Margaret Sanger. *Life*, the most popular magazine in the United States with a circulation of nearly 2 million, featured four pages on Sanger, with photographs (that she believed made her look old) of the epic moments of her crusade, along with her husband and Willowlake. The *Reader's Digest* planned an article on Sanger, and *True Confessions* published her short editorial entitled "Does the Public Want Birth Control?" Interviewed by the press and radio, Sanger hailed "the dawn of a new era" with birth control now freed from the outdated provisions of the Comstock Act. There was talk of a feature film on her life starring Greer Garson.

Privately Sanger worried about the outcome of the government's appeal in the Second Circuit Court of Appeals. She also recognized that there was more to do after this limited decision placed birth control in the hands of a largely obdurate medical profession. Now unsympathetic doctors controlled its delivery. Of course, Sanger's pragmatic strategy had medicalized birth control in the first place—from the time in 1922 when Judge Crane approved the doctor's exemption in *U.S. v. Sanger*, to her continuing commitment to the diaphragm, a form of birth control that required instruction by professionals, and even to her recent lobbying of the American Medical Association. The latter, after the *One Package* decision, endorsed birth control, recommending that its delivery be controlled by physicians and its techniques studied in medical schools.

Yet sixteen years after the physicians' exemption in the Crane decision, Sanger wanted a more expansive judgment reaching beyond simply treating disease. Encouraged by New Deal programs in public health, she recognized a new direction in which contraception could play a major role, during "the beginning of a new epoch in preventive medicine." She desired nothing less than the application of this legal sanction for contraception because children should be spaced for better health, because a family might not be able to afford another child, and because, for whatever reason, a married woman did not want another baby—all of the economic, social, and psychological reasons that still alarmed many Americans.[29]

Ernst, to Sanger's chagrin, had not pressed for such interpretations. Technically the *One Package* decision covered only a tariff act and was not necessarily applicable to postal or interstate commerce regulations. Nor did the decision apply to states beyond the jurisdiction of the Second Circuit Court. In his customary way, as he celebrated his triumph in *One Package*, Ernst exaggerated the importance of his victory. In the early 1930s he had compared his accomplishments in overturning the censorship of James Joyce's *Ulysses* and Radclyffe Hall's *The Well of Loneliness* to a New Deal for literature—a repeal of all sex taboos in letters. And he had successfully appealed Mary Ware Dennett's conviction on obscenity charges for her pamphlet *The Sex Side of Life*. Still, for Sanger, "Mr. Ernst has been too enthusiastic over his own victories in the court, and the fact that he made his victories on the article of contraception being used for disease gives him, in my estimation, an unwarranted satisfaction of those decisions," she grumbled, knowing that she deserved credit as well.[30] Ernst was more charitable, writing that Sanger's work had helped to change both judicial and medical minds.

Nearly a year after the initial ruling, in December 1936 the appeals court upheld the *One Package* ruling. To the panel of three judges—two of them the firm-jawed, scholarly, Harvard-trained cousins Augustus and Learned Hand—it seemed absurd that only unlawful articles on how to perform abortion would be excluded along with *all* contraceptives:

It is going far beyond such a policy to hold that abortions which destroy incipient life may be allowed in proper cases and that no measures may be taken to prevent conception even though a likely result should be to require the termination of pregnancy by means of an operation. It seems unreasonable to suppose that the national scheme of legislation involves such inconsistencies and requires the complete suppression of articles, the use of which in many cases is advocated by such a weight of authority in the medical world.

The legal landscape was changing, though Learned Hand tacked toward judicial restraint and congressional authority, noting that "many people have changed their minds about such matters in sixty years, but the act

forbids the same conduct now as then. A statute changes until a majority
would repeal it . . . Things which might intelligently be employed by conscientious and competent physicians for the purpose of saving life or promoting the well being of patients were never intended to be prohibited."[31]
Still, he was not prepared to dissent, and the third appeals judge, Thomas
Swan, had accepted physician-prescribed contraceptives as legitimate in a
previous case. All three noted that the Comstock Act had originally contained the exception of "a prescription of a physician in good standing given
in good faith," and they relied as well on the precedent-setting *U.S. v.
Sanger*. None of the judges specified the circumstances under which a doctor could legally prescribe birth control and so, as Ernst inferred, "as long
as a physician exercised his discretion in good faith the legality of his action was not to be questioned."[32]

Attorney General Homer Cummings abandoned any appeal to the U.S.
Supreme Court, which consistently refused to review cases involving birth
control until the 1960s. So ended what Sanger called "the drudgery of federal work." The courts had accomplished what all of her intense lobbying of
Congress had not. She disbanded the NCFLBC, which had consumed her
during the early 1930s, though familiar obstacles remained: "Of course the
R.C.'s [Roman Catholics] are not going to let it pass if they can do anything
about it & we must watch Congress to see that new bills are not run through
to cancel the Court decision . . . Now that the federal work is closing I am
going to give clinics a push & a good push too."[33] Birth control was, as Sanger
exulted, "free," and though preoccupied with its future, she was proud of
its past "efforts and accomplishments. In a short period it has made outstanding achievements, almost unparalleled in our social era."[34] In fact, in
the years between the world wars, Sanger's birth control movement emerged
as the most successful reform activity in the United States—almost the only
one not sponsored by the New Deal.

There remained legal skirmishes and some defeats, both at the federal
and state levels. In an action promptly overturned by the courts, the customs office seized copies of the Indian publication *Marriage Hygiene*, sent
to Dr. Norman Himes two years after the *One Package* decision. Judge Hand
tartly ruled that the courts "have twice decided that contraceptive articles
may have legal uses: the statute prohibiting them should be read as forbidding them only when they are unlawfully employed."[35] And the Post Office
confiscated a 1941 issue of *Consumer Reports* that evaluated condoms.

But in Massachusetts and Connecticut the birth control campaign stalled and even regressed. Both states, with large Catholic populations and disproportionate numbers of Catholic legislators, endured the most restrictive state versions of the Comstock law in the nation. In Massachusetts any publication or circulation of contraceptive information violated the law, as did the selling, giving, and lending of birth control materials and devices. Nor was there a physician's exemption. Connecticut went further, prohibiting even the use of contraceptives, an unenforceable, and indeed unenforced, provision. After a lecture tour in Connecticut, Sanger "had to rub my eyes to remember that this was the year 1932 and not back in the days of 1914." She felt as though "the Clock of Time had turned back . . . In New Haven they did stop the meeting in one place but the Protestants in the city arose indignantly & rented a theater & forced the Catholic mayor to give a permit for the meeting."[36]

Reacting to the *One Package* ruling, state authorities raided seven clinics run by the Massachusetts Birth Control League (MBCL). Similar actions took place in Connecticut. In both states after the familiar sting operation in which a policewoman disguised as a client received contraceptives, the police closed down the clinics, confiscated records, and arrested nurses and doctors on the charge of violating state Comstock laws. Slowly the cases moved through the appeals court, but unlike the New York judiciary, the Massachusetts and Connecticut Supreme Courts upheld statutes passed in the 1870s. Judges in both states considered the law absolute, noninterpretable, and devoid of ambiguity. The question of reasonableness of policy was irrelevant. Until the legislature nullified the law, the only consideration was that the statute was being violated, though the court levied a minimum fine on those doctors and nurses in the clinics who thought they were acting "as a benefit to humanity."[37]

Sanger remained hopeful that the U.S. Supreme Court would accept jurisdiction over one of these cases, and on review declare the statutes unconstitutional, thereby legalizing medically controlled contraception nationally. She worried that the decisions in Massachusetts and Connecticut were the beginning of a national effort to overturn *One Package* state by state. She complained that opponents never debated the physicians' exemption, but irrelevantly linked birth control to practices in the Soviet Union or cited the laws of nature or complained of the commercialism of contraception. Lacking money and resolve for a final appeal, the leaders of the MBCL, now sanitized into Maternal Health Clinics, withdrew their appeal. Sanger's hopes had been premature. Such a review by the U.S. Supreme

Court did not come until 1965, a year before her death, in *Griswold v. Connecticut*, when the Court, establishing a zone of privacy into which the government could not intrude, declared the Connecticut law forbidding the use of contraception unconstitutional. Not until 1972 was that right to contraception extended to unmarried women.

In the meantime the effects of the prohibitions were severe. In Connecticut there were no birth control services until 1961, and in 1942 the Connecticut Supreme Court upheld a law making it illegal to prescribe contraception even if a doctor believed a woman's life was in danger. In Massachusetts a few advocates continued to battle for the physicians' exemption, seizing on a bold new strategy: they would use the initiative and referendum procedures to change the law. Needing fifty thousand signatures to begin this cumbersome process, the leaders of the MBCL appealed to Sanger to lecture throughout the state. No one inspired like the icon of the movement; on the other hand, no one so aroused the hostility of the Catholic Church. The week before Sanger's arrival parish priests read proclamations from their pulpits denouncing "this nationally known defender of the detestable practice of birth control." Those sponsoring Sanger's lectures were "unpatriotic and a disgrace to the Christian community."[38]

Sanger arrived in the college town of Holyoke in 1940 expecting to speak in a Congregational church, only to find the church closed and no other public facility available. Local radio stations reported her lecture had been canceled. But with the determination of years past, Sanger informed reporters, who described her as looking old and tired, that she intended to speak in Holyoke. "Somehow I'll manage it. I will speak here."[39] Suffering from pneumonia, she later admitted, "The spirit was willing, but the old gal can't go at the same pace."[40] Eventually a former socialist hall, now the headquarters of the Textile Workers Union, was located. There, Sanger delivered her speech in front of a poster of Franklin Roosevelt, who was in the midst of his third campaign for the presidency.

Birth control, she said, saved the lives of women too old and sick to bear children. It prevented dangerous illegal abortions. Smaller families improved the lives of fathers and children as well; fewer mouths to feed allowed weekly wages to go further in these depressed times, and therefore decreased the number of those on public welfare. Sanger's ever malleable arguments for birth control now centered on its relevance for the economic improvement not just of individual families but of the nation as a whole.

Hers was a practical speech, and one she gave throughout the state without any more closed halls or personal harassment.

The Massachusetts initiative succeeded; polls indicated that a majority of state voters favored the legalization of birth control. But in the summer and fall of 1942, as the plebiscite on the referendum to change the birth control laws approached, fierce opposition from the Archdiocese began. In their Sunday sermons parish priests claimed new legislation would legalize abortion and establish state control over the number of children a family could have. Such propaganda proved successful. Catholics and conservatives turned out on Election Day, and the referendum failed by a vote of 505,000 to 691,000. Women in Massachusetts had to wait until the 1950s to obtain legal birth control from their physicians and, for those without private doctors, to have access to public clinics.

Sanger envisioned such setbacks as indications that the movement had gone astray. Fearful of losing momentum, she viewed the censorship of her books—even her *Autobiography*—and the closing up of clinics and lecture halls as evidence of a battle only half won. She invoked the militant past: "We need women who will keep the clinics open until every one of them is put in jail . . . God knows how weak and timid and full of fear, respectability has made the birth control movement. If we had just one-half the fighting spirit the Roman Catholics have we would lay them low & mow them down," she admitted.[41] But wealthy society women, whom Sanger had courted for their respectability and their money, did not volunteer for jail.

Sanger had more success with her birth control clinics, especially in the South. She had always believed that these facilities, so simple to open and organize, yet so expensive and time-consuming to maintain without the provocative advertising that made them suspect, defined the movement. Clinics offered women sex education, delivered birth control devices, and collected case studies for research. A good clinic, like her New York BCCRB, served as a laboratory for improvements in spermicides and other contraceptives. And to those who complained that clinics fostered immorality, she had a ready answer. Few unmarried women came to birth control clinics and besides, "if women are going to be promiscuous and immoral, it is better for society and the unborn child that this type of woman have contraceptive protection and not bring an innocent little child into an atmosphere to bear the scorn of an illegitimate birth."[42]

Despite their financial struggles, the number of contraceptive clinics in the United States doubled every three years in the 1930s, reaching 337 in 1937. Most did no research on the effectiveness of methods, although in Miami Dr. Lydia DeVilbiss served a diverse population in her Mother's Health Clinic, where she studied the reliability of her spermicidal powder, Fem-Foam, with its ever-changing ingredients. In Baltimore, the Johns Hopkins–trained and –affiliated obstetrician-gynecologist Dr. Bessie Moses established the Bureau for Contraceptive Advice, near the hospital, on the city's east side. With special days set aside for black and white patients referred by physicians, Moses intended the bureau to be a public health research center run by professionals, not, as Sanger preferred, a walk-in neighborhood clinic. Using data from her records, Moses published her results in 1936 in *Contraception as a Therapeutic Measure*. She concluded that the condom, still decorously referred to by some doctors as "an appliance placed over the male organ," was the contraceptive of choice.

Clinics could never be the ultimate solution, even if their number reached the three thousand Sanger thought desirable. "We must reach women on homesteads, on farms, in mining districts and millions of women in outlying rural districts where medical help is not available."[43] Sanger envisioned traveling caravans of contraceptive services supervised by public health nurses specializing in gynecology. Doris Davidson, a nurse trained at Sanger's clinic in New York, had absorbed the message. After finding doctors in Maine "too cautious," Davidson moved to West Virginia: "Oh!" she wrote to Sanger, "to reach the women in the tiny villages of the backwoods. How can it be done unless we go to them?"[44]

With her new ally Dr. Clarence Gamble, heir to the Procter and Gamble fortune, graduate of the Harvard Medical School, and father of five, Sanger began a campaign to introduce clinics and traveling nurses to the rural South. With more money to come, Gamble had inherited his first million dollars on his twenty-first birthday in 1915. It came with his grandfather's stipulation that 10 percent of any inherited money from the family company must go to charity. Recruited to birth control advocacy by Dr. Robert Dickinson—the Harvard Medical School curriculum did not include the teaching of birth control until the 1940s—Gamble surpassed any family-imposed tithing in his lifelong financial support for what he labeled as the "Great Cause and my monomania." And he was not a disengaged philanthropist; instead, Gamble nagged and pestered those working in headquarters, acknowledging that birth control advocates, because they were nonconformists, never got along with one another. Certainly he did not get along with them, in part because he intended to control the projects he funded, which at this stage involved testing the ingredients of various spermicides.

Within months of their first meeting, Sanger had appointed Gamble to a new position—medical field director of her BCCRB—and Gamble, whom she admired as "a lone prospector" in an age of bureaucrats, was at work on his "Outline for the Recent Field Work of the Birth Control Clinical Research Bureau." Like many doctors, Gamble was a eugenicist interested in increasing the birthrate of the fit, even as he, unlike some of his colleagues, sought contraception for the less fit. Among his projects was a prize honoring the American college class with the highest birthrate twenty years after graduation. Since Brigham Young University, followed by several Catholic colleges, always won, the Gamble Eugenics Fund was diverted to the establishment of birth control clinics. Full of ideas, Gamble hired young authors to write short stories for pulp magazines featuring young women whose futures were saved by using birth control.

Aware of the need for patients in order to test his spermicides, Gamble discovered Puerto Rico. After receiving the support of Ernest Gruening, the director of the U.S. Division of Territories and Island Possessions, Gamble successfully lobbied the Puerto Rican legislature to legalize birth control in 1937. He made his case in the name of negative eugenics: there were too many "unambitious and unintelligent groups." Soon the heavily Catholic protectorate of the United States had more birth control clinics than most mainland states. Voluntary sterilization, encouraged by a government-sponsored program, was also high, some said because only one confession to the priest was necessary. The advantage of a poor female population accessible through popular public health clinics was obvious to Gamble and Sanger, and Puerto Rico emerged as a laboratory available for the future.[45]

Gamble's first field project involved employing nurses to recruit women in both Puerto Rico and West Virginia into his "jelly program." Over a thousand women in West Virginia enrolled. Those who persisted in using his spermicide cut their fertility rates by nearly half, but in the universal challenge to all birth control providers, within a year at least half of the women stopped using this method. What came to be known as the refusal rate remained depressingly high. In another clinic in Berea, Kentucky, Gamble applied a different version of his foam powder and sponge method earlier tested on dogs' vaginas and eyes. First women dipped the sponge in water, next squeezed it out and sprinkled both sides with the spermicide powder, then kneaded the powdered sponge to start the production of foam, and finally inserted it into their vaginas. It was a cumbersome process, sometimes resulting in burning and itching. Sanger dismissed such hazards: "Women's organs are so sensitive that even a sponge alone without anything but water has been known to irritate and burn . . . the few who find it burning make such a noise that the few outcry the many . . . who find it successful & simple & cheaper than any other method."[46]

Gamble and Sanger next turned to North Carolina, the first state to have full-time county health officers and among the first to have a division of preventive medicine. But there were no public funds during the Depression to pay for doctors, traveling caravans, or supplies. Instead, for three years Gamble paid the salary of a nurse who worked under the direction of Dr. George Cooper, an official in the State Board of Health. Cooper had initiated what Sanger sought nationally—the incorporation of birth control information and services, under the supervision of a nurse, into county health programs. But when Sanger applauded North Carolina's policies and promised a visit, Cooper objected that she "did not have a dad-blamed thing to do with it and we don't want any part of Margaret Sanger's advertising and controversy." State officials, he warned, would never approve any program associated with her name; she was too noisy and pushy. Nor would they approve anything but physician-authorized birth control, and in segregated North Carolina their programs included only white women.[47]

Never one to let mistakes go uncorrected or attacks unanswered, Sanger, recuperating in Tucson from her gallbladder surgery, established her primacy as the leader of birth control in a response to Cooper: "I, its Director since 1916, advocated the principle that contraception must be in the hands of the medical profession . . . I have firmly stood by that idea, perhaps because of my training in the nursing field I had a better appreciation of the importance of the subject as a medical need . . . So that your ideas and mine are not far apart." Yet, in the justifications she pressed on Cooper, the reasons for contraception were not always medical and "may be economic and a woman may desire two children or ten children or no children at all, and I firmly believe that she should have the right to say something about this . . . [A woman] should go to her doctor for the best means to accomplish this result," an injunction that proved difficult for poor rural women. In any case, Sanger would come to North Carolina "entirely on my own . . . You are doing too good a job to have it in any way misunderstood by any outside groups."[48]

In October 1938 on her lecture tour in North Carolina, she reiterated her unorthodox, populist eugenicism, a version based on parental health:

We have got to change the inference that the quality of our population depends on the birth rate of college graduates. To me this is tinsel thinking. [There are] just as sound qualities in Arizona cowboys, mechanics and artists. Racial regeneration must come from within and be autonomous, self-directed and not imposed from without.[49]

Sanger did not openly challenge southern health officers such as Cooper on their exclusion of blacks from public clinics; although an opponent of segregation, she wondered why North and South Carolina did "not already give such information to their colored people." Nor did she believe that any African American projects should "be directed or run by white medical men."[50] For years, even in race-conscious Oklahoma, she had invited black physicians to her meetings, sometimes those held in private clubs. Building on her successful experience in Harlem, she recruited a national Negro Advisory Council whose members read like a who's who of black Americans and included the antilynching advocate Ida B. Wells, the activist W.E.B. Du Bois, and the historian Franklin Frazier. Now through her Division of Negro Services in the BCRCB, she initiated a southern program for blacks.

Gamble preferred demonstration projects as models for replication. Sanger disagreed, arguing not just for the prompt establishment of clinics but for the hiring of influential black ministers with social science backgrounds to serve as birth control evangelists traveling throughout the South. There was no better way to legitimize contraception. Sensitive to the perceived dangers felt by the black community, what some saw as efforts to destroy their race, Sanger informed Gamble in a letter that has been misrepresented, quoted only in part and taken out of context by her critics, "We do not want word to go out that we want to exterminate the Negro population and the minister is the man who can straighten out that idea if it ever occurs to any of their more rebellious members."[51]

When the wealthy philanthropists Albert and Mary Lasker, generous contributors to her "Negro Project" as well as personal friends, like many of Sanger's financial supporters, adopted Gamble's preference, Sanger surrendered. Eventually the project began and ended with a few demonstration

clinics for southern blacks, notably at Fisk University and Nashville's settlement house, the Bethlehem Center. Featured in national magazines such
as *Life* and *Look*, the spotless facilities were staffed by black physicians and
nurses, overseen by headquarters in New York. As Sanger had predicted,
there were only a few clinics and patients—only three thousand of the
latter by 1941.

Certainly Sanger was more racially tolerant than most Americans.
She despised segregation, protesting to the manager of the Gray Line
when her faithful maid, Daisy Mitchell, "a colored woman in my employ,"
was refused food service at various stations on the trip from Tucson to
New York.[52] She tried to answer the concerns of African Americans such
as Mable Staupers, head of the National Association of Colored Graduate
Nurses, and Dr. Dorothy Ferebee, who feared that the movement, so white
and upper middle class in its leadership and followers, would be seen as
trying to control the fertility of black women. Ferebee warned that some
blacks saw the cause—and Sanger—as paternalistic at best and enemies
of their race at worst. Uncertain about the way to lessen such fears save
through supportive black ministers, Sanger pushed ahead with her programs for African Americans. By the 1970s, held to higher standards than
other public figures of her generation after the civil rights movement, she
was unjustly labeled racist, often by pro-life groups intending to sully legal
abortion for black women.

In fact, to omit blacks from her lifelong, worldwide crusade for contraception would have testified to her prejudice. Sanger's efforts to establish
birth control services for blacks were inclusive, not neglectful and exclu-
sive, as was standard in this generation's nonviolent discriminations. No
one was ever forced into a Sanger clinic; instead, she intended, as with
white women, to improve the conditions in which all Americans lived. Presciently, if patronizingly, in 1941 she predicted:

> The Negro question is coming definitely to the fore in America, not
> only because of the war, but in anticipation of the place the Negro
> will occupy after the peace. I think it is magnificent that we are in
> on the ground floor, helping negroes to control their birth rate, to
> reduce their high infant and maternal death rate, to maintain better
> standards of health and living for those already born, and to create
> better opportunities for those who will be born.[53]

Four years later, in an interview with a reporter from the African American newspaper the *Chicago Defender*, Sanger spoke out in favor of integration. Declaring that discrimination was a universal failing to be opposed everywhere, she found its solution in the education of white men. "We must change the white attitudes . . . When you have Negroes working with whites you have the break down of barriers, the beginning of progress. Negro participation in planned parenthood means democratic participation in a democratic idea. Like other democratic ideas, planned parenthood places greater value on human life and the dignity of each person."[54]

Besides clinics, in the 1930s and 1940s Sanger and her associates eyed a number of potentially useful federal programs and agencies. She intended a "New Deal for mothers," believing that the Depression was an opportunity to give "a marvelous boost" to birth control. Under the Social Security Act of 1935, both the U.S. Public Health Service and the Children's Bureau served as funnels for public funds distributed to state and local departments. Here, beyond Sanger's previous imagining, was a historic opportunity to include childbearing as a matter of national health. But Washington officials proved intransigent. A resistant Katharine Lenroot, who ran the Children's Bureau in the Department of Labor from 1912 to 1951, prohibited the use of any funds for what was increasingly labeled "family planning." Letters of inquiry about sex and birth control went unanswered into her wastebasket, as did those to another female administrator, Mary Anderson, director of the Women's Bureau.

Both these women considered birth control too dangerous a personal and policy commitment. Exceptions among the male bureaucrats in New Deal Washington, Lenroot and Anderson worried that, with reputations sullied by association with Sanger and her cause, their bureaus and jobs would be absorbed into other agencies. Lenroot's annual National Conference on Better Care for Mothers and Babies informed social workers about breast-feeding, the care of premature babies, best nutrition practices, and how to raise a "crippled" child. Any mention of birth control, as attempted by Dr. Hannah Stone at a meeting in 1937, was ruled out of order. Only in 1967 under the Children's Health Act did a fixed percentage of funds for birth control's new appellation—family planning—become available.

Meanwhile, the U.S. Public Health Service, an agency in the Department of Labor, also controlled public funds. In 1935 under Title VI of the Social Security Act, the Public Health Service received $8 million and in

1938 another $5 million. Sought by Sanger for public health clinics, most of the money went instead to fight venereal disease through treatment centers using the new sulfa drugs. Such was the principal agenda of Dr. Thomas Parran, the surgeon general of the United States, a recognized authority on venereal diseases, the author of a popular book on the subject, *Shadow on the Land*, and a Catholic. Parran represented a new generation of professionals challenging the older moralistic precepts of social hygiene that previously rendered a health issue such as venereal disease invisible (except during wartime) and birth control obnoxious. As he explained the purposes of his bureau, "Modern society accepts as an obligation the provision of the necessities of life for those who cannot provide such necessities for themselves." In Parran's definition, medical service was "a necessity of life."[55]

Parran had refused to go on CBS Radio in 1934 when its producers informed him that he must not mention the words "gonorrhea" or "syphilis." But to birth control advocates such as Sanger, his approach, however modern to some, was hopelessly flawed. In 1939 with new funds allocated under the National Venereal Disease Control Act, not a single dollar went toward discussing—much less distributing—condoms, spermicides, and diaphragms. Instead, with venereal disease redefined as a national responsibility, money was used to establish clinics for study and treatment, diagnosis through blood tests, and vague discussion of abstinence as a preventive.

Information about contraception, obscured from the public by Parran's euphemism "venereal prophylaxis," promoted promiscuous behavior. "It is believed," he explained, "that such propaganda reaching all ages would have an ill effect which possibly could counterbalance the cases prevented."[56] Apparently Parran, an advisor to Congress on the 1939 National Venereal Disease Control Act, considered sexual diseases, particularly gonorrhea, as an unpreventable—but now possibly treatable—male problem. But more research was necessary, and the infamous Tuskegee syphilis study, in which black men with syphilis remained purposely untreated by penicillin, became Parran's legacy as surgeon general of the United States.

Sanger responded to this national attention to venereal disease with a series of pamphlets demonstrating high rates of maternal death and disease. Under her newly created Public Progress Committee of the BCCRB, she encouraged citizens to protest the omission of birth control from government programs. Parran countered that the "scientific and social factors of birth control" remained unproven. Sanger had heard this excuse before: it recalled "one of the earlier reports of the American Medical Association which also dealt at length with every sociological phase of birth control and scrupulously avoided discussion of the medical aspects—the only question on which they were competent to pass judgment."[57] Despite her criticism, her efforts to include birth control as preventive medicine funded by the federal government failed, though in 1942 the U.S. Public Health Service ruled that money allocated for local health services could be used for family planning despite fears of socialized medicine raised by doctors and persisting moral objections from the Catholic Church. But progress was slow: until the 1960s only fifteen states offered contraceptive counseling in public clinics.

Besides strategies for clinics and inclusion in federal programs, in the 1930s Sanger addressed another frontier that soon became her principal focus: the development of cheap, reliable birth control for women, some sort of pill, as she once said.[58] To that end, she continued to organize her signature meetings of physicians and research scientists. She called her 1936 meeting the Conference on Contraceptive Research and Clinical Practice. While such conferences among physicians and scientists proliferated during the 1930s, most were specialty-specific and in established fields. Surgeons met with surgeons and talked about new operations, such as the refinements of thyroidectomies, removing tumors in the sternum, and Dr. Allen Whipple's operations on the pancreas. They published their papers in the *Annals of Surgery*. Experts in tuberculosis met with their fellows and studied the *Bulletin of Tuberculosis*. Though less pervasive, similar specialization extended into the fields of zoology, physiology, and endocrinology. Birth control, neither broadly accepted as a medical topic nor understood for its scientific necessities, did not fit anywhere.

Sanger intended an interdisciplinary approach breaching territorial boundaries. She expected to bring together experts who shared information and listened to papers on the current state of contraceptive research. Most critically, she proposed to stimulate and somehow find the funds for more studies, whether on familiar topics within the paradigm of research such as "Physical Factors in the Efficacy of Contraceptive Jellies" and "The Value of the Diaphragm Inserter in Contraceptive Technique," or newer hormonal studies. All would be printed in the *Journal of Contraception* published by the BCCRB. She meant to encourage laboratory studies by specialists such as Dr. Raphael Kurzrok, a professor of obstetrics and gynecology at Columbia University who studied hormonal sterilization using the synthetic compound estradiol, not to impede fertility but to understand infertility.

Another of her favorites, Dr. Gregory Pincus of Harvard University, published his findings on rabbit and mice ovulation and the anovulant possibilities of hormones in his 1936 book *The Eggs of Mammals*, which was promptly reviewed in the *Journal of Contraception*.

Sanger's ally Dr. Robert Dickinson opposed such a conference on the grounds that there was not enough new material. Currently updating his comprehensive *Control of Conception*, Dickinson had surveyed the stagnant state of research in the field: "The cervix cover described nearly four thousand years ago is in principle the vaginal diaphragm of fifty years ago . . . the vaginal spermicide in an occlusive vehicle used by the early Egyptians we have made more portable and pleasant." And as in the past, half of those introduced to the Sanger-accredited method of diaphragm and jelly rejected the state-of-the-art female contraceptive as messy, inconvenient, and intrusive. And as for the repetitious spermicide investigations, the slight modifications of the ingredients of foam powders and jellies and their delivery, whether on cotton pads or from syringes, the shifting proportions of formaldehyde and the varieties of capsules did not conform to proper scientific methods now increasingly used in formal medical trials. Dickinson feared "exposing ourselves to ridicule for the meagerness of our results in these years when we have had scant funds for discovery and fear of censure denied us investigators."[59]

Sanger paid no attention, though other doctors objected on moral grounds. Dr. George Kosmak, a longtime Catholic adversary, complained of Sanger's "exaggerated and often hysterical dissemination of birth control propaganda." Though he acknowledged her "strength of will," like many physicians he deplored her conferences, clinics, independent action, and "loose thinking and false sentiments."[60]

By this time Sanger knew herself to be a talented organizer whose reputation encouraged the attendance of experts, and so she proceeded with the arrangements for a conference to be held in New York's Roosevelt Hotel in January 1937. In her introductory address to an assembly of two hundred, she noted that nine prestigious universities were represented among the authors of the papers. She spoke proudly about the past and, of course, the future. She praised the BCCRB, which had been visited by over fifty-six thousand women in thirteen years, its records now providing "a veritable human laboratory for research and correlations." After the recent *One Package* ruling, the birth control movement was no longer hampered by legal restrictions, nor was it a "hot bed of controversy . . . This means the field is cleared for the discovery of inexpensive, reliable methods for the control of human fertility."[61]

The time had come for a bold new agenda for "this youngest branch of science." Always dependent on physicians, Sanger now turned to another group of experts:

> Contraceptive research in both the laboratory and the clinic is now free to pursue its course emancipated from the stigma of prejudice . . . but we can not go much further alone. We cannot go either upward or onward without the help of the scientific mind . . . We must ask the scientist to come to our aid. We should place the scientist not only at the helm, but on the bridge as captain to guide humanity into the unknown future.[62]

A year after this meeting, while Margaret Sanger was recuperating in Arizona, two officers of the ABCL, the organization she had founded in 1921 and resigned from in 1928, traveled to Tucson. They came to discuss the state of the movement. Both, in a significant change in leadership, were men; Dr. Richard Pierson was head of the board of the ABCL and Kenneth Rose currently served as the national director of the ABCL and was a former executive of the John Price Jones Corporation, one of a group of firms that specialized in modern techniques of public relations, fund-raising, and consulting. Both told Sanger the same thing: it was time to merge the BCCRB, her special pride, with the ABCL. There was too much redundancy in a time of limited resources; there was too much overlap among the solicitation of prospects. The organization needed someone in New York to oversee day-to-day operations. Pierson and Rose reminded Sanger of the failure of the Birth Control Council of America, an interim group made up of members from both the ABCL and the BCCRB, charged with finding ways to lessen duplication and hard feelings between these two national organizations.

Sanger needed no reminding. She had resigned from the Birth Control Council of America in 1937, frustrated by its "personal narrow interests" and parochialism.[63] She meant by this the refusal of the ABCL executive board to approve decisions made by its delegates, specifically the merger of ABCL publications with her more substantial *Journal of Contraception*. The ABCL had also refused to sponsor a physician to work in the South. There were personal slights as well when she learned that the staff read letters addressed to her. The board had even declined to purchase discounted copies of her *Autobiography* to circulate among league members. The ever-loyal Florence Rose termed such actions "dirty work at the crossroads."[64]

As for the recent, unnecessarily expensive 242-page consultants' report, "I had the strong sense that whoever was writing the Report was doing his utmost and best to grab from the activities of other organizations credit to bolster up a case for the ABCL."[65] Sanger believed the league was unfairly taking credit for her contributions—the *One Package* decision, the federal lobbying work that had not changed the law but had influenced public opinion, and even the clinics that had been her priority since 1916. Some of its leaders were even spreading rumors that she had improperly used money raised for legislative lobbying for other purposes. Worst of all, they diminished her years of leadership by implying a lack of professionalism in any "one-woman operation."[66]

Sanger's allies Robert Dickinson and Clarence Gamble rallied to her defense. When the league asked Dickinson to encourage Sanger to retire from the merger efforts, he complained: "That Mrs. Sanger be urged to efface herself from the movement and turn over most of her activities to the League—the league that publishes no books, has no demonstration clinics, does no research and analyses, has few end results—is this amazing or amusing?"[67]

For years the ABCL had been one of Sanger's favorite targets: at first as a "pink tea social center for pleasant conversation and gossip," run by "drawing room lizards."[68] Later she condemned it as a feeble organization whose overpaid leaders—"good talkers but window dressing"—had forgotten the historic militancy of the movement, failing even to support a legal challenge after the arrests of clinic workers in Massachusetts and ending the street sales of pamphlets. When Clarence Little invited Sanger, for years birth control's best fund-raiser, to be on the sponsoring committee of a campaign, "I wrote him and said when the League had a vision large enough to embrace the whole movement and to cooperate with the activities of other groups that I would be willing to do as requested. I said a few other things that were on my mind and felt better after letting him know where I stood."[69]

But no matter what Sanger said, far away in Tucson and resistant to modern approaches of fund-raising and organization, she lacked authority. Negotiations between the two bureaus in New York ended in an agreement for a merger if three conditions were met: the new organization, renamed the Birth Control Federation of America, must hire a full-time male president, the chair of the board must not be an individual associated with either the ABCL or the BCCRB, and finally Margaret Sanger must be made honorary chair of the new board. *The New York Times* covered the negotiations on its second page: "Birth Control Rift Ended by Merger Restoration of Harmony. Will endeavor to relate the movement more broadly to the whole field of public health and family welfare and to the allied fields of population, education and eugenics."[70]

Having so long rejected any merger in which she would lose control of her clinic, the newly appointed honorary chair accepted the new arrangements, with reservations. She did not protest the installation of a male president. Pierson had persuaded her that birth control's agenda was best managed by men who negotiated more successfully than women with birth control's new constituencies of male legislators, hospital administrators, and doctors' associations. At Gamble's suggestion she agreed to a restructured committee system, though she refused to accept his advice that she avoid controversies with the Catholic Church. She abandoned her public objections to leaders inexperienced in the politics of birth control, even when, to her dismay, the new medical director, Dr. Woodbridge Morris, was a thirty-seven-year-old physician with no birth control background, but training in the emerging field of public health. Nor did she complain of her demotion to a position with no authority: "I am not going to return to be captain . . . It is not the same. It can never be the same. If it is going to die let it. When the merger took place, I spiritually left the front and joined the ranks."[71]

To her disappointed followers Sanger explained the necessity of moving "beyond a personal movement centered around MS or her personality or ideas or friends or coworkers," cautioning that there must be no public criticism. Success for the new organization would be a victory for all. But to friends she complained that the new organization had too many "boosters" and too few "kickers." Sixty years old in 1939, Sanger, who had never had the patience to groom a successor, surrendered to play the role of an aging, powerless critic with an inspiring name. She admitted to Florence Rose that her bad health had induced apathy. During her convalescence from surgery, Sanger had come to realize the degree to which her work had absorbed her life and "how selfish and narrow I had become . . . Now its done & I am free & happy & can kick up my heels in the pasture with the primroses looking on. It's a grand and glorious feeling."[72]

Practiced at transformative pivots in her personal and public life, for a time Sanger enjoyed a previously impossible leisure. She took up golf and piano lessons; she perfected her chicken curry and joined a watercolor class in Tucson. She learned how to drive an automobile, though, according to Grant and Stuart, never very well. She played with her beloved cocker spaniels, Pepper, Joy, and Beauty, convinced that dogs were more devoted and loving than humans. She traveled to Mexico, and in 1940 went on a cruise to Cuba and the Caribbean with Noah. She danced with fun-loving Angus Macdonald.

But Sanger remained suspicious of the new managers, especially when the board endorsed a resolution that the Birth Control Federation of America should avoid all controversies with the Catholic Church. Then in the ultimate heresy engineered by Kenneth Rose three years later, the Birth Control Federation of America was renamed the Planned Parenthood Federation of America over her strenuous opposition. For Sanger the term "birth control" had symbolic, historic, and literal meaning; it named the movement's purpose of giving women the power to regulate—to control—their fertility, without which none were free. Besides, it was the term she had assigned. "We will get no farther because of the title. Birth control was built on a strong foundation of truth, justice, right and common sense."[73]

As for the label "family planning," she wondered what it meant, perhaps anything from families planning summer vacations, as her niece Olive Byrne joked, to family finances and the infertility services that made birth control clinics into contradictions. Though occasionally she had used the term herself, Sanger remained a fierce critic of the inclusiveness of purpose and personnel in family planning: "With the name change [there were no] limitations of those in charge to whom you must bow the head & bend the knee. It begins to look as if some of us would have greater liberty to do good birth control work if we were not a part of the organization."[74]

Of course Sanger never abandoned the passion of her life. Instead, she moved into international work and in the United States shifted from an activist leader to an elder stateswoman, enjoying the reverence accorded when she attended annual meetings, but despising the low profile of the new organization, Executive Director Kenneth Rose's lack of aggressiveness, and her own lack of authority. Occasionally she commented on the natural progression of reform movements, explaining to Pearl Buck, "Organization work is routine, and has a deadly effect on all creative faculties. It only runs you down and gives nothing in return."[75] But when the new medical director, Dr. Morris, insisted that she submit her ideas to him before publicizing them, the rebuke came immediately: "It is utterly impossible for one of my temperament who after all has spent 25 years in fearlessly advising where I think the movement needs direction to refuse that advice or defer it."[76] Meanwhile, more persistently than anyone in headquarters, Sanger continued her search for a better contraceptive: "There is a definite lag in one important phase of the work—namely research. We have great need for more physicians with scientific background and a wide horizon of thinking to develop this major phase of our work in order that the medical profession may be prepared to meet the demands made upon them by an informed public asking for contraceptive advice."[77]

In the late 1930s, the world began to fall apart, and the well-traveled Sanger watched its destruction. She had always been a pacifist who connected militarism to population pressures and population pressures to the lack of contraception. But the emergence of the "madman Hitler," along with Franco and Mussolini, required a different set of principles. In the 1930s she observed a surge in anti-Semitic attitudes in Germany and "the vitriolic hatred of them spreading underground here is far more dangerous than the aggressive policy of the Japanese in Manchuria."[78] As early as 1936, Sanger had foreseen Europe's future in the civil war in Spain, a place of special affection, where, as she told Angus, she might have stayed forever with her anarchist lover Lorenzo Portet: "Fate played a game in sending me to USA instead of keeping me in Barcelona." Now republican Spain was "fighting for us . . . [in] a life & death struggle for her future & as I see it for the freedom & liberty in which we of this generation have breathed & developed. All of Europe is involved. The Catholic Church is locking arms with Fascist Germany & Italy."[79]

Even before the Germans invaded Poland in September 1939, Sanger had begun what Florence Rose called a "Refugee Bureau," her personal effort to help European friends gain entry into the United States. Immigration laws based on eugenically defined, numerically stringent quotas remained in place, with additional, Depression-related stipulations requiring a job or sponsor to prevent any immigrant from becoming a public charge. Such rules delayed the urgent requests of Jewish refugees fleeing the Nazis. Committed to those who had helped her in the past, Sanger supported the applications of a Jewish urologist from Poland, a German nurse, an Austrian gynecologist and obstetrician, and Ernst Grafenberg, the developer of the Grafenberg pessary ring. She helped her English friends as well. Across the Atlantic went sweaters for de Selincourt's grandson, along with Bundles for Britain to her aging English friends. Meanwhile, she wondered how "a fool like Hitler could hold 70 million people in his law made overnight as opposed to 100 years of enlightened progressive humane laws."[80]

Sanger was in Tucson when the Japanese attacked Pearl Harbor. Previously she had preached neutrality (with republican Spain an exception), arguing with Juliet Rublee, who did not think birth control "as important to mankind's progress as I do." In response Rublee wondered if Sanger would simply let Hitler dominate Europe, after Sanger opposed Roosevelt's destroyers for bases and lend-lease programs, the latter designed to aid Great Britain. While war loomed for the United States, Sanger held birth control—not preparedness—as "the key to civilized life and the world."[81]

Meanwhile, Rublee, living in London, where her husband was in charge of an international organization aiding refugees, worried about the lack of military organization in England and hoped that Hitler, like St. Paul, would somehow see a vision of Christ and convert. Sanger saw different threats: "The future of America is not threatened by Communists, Fascists, or Jews, but the power of Rome clutches at the throat of democracy through radio, public health welfare, the post office and part of the press and government. The Protestants have gone to sleep and the Jews and other non-Catholics are afraid."[82]

After listening to the news of the Japanese attack in December 1941 on the radio, Sanger despaired: "Nation after nation will now join in this madness & God only can keep our hearts true."[83] What had been lost for Sanger and many other Americans was the reformer's optimism that reasonable, progressive societies would adopt measures for the benefit of their peoples. Such was the underlying principle of birth control. Even during the war the control of reproduction remained for Sanger the cornerstone of an intelligent social order. But as was the case in World War I, there was government propaganda to increase the American population, and Sanger watched birthrates jump from 18 per 1,000 women in 1935 to 23 per 1,000 by 1944. Sanger's oft quoted phrase "the stork is the bird of war" proved correct, as Americans, including her sons, rushed to the altar and thereafter to the delivery room. And after the war, what would victory bring? In her version of the lessons of history, World War I had produced no just peace, in Germany only a transition from the Kaiser to Hitler, and in the Soviet Union from Lenin to Stalin. She held few hopes for a progressive postwar society. Stubbornly single-minded, she believed there would be no possibility for world peace until families had enough food. And that depended on controlling birthrates through contraception.

As the war disrupted lives, Sanger faced her own personal losses. In July 1939, just before the Germans invaded Poland, eighty-year-old Havelock Ellis died—"this simple, humble man," she called him in a radio interview. Sanger remembered his importance to the world and to women for his free thinking about sex. Forgiving Ellis's dismissal "of the American nurse" in his recent autobiography, she recalled his personal influence on her. "I have never felt about any person as I do about Havelock Ellis. I'd developed a reverence, an affection and a love which has strengthened over the years. To know him was a bounteous privilege; to claim him as my friend the greatest honor of my life."[84] Two years later the dependable Hannah Stone, who had run the clinic for fifteen years, succumbed to a heart attack at the age of forty-seven.

In 1943 her husband suffered a stroke and died. Sanger, so often absent in their marriage, had served as Noah's dutiful nurse for over a year, "listening to his calls and his buzzer." To his daughter, who like his other children attended neither his funeral in Tucson nor his burial in a cemetery near Willowlake, Sanger explained that he had wanted to die. He was tired of the "indignity of helplessness, hated to be bathed in bed and turned to keep him from bed sores."[85] But she made it clear to his children and to herself that her love for Noah Slee had transformed his life. The bickering of the last few years was forgotten as Sanger turned the page: "The petty irritations and annoyances are wiped out. Death removes them all. It wipes out the memories of the unreal. Only the goodness, kindness & loving things remain of my thoughts of J. Noah."[86] That same year her eldest brother, Joe Higgins—the home-based brother who never left Corning—died. And then in 1944 her beloved older sister Nan Higgins, who had scrimped and saved for Sanger's education at Claverack, died suddenly of a heart attack and was buried next to Noah. "Two dear graves side by side in Fishkill Cemetery," wrote a lonely Sanger in her diary.[87]

The resilient Sanger found family replacements, growing closer to the two younger brothers whom she had helped to raise during her mother's illness—Richard and Robert, the latter her favorite and an acclaimed football coach at Pennsylvania State University. According to Sanger, Robert was "the typical Higgins product of 11 centuries of the Irish Clan."[88] Her immediate family changed as well. Both her sons married—thirty-eight-year-old Stuart to Barbara Peabody, a nurse whom he had met at the Lahey Clinic. Their first child, a daughter named Margaret, was born in 1941, seven months after their marriage. Then, in a family notable for its health practitioners, Grant married Edwina Campbell, a wealthy graduate of Vassar and Columbia Medical School (one of ten women and a hundred men in the class of 1938) and a resident at Columbia-Presbyterian, whose professionalism Sanger admired. At first she worried that Edwina would never give up her career for motherhood, but she shortly found that this extraordinary new daughter-in-law who wanted to be a daughter—"not that anomalous creature of daughter-in-law"—and who addressed her as "mummy" was, in fact, a "breeder."[89] In 1943 Grant and Edwina's first son was born (the first of six children) and named Michael for the grandfather that Grant had grown to love during the summers in Truro.

By 1943 Stuart and Grant were overseas in the medical corps: Stuart in the Normandy landing and the Battle of the Bulge, Grant on an aircraft carrier and then a casualty ship in the Pacific. Now Sanger joined thousands of other anxious mothers. In December 1944, while listening to Christmas carols on the radio, she was "frantic to have word of Stuart. I've always said since Peggy's death that life could not hold me long if another of my children went before I did."[90] Negligent in the past in her attention to her sons, now Sanger devoted time and energy to her daughters-in-law and their infants, traveling to California to be with Edwina and to Florida to be with Barbara. In time some of her eight grandchildren called her Domah, the nickname used by their father for their grandmother Henrietta Sanger; others called her Mimi, the child's contraction of her entreaties "Come to me. Come to me." From her reading Sanger retained the anthropologists' detached view of grandmothers as a means of giving the wife's mother a place in the household, but to Dorothy Gordon she acknowledged that men "all laugh at us in that role of grandmother."[91] For a woman who hated growing old, such status made her feel unpleasantly ancient: "I only pray that I shall never grow old. It's too tragic & sad."[92] Sanger was still subtracting five years from her birth date, preferring, as she sparred with the editors of Who's Who in America, the dating of activities rather than any official chronology of her life.

One day during the war a letter came from the long-forgotten Bill Sanger, who had no idea where his sons were, though he thought his former wife might. In a rambling reminiscence Bill recalled their family life in

Hastings, asked Sanger to return a silver bowl and some furniture, and commented on how the war had become a revolution. Over the years he had never seen Stuart, he wrote, but Grant had occasionally visited. "They are in the service and now in my little corner I feel I am part of the big surge to win this war."[93] Meanwhile, with the consistent goodwill she displayed toward collateral relatives, Sanger enthusiastically recommended Bill's daughter Joan to Barnard College as a "hardworking responsible Protestant, whose father was an architect," though at the time Bill Sanger supported his wife and daughter by working in a low-paying job with the New York City Department of Water Supply, Gas and Electricity.

During the war Sanger included in what she called her "big interests" her work with Pearl Buck raising money for the latter's East-West Association, her painting, and, of course, birth control. In fact Sanger did very little birth control work, though she opposed calling off the cause for patriotism's sake. To do so reminded her of the mistaken surrender the suffrage movement had made during World War I. To fill her time Sanger wrote a pamphlet, *Should Women Have Babies During the War?*; she worked with the Tucson Birth Control League and raised money for a nondenominational hospital in Tucson to compete with the Catholic-run and -staffed St. Mary's. As a celebrity she publicized her opinions on everything from the discrimination against WACS, who, unlike male soldiers, were not given contraceptives, to the unfortunate bias that sent doctors into combat, but gave priests exemptions from the draft.

When Clarence Gamble asked if she had been as inactive as she seemed—a great loss, he believed, because "the mothers of the country need you"—the answer was that Sanger had been distracted by the war and her personal losses as well as her powerless status as honorary chair of an organization she believed had lost its way.[94] Characteristically, she looked forward: "If I am not too old when this war is over, [my] next epoch's work will be in China and India where pandemonium breaks out if one mentions the organs of a female body and its secretions."[95]

On Christmas Day 1945, the Sanger family was reunited in Tucson, where Stuart intended to establish his practice and live next door to his mother. To celebrate their peacetime reunion, eight Sangers—two-year-old Michael, five-month-old Peter, and their four-year-old-cousin Margaret, their parents and sixty-six-year-old grandmother—gathered to toast the future with champagne. After lunch Sanger included in her presents to her sons subscriptions to expensive medical journals, a testament to her pride in their chosen careers. And then as a surprise, she distributed shares of Dow Chemical and General Electric to her sons from her six-figure portfolio, inherited from her husband, so that Grant and Stuart could get "going and [have] a little security to give dignity and self-respect."[96] Meanwhile, their mother was already planning a trip to England.

10

WORLD LEADER

I forget the past as fast as I can make plans for the future.
— Margaret Sanger to Mary Valiant, January 18, 1947

In 1946, the war just over, thousands of American soldiers still overseas, and England on short rations, Sanger made plans for the first of many postwar trips overseas. The United States could not hold a woman who had long ago insisted that she had no country and who for years had recognized that access to birth control was a humanitarian necessity for women throughout the world. By this time Sanger had abandoned her occasional fantasies of a leisurely future, though she did describe herself as a "free agent in life."[1]

Of course, her friends knew that she would never give up birth control work; it was her lifelong passion. But now in her late sixties, Sanger briefly wavered: "Now as to the Conference on Population or the possibility of such a conference, if anyone wants to push the idea or organize it I'll help as much as I can but I will not be the one to direct its promotion."[2] Such intentions did not last long, and for the next fifteen years Sanger orchestrated the formation of what became the most significant and enduring privately funded association for sex education, family planning, and contraception— the International Planned Parenthood Federation (IPPF).

In her other major initiative during the 1950s, she became the enabling figure in the funding of research for the development of a cheap, effective birth control method, something that she had sought for years. Earlier, Sanger had anticipated the solution would come in some form of sperm immunization. But she soon recognized the possibilities of a birth control pill that prevented ovulation—an effective, easy-to-use method that would help all women limit the size of their families and would especially aid poor women, in "overcoming the lack of initiative, the hopelessness, the despair of that group in the lower strata of our world."[3]

Despite warnings about conditions in Europe, Sanger traveled by ship to England, where H. G. Wells was dying of liver cancer, Hugh de Selincourt was a self-described toothless mumbler, and Bessie Drysdale of the Neo-Malthusian League was weary and malnourished. Sanger did not stay long. But the next year she returned on her way to Stockholm for a population conference organized by the Nordic beauty Elise Ottesen-Jensen, the commanding figure in the Swedish birth control movement. Accustomed to being harassed and even spat upon for her efforts to teach young Swedes about reproduction, Ottesen-Jensen had founded the Swedish National League for Sex Education in the 1930s. By the 1950s the membership of the association had reached a hundred thousand.

Ottesen-Jensen privileged sex education over birth control, but both she and Sanger, forever in need of allies, tucked their agendas into anxieties about overpopulation. Sheltered by what became a mainstream global preoccupation, Sanger could now avoid the kind of moral and sexual questions that previously encumbered discussion of birth control for individuals. In time another form of criticism would center on the heavy-handed intrusion of governments into private affairs and the manipulation of the fertility of poor people. Sanger paid little attention to such reservations. As she had written to Wells before his death, "I am eager to get in touch with those scientists who would be interested in a world population conference to be held either in London or New York in 1947."[4] Committed to creating an organization that would address the management of human fertility as an international matter, Sanger traveled overseas eight times in the next ten years, sometimes by boat but increasingly by the new marvel of commercial overseas flight.

She had long been concerned about the possible collision of rising populations, stagnant food production, and limited space. Disgusted by the traditional patriotic fervor that trumpeted high birthrates as national power, Sanger insisted that both world wars were the result of overpopulation. In 1947 she decried "the world wide congestion of population which can not continue without worldwide misery, famine, & wars."[5] Such was the intellectual legacy of her friendships with the English Neo-Malthusians begun before World War I, and lasting, through her careful tending, for a lifetime.

After World War I, under her direction, the American Birth Control

League had sponsored the International Neo-Malthusian and Birth Control Conference, held in New York in 1925. The more than a thousand participants from sixteen countries had included Norman Thomas, perennial presidential candidate of the Socialist Party U.S.A., Dr. Aletta Jacobs, from the Netherlands (who years before had dismissed Sanger as an ignorant nurse), and from England, the eugenicist Charles Drysdale and the famous economist John Maynard Keynes, along with 150 specialists in medicine, economics, and the emerging discipline of demography. Recruited by Sanger, they delivered papers on differential fertility rates among rich and poor nations and the pressures of exploding populations on food sources.

With the success of the conference, Sanger's reputation soared. She was becoming the most important international figure in the contraceptive movement, as leadership of population causes and birth control research, previously centered in England, France, and Germany, crossed the Atlantic to the United States. In her greeting to the conference, Sanger made contraception less radical by attaching it to the concerns of experts: "The scientific flavor of our work will perhaps help make the idea more acceptable to statesmen."[6] Two years later Sanger organized an international conference in Geneva, where similar issues were discussed. What she had first elaborated as birth control for individual women was being reshaped into a respectable global intention to influence populations through targeted annual birthrates.

Never one to let an opportunity escape, Sanger created an international organization in the 1930s, using money from the Milbank Memorial Fund, whose directors had long been interested in population issues. The result had been the formation of the Birth Control International Information Centre in London, where an overworked Edith How-Martyn struggled to keep up with the correspondence, send out contraceptive information, and raise money, once organizing a Malthusian Ball and contributing its meager proceeds to the Centre. Sanger had helped, sending small sums of money to establish clinics throughout the world. Among the recipients was her friend the radical journalist Agnes Smedley, who was living in Shanghai in the early 1930s. Smedley predicted that birth control work in China would never come until there was a revolution "that will wipe out the whole capitalist class, the land-owner class and foreign imperialists."[7] But Sanger wanted more than simply a clearinghouse dispensing population information and educating individual clients in the best contraceptive methods.

By the late 1940s, even after a world war in which 56 million people had died, population concerns absorbed philanthropists such as John D. Rockefeller III; politicians, including President Harry Truman; and academics in ivory towers. Truman had warned in his 1952 message to Congress that overpopulation was "one of the gravest problems arising from the present world crisis."[8] Two international wars in two decades had broadened national perspectives into global considerations. But while American women were encouraged to have more children during the cheaper-by-the-dozen baby boom of the 1950s—four was the perfect number, according to the magazines of the decade—the Western press noted disturbing increases in Japan. The five years from 1945 to 1950 had increased the Japanese population by 12 million. In India there had been a gain of 43 million in just a decade. In the boardrooms of wealthy foundations, talk of a population "bomb," an "explosion" of people, and the resulting famines, mostly predicted for India, China, and Japan, laid the groundwork for private organizations, modeled after the United Nations. Their intention was to assist governments in efforts to regulate fertility and establish population goals.

A "population establishment" emerged in Princeton University's Office of Population Research under Frank Notestein, in the Rockefeller's Population Council, and in the British Eugenics Society, led by Dr. C. P. Blacker, the latter association now replacing its previous eugenic concerns for quality persons with attention to the quantity of people. Humans were now considered not so much as individuals but as populations.[9] Although Sanger had successfully raised money from the Rockefeller family for years, triply marginalized as a woman, as without credentials, and as a propagandist, she was never included in meetings of population experts such as John D. Rockefeller's invitation-only Conference on Population Problems held in Williamsburg in 1952. Here, apprehensive discussions about the political survival of "westernized groups," the possible infiltration of Communism in crowded India, and a version of international race suicide led to the formation of the Population Council.

There was disagreement among these experts about what to do, but a comforting academic concept, "demographic transition theory," emerged, based on the idea that birthrates rose in undeveloped countries, only to stagnate during a transitional phase and then level off and decline after modernization—the latter a popular concept borrowed from economists that synthesized into the single word "modernization," the simultaneous process of increasing urbanization, improved transportation, new technology, and substantial capital investment. But too large a population blocked opportunities for growth and stalled industrialization in what was now dubbed "the Third World." As expressed in frightening, easily absorbed numbers, it had taken all of human history to reach a billion people, but only 130 years for the second billion, and in thirty years another billion would be added. Time was running out.

The tools used to study such matters developed from sophisticated statistical measures of gross national product, per capita income, and heightened interest in the effect of declining mortality rates on rising populations. The postwar application of the insecticide DDT to wipe out malaria-carrying mosquitoes provided a useful case study of the impact of lengthened life spans in nations such as Ceylon with limited ability to increase food production. While these specialists debated policy, Sanger already had her solution: "The overarching name Population is all to the good if it will arouse the public interest and get a better understanding of birth control."[10]

In Sanger's view, just as public health agencies must become the sites for national family planning clinics, so the United Nations, particularly through its agencies UNESCO and the World Health Organization, was the logical place for action. She was soon disappointed. UN officials did organize two conferences on family planning during the 1950s, one in Rome, which, given its setting in the heartland of Catholicism, was doomed to failure from the start, and the second in Belgrade, where, after much disagreement, only one session was devoted to contraception. At every level, the UN was rapidly disintegrating into a stalemate between East and West, and, in population matters, between Catholic and non-Catholic nations and delegates.

The Soviet bloc denied the premise of Westerners that population control was necessary for the world's future. Arguing instead that poverty caused large populations, not the reverse, Communist nations sought economic solutions: an increase in the proletariat was essential for socialist revolution. Meanwhile, delegates from Catholic nations threatened boycotts if any action was taken to promote family planning clinics with birth control services, though Sanger's English admirer the biologist Dr. Julian Huxley, now the director of UNESCO, publicized his view that population must be balanced against resources or civilization would perish. Contraception and sterilization were better solutions than continence and disease, Huxley had long ago concluded. And he placed birth control, imperfect as it might be, as a major event in the world's history—"one step in mankind's mastery over the blind forces of nature, a measure of his civilization and growth to maturity."[11]

The World Health Organization did commission a study of the rhythm method, and Dr. Abraham Stone, the director of the Margaret Sanger Research Bureau since his wife Hannah's death, traveled to India to set up pilot programs to teach women the intricacies of their reproductive cycles. The practical Stone developed a string of beads with different colors denoting days of fertility and infertility, only to be repudiated by Sanger, who had always believed so-called timed abstinence "a joke." "Personally I disagree with [the rhythm method] violently from the point of view of biology. The female animals in the field have long ago rejected it," by which, using undocumented folklore about women's sexuality, she meant that women were most interested in sex when they were most likely to conceive.[12]

Sanger had her own international agenda. In Stockholm in 1948, she pressed for another meeting to be held in England and the formation of an interim executive committee. Two years later, in the charming town of Cheltenham, which advertised itself as the gateway to the Cotswolds, 250 delegates from twenty nations, including two American students of reproductive biology—Dr. Earl Engle of Columbia and Dr. John Rock of Harvard—attended a weeklong meeting with the heady title International Congress on Population and World Resources in Relation to the Family. Sanger, who rarely made comments from the floor or questioned speakers at these meetings, delivered her standard lecture on the history of birth control but with a new ending that highlighted exciting research in endocrinology along with a complaint: "It seems absurd to me that we have been able to make the atom bomb, yet we have not got a really simple good and harmless contraceptive."[13] But she had hopes for the future.

Ever alert to the uses of the rich and famous, she convinced Lord Horder, physician to royalty and the head of the British Family Planning Association, to preside over the conference. The real celebrity at this meeting was the distinguished Scots physician and Nobel Prize winner Sir John Boyd Orr, who heralded the arrival of postwar internationalism directed by nongovernmental bodies: "Governments are always at least a decade behind intelligent, thinking people. Social measures began long before governments took them up . . . we have to think of the world as a whole . . . When people meet here, the programme of the future gets born."[14] Earlier, Sanger had solicited papers with explicit instructions about deadlines and the required 2,500-word length. At the conference she chaired a session on population trends, encouraged more study groups, hosted a party, and paid the bills with money raised from foundations, including a new one established by Ellen and Indian-born Goa Watumull of the department store chain in Hawaii. On the perplexing matter of how to move talk to action, Sanger proclaimed private clinics too expensive a solution and argued instead, as she had since the 1930s, for the delivery of contraception through government-run public health facilities.

And while the delegates talked, in her hotel room Sanger was lining up support for a future meeting and the creation of a structure—a secretariat modeled after the United Nations—that would provide permanency for an international movement. The last day delegates declared the right of parents to decide upon the number of their children, along with the right of all people to obtain scientific information on the control of conception and the treatment of infertility, the latter never one of Sanger's concerns. Still, such pronouncements diminished the uproar over her comment to reporters that "English women should declare a moratorium on babies for ten years; let none get born in any country until hunger is conquered. And let the excess emigrate to places with more room." The English press was outraged; the *Daily Mail* predicted that "Nature will frustrate a million Mrs. Slees."[15]

Cheltenham was the beginning of a series of Sanger-orchestrated international conferences that took place in Stockholm, Bombay, Tokyo, and New Delhi in the coming years. During the 1950s family planning advanced more rapidly under the direction of private groups than under that of public ones such as the UN and national governments. These conferences, like the ABCL she had created in 1921, supported special projects, provided a forum for new advances in technology, and created global links among activists. Sanger organized and attended every one of these meetings, along with the new species of specialist—population experts—who were examining birth and mortality rates with alarm, especially in India and Japan, the favorite sites for dire predictions of future catastrophe. Sanger made sure that Dr. Gregory Pincus and Dr. John Rock, the scientists closest to the development of a chemical contraceptive, reported on their work on the anovulant hormone, progesterone. With money donated by the patron of contraception research, Katharine McCormick, Sanger paid their travel expenses, even hiring Pincus's daughter in 1959 to act as her companion and secretary.

Previously invisible to some experts, birth control as an essential part of family planning now became the weapon of choice in the battle against overpopulation. Sanger's longtime financial supporter Dorothy Brush described Sanger's role in its postwar advocacy: "Almost single-handed, she created this conference, and those that followed out of nothing but willpower. She was unyielding, relentless and egotistical in a way that was wonderful to behold . . . not for herself only, but for the objectives with which she was completely identified."[16] Of course, Brush was a close friend, and out of earshot there was grumbling about a one-woman operation run by an amateur who could not work with committees and wanted her own way.

Even her inner circle found Sanger increasingly difficult. After an argument over modern art, with Juliet Rublee opposed and Sanger in favor, in a letter addressed to "Darling Margaret," Rublee aired a general complaint: "It is impossible to discuss anything with you, except your great subject & marvelous achievement in Birth Control . . . Your letters were so violent, so passionate, so definitely abusive of me & angry that I felt hopeless . . . And I wonder whether you have ever admitted that you were wrong about anything or said you were sorry about anything you have ever done."[17] Such imperious behavior leached into Sanger's public life. In the minutes of her international conferences several contentious matters were resolved simply by referring the matter to Mrs. Sanger, as often to avoid a confrontation as to take advantage of her undiminished executive talents.

Four years after Cheltenham, 487 delegates from twenty-two countries met in Bombay's Sir Cowasji Jehangir Hall to be greeted by a message from a supporter—Prime Minister Jawaharlal Nehru of newly independent India. Sanger, with her practiced cultivation of the rich and powerful, had made a point of meeting Nehru in London in 1935 and entertaining his sister and nieces in Tucson. Now she listened as the newly elected leader of free India, the only government at this point to support family planning, acknowledged the desperate need for his country to limit its population growth in a Five-Year Plan. After four days of discussion Sanger achieved her goal: the creation of a permanent organization named, after endless discussion, the International Planned Parenthood Federation, with its headquarters in London on Eccleston Square, an executive director in the devoted Neo-Malthusian psychiatrist who supported sterilization, Dr. C. P. Blacker, and one full-time employee, Vera Houghton.

The organization's constitution expanded earlier rationales for its existence: "The knowledge of planned parenthood is a fundamental human right and . . . the balance between the population of the world and its natural resources is a necessary condition of human happiness, prosperity and peace." The central tools to achieve these goals were sex education and contraception. The federation existed to advance "the education of the countries of the world in family planning, to promote . . . sex education and marriage counseling, to simulate research, and to investigate the biological and demographical implication of human fertility and methods of contraception." To further the latter, a medical subcommittee was formed to assist in the development of practical birth control techniques and research.[18]

With Sanger and India's aristocratic Lady Rama Rau as honorary co-presidents, members intended to set up model contraceptive projects for replication, pressure national governments, and work when possible "in a consultative fashion" with the UN. A newsletter, *Around the World News of Population*, with Dorothy Brush as its editor and chief financial supporter, was approved. A relieved Sanger wrote to Juliet Rublee, "The Conference is over—It was a huge Success good publicity in all the papers—good full attendance through every session—much hospitality."[19]

On her way to India, Sanger had flown to Japan from Honolulu and had been greeted rapturously by a motorcade with sound trucks blaring, "Sanger is here! Sanger is here!"—her name, as pronounced in Japanese, now the eponym for birth control. She had spoken to the Japanese Diet about family planning, the first woman to address that body, discussed birth control with groups of women, and educated doctors about its techniques. Sometimes depressed at home, in Japan "the more I worked & interviewed the younger I looked & was never tired."[20] If the trip was a triumph, it came with an unpleasant reminder.

Three years earlier Sanger experienced the type of setback that made her wary that for all the advances of birth control—its legality, its growing acceptance among the public, and its prospects for a breakthrough technology—the possibility of regression forever lurked, perhaps with a change in judges or a new Congress or even the growing influence of the Catholic Church. Such feelings replayed lifelong fears of having to return to Corning, the birthplace she had fled as a young adult. Throughout her life she experienced visceral panic when she traveled near the place that represented her past.

Shortly after the war, Sanger's friend Shidzue Kato, no longer the wife of Admiral Ishimoto but now divorced, remarried, and a member of the Japanese Diet, had invited Sanger to visit Japan, where the abortion rate was high and the population had increased by 12 million in five years. Several newspapers and a collection of activists who remembered Sanger's two earlier visits also extended invitations. From Sanger's perspective, Japan seemed a natural site for a future international meeting. Accordingly, she applied for the necessary visa but was refused by General Douglas MacArthur, the supreme commander of the Allied forces in Japan. The general believed that birth control was a social matter for the Japanese to decide for themselves. As he informed the many Americans who intervened on Sanger's behalf, "Any interference by occupying forces would be viewed as genocide. Activists should stay at home and work in Massachusetts."[21] Besides, Sanger was no more than a propagandist, though she could certainly enter Japan as a tourist.

"I do not want to go as an ordinary tourist and only be allowed to look at the gardens and the sights. I want to be able to speak and join in with those who invite me to come to visit Japan. If the general refuses, I will make a noise to high heaven," responded the ever militant Sanger.[22] Experienced in transforming censorship into favorable publicity, she sent a statement to various newspapers: "I refuse to accept as final the decision of General MacArthur that I may not come to Japan at the invitation of the Japanese. That an American can be barred from a perfectly proper mission by the bigotry and whim of other Americans is intolerable."[23]

Influential supporters took up her case. A recent convert, Eleanor Roosevelt, weighed in with a newspaper column. So, too, did friends with contacts in the State Department. Sanger framed the battle as one against government repression and, as well, her traditional enemy the Catholics, a small minority in Japan, although a Catholic Woman's Association had urged MacArthur to reject Sanger's application. In fact, the general was playing politics: anticipating a presidential campaign in 1952, he had no intention of offending not so much Japanese Catholics but the critical voting bloc of American Catholics. By 1951 the general, commanding forces in Korea, had his own battles to wage: his call for air strikes against China and his persistent criticism of military strategy led Truman to relieve him for insubordination. By 1955 Sanger had the last word when the fifth meeting of the IPPF took place in Tokyo, and at her insistence, Dr. Gregory Pincus delivered a paper titled "Some Effects of Progesterone and Related Compounds upon Reproduction and Early Development in Mammals." Although his trials were on rabbits and rats, Pincus carefully concluded that "a foundation has been laid for the useful exploitation of the problem on an objective basis."[24]

In the late 1950s, between meetings, Sanger worked unsuccessfully to organize an international conference in Washington, which her more cautious American colleagues opposed on the basis that population control must not emanate from Washington. Besides, there was hope that the Catholic Church might moderate its position on contraception, and such a meeting would only antagonize its bishops. Still, at a conference on her home ground, Sanger hoped to revise the structure of the federation. She would replace regional arrangements with national subcenters reporting to the central field office in London. Attuned to the details of the IPPF, she opposed the Western Hemisphere's policy of using nurses as field workers in places such as Mexico. "The most important thing in a new country—especially a Roman Catholic dominated country—is to get the medical profession together in a conference or committee meeting in their countries where they can make decisions. Without such support no field worker is successful or even safe no matter how much money is behind her . . . a woman going around alone without the support of the medical profession in South America is in an entirely different situation than in the USA or in English speaking nations."[25] No doubt Sanger was correct, but by the late fifties she lacked the influence to install reforms in the organization she had created.

More often in Tucson, between her overseas trips, and now free from any official obligations to the Planned Parenthood Federation of America save for fund-raising, Sanger remained the voice of the American family planning movement. In her first appearance on television in 1952, she debated two Catholic women on the popular show *Freedom Forum* in Los Angeles, furious that she was constantly interrupted. "They were told not to allow me to talk & they succeeded, alas," she reported to Dorothy Brush. "I was downed with noise, shouting, contradictions every time I started to talk—Finally I had the last minute & I gave them & their religion a mouth full." Most observers agreed. Even the host of the program, Freeman Lusk, described the event as an ordeal and asked Sanger to appear again to debate more qualified, "civilized" opponents. Still, Sanger was so discouraged at "my own reflexes & lack of 'come-back' that I have almost decided not to attempt any more public speaking ever again."[26]

After a half century, Sanger enjoyed the honors and plaudits of a life's work, proudly accepting not just the prestigious Lasker Award in 1950 but an honorary degree from Smith College the year before. The Smith citation praised Sanger as a "leader in the world-wide study of population problems . . . with deep sympathy for the oppressed and disinherited who has made a conspicuous contribution to human welfare through her integrity, courage, and social vision." Sanger called it the "highest honor and distinction of my career" and promptly gave Smith her personal papers, after earlier donating her public ones to the Library of Congress.[27] She found it ironic that she was receiving an honorary doctorate in Massachusetts, where it was still illegal to buy contraceptive devices and where the governor had just lost an election, in part because he had supported legislation to overturn the state's ban on contraception. In her public response, Sanger saluted Smith for its vision and hoped her award might inspire future pioneers among its young women. Privately she praised the college for its courage in recognizing a pariah during a capital campaign.

There was, as well, her nomination for the Nobel Peace Prize by fervent loyalists who recognized how unlikely it was that such a distinction would be bestowed on her but who were determined to try anyway. With the 1931 Nobel Peace Prize Award to Jane Addams for her work in the Women's International League for Peace and Freedom as a precedent, Dorothy Brush, Ellen Watumull, and Clarence Gamble began the tedious process of soliciting letters, encouraging a focus on Sanger's international work and her expansive interpretation of birth control as a public health measure and human rights issue that would lead to world peace. "If the committee feels that Mrs. Sanger is a controversial figure," wrote one advocate, "let us recall certain scribes and pharisees, all honorable men and patriots, who failed to recognize an even more controversial figure."[28] For the next decade the effort sputtered on, eventually failing.

There were plans for a different kind of honor—a movie with the working title of "First Woman of the Century," based on Sanger's 1938 *Autobiography*, with Ida Lupino starring as Sanger. For dramatic effect the screenplay required that Margaret, not her sister Ethel Higgins Byrne, be "the Hunger Strikee which I would have been had my trial been first," according to the appeal Sanger made to her sister. The release stated that Ethel agreed not to be in the film at all and that "Mrs. Sanger engaged in the famous hunger strike instead of myself."[29] Suffering from the effects of a stroke, Ethel eventually signed, though the delay was not from opposition to this familiar imposition by her older sister, who for years had appropriated her birth date, but rather from indifference. There was a more serious challenge, given the authority of the Catholic director of the Motion Picture Production Code, Joseph Breen, whose approval was necessary if any movie on Margaret Sanger's life was to be screened in theaters across America. Though such censorship often emboldened her, Sanger grew dissatisfied with the script and eventually terminated the contract.

In a further measure of her contested prominence during the 1950s, Sanger was interviewed by a confrontational Mike Wallace on his popular ABC television Saturday night show. Wallace had infuriated Sanger when he canceled an earlier date, explaining that two Catholic priests had discouraged any show about "the murder that was birth control." They had also approached his sponsor Philip Morris and ABC. Sanger responded with her own pressure, and Wallace was soon portrayed in the press as capitulating to Catholic influence. By September 1957 Wallace had relented and the program took place on a dark, empty stage, with a photograph of Sanger behind Wallace.

In the unflattering light Sanger, who celebrated her seventy-eighth birthday a week after the interview, looked her age. A novice at television, she answered Wallace's occasional badgering slowly, hesitantly, and uncertainly, as he presented her motives as "driven emotionally toward the birth control movement because of antagonism toward the church, because that was a way to fight the church." He quoted a newspaper article that her work was intended to find ways for single women to avoid having "illegitimate" children. He asked about her religious beliefs and her divorce. He quoted from her *Autobiography* about the influence of Havelock Ellis, "which you cannot disavow," and questioned her living arrangements with J. Noah Slee. Near the end Wallace posed the question "Could it be that women in the United States have become too independent, that they've followed the lead of women like Margaret Sanger by neglecting family life for a career?"[30] Sanger had little time to answer such a loaded proposition, and the half-hour program ended on an unlikely note when Sanger asked Wallace if he wanted to see a photograph of her children and grandchildren.

Sanger's friends and family found her performance disheartening, but the program prompted letters from new clients anxious for more information about birth control. Critics, also aroused by the program, launched familiar insults: "It's just too bad your mother didn't practice birth control 95 years ago when she had you."[31] Sanger insisted that she "had a good time," dismissing the interview as "a riot. He got a few replies that knocked him pale in the face." But such bravado never dispelled her fears that as she aged, her responses came too slowly for the rapid give-and-take of public life. Unlike Wallace, who acknowledged his sponsor Philip Morris several times and who sent the now nonsmoking Sanger a cigarette box for Christmas, she had been unable to advertise birth control: "The time was wasted as far as Birth Control was concerned."[32] *The New York Times* agreed: "Mr. Wallace seemed determined to explore the personal life of Mrs. Sanger rather than the truly significant aspects of her career . . . Mrs. Sanger is far more stimulating to meet than Mr. Wallace's program suggested."[33]

Even as she received other honors—a profile in the *Reader's Digest*, a radio address in New York, plaudits from around the world, she kept in touch with the PPFA, becoming ever more scornful of the national organization's leadership and policies. To her friend Katharine Dexter McCormick, whose resources she was cultivating for a new project, Sanger explained that "the PPF are rather marking time and just holding their own."[34] Overhead expenses were too high in the headquarters on Fifth Avenue; the amount of the resigning director Kenneth Rose's severance pay was outrageous. Fund-raising was inefficient, she believed, and there remained a constant turnover of personnel in a poorly run office. The administrative overhead subtracted from grants and donations was far too high, enough to advise McCormick to contribute elsewhere. More critically, the federation had abandoned efforts to establish contraceptive services through public health agencies; in fact, to Sanger's chagrin, only seven states currently offered birth control through state-supported agencies by the mid-1950s.

When a pending change in the U.S. Criminal Code extending the ban on lewd phonograph recordings was dismissed by the PPFA president, Charles Scribner, as not affecting birth control, Sanger disagreed. Scribner might be correct legally, but such a response revealed "feeble, weak, unstable leadership in the group which is deplorable and unworthy of financial support . . . Don't allow inaction."[35] And worst of all, in her least favored of activities, she was forced to raise money for her beloved but financially insecure Margaret Sanger Clinic.

Sanger had always recommended term limits for organizational service: "I am one who believes that each of us fulfills a mission in any organization and when we know this we should get out and let the movement stand, fall or grow."[36] Yet she found it impossible to follow her own advice and so continually offered critical suggestions to the officers of the PPFA. Even after she sold the three-story brownstone at 17 West Sixteenth Street, which for so long had been the showpiece of her movement and the home of the clinic, Dr. Abraham Stone received detailed suggestions about personnel and policy.

Nor, to her disappointment, did either of her two sons show any interest in birth control work, though Grant was briefly on the advisory board of the Margaret Sanger Clinic. Perhaps both resented the movement for taking their mother's time. In any case, "the boys don't want to be in the birth control movement. Grant is getting into it . . . at least to pace along with some of the older men. Neither he nor Stuart will ever push themselves to the forefront and they will have to be coaxed along . . . of course I want them to be active."[37] Her sons, she decided, in a rare introspective moment, did not have her "patience—on hearing the same objections, questions, suggestions, I am ever interested and never bored nor toss the question back to the person as a dumbbell . . . My sons would not bother to reply."[38]

Sanger never abandoned her support of eugenicism. The certainty that had driven her ascension from a poor Irish girl in Corning through the years of ridicule and imprisonment to her status as a world figure made it impossible for her to change her mind about a matter such as involuntary sterilization. No matter that by the late 1930s a new breed of American geneticists had disavowed the earlier determinations of the scientific community that the deficiencies of parents were genetically bestowed upon their children. Sanger paid little attention.

In 1950 she used a high-profile speech when accepting the prestigious Lasker Award—given for her longtime service "to achieve balanced populations"—to promote the idea of government subsidies for those with defective heredity who agreed to be sterilized. When David Loth, the PPFA's director of communications, objected to what he characterized as "a bribe," Sanger countered: "Sterilization is not a horrible idea no matter under what the conditions." By her calculation, pensions for the unfit were no different from those for veterans, both awarded to Americans who contributed to society. But Sanger made clear that involuntary sterilization must never be practiced on targeted groups, as the Nazis had done.

"To have a pension or financial support of the feeble-minded and the defective to save the country from a multiple of their offspring is a sound investment. . . . The indignity of it can be quite repulsive if we are looking upon humanity from the individual point of view, but I am not looking on it that way, for I believe that many who should be sterilized would agree to be sterilized if they knew something about the simplicity of the operation." The amount of the pension should be comparable to "the old age pensions today, say $75 a month which such couple would receive ultimately at 65 anyway." Besides it was "an investment for our children's children," she informed Loth. "We know quite well . . . of [the] neglect, abandonment, killings and burning alive of children by their parents who have no right to bring innocent victims into the world."[39] As evidence, she cited the recent California case of a young mother who had beaten her seven-month-old baby to death. After the judge had encouraged her to give up "her rights of mother-hood," young Georgette Bruch had "voluntarily" asked to be sterilized.[40]

Of course, Sanger was not alone in these proposals. Even after the horrors of the Holocaust were publicized, nearly half of all Americans still supported involuntary sterilization, and in some states officials continued to sterilize the institutionalized dysgenic without their permission. In fact, involuntary sterilizations, performed to advance eugenic purposes, accelerated after 1948 in four states—Georgia, Nebraska, North Carolina, and Iowa. By this time Sanger had discovered the informal restrictions on voluntary sterilizations—the increasingly popular, ultimate birth control of choice for middle-class women.

In hospitals and doctors' offices across the country, women who wanted to be sterilized were denied what was now a simple surgical procedure by virtue of the 120 rule, installed by pronatalist doctors and promoted by the American Medical Association. If the number of a mother's children multiplied by their age did not reach 120, they were denied the operation. In these subterranean applications of earlier race suicide policies, supposedly unfit women, especially poor black women in the South, were involuntarily sterilized in what became known as "Mississippi appendectomies," while white women judged to be fit who wanted to be sterilized could find neither doctor nor hospital to perform the procedure.

Meanwhile, to Sanger's further dismay, Catholic hospitals were revoking the privileges of doctors who performed sterilization procedures or even advised birth control. In a letter to the director of the American Medical Association, Sanger urged an investigation of "parochial hospitals' defiance of medical practice and court decisions that prevent physicians from maintaining medical standards."[41]

With time on her hands between her international conferences and occasional lectures, Sanger pondered her personal future, sharing her anxieties with her longtime lover Angus Macdonald: "As life shortens—questions arise . . . What am I to do? Am I to live alone? Am I to couple up with someone else who? You are not free—Others are free—the artist—the lawyer at the Plaza. A Hermit in the mts of Vermont—all old Suitors asking to be favored . . . I at present am not in love with anyone (maybe) never will be again."[42] Nearly seventy years old when she wrote this letter, hers was an impressive list of lovers, and it included a new conquest.

Sanger had met Hobson Pittman, an artist, during a visit to her brother Bob at Pennsylvania State University in 1945. During the summer she had taken a course with Pittman, a well-known painter who had just been featured in the periodical *American Artist*. Sanger admired his pastel and charcoal drawings and invited him to Willowlake, where she fell in love after one "glorious night." The equally enraptured Pittman proposed, and Sanger must have remembered the other artist in her life—William Sanger— and his impetuous pursuit. Now she hesitated and asked Macdonald for advice, admitting that "only a crude Yankee" would tell one man she was in love with another. Of course the issue was not "a sex problem," she wrote. She had none of those. Rather, Pittman was "an artist—one of the tops— vital, sensitive, well just all the qualities—(even dancing) that I feel at one with. But—here is where your advice is needed—younger. Also I don't want to get married at all. He does & at once."[43]

Even in her seventies, she held to the central conviction of her long, passionate life that "one should always be in a state of love—to live joyously."[44] To Dorothy Brush she acknowledged her exceptional sexuality: "You know that I am not like other women sexually. It may be sad, but in some ways it's a blessing too. It has made the mental and spiritual experience infinitely rich."[45]

Pittman was twenty years younger than Sanger, but it was not the age difference that bothered Sanger; violation of conventional behavior had never inhibited her. Rather, it was Pittman's prudishness. When she met him in Paris after the Cheltenham Conference and they traveled together, he worried about possible gossip and later declined her invitation to Tucson. "I go to State Coll. each year and I do not care to face the innuendoes that would normally arise from such an arrangement. So my dear I'm afraid I must be counted out this time."[46] Sanger was stunned; for years even as a celebrated advocate of women's sexuality, she had traveled with men, often in lengthy automobile trips from New York to Tucson. "So far in my tempestuous life, there has been no insinuation about my morals either here or abroad where I am fairly well known . . . We are all adults." Pittman was the first man to be "ashamed" of such arrangements: "It never occurred to me that your reputation at Penn State was more important than mine in England . . . I see now that [what] is important to you [is] not a reputation as a great artist but a reputation of a Puritan."[47]

Exaggerating his health problems as Sanger diminished hers, Pittman did not need a wife. Asked for advice, Juliet Rublee exploded. He needed a mother! In a few years the relationship dwindled into an exchange of letters rather than a passionate sexual affair. Sanger remained single for the rest of her life, replacing loneliness and a comforting, routinized husband's intimacy with connections to friends, family, and, to the distress of her sons, a male administrative assistant, Jonathan Schultz. Though friends and family worried about the young attorney's influence—the relationship seemed the classic setting for exploitation—Schultz relieved Sanger from worry about the future of the still-fledgling IPPF. He took care of her correspondence, wrote her speeches, and attended to the exhausting details of the arrangements for the upcoming international conference in New Delhi.

After two husbands and multiple lovers, Sanger's expectations of marriage, but not sex, had dwindled into an unromantic arrangement that "saves one from decisions." As her life stretched into her eighties—well beyond the yardstick of demographers—Sanger discovered an unpleasant, but omnipresent, new companion. Writing to a biographer, she paraphrased Elizabeth Browning: "Death is a face-to-face intimacy. Age is a thickening of the mortal mask. So I hate it . . . Put it away from me. Why tell of age when it's just an appearance, when we are all young in soul and heart."[48]

In the summer of 1949 Sanger suffered the first of several heart attacks. She had been rushing for a plane when she suffered a coronary thrombosis—a blood clot in an artery in her heart—and in the cardiac therapy of the times was sent to bed for six weeks in Tucson. As she had done so often in the past, she dismissed her condition, instructing a secretary to write letters "in my language" and to never say she was ill. Offhandedly, she referred to "the pump acting up," though she had been diagnosed with a painful case of angina pectoris due to inadequate blood flow to her heart. At first aspirin helped the "pain & jumping throbbing heart beat," but even in the hospital "the flooding every day nearly kills me as my veins are deep & small, but the new process of dissolving & preventing clots needs careful technical watching & so I am in for it," she explained to a friend.[49] Intending to travel overseas in the fall, she pressed her doctors for an early release from the hospital, but she also consulted her friends in Unity, the Rosicrucian association, for horoscope readings.

After her signs dictated "taking it easy" at least until the new moon and Jupiter and Saturn aligned with Aries to create the favorable sign of the pioneer, a physically improved Sanger traveled to Chicago for a lecture to the pioneers of the movement, on the twenty-fifth anniversary of their organization. Here she celebrated birth control rather than its cluttered new derivative—family planning. In her later years Sanger insisted that she never wanted to talk to another audience, likening her lecturing to a battery that runs down in a car. "Audiences take a great deal out of me."[50] Yet if the occasion was important and her body strong enough, Sanger responded as an expression of loyalty to those who, in the earlier, endangered days of her movement, had been faithful to her.

The next year Sanger suffered another heart attack, this time while on a fishing trip with Stuart and his family in the White Mountains in eastern Arizona. Again hospitalized, she was put in an oxygen tent and given the blood thinner dicumerol, along with the highly addictive painkiller Demerol, on which she became intermittently dependent for the rest of her life. Her friends saw this addiction as the reason for her irritability, mood swings, and confusion. Although she proclaimed her dislike of pills, Sanger now depended on nitroglycerin, which she likened to an explosive TNT, blood thinners for her heart, Seconal for insomnia, and Demerol for pain. As always, she dismissed the seriousness of her condition—joking to others, if not herself: "Got an oxygen tent, three nurses, & at once I felt relieved & better & am practically OK now. The 8,000 feet was too much for this hot house orchid & now the oxygen tent is too cool for the bronchial tubes . . . Really," she assured Abraham Stone, "I am in good form."[51]

For the rest of her life Sanger suffered from coronary artery disease marked by atrial fibrillation, a difficult illness for someone "as peppy as I am." This would be the condition that Sanger would never defeat, though she would not die of it, and like her earlier tuberculosis and gallbladder disease, the attacks were infuriatingly incapacitating for a woman with public commitments. In 1953, in Los Angeles the night before a speech to the Severance Club, "at 1:15 AM I awoke ready to die!!! Pain—breathless, irregular pulse pounding—I crawled into [Ellen Watumull's] room . . . We decided not to call a Doctor at that awful hour & I gave her a lesson in First aid." The next day Sanger somehow delivered a successful speech without notes: "I was singing in my heart like Poetry."[52]

Despising the infantilization practiced by doctors "who treat me like a child," Sanger tried new therapies, including radioactive iodine treatments. She even considered heart surgery, a specialty then in a primitive state, in which the surface of the heart was irritated in order to increase blood flow.[53] Her sons found her a difficult patient. "Do you think you can rearrange

your life so you are not running around the world at such speeds?" Grant
inquired.[54] By this time he knew the answer.

Even before her debilitating heart disease, Sanger had begun a new
project: the building of a new home on prime residential property in Tucson, purchased years before by Noah Slee, who had an investor's eye for
real estate. Sanger took an interior design course in anticipation and, according to one friend, treated the project like a new lover. Then she invited
her friend Frank Lloyd Wright, living in nearby Scottsdale, to create "a fitting house for my soul's development."[55] Wright declined. Any house on
such a small lot would be no more than "a pig's sty" and certainly did not
interest one of America's greatest architects. Instead, under the direction
of a local architect, she signed a contract for $35,000 (and spent close to
$46,000, in today's money over $250,000), using funds from the sale of
Willowlake for an innovative glass-encased home with a dramatic forty-
foot-long living room and steel fireplace, a second-floor study, and a polished aluminum roof. From the air it resembled a fan, with rooms stretching
out from a central hall and an interior pool. Asked what he thought of her
new house, Frank Lloyd Wright replied that it did not matter: it was Margaret's home.

The house, completed while Sanger was recovering from her first heart
attack, was next door to the home of Sanger's son Stuart, his wife, Barbara,
and their two daughters. Presently she undertook her new role of grand-
mothering. Never given to traditional mothering—she still encouraged her
friends to let go of their children and not cling to them—Sanger became a
memorable presence in the lives of young Margaret and Nancy. She told
stories and wrote plays for the neighborhood children to be performed with
costumes from her wardrobe. She instructed the children in a skill that
had been critical to her career: how to project their voices. She introduced
Margaret and Nancy to visiting celebrities. When Helen Keller arrived for
a visit, the sightless Keller ran her hands over young Margaret's face and
body (younger sister Nancy was too frightened) and pronounced her a fine
child. But Sanger was not a babysitter on call who took the children at her
sons' request: her involvement was on her own terms.

She saw less of Grant and Edwina Sanger, though she usually traveled
to their home in Mt. Kisco to spend Christmas with their ever-increasing
family. Once, she spent a restless month in Fishers Island, where Grant's
family summered. "It is not a wild or gay place," she described the island off
the coast of Connecticut in Long Island Sound, "but quiet and glorious

for children. When people launch their boats, they are really yachts; then things are gay." She invited Pittman, but he remained worried about his reputation, even when she repeated, "I am like Caesar's wife, above suspicion."[56]

Usually she visited after the birth of each child, increasingly bemused, then somewhat irritated, and finally complacent about the size of her son's family. Certainly the six children delivered by Edwina in ten years violated Sanger's best practices of spaced pregnancies and maternal health. When baby Alexander followed Stephen by eleven months, Sanger, perhaps joking, informed her daughter-in-law that she "had disgraced her in public and that she was going abroad until it was all over."[57] Neither parent relished calling "Domah" to announce another prospective arrival. To her friends, a self-described "blushing" Sanger explained that Edwina liked to have children in pairs, and besides, there were sufficient resources to raise them. Still, there were questions about the size of her son's family. Was Grant displaying his independence from the cause to which he had so often played second fiddle? Or did Edwina keep having children in order to have (eventually) a daughter after five boys? Or were both parents simply swept up in the postwar baby boom of the 1950s?

When she visited, Sanger never stayed long. No one knew exactly how long this would be, though it was usually a shorter time than anticipated. Heralded in the Sanger household with cries of "The Queen is coming," she was a difficult guest. She painted in bed, let the children color on the sheets, and ruined the children's schedules with trips to sometimes inappropriate movies. But as with Stuart's children, she was also a mesmerizing figure who told dramatic stories, arranged games, and played cards. Some of these children separated what they considered her absentee parenting of their father from Sanger the generous grandmother. As early as 1947, with her own finances uncertain, she had written to Edwina's brother, Bill Campbell, to set up an education fund "for the growing family."[58] To one of these children she also left a precious legacy: a lifetime interest in her life and cause; Alexander, the fourth of the six children, wrote his senior thesis at Princeton on his grandmother's early life. Formerly president of the New York Birth Control League, Alexander Sanger is currently the chair of the International Planned Parenthood Council, International Planned Parenthood Federation/Western Hemisphere Region.

Living mostly in Tucson after World War II, Sanger emerged as a local social and political force. "My life is less hectic, but just as active and unpredictable in spots as it can be," she wrote to Angus Macdonald, who, now with a pilot's license, wanted to visit more often.[59] Sanger raised money for a new hospital, joined the Tucson Watercolor Guild, and was well known for her New Year's Day reception and her theme parties. When she served a Japanese sukiyaki feast, guests were told to remove their shoes, put on slippers, and give a proper bow to the host. Of course, a woman who held as one of her mottoes that life is too short to spend over a stove employed a cook and a maid. As her granddaughter described, "Mimi always dressed for dinner in lovely dresses with long trains. She'd get up from her nap, have a cocktail, and then have dinner usually with guests. Her house was a magical place."[60] One morning an astonished Margaret observed her seventy-one-year-old grandmother, seventy-six-year-old Juliet Rublee, and seventy-year-old Elizabeth Arden, nightgowns tied around their legs, standing on their heads, their legs against the wall—to improve their complexions, they explained.

Locally, Sanger's primary focus remained the clinics that she had helped establish in the Southwest, now stretching from El Paso to Phoenix. She served as a financial supporter and a consultant for organizations that she nevertheless criticized as "spineless and so mundane in their activities, so cautious, so circumspect, that they will never fight back when the opposing forces come down upon them." Local groups, she discovered, were especially sensitive to "political and religious objections, criticism and influence." In Phoenix, when Catholic priests demanded that all those connected with Planned Parenthood be removed from leadership in the Community Chest, the president of the local Maternal Health Clinic, in Sanger's description, "quivered and shook, grew pale and remained seated." Later, Peggy Goldwater explained that she feared that her husband Barry Goldwater's department store might be boycotted.[61] "We have," Sanger wrote to Paul Blanshard, the author of a popular indictment of the Catholic Church's intrusiveness in secular affairs, "fought for independence from Great Britain. Now we are enslaved to the Vatican in Rome."[62]

In 1953 Lawrence Lader, a young journalist and biographer, traveled to Tucson intending to write a biography of Sanger. It had been fifteen years since her *Autobiography* had been published, and what she had written then was at best incomplete propaganda. Besides, a great deal of progress had been made since that time, particularly in relation to her leadership of the international family planning movement. Sanger had wanted to tell the story herself, but "expressing the deep feelings of childhood and of the early experiences of the birth control movement did something to me . . .

the prying went deeper and deeper into my experiences. The result left me with an empty creativeness." It was a condition she had observed in other writers who "felt that the past had been finished and they were sort of marking time for some new creative spark that never took."[63] She would not use herself up in remembrances: someone would have to write her life story, as she looked forward, not backward.

At first the thirty-four-year-old Lader seemed too young, too unsophisticated, and much too intent on searching out aspects of her personal life better left untouched: "I am not certain that he has lived enough or suffered or loved enough to know a woman's life as I have lived it."[64] Eventually Sanger agreed to his proposal, insisting that she did not like to talk about herself—only the movement—and paying Lader an advance with the royalties to go to the Margaret Sanger Research Bureau. Of course, she insisted on controlling the manuscript after it was completed.

The initially starstruck Lader worried that he could not "put over the radiance and inexhaustible flame of your own driving force."[65] Certainly the biography of Margaret Sanger became the most difficult but rewarding project of his life. She refused to have her birth date included, though, as Lader pointed out in a losing battle, the correct date—1879—was a minimal requirement for any biography. William Sanger did not want to be mentioned in any biography of his former wife, and certain informants were off-limits. Others, especially the English triumvirate of Ellis, de Selincourt, and Wells, were dead, and she declined to have information about the sexual practices of the Wantley group included. Meanwhile, Lader seemed to view her liaisons as simply arrangements of "the tumble into bed," and not "the glorious friendship and spiritual love between men and women" that animated all her sexual relationships with men.[66] When Lader asked questions about Sanger's domestic past—who took care of the children in 1914 when she was in England for a year and whether she felt guilty about Peggy's death in 1915—Sanger invoked her first rule of biography: good biographies leave out personal lives except as "it touches their undomestic interests."[67] Of course she did not want "a glamor book," she informed Lader, although that is what she got. The reviewer in *The New Yorker* complained that "a whole book of panegyrics can get monotonous."[68]

Later, Lader recalled Sanger's isolation—her insistence that he live nearby and spend hours, sometimes into the night, interviewing her. She referred to her house as the well of loneliness, pouring out intimate memories after too much champagne and Demerol. She flirted with him, calling him "her sweet prince," perhaps, he decided later, as a means of getting him to accept her views. Certainly she used Lader's biography to correct the slight incurred by Havelock Ellis, who had dismissed her as the little American nurse in his autobiography. Yet after disclosures about her private life, the next day she regretted "the torture of exploring the past."[69] And she came to dislike him; even talking on the phone raised her temperature.

Throughout their collaboration, Sanger wondered what his theme was, even as she made clear that she was not "the nice MS who in all truth was not a simple nurse with arms around everyone & to whom all & sundry were waving kisses. She had more iron in her makeup—more conflicts & emotions—than could be dramatized ever."[70] For his part Lader struggled with the integration of the public and private Sanger. Eventually, in *The Margaret Sanger Story*, he described a contradiction—a militant, pragmatic visionary—though she told him more than once that she was just the woman who pressed the button to turn on the electric light and was not responsible for the wiring or the mechanism of the lighting. But she made clear, in her inveterate rule, that she would not "usher the public" into her bedroom.[71]

When Lader complained about her refusal to include certain biographical details—for example, her brother Joe Higgins's jailing for robbery as a young boy and her sister Ethel's divorce—she clarified her views. "Why don't I like the past? [On trains] Havelock rode backwards to see what scenes that had passed, while I liked to see what lay before us."[72] "But why the past? The present and future are important," she later repeated.[73] Years before, Sanger had maintained that her biography would be harder to write than her beloved Havelock's, because, ever living in the future, she kept much of her present and past self hidden.

In 1950 Sanger's future arrived in a letter from Katharine McCormick. The two women had known each other for thirty years, but they still greeted each other formally as Mrs. Sanger and Mrs. McCormick. Six years later, as their partnership deepened and their excitement grew, to each other they became Kay and Margaret. Four years older than Sanger, McCormick was a formidable presence—physically, intellectually, and financially, the latter as the heir to a large fortune in her own right. In 1947 her husband, Stanley, had died after years of nursing care for his schizophrenia. After the competing claims by his relatives to his estate had been settled and taxes paid, McCormick controlled $15 million to be added to the $10 million she had inherited from her own family. And she was ready to return to birth control work. Now she questioned Sanger about two things: where the need was greatest and what the status of birth control research was.

In her prompt response Sanger indicated a broad range of needs that included support of her nascent international conferences as well as "five or six university laboratories in this country, in England or in Germany, definitely to be applied for contraceptive control." For years Sanger had followed the science of birth control in part because she read, and sometimes edited, the scientific papers delivered at her conferences. Her search for a simple, cheap, safe contraceptive never flagged.[74] Having foreseen the possibility of an oral contraceptive in the 1930s and having more than once mentioned "a magic pill," she knew all about the chemical messengers in the blood called hormones and their contraceptive possibilities, although to her chagrin, most scientists, constrained by contemporary attitudes, remained focused on infertility, not on her life's passion of controlling fertility.

Sanger was also aware of the possibilities for new technology. With McCormick's money, which was the best project? Some scientists were investigating the process of how the egg was transported through the Fallopian tubes to the uterus, but this seemed basic physiology to Sanger, who craved applications. Others studied the vitality of sperm, and a smaller group, under Dr. Georgeanna Seegar Jones at the Johns Hopkins Medical School, was studying endocrine factors explaining the infertile days of a woman's reproductive cycle. Dr. Nicholas Eastman of Hopkins investigated spermatoxins, using grants from wealthy pharmaceutical companies, who now had money to spend after the profitable marketing of antibiotics. But Sanger had spent a lifetime frustrated by the ever-changing recipes for sperm-killing jellies and powders.

Dr. Donald Hooker, also of Johns Hopkins, had received grants to study the use of radiation as a means of sterilizing the ovaries of monkeys, but the effects of such treatments on humans were unknown and potentially dangerous. At Columbia University, in research funded by the Rockefeller-supported Population Council, the gynecology department focused on the IUD, the intrauterine device that could be permanently inserted into the uterus, preventing the fertilization of eggs, though no one knew exactly why. But IUDs, Sanger knew, sometimes led to lethal infections.

In Boston, Dr. John Rock, a Harvard-trained clinical gynecologist who specialized in infertility, found that sexual ignorance was the reason that some couples were childless. Using his knowledge of the rhythm method and progesterone, he advised some infertile couples to have sexual relations in midcycle—the Catholic-approved method used for the opposite purpose. By 1950 Rock understood that the hormones he was using for fertility could also create a condition of temporary infertility. But Sanger, suspicious of his Catholicism, could never approve any approach that encouraged pregnancy.

Forty miles away, in Worcester, Massachusetts, the Jewish refugee from academia who, with his bushy brows, resembled a sad rabbi, and who had not received tenure at Harvard, Dr. Gregory Pincus, along with his assistant, Dr. Min Chueh Chang, were continuing their experiments on mammalian eggs and sperm and the central role of the hormone progesterone. By the late 1940s Pincus's privately supported Worcester Foundation for Experimental Biology had received fourteen thousand dollars from the PPFA, along with money from the Searle pharmaceutical company, to study how steroids could be used to treat arthritis. His results seemed meager in terms of their practical applications to humans. Searle cut his funding: "You haven't given us a thing to justify the half-million we have invested in you . . . your record as a contributor to the commerce of the Searle Company is a lamentable failure, replete with false leads, poor judgment and assurances from you that were false. Yet you have the nerve to ask for more," went the searing dismissal from the drug company.[75] Dr. William Vogt, then the director of the PPFA, was similarly discouraged and looked to other projects.

During 1950 and 1951 Sanger met and corresponded with McCormick; in 1952 she spent an entire summer in one of McCormick's cottages in Santa Barbara. She visited Pincus in Worcester and invited him to dinner in New York, along with Abraham Stone, who had become an enthusiast for hormonal contraception. Later, Pincus remembered that Sanger "came to see me in 1950 and we started a conversation that I shall remember for the rest of my life. She told me of the misery and suffering of women and said it was time to have an effective contraceptive. [She asked] do you think it would be possible to develop an efficient contraceptive which would be easy to take, for example, a cheap pill. I answered 'I think so.' Immediately she sent $2300."[76]

In the early 1950s the activist Sanger and the philanthropist McCormick, neither with medical or scientific degrees, though McCormick had majored in biology at MIT, pondered their choice: which program and which approach would lead to the oral contraceptive they had defined as their short-term goal—and an immediate one, for they were both in their seventies?

By 1953 they had decided. In an epic meeting they traveled together in McCormick's chauffeur-driven limousine to the plain one-story lab of Gregory Pincus, outside of Worcester. Within hours McCormick had written a check for $10,000, promising, after getting in touch with "my money man," another $150,000 for the rest of the year. By 1967 she had donated $2 million, with an additional million designated in her will. These grants, given by a private individual and not in the customary fashion by a private association such as the PPFA or the National Research Council, initiated McCormick's lifetime support of Pincus and, later, Dr. John Rock.

Rock had actually begun human trials using progesterone. At a time of little regulation by the Food and Drug Administration, only the conscience and knowledge of the investigator protected volunteers. In his private practice Rock had given "courageous" infertile women synthetic progesterone for a different reason: in order to prevent the ovulation of immature eggs which did not grow to maturity, after which he stopped the hormone, anticipating the development of an awakened healthy egg and a subsequent pregnancy. What Rock called a "felicitous" result (thirteen of eighty patients were soon pregnant after stopping the progesterone) became known as the "Rock rebound," and soon McCormick and Sanger were visiting him in the crowded lab he called "the hovel." Investigating infertility, Rock had proved, in one of those serendipitous scientific findings that punctuate advances in medicine, that progesterone stopped ovulation not just in rabbits and rats but in humans.

When they first visited, Rock thought McCormick a dabbling society woman, and did not realize that her livelier companion was the famous Margaret Sanger. She found him handsome as a god, though Sanger remained suspicious of this Catholic father of five. Yet Rock's patients were the first to demonstrate the effectiveness of progesterone, and he needed a larger laboratory, which McCormick soon provided. Soon he and Pincus were partners in the search for a contraceptive to be delivered by mouth.

With his new resources Pincus, who had earlier worked in the general field of steroids, now concentrated entirely on a chemical means of contraception to be delivered, as both women insisted, by means of a pill ingested by mouth. Not everyone in the field was convinced. Dr. William Vogt, who had never visited Pincus and in any case disliked experimental research, ridiculed support of a marginalized scientist who had lost the confidence of the drug houses. Vogt also insulted McCormick with his criticism of her funding of Rock's new "animal house." By this time Sanger had dismissed the PPFA and its leader: "If the Federation is slowing down on scientific research for a simple contraceptive, they might as well close it down." Besides, Vogt's power, typical of those new to authority, "had gone to his head."[77]

Their minds made up, Sanger and McCormick never wavered in their single-minded support of Pincus and Rock. Rejecting the approach of private foundations who spread their money over several projects, McCormick funded the Worcester Lab, though, as she wrote Sanger in late 1953, "this, of course, is desperately slow business—& I have asked them both if there is no way by which they can enlarge (increase) their testing experiments."[78] The two women were not deterred as the project moved from animals in cages to humans in clinic rooms. Sanger believed that the opposition to the project only displayed the perpetual criticism of birth control that she had so long endured and transcended.

For Pincus and Rock, there were reasons for delays that took more than money to solve. First Pincus needed more progesterone, which was difficult to extract from animals and so expensive, at a thousand dollars an ounce, that it was reserved for increasing the fertility of only the best Thoroughbred broodmares. Some chemists were beginning to use plants that mimicked progesterone in their molecular structure. One project by Dr. Russell Marker in Mexico employed the roots of yamlike cabeza de negro in a tedious process of picking, drying, grinding, and heating the roots, though it took nine tons of roots to produce five kilos of progesterone. More promising was the work of chemists employed by Searle who manipulated the organic molecules of steroids to produce different syntheses of pure crystalline progesterone. Of these compounds Pincus eventually chose norethynodrel, which appeared strong enough to be delivered orally. By 1954 he was ready to move to human trials.

But such trials required humans willing to have their urine tested and to undergo periodic endometrial biopsies. Even in the earlier record keeping in her clinic, Sanger had trouble getting clients to follow the necessary regimen for data collecting. "Human females," agreed McCormick, "are not so easy to investigate as are rabbits and mice in cages. The latter can be intensively controlled all the time [whereas] the human females leave town at unexpected times & so cannot be examined at a certain period; & they also forget to take the medicine sometimes—in which cases the whole experiment has to begin over again."[79]

By 1954, with issues remaining of how much progesterone and estrogen were needed to prevent bleeding, the human trials began, first on Rock's eager infertile private patients and next on twenty-eight patients from the Worcester State Hospital, in an unsavory arrangement in which the superintendent of the hospital received funds from McCormick to be used on improvements of the asylum. Both the investigators and Sanger were worried less about violating safety standards for human experimentation than they were about violating state laws. The politics of birth control required that the studies be described as investigations of menstrual disorders and infertility; in Massachusetts anyone who dispensed birth control information was still subject to a felony charge and if convicted faced the possibility of five years in jail and a thousand-dollar fine for each infraction.

But Pincus needed more volunteers for a large-scale demonstration. Puerto Rico, with its clinics already in place, a sympathetic administration, no laws against contraception, and a poor population with large families, was an obvious choice, and despite various hazards, over a thousand women volunteered after being advised informally of various risks. (So, too, did nurses and a few doctors.) Meanwhile, in the perfect completion of a life's work, Sanger hoped that the Margaret Sanger Research Bureau could be an additional site for the trials. It was, she informed Pincus, "the oldest birth control clinic in the country, with already one hundred and thirty thousand records in their files, with a splendid staff of gynecologists, why the M.S. Bureau would not be the perfect place in the U.S.A. to start the injection of progesterone on one hundred women."[80] But Pincus, a meticulous laboratory scientist, demanded "sophisticated supervision" with well-trained technicians familiar with vaginal smear techniques. Besides, he needed larger trials than the Sanger clinic could provide.[81]

Undeterred, Sanger encouraged Pincus to deliver his results in a paper at one of her international meetings and to send five hundred kilos of progesterone to Japan, which arrived in time for Sanger's conference in Tokyo in 1955. It might be, she believed, possible to set up large-scale trials in Japan. "While most of the people in Asia hesitate to be what they call 'guinea pigs,' the fact that Puerto Rican health authorities are willing to initiate an experiment with a substance that you have found harmless, would I believe be most welcome."[82]

Sanger also insisted that Pincus chair the Biomedical Aspects of Fertility Control Committee, a subcommittee of the IPPF's medical group, though Pincus tried to decline, proclaiming himself not a "worthwhile person" to do so. He also chafed under McCormick's mandate that he submit reports every two weeks and protested, in 1957, that he was not ready to recommend the universal use of the pill, though he believed its adverse effects largely psychological. Sanger explained her intrusions: "You are really in our cause and that means that you are bound to be imposed on now and then." And as she pressed him to deliver his results, a resigned Pincus acknowledged, "You have certainly stirred up a good deal of activity."[83]

Field trials, sometimes repeated because of the changing proportions of progesterone and estrogen, as well as mistakes in record keeping in the clinics and the number of dropouts, made the process agonizingly slow to the impatient McCormick and Sanger. In 1955 Pincus still spoke of the need for more investigations, though in an obscure public reference he acknowledged that "the delicately balanced sequential processes involved in normal mammalian reproduction are clearly attackable. Our objective is to disrupt them in such a way that no physical cost is involved."[84] Finally Sanger applauded that "the conspiracy of silence has been broken."[85] Yet before 1960, Enovid, the trade name for this first generation of the pill, came with the inviting contraceptive advertisement that it regulated menstruation. By 1959 over a half million women were taking Searle's oral contraceptive, supposedly for menstrual problems. "We have a new 'slogan' here in backwards Massachusetts," wrote McCormick to Sanger, "take Enovid for the rhythm method."[86]

In 1957 the pharmaceutical company Searle filed for a license, this time for a contraceptive, presenting as data Pincus's evidence from 897 women and 10,427 cycles of no ovulation. A somnolent Food and Drug Administration required only that the product be safe, not created for fraudulent purposes, and used for its declared purpose, though the thalidomide scandal simmering in Europe had led to more caution. But it was not caution that delayed approval. Instead, there were the usual moral and religious objections. Catholic watchdogs, describing a "death pill," objected that it would make extramarital sex easier for women. Even some non-Catholics, in this dawning of a new age in preventive medicine, feared the effects on healthy women of taking a powerful hormone for many years, as the pill became the first of many lifestyle drugs prescribed by doctors.

Approval stalled until an angry Rock persuaded the reviewer at the FDA, Dr. Pascale DeFelice, a practicing Catholic and obstetrician-gynecologist with little experience in hormones, to support the license, even shaking him by the shoulders at one point in their discussions. Later there would be complaints about the effects of the pill, but prior to this time no medicine in the United States had received such extensive field trials. Having long ago answered any moral objections to birth control, Sanger knew that Enovid carried a lower health risk to women than pregnancy or abortion, which was still illegal.

As early as 1956 Sanger acknowledged McCormick's contributions to a new era of reproductive freedom in a letter she might have written to herself:

> You must, indeed, feel a certain pride in your judgement. Gregory Pincus had been working for at least ten years on the progesterone of reproductive process in animals. He had practically no money for this work and Dr. Stone and I did our best to get a few dollars for him and I think that that amount we collected went to pay the expenses for Chang. Then you came along with your fine interest and enthusiasm and with our faith and wonderful directives things began to happen.[87]

In 1959 Sanger attended her last international conference of the IPPF, this time in New Delhi, where 750 delegates from twenty-eight nations gathered to hear fifty papers and share ideas in the study groups that Sanger recommended. In the dramatic opening ceremony the curtains parted and Sanger walked slowly onto a grand stage, leaning on Prime Minister Nehru's arm. The delegates stood and cheered as eighty-year-old Sanger, wreathed in garlands of jasmine and roses, acknowledged Nehru, whose government had pledged $10 million for family planning. In a tremulous voice she ended with the convictions that had always underwritten her crusade, an admonition to doctors that they "be sympathetic to the shy, simple woman who comes to them, asking for information as to how to space her pregnancies and how to take care of the children she has already borne."[88] It was, as Ellen Chesler has written, "a final opportunity to reiterate her view that how an individual woman perceives her own self-interest may be as important to her decisions about fertility as larger economic and social conditions."[89] With perception gained from fifty years of experience in the birth control field, Sanger recognized the centrality of what experts would later acknowledge: the choices of individual parents to determine the number of children a family will have was grounded in the availability of contraception as well as social and economic incentives.

Sanger's two initiatives of the postwar period converged in New Delhi— the establishment of an international planned parenthood federation and a report on an effective oral contraceptive. But she was too exhausted to hear Gregory Pincus dedicate his detailed conclusions from "Field Trials with Norethynodrel as an Oral Contraceptive" to Margaret Sanger. His research was, he said, the product of her pioneering resolution. Four days later Sanger returned home in a wheelchair from her last trip overseas.

EPILOGUE: LAST YEARS

Life slips past us . . . It does not wait. Each of us has a cycle of his own. That cycle closes itself off even before we have fulfilled its course unless we cooperate with nature.

—Margaret Sanger to Hobson Pittman, November 14, 1948

In early 1960 the handsome young Democratic senator from Massachusetts, John F. Kennedy, emerged as a contender for his party's presidential nomination. Urged by her friend Norman Thomas, Sanger, who rarely paid attention to partisan politics, glimpsed an opportunity to gain support from a rising star. Kennedy had earlier insisted that he separated his Catholic religion from positions he took on public matters, which he would approach from the perspective of his conscience and the national interest. If so, to Sanger's mind, he must denounce state prohibitions on birth control and public health programs that omitted family planning. In January Sanger wrote to the senator, explaining what Kennedy no doubt knew: his home state of Massachusetts "has been under the pressure of the Roman Catholic Hierarchy where any means of Birth Control information considered artificial is absolutely forbidden by law." The church was employing its power over legislation "to make a crime out of that which is no crime at all, but rather a social virtue in the eyes of many citizens. Have you looked into this law or disapproved of it in any way?"[1]

There is no record of Kennedy's response. But throughout the 1960 campaign he made clear a politically expedient departure from orthodox Catholic positions, disapproving of funding parochial schools from tax dollars, and in a famous speech in the spring, he repeated that he was not the

Catholic candidate for president. No one in the church spoke for him, nor he for the church. But he remained avoidant and equivocal on the matter of birth control. Soon, despite suggestions from friends that she "go easy" on Kennedy because he "was a sympathetic liberal man," Sanger denounced him as "neither Democrat nor Republican. Nor American, nor Chinese. He is a Roman Catholic."[2]

Kennedy was following the precedents established by Protestant presidents, especially his immediate predecessor, Dwight Eisenhower. During his second administration, as U.S. spending on foreign aid increased, Eisenhower became dissatisfied with the results. Sufficiently aroused, he appointed his friend, former undersecretary of the army William Draper, to head a commission investigating military aid. In a connection that revealed this generation's anxiety about overpopulation, the commission recommended that the United States fund requests for maternal and child welfare, "a fig leaf," writes Matthew Connelly, "for members who still could not countenance explicit mention of contraception."[3] For the Draper Commission, the Cold War linked two seemingly disparate things—military aid and family planning. In this new climate, a nation's opposition to communism was profoundly affected by its economic stability, which in turn was shaped by poverty and overpopulation.

At first Eisenhower had seemed receptive to such an analysis. Concerned with what he called "exploding population growth," the president found "an effective two cent contraceptive" the only solution to growing pressures of people on resources. Promptly made aware of the toxicity of the issue by Catholic bishops, Eisenhower rejected the Draper report in a public statement: "I cannot imagine anything more emphatically a subject that is not a proper political or governmental activity or function or responsibility [than birth control]."[4] In response to this widely reported pronouncement, in a letter to *The New York Times*, Sanger protested both Catholic interference and this president's inability to understand that population control was vital for world peace, with birth control the essential battle weapon. She was ready, she wrote, to debate Eisenhower in order to "straighten him out."[5] By the late 1950s public opinion supported contraception, though not necessarily its federal funding. Still, Eisenhower's rejection of the Draper report engendered counterattacks, and financial support for the IPPF increased. Sanger's longtime rule that a cause is won by its enemies applied, but as she understood from the past, winning took time.

As the presidential year of 1960 continued, Kennedy avoided the specific question of his position on contraception, taking cover in the useful protection of an alleged backlash from abroad: Americans should not appear "to advocate limitation of the black or brown or yellow peoples whose population is increasing no faster than in the United States."[6] Now Sanger lost patience. By the fall she informed reporters that if Kennedy were elected, she would leave the United States and find another place to live. It was the kind of attention-getting, combative, rhetorical ire that she often employed and rarely regretted. When Kennedy won in November and the Associated Press asked if she was actually going to leave the United States, she backtracked, explaining that friends who were very close friends with the Kennedys "have told me that they are both sympathetic and understanding toward the problem of world population . . . I will wait out the first year of Senator Kennedy's Administration and see what happens. I will make my decision then."[7] In the hate mail she continued to receive, someone inquired, "Would anyone really miss you?"[8]

There was reason to believe that the Catholic position on birth control might moderate, with such a transformation coming from the Vatican, not the Catholic bishops and priests of America who dealt with the popularity of contraception among their disobedient flock. In 1957, just before his death the following year, Pope Pius XII had sanctioned the therapeutic use of the pill, on the advice of a physician, as an appropriate remedy in the case of disease or infertility. In 1964, Pope John XXIII created a Papal Commission on Population, the Family and Natality, whose very name gave rise to optimism. Sanger's Catholic friend Dr. John Rock had already begun his lonely campaign to push his church to accept the pill as a contraceptive, which, he argued, was not an artificial, mechanistic device that killed or blocked the passage of sperm. Progesterone was a natural secretion of the ovaries. It prevented ovulation and, besides, was already accepted as a means of treating infertility. Its synthetic creation merely mimicked a natural substance in the blood, argued Rock in his 1963 bestselling book, *The Time Has Come: A Catholic Doctor's Proposals to End the Battle over Birth Control.* Surely the next step was possible: the pill (and for Americans of this generation and thereafter, there was only one "the pill") was a morally permissible application of the already approved rhythm method.

Sanger was hopeful as well, but she remained suspicious of her lifelong archenemy. In one of her last interviews, she noted to a Tucson reporter the "apparent change in the attitude by the Catholic Church with which [I] have had many battles."[9] She was dead by the time that Paul VI's Encyclical

Letter to his Venerable Brothers, *Humanae Vitae*, repeated the church's ancient proscriptions, as the new pope, like Eisenhower, overruled the conclusions of his own appointed commission: "Every marriage act," wrote the pope, who used the occasion to emphasize his papal authority over an issue that was dividing the church, "must remain open to the transmission of life . . . Just as man does not have unlimited dominion over his body in general, so also he has no such dominion over his specifically sexual faculties, for these are concerned by their very nature with the generation of life, of which God is the source." Contraception rendered men vulnerable to infidelity and the lowering of moral standards. Women would become "mere instruments of selfish enjoyment." Abstinence proved true love and the use of any form of birth control remained a sin.[10] *Humanae Vitae* repeated the mandates of thirty years before, as well as the proscriptions of Augustine in the fourth century. Sanger's lifetime battle with the church remained unresolved, but she knew from her clinics that many Catholic women used contraception. Like other American women in the 1960s—some 10 million in 1966—they depended on the pill, not to treat but to establish infertility.

Sanger did not comment on the new age of women's reproductive freedom that dawned after Kennedy's assassination. It arrived with President Lyndon Johnson's support of federally tax-funded birth control programs included in his War on Poverty. Unlike Eisenhower and Kennedy, Johnson often spoke about the importance of research directed toward world population issues. He linked limited resources and even disastrous environmental effects to the explosion of the number of human beings, and a month before Sanger's death, Lyndon Johnson received the Margaret Sanger Award from the PPFA. But as she always feared, advances in women's reproductive freedom were never secure and soon became partisan matters subject to reversal.

Nor did Sanger play any role in the crusade to make abortion legal, a movement beginning to gain prominence among a group of pioneers. Among them was Dr. Alan Guttmacher, a Johns Hopkins–trained gynecologist and obstetrician, and the medical director of PPFA in 1960, who publicly denounced antiabortion laws. Like Sanger, Guttmacher's advocacy developed from searing personal experiences: having to deliver the baby of a twelve-year-old girl whose father had raped her, because her health was not in danger and therefore Maryland's district attorney would not give him legal permission to perform an abortion. Sanger had always considered birth control the solution to abortion, but she was too ill to be aware of this new movement for women's rights. Given her priorities, she would doubtless have argued that the proper use of birth control made abortion unnecessary, but because all women needed autonomy over their bodies, in the case of oversight or failure they had the right to end a pregnancy.

Sanger was most likely aware of the 1961 legal challenge initiated by Estelle Griswold, the executive director of Planned Parenthood in Connecticut. Born a Roman Catholic, Griswold had revived a clinic in New Haven and a dispirited state movement when she became the head of the Connecticut Birth Control League in the 1950s. After several efforts to overturn restrictive legislation, she and her ally Dr. Lee Buxton, the director of the Yale University infertility clinic, concluded that revision of the Connecticut laws that made contraception illegal was impossible. Even a bill empowering a physician's right to give contraceptive advice had been defeated. The state courts provided no help. As late as 1959 the Connecticut Supreme Court unanimously upheld the state's 1879 version of the Comstock law, which criminalized counseling or using birth control. Yet among the justices of the United States Supreme Court, who earlier had avoided any review of appeals in contraceptive cases, there had been progress. In 1959 the justices accepted a Connecticut case, *Poe v. Ullman*, and heard arguments involving the use of physician-prescribed contraception, before dismissing the matter on technical grounds.

In 1961 Griswold and Buxton tried again. Arrested and charged with "assisting, abetting, counseling, causing and commanding certain married women to use drugs, medicinal articles and instruments for the purpose of contraception," Griswold and Buxton were found guilty and fined in a decision upheld in the state courts. After appeals in the state courts, the U.S. Supreme Court accepted the case; at the end of its session in 1965, a year before Sanger's death, the court reversed the convictions of Estelle Griswold and Lee Buxton, and held the Connecticut Comstock law unconstitutional on the grounds that, in Justice William O. Douglas's famous expansion of American liberty, "the First Amendment has a penumbra where privacy is protected from governmental intrusion."[11]

Other justices found grounds based on the Fourteenth Amendment and the Ninth Amendment's clause that the enumeration of certain rights by the Constitution neither "denied nor disparaged others retained by the people." Two dissenters, Hugo Black and Potter Stewart, could find no constitutional guarantee that the Connecticut law infringed. But the majority now believed that the right to privacy, and therefore the use of contraceptives, was inherent in the right to liberty. Thus Sanger's life spanned—from her birth in 1879, six years after the passage of the Comstock law, to 1966 and its overturning—the entire judicial history of contraception's legal course, though at first such rights were extended only to married Americans. It wasn't until 1972, in the case of *Eisenstadt v. Baird*, that the right to use birth control was guaranteed to the unmarried.

Achieved in the courts and in the halls of public opinion, now birth control was unassailably legal, and on grounds that mirrored some of the arguments made years before by Sanger's attorneys Jonah Goldstein, in 1917, and Morris Ernst, in the 1920s. These two had argued that prohibitions on contraception denied liberty to women whose pursuit of happiness was infringed upon by the restrictions on birth control. A woman's right to intercourse—her free exercise of conscience—was transgressed if pregnancy must follow. In 1928 Justice Louis Brandeis enunciated his version of this broadened interpretation: "The makers of the constitution had intended to secure conditions favorable to the pursuits of happiness . . . They sought to protect Americans in their beliefs, thoughts, and their sensations. They conferred . . . the right to be left alone . . . against the unjustifiable intrusion by the government upon the privacy of the individual. To protect that right, every unjustifiable intrusion by the government on the privacy of the individual must be deemed a violation of the Fourth Amendment."[12]

Five years before her death, Sanger made her last appearance after over a half century in public forums. In 1909 she had stood on wooden cartons, giving short speeches about the evils of capitalism in Manhattan. She had moved on to longer presentations on birth control and sex education delivered throughout the United States. She had taken her message overseas to Asia in the 1920s. In the 1930s she had begun international work that continued in lectures to large crowds in Japan and India. Now, in May 1961, she traveled to New York to receive a final tribute from the World Population Emergency Campaign (WPEC), which was established in 1960 and affiliated with the IPPF, its purpose to raise money and lobby politicians about the blight of overpopulation. What better way, its leaders decided, than to honor Margaret Sanger. With her son Stuart, for she could no longer travel alone, she flew to New York to receive the award.

Not everyone in the audience gathered in the Waldorf Astoria ballroom could hear this last speech. The microphone had not been adjusted to her

height; her voice, never strident, had lost its clarity and volume. An assidu-
ous record keeper throughout her life, Sanger kept no copy of these last
remarks, though she apparently thanked the friends of old who "stood by
all the difficult periods with kindness, understanding and affectionate support." She spoke of the newer friends "who have come to us in later decades,
giving us all the feeling that our Cause is important to human progress and
they are with us . . . I thank you with all my heart. I am grateful. I am thank-
ful."[13] One of those friends of old, Robert Parker, saluted what he called "a
glorious, victorious vindication! . . . For me you never spoke more eloquently—
simple, honest, direct and with no compromise." Viewing Sanger from a
different perspective, the editor of *Vogue* praised her appearance, noting to
Parker that "she had kept her little figure."[14]

After she returned to Tucson, Sanger's mind continued to deteriorate in
a process that had begun in the late 1950s, though she still had moments
of lucidity. When in 1960 Dr. Alan Guttmacher, the head of the Margaret
Sanger Bureau's research division, wrote in the *Saturday Review* that "the
diaphragm was brought to this country by the *late* Margaret Sanger [em-
phasis added]," Sanger demanded Guttmacher's resignation over "this un-
forgivable error . . . a man who would make such an error should not be
connected in any way with the Margaret Sanger Bureau."[15] Guttmacher
apologized but remained in his position as an important force in the battle
for contraceptive and abortion rights. Later he provided a compelling obit-
uary of "a bright, witty, attractive, dynamic, titian-haired woman who convinced America and the world that control of human conception is a basic
human right and like other human rights must be equally available to all."[16]

By 1962, struggling against the new enemy of leukemia, Sanger was
mostly bedridden, confused and unable to take care of herself. The woman
who looked to the future had no future. In the past she had been a member
of the Euthanasia Society of America, opposing "doctors just keeping people
alive. Why don't you give them something to put them out of their misery?"
Yet in her old age, according to her son Grant, she clung to life.[17] One doctor reported that she suffered "from senility, advanced arteriosclerosis of
the brain, resulting in poor memory, forgetfulness, failure of judgment
concerning money matters, irritability, disorientation, misidentification of
persons and periods of great agitation."[18] Stuart petitioned the Pima County,
Arizona, court to have his mother declared incompetent and to become her
conservator. In July 1962, against her will, Sanger was placed in a nursing

home. Her granddaughter Margaret Sanger Marston Lampe remembered her suspiciousness as Stuart drove to the facility outside of Tucson. She clapped her hands in her imperious fashion and demanded that her son take her home, but the car moved on.[19]

Sanger had begun her life in miserable circumstances in Corning, and in another period beyond her control, she ended her days in similar conditions in an institution. There were affirming moments. Grant and Edwina visited during Christmas of 1964, with their children, though Sanger could not remember all their names. Friends came, bringing her favorite champagne and chicken sandwiches for lunch. In one poignant visit, her granddaughter Margaret Sanger Marston came with her baby, also named Margaret but called, in an echo from the past, Peggy. Sanger held the baby, whispering, "Yes, it's my little Peggy. My own little Peggy, come back."[20]

Never easy family business, the decision to institutionalize Sanger outraged her friends, who insisted that she could have stayed at home with nurses or at least have been confined in a better facility. Some even accused Stuart of trying to appropriate her assets, while Stuart complained that his mother stirred up such reactions. A few local friends consulted, but did not hire, an attorney about contesting the incompetency ruling. To such complaints Stuart responded in a letter to Dorothy Brush: "My mother was declared incompetent because of her behavior . . . financially she was absolutely irresponsible . . . at times she is of course completely rational and can converse nicely. Other times . . . she is confused and muddled. At the present time she is incontinent . . . and has a rather large tumor in the left quadrant of her abdomen."[21] To hire nurses around the clock might deplete resources needed for an indeterminate lifetime, though when her will was probated she left an estate valued at $111,891 (nearly $700,000 in today's valuation). Elizabeth Grew Bacon, one of the pioneers of the movement, expressed the dismay of many: "For a world figure, who has been brave, courageous, and single-minded in fighting for freedom and the betterment of mankind, it is too terribly sad for the last days to be publicly and officially decreed incompetent."[22]

On September 6, 1966, just before her eighty-seventh birthday, Margaret Sanger died. Described as eighty-three in most national and international press coverage, she had won the public skirmish over her age. Even her grandsons were surprised at the extent of the coverage of her death. Obituaries appeared in small local papers throughout the United States, with *The New York Times* summarizing the general point of view: "The birth control movement grew out of one woman's outrage at the suffering she saw among the poor. It grew into a view of family planning accepted and practiced in a majority of American homes, a cause wisely promoted throughout the world and an international consensus that population control is necessary to human welfare and global peace."[23] Some papers, especially those in Tucson, emphasized her contribution to the lives of women, while others chronicled her personal story. Acknowledging her dislike of her hometown, the *Corning Leader* praised her struggles for an unpopular cause, and there was general agreement that after Sanger, the decision a woman made to bear a child was a separate matter from that of engaging in sexual intercourse.[24]

Funeral services were held in an Episcopal church in Tucson, and later that month Sanger was remembered in a memorial service in New York's Episcopal St. George's Church in Stuyvesant Square, with Rose Halpern, one of her first patients in the Brownsville clinic, in the congregation. An imperial organ and full choir filled the church with Bach's Choral Introit. The congregation joined in the familiar Old Hundred, "All people that on earth do dwell," singing as well the appropriate hymn "Once to Every Nation / Comes the Moment to Decide." Hobson Pittman and Morris Ernst delivered eulogies. Ernst spoke of Sanger's achievement in giving women hope that they could decide when and how many children they would have. Because of Margaret Sanger, intoned Ernst, women understood that conception did not just happen; rather, it was an element of their lives that they could control. The day of Sanger's funeral was stormy, and so among the rolls of thunder and torrents of sweeping rain, Ernst concluded, "And so a stormy day ends a stormy career." Later that week Margaret Sanger was buried in a cemetery near Willowlake in Fishkill, New York, next to her sister Nan Higgins, her maid Daisy "Old Faithful" Mitchell, and her husband Noah Slee. Her cause, redeemed by her persistent, courageous, and often sacrificial efforts to publicize and legalize birth control and make it available to all women, lives on.

NOTES

1: MAGGIE HIGGINS: DAUGHTER OF CORNING

1. Margaret Sanger, *The Autobiography of Margaret Sanger* (New York: Mineola Publications, 1971), 29.
2. Margaret Sanger, *My Fight for Birth Control* (New York: Farrar & Rhinehart, 1931), 4. Anne Higgins was fifty, not forty-eight.
3. Sanger, *Autobiography*, 12; Ellen Chesler, *Woman of Valor: Margaret Sanger and the Birth Control Movement in America* (New York: Simon & Schuster, 1992), 468–69; Harold Hersey, "Margaret Sanger: The Biography of a Birth Control Pioneer," manuscript in the Rare Books Division, New York Public Library. Anne Purcell is listed as having been born in Ireland in the 1860 and 1880 censuses.
4. Chesler, 475.
5. Irene Neu, *Erastus Corning, 1794–1872* (Ithaca, NY: Cornell University Press, 1960).
6. Sanger, *My Fight*, 21.
7. Ibid., 5.
8. *Corning Daily Democrat*, December 7, 1888.
9. Sanger, *My Fight*, 5.
10. Robert McNamara, *A Century of Grace: A History of St. Mary's Roman Catholic Parish, Corning, New York, 1848–1948* (Corning: St. Mary's Church, 1948), 34. There is some controversy over where Margaret Sanger went to school. She refers to the public school and it was public, though nuns taught there.
11. Michael, Joseph, and Mary appear in the 1900 Corning directory. And that year Margaret is listed as a schoolteacher boarding at 256 First Street. See also Boyd's *Elmira and Corning Directory*.
12. W. Cuttens Wilbur to Margaret Sanger, August 10 and 30, October 12, 1936, Margaret Sanger Papers Microfilm Edition: Smith College Collections, hereafter MSPSCC.
13. "Corning's Margaret Higgins Sanger," *Andaste Inquirer* 7, no. 1 (1978), 9–19, Painted Post Historical Society of Corning, Corning, New York; oral history, Mrs. Rudolph Shafer, April 28, 1977, Painted Post Historical Society.
14. C. H. Cramer, *Royal Bob: The Life of Robert Ingersoll* (New York: Bobbs-Merrill, 1952); Orvin Larson, *American Infidel: Robert Ingersoll* (New York: Aradel Press, 1962).
15. McNamara, *St. Mary's Parish*.
16. Sanger, *My Fight*, 8.

17. McNamara, *St. Mary's Parish*, 93; Madeline Gray, *Margaret Sanger, A Biography of the Champion of Birth Control* (New York: Richard Marek, 1979), 44–45.

18. Sanger, *My Fight*, 20.

19. Ibid., 12, 14.

20. For various interpretations of this story, see Chesler, *Woman of Valor*, 28; and David Kennedy, *Birth Control in America* (New Haven: Yale University Press, 1970), 3.

21. Sanger, *My Fight*, 9.

22. Ibid.

23. Ibid., 16.

24. Sanger, *Autobiography*, 16.

25. *Andaste Inquirer* 7, no. 1 (1978), 12.

26. Sanger, *My Fight*, 3.

27. Sanger, *Autobiography*, 494.

28. The following description is based on material from the Claverack Free Library, Claverack, New York, which has extensive source material, including catalogs, registers, and other materials about Claverack College, carefully tended by the librarian Sally Alderdice.

29. Brochures of Claverack College, Claverack Free Library, Hudson, New York.

30. Sanger, *Autobiography*, 38.

31. Sanger, *My Fight*, 27.

32. Margaret Sanger (hereafter MS) to Hugh de Selincourt, n.d., ca. 1927, Margaret Sanger Papers on microfilm, Library of Congress edition. Hereafter MSPLC.

33. Sanger, *Autobiography*, 40.

34. Ibid., 41.

35. Sanger, *My Fight*, 29.

36. Quoted in Lawrence Lader, *The Margaret Sanger Story* (New York: Doubleday, 1955), 16.

2: MRS. WILLIAM SANGER OF HASTINGS-ON-HUDSON

1. MS to Mary Higgins, undated, MSPSCC.

2. Sanger, *My Fight*, 32.

3. Clara Weeks-Shaw, *A Text-Book of Nursing* (New York: D. W. Appleton, 1896), 6.

4. Ibid., 210.

5. Maryanne Lewis and Sylvia Barker, *The Sinai Nurse* (New York: Phoenix Publishing, 2001); Doris Lippman, *The Evolution of the Nursing Textbook in the United States from 1873–1953* (New York: Columbia Teacher's College, 1980), 35.

6. Lippman, 35; Janet Wilson, "Isabel Hampton and the Professionalization of Nursing in the 1890's," in *The Therapeutic Revolution: Essays in the Social History of American Medicine*, ed. Morris J. Vogel and Charles E. Rosenberg (Philadelphia: University of Pennsylvania Press, 1979), 201–45.

7. MS to Aubrey Williams, February 12, 1940, MSPLC.

8. MS to Mary Higgins, June 20, [1900], MSPSCC.

9. Sanger, *Autobiography*, 48.

10. Ibid., 48.

11. MS to Mary Higgins, June 2, 1901, MSPSCC.

12. Sanger, *My Fight*, 32–33.

13. MS to Mary Higgins, June 20, n.y., MSPSCC.

14. MS to Mary Higgins, December 29, 1900, MSPSCC.

15. MS to Mary Higgins, June 2, 1901, MSPSCC.
16. M. Scott Carmichael, "Tuberculosis of the Tonsil Associated with Tuberculosis Glands of the Neck" (paper read at the Edinburgh Meeting, June 16, 1909, in possession of Dr. Richard Ross).
17. William Sanger to MS, March 12, 1914, MSPSCC.
18. Sanger, *Autobiography*, 57.
19. MS to Mary Higgins, n.d., MSPSCC.
20. William Sanger to "dearest," n.d., MSPSCC.
21. Relevant Sanger immigration records are in the Port of New York Immigration Records; and in the National Archives, Washington, DC. Eleazar Sanger was naturalized on February 6, 1891.
22. Sanger, *Autobiography*, 36.
23. MS to Virginia Gildersleeve, May 10, 1944, MSPSCC.
24. U.S. Census, 1880, 1920. Ellen Chesler, in her 1992 biography *Woman of Valor*, is the first biographer of Sanger to have researched the Jewish roots of William Sanger. See pages 478–79.
25. MS to Mary Higgins, n.d., ca. 1902, MSPSCC.
26. MS to Anna (Nan) Higgins, August 1902, MSPSCC.
27. William Sanger to Mary Higgins, July 27 and August 18, 1902, MSPSCC.
28. The following material is based on Rene and Jean Dubos, *The White Plague: Tuberculosis, Man and Society* (New Brunswick, NJ: Rutgers University Press, 1996); Katherine Ott, *Fevered Lives, Tuberculosis in American Culture Since 1870* (Cambridge, MA: Harvard University Press, 1996); interview with and materials provided by Dr. Richard Ross of the Johns Hopkins University School of Medicine, including "Tuberculosis of the Tonsils," *Indian Journal of Tuberculosis*; S. A. Knopf, *Tuberculosis as a Disease of the Masses and How to Combat It* (New York: M. Firestack, 1901); Mark Caldwell, *The Last Crusade: The War on Consumption, 1862–1951* (New York: Macmillan, 1998); Edward Trudeau, *An Autobiography* (New York: Doubleday, 1916).
29. Robert Taylor, *Saranac: America's Magic Mountain* (Boston: Houghton Mifflin, 1986).
30. Sanger, *Autobiography*, 58.
31. Dr. Byron Caples to MS, February 6, 1930, MSPSCC.
32. Sanger, *My Fight*, 37.
33. Sanger, *Autobiography*, 60.
34. Sanger, *My Fight*, 38.
35. Sanger, *Autobiography*, 61.
36. On Stanton, see Jean H. Baker, *Sisters: The Lives of America's Suffragists* (New York: Hill and Wang, 2005), 135.
37. *Messages and Papers of the Presidents* (New York: Bureau of National Literature), 16:6984; Theodore Roosevelt, *Outlook*, April 8, 1911, 765; Theodore Roosevelt to Cecil Spring Rice, August 11, 1899, in *The Letters of Theodore Roosevelt*, ed. Elting Morison, 8 vols. (Cambridge, MA: Harvard University Press, 1951–54), 2:1053.
38. The best discussion of Knowlton is in Helen Horowitz, *Rereading Sex: Battles over Sexual Knowledge and Suppression in 19th Century America* (New York: Knopf, 2002), 73–85.
39. Carl Degler, *At Odds: Woman and the Family in America from the Revolution to the Present* (New York: Oxford University Press, 1980), 222; Mosher Survey, Clelia Mosher Papers, Stanford University Archives, online version.
40. Sanger, *My Fight*, 39.
41. Ibid., 43.

42. Sanger, *Autobiography*, 64; Sanger, *My Fight*, 43–44.
43. Sanger, *My Fight*, 42, 43.
44. Bill Sanger to Grant Sanger, October 21, 1952, MSPSCC.

3: COMRADE SANGER

1. Lawrence Lader, *The Margaret Sanger Story* (New York: Doubleday, 1955), 34.
2. Sanger, *My Fight*, 44.
3. Walter Lippmann, *Early Writings* (New York: Liveright, 1970), 294.
4. Quoted in Irving Howe, *World of Our Fathers* (New York: Simon & Schuster, 1976), 69.
5. *New York Call*, September 3, 1910; also in Esther Katz, *The Selected Papers of Margaret Sanger* (Urbana: University of Illinois Press, 2003), 1:20–21.
6. *New York Call*, March 30 and April 1, 1911.
7. Sanger, *My Fight*, 49.
8. Sanger, *Autobiography*, 86.
9. Sanger, *My Fight*, 52–55; Sanger, *Autobiography*, 90–91.
10. Sanger, *Autobiography*, 92; Sanger, *My Fight*, 56.
11. Sanger, *My Fight*, 56.
12. Description of Goldman based on Ross Weitzman's lively *Republic of Dreams: Greenwich Village: The American Bohemia, 1910–1960* (New York: Simon & Schuster, 2002), 202–20.
13. Sanger, *My Fight*, 57.
14. Ibid., 60.
15. Sanger, *Autobiography*, 75.
16. Ibid., 69.
17. *New York Call*, March 24 and August 24, 1911.
18. Ibid., November 5, 1911.
19. MS to my dear Comrade Gerber [probably December 9, 1911], in Katz, *Selected Papers*, 1:23.
20. Sanger, *Autobiography*, 70.
21. Ibid., 76.
22. *New York Call*, November 7, 1911; other coverage, October 5, 1910.
23. *New York Call*, March 22, 1911.
24. Ibid., December 9 and 11, 1911.
25. Sanger, *Autobiography*, 81.
26. Ibid., 82.
27. *New York Call*, February 15, 1912.
28. *Hearings Before the Committee on Rules, 62nd Cong., 2nd Sess., March 2–7, 1912* (Washington, DC: Government Printing Office, 1912), 226–30.
29. Katz, *Selected Papers*, 1:49.
30. Sanger, *Autobiography*, 85.
31. T. S. Eliot in *Cambridge Review* 49 (1928), 488; Sanger, *Autobiography*, 73.
32. Sanger, *Autobiography*, 108–109.
33. Mabel Dodge Luhan, *Intimate Memories: The Autobiography of Mabel Dodge Luhan* (Albuquerque: University of New Mexico Press, 1999), 119–20. See also Sanger, *Autobiography*, 73.
34. Mabel Dodge Luhan, *Movers and Shakers* (Albuquerque: University of New Mexico Press, 1936), 69–71.

35. Sanger, *Autobiography*, 66; Sanger, *My Fight*, 43.

36. Judith Schwarz, *Radical Feminists of Heterodoxy, Greenwich Village, 1912–1940* (Norwich, VT: New Victorian Publishing, 1986), 66.

37. Luhan, *Movers and Shakers*, 61.

38. John Rompapas to Dearest Margaret, n.d., MSPLC. See also Katz, *Selected Papers*, 1:49–52.

39. Interview with Anne Sanger Gager, New London, CT, July 2006; on nymphomania as a cultural construction (it is no longer considered an organic or physiological disorder), see Carol Groneman, *Nymphomania* (New York: Norton, 2000).

40. Sanger, *My Fight*, 57.

41. Margaret Sanger, "What Every Mother Should Know, or How Six Children Were Taught the Truth," MSPLC.

42. Emma Goldman, "The Tragedy of Woman's Emancipation," in *Anarchism and Other Essays* (New York: 1910) 236–37.

43. Timothy Gilfoyle, *City of Eros: New York City, Prostitution, and the Commercialization of Sex, 1790–1920* (New York: Norton, 1992), 197–212.

44. "The Unrecorded Battle," MSPLC.

45. Anthony Comstock, *Traps for the Young*, ed. Robert Bremner (Cambridge, MA: Harvard University Press, 1967), 133, 241.

46. Helen Horowitz, *Rereading Sex: Battles over Sexual Knowledge and Suppression in 19th Century America* (New York: Knopf, 2002), 382. The Comstock Act reads, "Every obscene, lewd, or lascivious, and every filthy book, pamphlet, every picture, paper, letter, writing, print, or other publication of an indecent character, and every article or thing designed, adapted, or intended for preventing conception or producing abortion or for any indecent or immoral use; and every article, instrument, substance, drugs, medicine, or thing which is advertised or described in a manner calculated to lead another to use or apply it for preventing conception or producing abortion or any indecent or immoral purpose."

47. *New York Call*, December 29, 1912; also in *What Every Girl Should Know* (New York: Rabelais Press, 1914, reprinted 1974 by Arno Press).

48. On the competition of Sanger and Goldman, Chesler, *Woman of Valor*, 88.

49. MS to T. J. Mead, September 27, 1939, MSPLC.

50. Bill Sanger to MS, February 6, n.y., MSPSCC.

51. Ibid.

52. Bill Sanger to Peg Dear Heart, March 12, 1914, MSPSCC.

53. MS to Nancy Brushman, November 4, 1912, cited in Katz, *Selected Papers*, 1:39.

54. Hutchins Hapgood, *A Victorian in the Modern World* (Seattle: University of Washington Press, 1939), 170.

55. Sanger, *Autobiography*, 94.

56. Ibid., 76.

57. Quoted in Madeline Gray, *Margaret Sanger: A Biography of the Champion of Birth Control* (New York: Richard Marek, 1979), 61.

58. Sanger, *My Fight*, 58.

59. Ibid.

60. Bill Sanger to Sweetheart, February 6, 1914, MSPSCC.

61. Bill Sanger to Peg my Dear Heart, March 12, 1914, MSPSCC.

62. Bill Sanger to my Peg, September 3, 1913, MSPSCC.

4: CREATING MARGARET SANGER

1. Bill Sanger to MS, December 28, 1913, and January 11, 1914, MSPSCC.
2. Sanger, *Autobiography*, 108; Sanger, *My Fight*, 62.
3. Caroline Nelson to Margaret Sanger, June 15, 1915, MSPSCC.
4. *Woman Rebel*, March 1914.
5. Quoted in Baker, *Sisters*, 118.
6. *Woman Rebel*, March 1914.
7. Ibid.
8. Ibid., September–October 1914.
9. Ibid., June 1914.
10. Ibid., May 1914.
11. *Masses*, May 1914.
12. Max Eastman, "Is the Truth Obscene?" *Masses*, March 15, 1914.
13. *Atlantic Monthly*, March 1914, 298.
14. Emma Goldman to My Dear Margaret, April 9, 1914, MSPLC.
15. Bill Sanger to MS, March 3, 1914, and September 3, 1915, MSPSCC.
16. Ibid., March 3 and 19, 1914; January 5, 1915, MSPSCC.
17. Bill Sanger to MS, December 28, 1913, January 11 and 20, April 12, June 1 and 17, December 8 and 25, 1914, MSPSCC.
18. Walter Roberts undated correspondence, MSPSCC; see also Walter Roberts to MS, May 13, 1914, MSPSCC.
19. Quoted in Bertram Wolfe, *A Life in Two Centuries* (New York: Stern and Day, 1981), 27.
20. MS to Steven Haweis, April 19, 1914, MSPLC.
21. *Woman Rebel*, August 1914; MS to Stephen Haweis, July 23, 1914, MSPLC.
22. *Woman Rebel*, July 1914.
23. Ibid.
24. Sanger, *Autobiography*, 114–15; Sanger, *My Fight*, 90; *People v. Margaret Sanger*, copy in MSPLC.
25. Sanger, *Autobiography*, 115.
26. Sanger, "Contemplating Defense for Trial," MSPLC.
27. Quinine, the antimalarial powder, was widely viewed as effective in initiating labor contractions and therefore was used by the public as an abortifacient, though large doses were toxic.
28. Margaret Sanger, *Family Limitation*, 1st ed., 1914, copy in MSPLC. First edition is also included in Joan Jensen, "The Evolution of Margaret Sanger's *Family Limitation Pamphlet, 1914–1921*," *Signs* 6 (Spring 1981), 548–67.
29. Sanger, *Family Limitation*, 562.
30. Federal Trial Scrapbook, MSPLC.
31. Sanger, *Autobiography*, 119.
32. MS to Comrade Sinclair, September 23, 1914, MSPSCC.
33. Sanger, *Autobiography*, 118, 119.
34. "Comrades and Friends," October 28, 1914, MSPLC.
35. Katz, *Selected Papers*, 1:98.
36. MS, Diary, December 17, 1914, MSPLC.
37. MS, Diary, November 3 and December 13, 1914, MSPLC.
38. Ibid.

39. Sanger, *Autobiography*, 134, 141.
40. Havelock Ellis to MS, December 30, 1914, MSPLC.
41. Quoted in Chesler, *Woman of Valor*, 113.
42. Havelock Ellis, *Little Essays of Love and Virtue* (London: Black, 1922), 123.
43. Havelock Ellis to MS, December 26, 1914, MSPLC.
44. Ibid., October 26, 1915, MSPLC.
45. Ibid., January 5 and September 1, 1915, MSPLC.
46. Françoise Cyon to MS, October 29, 1946, MSPSCC; Havelock Ellis to MS, n.d., MSPLC.
47. Havelock Ellis, *My Life* (New York: Houghton Mifflin, 1939), 520.
48. MS to Hugh de Selincourt, November 11, 1945, MSPSCC.
49. MS to Bill Sanger, May 31, 1915, MSPSCC.
50. Bill Sanger to Dear Peg, December 8, 1914, MSPSCC.
51. Bill Sanger to Peg, January 21, 1915, MSPSCC; *Jailed for Birth Control: The Trial of William Sanger*, ed. James Fawcett (n.p., 1917), 13.
52. MS to Nan, n.d. [1915], MSPLC.
53. Katz, *Selected Papers*, 1:123.
54. MS, Diary, December 1914, MSPLC.
55. MS to Nan, February 22, 1915, MSPSCC.
56. MS to Stuart, March 29, 1915, MSPSCC.
57. Fawcett, *Jailed for Birth Control*, 13–14; *New York Times*, September 5 and 11, 1915.
58. *New Republic*, September 24, 1915, 195.

5: ON TRIAL

1. Paul Avrich, *Modern School Movement: Anarchism and Education in the United States* (Oakland, CA.: AK Press, 2006).
2. John M. Barry, *The Great Influenza* (New York: Penguin Books, 2004), 316–20, 390; Sir William Osler, *Principles and the Practice of Medicine Designed for Practitioners and Students of Medicine* (New York: Appleton, 1912); *Osler's Textbook Revisited*, ed. A. McGehee Harvey and Victor McKusick (New York: Appleton Century Crofts, 1967).
3. Sanger, *My Fight*, 127.
4. MS Recollections, 1953, MSPSCC.
5. MS to Lawrence Lader, December 3, 1953, MSPSCC.
6. J. Hewitt McKenzie, *Spirit Intercourse: Its Theory and Practice* (New York: Mitchell Kennerley, 1917), 177.
7. Sanger, *Autobiography*, 199; Sanger, *My Fight*, 128.
8. McKenzie, *Spirit Intercourse*, 184–85.
9. Bessie D. to My Dear Poor Friend, November 26, 1915, MSPSCC; Emma Goldman to My Dear Girl, December 12, 1915, MSPLC.
10. Harold Content to My Dear Mrs. Sanger, October 13, 1915, MSPLC.
11. Quoted in Katz, *Selected Papers*, 1:171; Morris Kahn to Whom It May Concern, December 30, 1915, MSPLC.
12. *New York Call*, January 8, 1916.
13. Speech in Katz, *Selected Papers*, 1:179.
14. *New York Sun*, January 17, 1916; also quoted in Sanger, *Autobiography*, 186.

15. Harold Content to Mrs. Sanger, February 15, 1916, MSPLC.
16. *United States v. Margaret Sanger,* newspaper clippings in MS, Federal Trial Scrapbook, MSPLC; *New York Times,* February 19, 1916.
17. H. G. Wells, Marie Stopes, et al. to the President of the United States, September 1916, copy in MSPLC.
18. U.S. Attorney H. Snowden Marshall to Attorney General Thomas Gregory, February 18 and July 13, 1916, copy, MSPLC.
19. MS to the Editor of *Mother Earth, Mother Earth,* April 16, 1916.
20. Thomas Gregory to Snowden Marshall, July 17, 1916, copy, MSPLC.
21. Sanger, *My Fight,* 189.
22. MS to Charles and Bessie Drysdale, August 9, 1916, in Katz, *Selected Papers,* 1:188.
23. Marie Equi to MS, Saturday, n.d., MSPSCC.
24. MS to Charles and Bessie Drysdale, August 9, 1916, in Katz, *Selected Papers,* 1:187.
25. Ibid., 189.
26. Anthony Comstock to Mrs. Clara Gruening, April 28, 1915, Mary Ware Dennett Papers, Schlesinger Library, Cambridge, MA.
27. Sanger, *My Fight,* 157.
28. MS to the Editor, *Medical World,* November 1917, cited in Katz, *Selected Papers,* 1:199. The man who was "an expert" is the famed Johns Hopkins gynecologist and adamant opponent of birth control Dr. Howard Kelly.
29. Sanger, *My Fight,* 155.
30. Ibid., 154.
31. Ibid., 144.
32. *New York Call,* October 22, 1916.
33. Cited in Katz, *Selected Papers,* 1:201.
34. *Brooklyn Daily Eagle,* October 26, 1916, cited in Chesler, *Woman of Valor,* 151.
35. Sanger, *My Fight,* 189–90.
36. Ibid., 159.
37. Sanger, *Autobiography,* 222–23; Sanger wrote two somewhat different descriptions of this scene. See also Sanger, *My Fight,* 160.
38. *New York Tribune,* November 27, 1916.
39. *New York Call,* October 22 and 27, 1916; *New York Times,* November 16, 1916.
40. Sanger, *Autobiography,* 222.
41. MS, Diary, April 27, 1919, MSPLC. For evidence on Sanger's romance with Goldstein, see Gray, *Margaret Sanger,* 153–56.
42. MS, Diary, April 27, 1919, MSPLC.
43. Birth Control Meeting in Honor of Margaret Sanger, 1916, MSPLC.
44. *The People of New York, Plaintiff, v. Margaret H. Sanger, Defendant,* Court of Special Appeals in National Archives Record Group 267, National Archives, Washington, DC.
45. Sanger, *Autobiography,* 235.
46. Ibid., 237; *New York Times,* February 3, 1917.
47. MS to Ethel Byrne, n.d., [ca. Feb, 1917], MSPLC.
48. Ibid., February 21, 1917, MSPSCC.
49. MS, Diary, February 6, [1917], MSPLC; also in MS, *My Fight,* 181.
50. Sanger, *My Fight,* 182.
51. MS to Herbert Sturges, February 23, 1917, MSPSCC.

52. Quoted in Chesler, *Woman of Valor*, 506; See also *People of New York, ex.rel. Margaret H. Sanger, Fania Mindell, and Ethel Byrne Against Warden and Keeper* (New York: Hecla Press, 1917).
53. Sanger, *My Fight*, 185.
54. Sanger, *Autobiography*, 251.
55. MS to Bill Sanger, March 21, 1917, MSPSCC.
56. Ibid., October 13, 1915, MSPSCC.
57. Ibid., March 24, 1917, MSPSCC.

6: *THE BIRTH CONTROL REVIEW*

1. Sanger, *Autobiography*, 255.
2. *Birth Control Review*, June 1917; hereafter *BCR*.
3. The story of these farmerettes is told in Elaine Weiss's *Fruits of Victory: The Womans' Land Army in the Great War* (Washington, DC: Potomac Books, 2008).
4. Carrie Catt to My Dear Mrs. Sanger and Mrs. Rublee, November 24, 1920, MSPLC.
5. Allen Brandt, *No Magic Bullet: A Social History of Venereal Disease Since 1880* (New York: Oxford University Press, 1985), 77.
6. Quoted in ibid.
7. *BCR*, October 1918. For a discussion of birth control and the U.S. Army during World War I, see John D'Emilio and Estelle Friedman, *Intimate Matters: A History of Sexuality in American History* (New York: Harper & Row, 1988), 211; Brandt, *No Magic Bullet*. On the treatment of women during the war, see John Parascandola, *Sex, Sin, and Science* (Westport, CT: Praeger, 2008).
8. *BCR*, February 1919.
9. U.S. Dept of Justice, FBI files, cited in Chesler, *Sanger: Woman of Valor*, 507. My request for access to these materials under the Freedom of Information Act has not been acted upon.
10. Sanger, *Autobiography*, 252.
11. *BCR*, February 1917.
12. *BCR*, February 1917, and July 1919.
13. Sanger, *Autobiography*, 257.
14. Sanger, *My Fight*, 192.
15. *BCR*, January 1918.
16. Lader, *The Margaret Sanger Story*, 138; Havelock Ellis to MS, May 19, 1918, MSPLC.
17. *BCR*, April–May 1917, and April 1921.
18. *BCR*, June 1917.
19. Ibid., February 1919.
20. Theodore Roosevelt to Bessie Van Vorst, October 18, 1902; Roosevelt to Whitelaw Reid, September 11, 1905, in *The Letters of Theodore Roosevelt*, ed. Elting Morison (Cambridge, MA: Harvard University Press, 1951), 3:355, 4:18. For similar comments by Roosevelt see ibid., 2:1053, 1112.
21. Chesler, *Woman of Valor*, 164.
22. *BCR*, October 1917, January 1918; *Metropolitan Magazine*, October and December 1917.
23. *BCR*, January 1918.
24. Ibid., February–March 1918.

25. Quoted in William Castle, Charles Davenport, et al., *Heredity and Eugenics* (Chicago: University of Chicago Press, 1912), 309.
26. On results of intelligence tests for recruits, see Robert Yerkes, *Psychological Examining in the U.S. Army* (Washington, DC: National Academy of Sciences, 1921).
27. *BCR*, April–May 1917. For biologists in this generation, the term "race" referred to a branch of study that concentrated on the genetic basis of racial diversity; for the public the term included various ethnic groups as well as colors.
28. Havelock Ellis, *The Task of Social Hygiene* (London: Constable, 1912), 32.
29. *BCR*, January 1920.
30. Ibid., February 1919.
31. Ibid.
32. For the foremost exponent of new philosophical approaches to this matter, see Peter Singer, *Practical Ethics* (New York: Cambridge University Press, 1993).
33. Quoted in Lader, *The Margaret Sanger Story*, 142.
34. Billy Williams to MS, undated letters, MSPSCC.
35. Sanger, *Autobiography*, 265.
36. Ibid., 266.
37. Grant Sanger to Dear Mother; Stuart Sanger to Dear Mother, n.d., ca. 1918, MSPSCC; Gray, *Margaret Sanger*, 152.
38. Grant to Dear Mother, February 20, March 6, and November 17, 1918; Stuart to Dear Mother, February 16 and other February letters, 1918, MSPSCC.
39. Juliet Rublee to MS, August 6, n.y., MSPSCC.
40. MS to Juliet Rublee, August 10 [probably 1918], MSPSCC.
41. MS to Juliet Rublee, n.d. [probably Nov. 1919].
42. Ibid.
43. *New York Times*, November 9, 1919.
44. MS to Bill Dear, December 1, 1919, MSPSCC.
45. MS, Diary, April 7, 1919, MSPLC.
46. MS, Diary, February 19, 1919.
47. *BCR*, March 1917.
48. Sanger, *Autobiography*, 257.
49. MS to Gertrude Pinchot, April 16, 1917, in Katz, *Selected Papers*, 1:214.
50. MS to Juliet Rublee, July 13, 1917, MSPSCC; Sanger, *Autobiography*, 254.
51. Frederick Blossom to MS, October 11, 1917, MSPLC.
52. Ibid., October 18, 1917, MSPLC.
53. Sanger, *Autobiography*, 259.
54. Quoted in Lader, *The Margaret Sanger Story*, 145.
55. Sanger, *Autobiography*, 260.
56. *People of New York v. M. Sanger Defendant*; M.Sanger, *Appellate v. People of New York, People of New York Respondent v. Margaret Sanger Defendant-Appellate*, Appellate Case Files, Record Group 267, Box 6193, National Archives, Washington, DC.
57. MS, Diary, July 1919, MSPLC.

7: VOYAGES

1. Billy Williams to Margaret Sanger, n.d., [ca. 1920], MSPLC.
2. MS to Juliet Rublee, July 30, 1921, MSPSCC.
3. MS to Hugh de Selincourt, February 23, 1927, MSPSLC.

4. Margaret Sanger, *The Pivot of Civilization* (Kessinger reprints, New York: Brentano, 1922), 16; Margaret Sanger, *Woman and the New Race* (New York: Truth Publishing, 1920), 45.

5. Sanger, *Woman and the New Race*, 1.

6. Quoted in Sanger, *Pivot*, 82.

7. Sanger, *Woman and the New Race*, 57, 87–88; Sanger, *Pivot*, 16.

8. Sanger, *Woman and the New Race*, 94; Sanger, *Pivot*, 38.

9. Sanger, *Pivot*, 26.

10. Ibid., 38, 91.

11. Ibid., 46.

12. Ibid., 47; MS, Diary, November 12, 1935, MSPLC.

13. Sanger, *Pivot*, 46, 47.

14. Ibid., 81.

15. Ibid.

16. Quoted in Eugene Black, *War Against the Weak: Eugenics and America's Campaign to Create a Master Race* (New York: Four Walls, Eight Windows, 2003), 139–40.

17. MS to Juliet Rublee in Katz, *Selected Papers*, 1:307.

18. Ibid., 1:96. On the development of research on female reproduction and hormones, see Adele Clarke, *Disciplining Reproduction: Modernity, American Life Sciences, and the Problems of Sex* (Berkeley: University of California Press, 1998).

19. Sanger, *Pivot*, 117.

20. Hugh de Selincourt to MS, September 14 [ca. 1921], MSPCC.

21. Harold Child to MS, quoted in Lader, *The Margaret Sanger Story*, 160.

22. MS to Juliet Rublee, July 14, 1921, MSPSCC.

23. Janet de Selincourt to MS, October 20, 1924, MSPSCC.

24. MS to Juliet Rublee, June 22, 1921, MSPSCC.

25. H. G. Wells, *Secret Places of the Heart* (New York: Cassell and Company, 1922), 58, 60.

26. H. G. Wells to MS, n.d. [ca. 1920], October 8, 1924, MSPLC.

27. MS, Diary, July 26, 1920, MSPLC.

28. MS to Hugh de Selincourt, June 1920, MSPLC.

29. MS to Juliet Rublee, August 8, n.y., MSPSCC.

30. MS to Hugh de Selincourt, January 27, 1922, MSPLC.

31. MS to Juliet Rublee, June 22, 1921, MSPSCC.

32. Quoted in Gray, *Margaret Sanger*, 206.

33. U.S. Department of Labor, *Annual Report of the Commissioner-General of Immigration to the Secretary of Labor* (Washington, DC: Government Printing Office, 1923), 3–4.

34. Mary Ware Dennett to MS, July 29, 1921, MSPLC.

35. MS to Marie Stopes, July 29 n.y., MSPLC; Katz, *Selected Papers*, 1:273.

36. Marie Stopes to MS, October 28, 1921, MSPLC; MS to Marie Stopes, October 29, 1921, MSPLC.

37. John Haynes Holmes to Mary Ware Dennett, December 8, 1925, Mary Ware Dennett Papers, Schlesinger Library, Cambridge, MA.

38. Sanger, *Autobiography*, 299–300.

39. Quoted in Katz, *Selected Papers*, 1:323; See also *Birth Control—What It Is, How It Works, What It Will Do; Proceedings of the First American Birth Control Conference* (New York, 1921).

40. Sanger, *My Fight*, 213.
41. *New York Times*, November 17, 1921.
42. Sanger, *My Fight*, 217; Sanger, *Autobiography*, 304.
43. *New York Tribune*, November 18, 1921.
44. Sanger, *Autobiography*, 306.
45. Ibid.
46. Ibid., 307.
47. *BCR*, January 1922.
48. Sanger, *My Fight*, 240.
49. Ibid., 233.
50. MS to Juliet Rublee, n.d. [ca. 1922], MSPSCC.
51. MS, Speech in Carnegie Hall [ca. 1922], MSPLC.
52. MS to Juliet Rublee, July 14, 1921, MSPSCC.
53. MS to Noah Slee, n.d. [ca. 1923], MSPSCC.
54. Noah Slee to MS, May 20, n.y., MSPSCC.
55. MS to Noah Slee, March 1, n.y., in Katz, *Selected Papers*, 1:387–88.
56. Noah Slee to MS, May 20, n.y., MSPSCC.
57. MS to J. Noah Slee, n.y., MSPSCC.
58. Olive Byrne Richards oral history, unmicrofilmed collection of MSPSCC.
59. MS to J. Noah Slee, October 23, n.y., MSPSCC.
60. MS to Dorothy Brush, August 20, 1949, MSPSCC.
61. MS to Havelock Ellis, December 1933, MSPLC.
62. MS to Hugh de Selincourt, July 17, 1924, MSPLC.
63. Ibid., December 25, 1921, MSPLC.
64. Ibid., February 24, n.y., MSPLC.
65. MS to Juliet Rublee, Monday, n.d., MSPSCC.
66. Margaret Sanger, "The Meaning of Birth Control," in Katz, *Selected Papers*, 1:385.
67. Sanger, *Autobiography*, 190.
68. *BCR*, July 1920.
69. Dr. Robert Dickinson to MS, March 19, 1926, MSPLC.
70. Robert Dickinson, *Control of Conception* (Baltimore, MD: Williams and Wilkins, 1938), 163; Presidential Address to the American Gynecological Society, *American Journal of Obstetrics and Gynecology* 1 (October 1920).
71. MS, Address in Chicago, MSPSCC.
72. Lader, *The Margaret Sanger Story*, 210.
73. Dickinson, *Control of Contraception*, 316. In 1920 there were 7,229 women graduates of medical schools and 144,977 men.
74. MS to Dr. Bocker, October 17, 1921, MSPLC.
75. Quoted in Rosemarie Holz, "The Birth Control Clinic in America: Life Within, Life Without, 1923–1972" (unpublished diss., University of Illinois at Urbana-Champaign, 2004), 42. On birth control clinics, see also Cathy Hajo, "What Every Woman Should Know: Birth Control Clinics in the United States, 1919–1939" (unpublished diss., New York University, 2006), and Cathy Hajo, *Birth Control on Main Street: Organizing Clinics in the U.S., 1916–1939* (Champaign: University of Illinois Press, 2009).
76. *BCR*, January 1927.
77. MS, Diary, January 1, 1925, MSPLC.
78. Quoted from *The Group*, in Chesler, *Woman of Valor*, 288–89.

79. Raymond Pearl to MS, November 13, 1924, MSPLC.
80. ABCL press release, March 31, 1925, MSPLC.
81. Edward East to Margaret Sanger, May 15, 1925, MSPLC.

8: SPREADING THE WORD

1. MS to Juliet Rublee, June 28, 1928, MSPSCC.
2. *New York Times*, September 28, 1928.
3. *BCR*, December 1931.
4. MS to Juliet Rublee, May 5, 1929, MSPSCC.
5. MS to Havelock Ellis, February 19, 1929, MSPLC.
6. MS to Penelope Huse, January 31, 1929, MSPSCC.
7. MS to Edith How-Martyn, May 21, n.y., MSPLC.
8. Comment on back of a letter to Robert Dickinson, April 22, 1932, Smith College unfilmed collection of MSP.
9. MS to Juliet Rublee, Friday 26, n.y., MSPSCC.
10. Sanger, *Autobiography*, 407.
11. Ibid., 408.
12. MS to Juliet Rublee, August 10, n.y., MSPSCC.
13. Dickinson, *Control of Contraception*, 124.
14. MS to Havelock Ellis, August 1, 1933, MSPLC.
15. Clarence Little to MS, October 26, 1925, MSPLC.
16. MS to Mr. Waldman, July 2, 1929, quoted in Katz, *Selected Papers*, 2:34.
17. W.E.B. Du Bois, "The Damnation of Women," in *Dark Water: Voices from the Veil* (New York: Harcourt Brace, 1920), 164–65.
18. W.E.B. Du Bois, "Black Folks and Birth Control," *BCR*, June 1932.
19. Edward East to MS, December 31, 1929, MSPSCC.
20. Quoted in Katz, *Selected Papers*, 2:213.
21. Quoted by MS to Norman Himes, January 10, 1933, MSPLC.
22. Ibid.
23. MS to Hugh de Selincourt, August 4, 1930, MSPLC.
24. Ibid., January 31, 1932, MSPLC.
25. Ibid., March 12, 1933, MSPLC.
26. MS to Havelock Ellis, December 3, 1933, MSPLC.
27. MS to Françoise Cyon, September 24, 1931, MSPLC.
28. MS to J. Noah Slee, November 17, 1934, MSPSCC.
29. MS to Noah, October 3, 1927, Ibid.
30. MS to Noah, February 18, n.y., MSPSCC.
31. *People*, April 1931, quoted in Katz, *Selected Papers*, 2:59.
32. MS Speech in Washington, DC, February 1935, MSPLC; Hazel Moore Lobbying Reports, NCFLBC materials, MSPLC; *New York Times*, February 13, 1935.
33. MS to Florence Rose, February 2, 1933, MSPSCC; Hearings on Birth Control, U.S. Senate, 72nd Cong., Senate Bill 4436, May 12, 19, and 20, 1932 (Washington, DC: Government Printing Office, 1932).
34. MS to Mrs. Foster Hunt, December 16, 1933, MSPLC.
35. MS to F. R., February 2, 1933, MSPSCC.
36. *New York Times*, June 14, 1934.
37. MS to George Bernard Shaw, January 27, 1932, MSPLC.

38. Pope Pius XI, "Encyclical of Pope Pius XI on Christian Marriage," December 1931, available at the Papal Encyclicals Online, www.papalencyclicals.net.

39. MS Replies to the Pope, interview with the press, January 13, 1931, MSPLC.

40. MS to George Bernard Shaw, January 27, 1932, MSPLC.

41. Quoted in Katz, *Selected Papers*, 2:115; Hazel Moore Lobbying Reports, MSPLC.

42. Hearings on Birth Control Bill 4582, Subcommittee of the Senate, 72nd Cong., February 13 and 14, 1931 (Washington, DC: Government Printing Office, 1931).

43. Hearings on Birth Control Bill 11082, Subcommittee of the Ways and Means Committee, U.S. House of Representatives, 72nd Cong., May 1932 (Washington, DC: Government Printing Office, 1932).

44. Ibid. Norton, later dubbed "Fighting Mary of Newark," although a member of the House of Representatives, also testified in the Senate hearings.

45. Hearings on Birth Control Bill 5978, Subcommittee of the Ways and Means Committee, U.S. House of Representatives, 73rd Cong., January 18–20, 1934.

46. Katharine Hepburn to MS, January 29, n.y., quoted in Katz, *Selected Papers*, 2:268.

47. Hearings on Birth Control Bill 1142, U.S. Senate, 73rd Cong., January 1934; Hearings on Birth Control Bill 11082, May 19 and 20, 1932; Sanger, *Autobiography*, 426.

48. MS to Dr. Prentiss Willson, November 19, 1934, MSPLC.

49. Hearings on Birth Control Bill 1842, Subcommittee of the Judiciary, U.S. Senate, 73rd Cong.; Hearings Before a Subcommittee of the Judiciary Committee on Senate Bill 4582, 72nd Cong., Feb. 13, 1931.

50. Hearings on Birth Control Bill 4582, Subcommittee of the Judiciary, February 13 and 14, 1931.

51. Hearings on Birth Control Bill 11082, Ways and Means Committee, U.S. House of Representatives, 72nd Cong., May 19 and 20, 1932.

52. Mary Ware Dennett to MS, February 28, 1931, MSPLCC.

53. Margaret Sanger, "National Security and Birth Control," *Forum*, March 1935, 140.

54. Mary Ware Dennett to MS, February 15, 1930, MSPLC.

55. MS to Mary Ware Dennett, February 21, 1931, MSPLC.

56. Jessie Ames Marshall to MS, May 12 and June 29, 1934, MSPLC.

57. MS to Mrs. Marshall, June 1, 1934, MSPSCC; Jessie Marshall to MS, June 29, 1934, MSPLC; see also Katz, *Selected Papers*, 2:300–301.

58. MS, Ford Hall Speech, in Katz, *Selected Papers*, 2:25.

59. Ibid., 24.

60. Margaret Sanger, *Happiness in Marriage* (New York: Blue Ribbon Books, 1926), 132.

61. Ibid., 56, 132.

62. Ibid, 112; see also 183–84.

63. Ibid., 153–54.

64. *New York Times*, July 4, 1926.

65. Sanger, *Happiness in Marriage*, xvii.

66. MS to Otto Kahn, December 28, 1928, MSPLC.

67. The one exception is Ellen Chesler's *Woman of Valor*, though her excellent, balanced portrayal of Margaret Sanger was published after Sanger's death.

68. "A Review by Dr. Fred Hankins," *BCR*, November 1931.

69. Margaret Sanger to the Editors, *BCR*, November 1931; italics mine.

70. MS to Hugh de Selincourt, October 30, 1931, MSPLC.

71. MS to Dear—, August 30, 1934, MSPSCC; Sanger, *Autobiography*, 436.

72. MS to Juliet Rublee, January 9, n.y., MSPSCC.

73. Quoted in Adele Clarke, *Disciplining Reproduction: Modernity, American Life Sciences, and the Problems of Sex* (Berkeley: University of California Press, 1989), 190–91.
74. Quoted in Clarke, *Disciplining Reproduction*, 193.
75. MS to Katharine McCormick, July 31, 1928, MSPLC.
76. Quoted in Clarke, *Disciplining Reproduction*, 190.
77. Quoted in Merrilly Borell, "Biologists and the Promotion of Birth Control Research," *Journal of the History of Biology* 20 (Spring 1987), 78.
78. Quoted in Daniel Kevles, *In the Name of Eugenics* (New York: Knopf, 1985), 116.
79. *Buck v. Bell*, 274 U.S. 200 (1927).
80. MS, "My Plan for Peace," January 1934, MSPLC.
81. Sanger, *Autobiography*, 387.
82. Ibid., 385. See also Margaret Sanger, ed., *Proceedings of the World Population Conference* (Geneva, 1927).
83. *New York Times*, February 13, 1935.
84. Quoted in Katz, *Selected Papers*, 2:209.
85. MS to Dear F.R., n.d. (ca. 1932), MSPSCC.
86. MS Speech in Washington [February 1935], MSPLC.
87. Ibid.
88. MS to Noah Slee, April 20, May 7, 1935, MSPSCC.
89. MS to Hugh de Selincourt, December 25, 1925, MSPLC.
90. MS, Diary, January 11, 1926, MSPLC.
91. MS to Angus Macdonald, n.d., MSPSCC.
92. MS to Juliet Rublee, n.d., MSPSCC.
93. Angus Macdonald to MS, June 9, 1933, MSPSCC.
94. MS to Angus Macdonald, n.d., MSPSCC.
95. MS to Juliet Rublee, n.d. [ca. 1932], MSPSCC.

9: ALL THINGS FADE

1. See M. K. Gandhi to MS, July 8, 1925, MSPLC.
2. Figures on press coverage in Chesler, *Woman of Valor*, 561; see also MS, India Journal, MSPLC.
3. MS to Kate Ripley, July 21, 1936, MSPLC.
4. MS to Noah Slee, February 3, 1936, MSPSCC.
5. MS, India Journal, MSPLC.
6. Sanger, *Autobiography*, 465–66.
7. Ibid., 470.
8. Rudrangshu Mukherjee, ed., *The Penguin Gandhi* (New York: Penguin Books, 1993), 191, 188.
9. Mukherjee, *The Penguin Gandhi*, 190; "Gandhi and Mrs. Sanger Debate Birth Control," *Asia* (November 1936), 699–70; see also MS, "Greetings Everybody," January 2, 1936, material on India trip, MSPLC.
10. MS, India Journal, MSPLC.
11. MS to John and Mabel Kingsbury, February 18, 1936, MSPSCC.
12. Margaret Cousins to MS, May 15, 1936, MSPLC.
13. MS to Noah Slee, March 5, [1936] MSPSCC.
14. MS, India Journal, 1936, MSPLC.
15. MS to Florence Rose, March 3, 1936, MSPSCC.

16. MS, India Journal, MSPLC.

17. MS to Angus Macdonald, January 14, 1936, MSPSCC.

18. Shidzue Ishimoto to MS, September 18, 1937, MSPLC.

19. MS to Havelock Ellis, March 21, 1936, MSPLC; MS to Ethel Clyde, April 25, 1936, MSPSCC.

20. MS to Noah Slee, Sunday Morning, n.d. [ca. 1934], MSPSCC.

21. Ibid., October 1937, MSPSCC.

22. Quoted in Lader, *The Margaret Sanger Story*, 305.

23. MS to Noah Slee, October 29, 1937, MSPSCC.

24. Ibid., November 1, 1937, MSPSCC.

25. MS to Edith How-Martyn, October 16, 1934, MSPLC.

26. *Ladies' Home Journal* 55 (March 1938), 14–15.

27. MS to Dorothy Gordon, June 24, 1933, MSPSCC.

28. *U.S. v. One Package*, 86 F.2d 737 (2nd Cir. 1936), and 13 F. Supp. 334 (E.D. N.Y. 1936); see also Morris Ernst and Alexander Lindey, *The Censor Marches On* (New York: Doubleday, 1940), 164.

29. Margaret Sanger, "Statement on the American Medical Association Action," quoted in Katz, *Selected Papers*, 2:405.

30. MS to Charles Scribner, April 24, 1936, MSPLC.

31. *U.S. v. One Package*, 86 F. 2d, 738–39; See also NCFLBC, "Summary of Correspondence and Important Steps in Case of *U.S. v. One Package*," October 1936, MSPLC.

32. Ernst and Lindey, *The Censor*, 2.

33. MS to Edith How-Martyn, December 12, 1936, MSPLC.

34. MS, "Birth Control," "Momentous Decision," February 1937, MSPLC.

35. Quoted in *Journal of Contraception* 4 (June–July), 1939.

36. MS to Havelock Ellis, n.d., MSPLC.

37. *Journal of Contraception* 4 (March), 1939.

38. Quoted in Gray, *Margaret Sanger*, 383.

39. Ibid., 385.

40. MS to the Kingsburys, January 26, 1940, MSPLC.

41. MS to Dr. Clarence Gamble, April 11, 1940, MSPLC.

42. MS to Betty-Mary Goetting, January 1938, MSPSCC.

43. Margaret Sanger, "The Future of Contraception: Address to the Delegates," *Journal of Contraception* 2 (January), 1937.

44. Doris Davidson to MS, January 23, 1933, MSPLC.

45. Quoted in Doone Williams and Greer Williams, *Every Child a Wanted Child: Clarence Gamble and His Work in the Birth Control Movement,* ed. Edith Flint (Cambridge, MA: Harvard University Press, 1978), 221, 236.

46. MS to Edith How-Martyn, December 1, 1938, MSPLC.

47. Quoted in Katz, *Selected Papers*, 2:433.

48. MS to Dr. George Cooper, February 12, 1938, MSPSCC.

49. Quoted in Carole McCann, *Birth Control Politics in the United States, 1916–1945* (Ithaca, NY: Cornell University Press, 1994), 118.

50. MS to Clarence Gamble, November 26, 1939, MSPSCC.

51. Ibid., October 19, 1939, MSPSCC.

52. MS to General Manager of the Gray Line, June 19, 1939, MSPLC.

53. MS to Albert Lasker, July 9, 1942, MSPSCC; see also McCann, *Birth Control Politics in the United States*, 162–64.

54. *Chicago Defender*, September 22, 1945, quoted in *Margaret Sanger Papers Newsletter* 42 (Spring 2006), 5-6.
55. Thomas Parran, "The Aims of the Public Health Service," *Smithsonian Annual Report*, 1937-38, 437.
56. Quoted in Brandt, *No Magic Bullet*, 125.
57. MS to Willystine Goodsell, May 24, 1938, MSPLC.
58. See MS to Edith How-Martyn, January 10, 1932, MSPLC.
59. Dr. Robert Dickinson to MS, October 28, 1936, MSPLC.
60. Dr. George Kosmak, editorial in *Journal of the American Medical Association*, 112, October 21, 1939.
61. Margaret Sanger, "Address to the Delegates," *Journal of Contraception* 2 (January), 1937.
62. Ibid.
63. MS to Florence Rose, January 6, 1938, MSPSCC.
64. Florence Rose to MS, December 12, 1937, MSPSCC.
65. MS to Penelope Huse, December 20, 1937, MSPSCC.
66. John Price Corporation, "Report on the ABCL," MSPLC; Florence Rose to MS, December 10, 1937; MS to Penelope Huse, December 20, 1937, MSPSCC.
67. Robert Dickinson to ABCL Directors, March 23, 1937, MSPLC; see also Katz, *Selected Papers*, 2:400.
68. MS to Clarence Gamble, April 13, 1937, MSPLC.
69. MS to Edith How-Martyn, February 1, 1938, MSPLC.
70. *New York Times*, January 19, 1939.
71. MS to Cele Damon, December 27, 1939, MSPLC.
72. MS to Florence Rose, n.d. [ca. 1939], MSPSCC.
73. MS to Robert Dickinson, February 20, 1942, MSPLC.
74. MS to Clarence Gamble, quoted in Williams and Williams, *Every Child a Wanted Child*; Margaret Sanger, "Proceedings of the BCFA," June 30, 1941, MSPSCC; MS to Kenneth Rose, January 22, 1942, MSPLC.
75. MS to Pearl Buck, October 23, 1944, MSPSCC.
76. MS to Woodbridge Morris, March 3, 1940, MSPLC.
77. MS to Herman Rubinraut, November 19, 1938, MSPSCC.
78. MS to Edith How-Martyn, May 21, 1933, MSPLC.
79. MS to Angus Macdonald, September 3, 1936, MSPSCC.
80. MS to Florence Rose, December 7, 1938, MSPSCC.
81. MS to Juliet Rublee, August 8, 1941, MSPSCC.
82. MS to Dr. Fenson, July 17, 1939, MSPLC.
83. MS, Journal, 1941, MSPLC.
84. MS, "Let's Talk It Over," July 17, 1939, MSPLC.
85. MS to Elizabeth Slee Willis, June 2, 1943, MSPSCC.
86. MS to Dorothy Brush, June 26, 1943, MSPLC.
87. MS, Diary, October 24, 1944, MSPLC.
88. MS to Dorothy Gordon, August 1941, MSPSCC.
89. Edwina Sanger to MS, August 2 and November 18, 1939, MSPSCC.
90. MS, Diary, December 22, 1944, MSPLC.
91. MS to Dorothy Gordon, December 11, 1942, MSPSCC.
92. MS to Angus Macdonald, June 17, 1943, MSPSCC.
93. Bill Sanger to MS, September 18, 1942, MSPSCC.

94. Dr. Clarence Gamble to MS, December 2, 1942, MSPLC.
95. MS to Clarence Gamble, n.d., MSPLC.
96. MS, Diary, 1945, MSPLC.

10: WORLD LEADER

1. MS to Margaret Valiant, January 12, 1947, MSPSCC.
2. Ibid.
3. MS to Roslyn Weir, March 2, 1950, MSPLC.
4. MS to H. G. Wells, August 5, 1946, MSPSCC.
5. MS to Ada McCormick, n.d. [ca. 1947], MSPLC.
6. MS to Edith How-Martyn, July 4, 1926, MSPSCC.
7. Quoted in Matthew Connelly, *Fatal Misconception: The Struggle to Control World Population* (Cambridge, MA: Harvard University Press, 2008), 87.
8. Harry Truman, "Special Message to Congress," *Public Papers of the Presidents of the United States* (Washington, DC: Government Printing Office, 1966), 209.
9. Discussed in Connelly, *Fatal Misconception*, 155.
10. MS to Elise Ottesen-Jensen, August 2, 1949, MSPLC.
11. Margaret Sanger and Edith How-Martyn, *Round the World for Birth Control* (London: 1937), 3.
12. MS to Edward Steel, March 31, 1953, MSPSCC.
13. Beryl Suitters, *Be Brave and Angry: Chronicles of the International Planned Parenthood Foundation* (London: IPPF Publications, 1974), 95; see also Margaret Sanger, "Survey of the Birth Control Movement," August 24, 1948, MSPSCC.
14. Quoted in Family Planning Association of Great Britain, *Proceedings of the International Congress on Population and World Resources* (London: H. K. Lewis), 18.
15. Suitters, *Be Brave and Angry*, 23–24.
16. Quoted in Lader, *The Margaret Sanger Story*, 322.
17. Juliet Rublee to MS, November 15, 1946, MSPSCC.
18. Suitters, *Be Brave and Angry*, 398.
19. MS to Juliet Rublee, December 1, 1952, MSPSCC.
20. Ibid., January 1953, MSPSCC.
21. General Douglas MacArthur to Mr. Bosworth, April 6, 1950, MSPSCC; also MS to Charles Scribner, February 24, 1950, MSPCC, *New York Times*, February 13, 1950.
22. MS to Edna McKinnon, February 1950, MSPSCC.
23. *Churchman*, March 3, 1950; *New York Times*, February 13, 1950.
24. The Fifth International Conference on Planned Parenthood, *Report of the Proceedings, 24–29 October, 1955* (London: IPPF, n.d.), 184.
25. MS to Pip (C. P. Blacker), July 18, 1957, quoted in Avadia Wada, *The Light Is Ours: Memoirs and Movements* (London: IPPF Publications, 2001), 156.
26. MS to Dorothy Brush, January 14, 1952, MSPSCC; see also Freeman Lusk to MS, May 10, 1952; *Los Angeles Times*, March 14, 1952.
27. MS to Annetta Clark, March 12, 1949, MSPSCC.
28. Elinor Cutts to the Nobel Committee, January 24, 1952, MSPSCC.
29. MS to Ethel Byrne, January 22, 1952, MSPSCC; Ethel Byrne to Women's Producers Group, January 1952, MSPSCC.
30. Quotes from 1957 videotape of MS interview with Michael Wallace, MSPSCC.

31. D. Savoie to MS, September 21, 1957, in Katz, *Selected Papers*, 3:438.
32. MS to Ellen Watumull, October 9, 1957, MSPSCC.
33. *New York Times*, September 23, 1957.
34. MS to Katharine Dexter McCormick, October 27, 1950, MSPSCC.
35. MS to Charles Scribner, February 1950, MSPSCC.
36. MS to David Loth, April 12, 1951, MSPSCC.
37. MS to Abraham Stone, February 23, 1939, MSPLC; MS to Lawrence Lader, April 12, 1953, MSPSCC.
38. MS to Lawrence Lader, April 12, 1953, MSPSCC.
39. MS to David Loth, February 4 and April 12, 1951, MSPSCC.
40. *Washington Post*, January 28, 1949.
41. MS to the American Medical Association, February 5, 1952, MSPLC.
42. MS to Angus Macdonald, n.d. [ca. 1949], MSPSCC.
43. Ibid., September 28, 1945, MSPSCC.
44. Ibid., November 12, 1945, MSPSCC.
45. MS to Dorothy Brush, September 18, 1949, MSPSCC.
46. Hobson Pittman to MS, June 16, 1948, MSPSCC.
47. MS to Hobson Pittman, n.d. [ca. 1948], and June 15, 1948, MSPSCC.
48. MS to Larry Lader, "Autobiographical Material for Larry Lader, 1953-4," MSPSCC.
49. MS to Cele Wright, August 5, 1949, MSPSCC.
50. MS to Edith Clyde, April 12, 1936, MSPLC.
51. MS to Abraham Stone, August 17, 1950, MSPLC.
52. MS to Juliet Rublee, January 1953, MSPSCC.
53. MS to Dorothy Brush, August 8, 1949, MSPSCC.
54. Grant Sanger to MS, August 7, 1949, MSPSCC.
55. MS to Frank Lloyd Wright, April 19, 1949, in Katz, *Selected Papers*, 3:243.
56. MS to Hobson Pittman, May 16, 1951, MSPSCC.
57. Edwina Campbell Sanger, *My First Ninety Years* (privately printed), 44.
58. MS to Bill Campbell, October 17, 1947, MSPSCC.
59. MS to Angus Macdonald, June 14, 1949, MSPSCC.
60. Margaret Sanger Marston Lampe, *Mimi and Me* (Canada: Art Bindery, 2006), 21.
61. MS to Roslyn Weir, March 2, 1950, MSPLC.
62. MS to Paul Blanshard, December 7, 1953, MSPSCC.
63. MS to Edna Ferber, October 26, 1953, quoted in Katz, *Selected Papers*, 3:341.
64. MS to Abraham Stone, April 2, 1953, MSPLC.
65. Lawrence Lader to MS, July 25, 1953, MSPSCC.
66. MS to Françoise Cyon Delisle, November 1, 1954, MSPSCC.
67. MS to Lawrence Lader, July 14, 1953, MSPSCC.
68. *New Yorker*, May 14, 1955.
69. Larry Lader, "Margaret Sanger, Militant, Propagandist, Visionary," *Issues* (Spring 1990), 8.
70. MS to Leighton Rollins, July 2, 1949, MSPSCC.
71. MS to Lawrence Lader, n.d. [ca. 1953]; MS to Hugh de Selincourt, October 31, 1931, MSPLC.
72. MS to Lawrence Lader, n.d. [ca. October 1953], MSPSCC.
73. Ibid., April 12, 1953.
74. MS to Katharine McCormick, October 27, 1950, MSPSCC.

75. Quoted in James Reed, *From Private Vice to Public Virtue: The Birth Control Movement and American Society Since 1830* (New York: Basic Books, 1978), 332.
76. Interview with Gregory Pincus in the *Sydney Sun*, January 11, 1967, in Gregory Pincus Papers, LC.
77. MS to Marion Ingersoll, March 15, 1954, MSPSCC.
78. Katharine McCormick to MS, November 13, 1953, MSPLC.
79. Ibid.
80. MS to Dr. Gregory Pincus, March 29, 1954, Pincus Papers.
81. Gregory Pincus to MS, March 23, 1954, Pincus Papers.
82. MS to Dr. Pincus, March 18, 1954, MSPLC.
83. MS to Gregory Pincus, February 7, 1957; Pincus to MS, September 14, 1954, Pincus Papers.
84. Suitters, *Be Brave and Angry*, 128.
85. MS to Katharine McCormick, December 12, 1956, MSPSCC.
86. Katharine McCormick to Sanger, January 2, 1960, MSPSCC.
87. MS to Katharine McCormick, December 12, 1956, MSPSCC.
88. International Planned Parenthood Federation, *The Sixth International Conference on Planned Parenthood, Report of the Proceedings, February 14–21, 1959* (London, 1959), 10; Suitters, 163–66.
89. Chesler, *Woman of Valor*, 450.

EPILOGUE: LAST YEARS

1. MS to Senator Kennedy, January 11, 1960, in Katz, *Selected Papers*, 3:460.
2. Ibid., 3:467–68.
3. Connelly, *Fatal Misconception*, 186.
4. Connelly, *Fatal Misconception*, 185–86.
5. MS to *New York Times*, January 11, 1960.
6. Connelly, *Fatal Misconception*, 187.
7. *New York Times*, November 10, 1960.
8. Mrs. Barbara Benoit to MS, July 18, 1960, in Katz, *Selected Papers*, 3:406.
9. Katz, *Selected Papers*, 3:486.
10. Online version of "Encyclical Letter Humanae Vitae of Supreme Pontiff Paul VI to His Venerable Brothers," available at the Papal Encyclicals Online, www.papalencyclicals.net; see also John Noonan, *Contraception: A History of Its Treatment by Catholic Theologians* (Cambridge, MA: Belknap Press, 1965), 467–69, 502–504.
11. Quoted in David Garrow, *Liberty and Sexuality: The Right to Privacy and the Making of Roe v. Wade* (New York: Macmillan, 1994), 253. Garrow includes extensive coverage of these events.
12. Melvin Urofsky, *Louis Brandeis: A Life* (New York: Pantheon, 2009), 630–31.
13. MS to Harold Oram, May 3, 1961, MSPSCC.
14. Robert Parker to MS, May 15 1961, MSPSCC.
15. *Saturday Review*, February 6, 1960; MS to Dr. Alan Guttmacher, February 22, 1960, MSPSCC.
16. Quoted in Katz, *Selected Papers*, 3: 491–92.
17. Grant Sanger interview with Ellen Chesler, 1987, MSPSCC.
18. Gray, *Margaret Sanger*, 440.
19. Margaret Lampe, *Mimi and Me*, 30.

20. Gray, *Margaret Sanger*, 442.
21. Stuart Sanger to Dorothy Brush, February 8, 1963, MSPSCC.
22. Quoted in Katz, *Selected Papers*, 3:481.
23. *New York Times*, September 11, 1966.
24. Obituaries and description in unfilmed material in MSPSCC.

ACKNOWLEDGMENTS

Like most authors, from the very beginning of my research, I was indebted to colleagues, librarians, Sanger relatives and specialists, and, as ever, my family. Sally Alderdice of the Claverack Free Library spent a day with me, helping me sort through the abundant materials on the Claverack College and Hudson River Institute, which Margaret Sanger attended. She even retrieved me from and returned me to the train station. My friend and colleague Dr. Esther Gibbs was present at the beginning, and at the end, of my research. A former resident of Elmira, New York, she served as a native informant about nearby Corning, where Sanger was born and grew up. Later, as I confronted the chemistry of the birth control pill, Dr. Gibbs, a distinguished professor of chemistry at Goucher College, helped me understand the process of synthesizing hormones.

Because the bulk of Margaret Sanger's papers are on microfilm, the librarians at Goucher College responded to endless interlibrary loan requests. Librarians at the Sophia Smith Collection at Smith College proved hospitable and knowledgeable during my visits there, and later in processing my requests for images. As has not always been my experience on other historical projects, I found two Sanger experts enthusiastically willing to share their insights. I spent a morning with Professor Ellen Chesler, whose biography *Woman of Valor: Margaret Sanger and the Birth Control Movement in America* stands as a monument to its subject. Dr. Esther Katz, the indefatigable editor of the Margaret Sanger Papers Project, which has a fourth volume on the way, offered her profound wisdom about Sanger. Meanwhile, the Sanger family, including Sanger's grandchildren Margaret Sanger Lampe and Nancy Sanger Pellison, provided the kind of intimate memories that only relatives can. During our teas together, Martha Frick Symington Sanger, herself a biographer, offered stimulating insight into the relationships between various Sangers, and both Anne Sanger Gager and Alexander Sanger were generous with their time during my interviews.

Thanks as well to my publishing home of Hill and Wang, and especially to Thomas LeBien and Dan Crissman.

Finally, I am grateful to my family, particularly my husband, Dr. Robinson Baker, whose background as a physician assisted my understanding of various medical matters so significant in Sanger's life. Hardly a researcher's widower, he was a writer's companion, and our mutual love and affection have sustained me.

INDEX